THE DEMOCRATIC STATE

STUDIES IN
GOVERNMENT AND PUBLIC POLICY

Charles H. Levine, Series Editor

THE
DEMOCRATIC
STATE

Edited by
ROGER BENJAMIN
and
STEPHEN L. ELKIN

UNIVERSITY PRESS OF KANSAS

Published by the University Press of Kansas (Lawrence, Kansas 66045),
which was organized by the Kansas Board of Regents and is operated
and funded by Emporia State University, Fort Hays State University,
Kansas State University, Pittsburg State University,
the University of Kansas, and Wichita State University

Library of Congress Cataloging in Publication Data
Main entry under title:
The Democratic state.
(Studies in government and public policy)
Bibliography: p.
Includes index.
1. Democracy.   2. Liberalism.   3. Capitalism.
I. Benjamin, Roger W.   II. Elkin, Stephen L.
III. Series.
JC423.D4418 1985   321.8   84-21963
ISBN 0-7006-0263-1
ISBN 0-7006-0262-3 (pbk.)

Printed in the United States of America

Contents

List of Tables

1

Between Liberalism and Capitalism: An Introduction to the Democratic State

Stephen L. Elkin

A book devoted to the "democratic state" must begin with the concept itself. For as George Kateb says, the concept is "alien to the spirit of representative democracy" (1979, p. 2).[1] After all, the variety of liberal theory that provides the principal justifying account of contemporary representative or liberal democracy argues that government is a contract for the safety, convenience, and prosperity of the contracting parties. It has only the life that these persons breathe into it, and it can make no claims on them except ones that they authorize. Indeed, in one version of liberal theory, government can do nothing for citizens that a complex array of mutual-benefit societies could not in principle do better and less coercively. Any argument that liberal democratic governments are "states," whether it is made by way of explanation or justification, is then unwelcome to many liberals because it implies that the basis of such governments is something other than or in addition to contract and consent. The study of the democratic state is likely then to be widely perceived as an unwise and peculiar enterprise, plagued by contradictions.

The events of the last fifty years have also done little to encourage the development of a political science built around a conception of the state. As George Armstrong Kelly notes, theories of the state have become associated both with the organized evil of fascism and with what is thought of as a "superannuated idealism of the nation's corporate will" (1979, p. 21). If this were not enough, in the hands of some Marxists the state has been understood as the "executive . . . committee of the . . . bourgeoisie" in a sufficiently literal way to put off all but the most intrepid and committed theoretical workers in the Marxist vineyard (Marx and Engels, 1955, pp. 11–12).

What then accounts for the renewed interest in the state and particularly the democratic state?[2] It is possible to get along without a discussion of the state as long as we believe that the direction of public action is defined by the choices of private individuals.[3] Society directs government, we might say, and the apparatus of popular control is the principal means by which it does so. But several features of twentieth-century democratic political economies have made this view of the connection between society and the state increasingly problematic. These features have encouraged state-centered formulations that highlight the ability of the state to shape society in directions that cannot be easily traced to direct expressions of citizen opinion.[4]

An introduction to the democratic state can usefully begin by looking at the features of contemporary societies that have invited these formulations and then turn to the formulations themselves. We will then be in a position to consider the responses made by students of politics to the rise of the democratic state, particularly its relation to the liberal theory that is at the heart of our thinking about Western societies. The discussion as a whole will provide the necessary foundation for characterizing the five essays that follow.

POLITICAL FEATURES
OF CONTEMPORARY LIBERAL DEMOCRACIES

The features to be considered are in varying degrees common to virtually all liberal democracies. But they will be discussed with an eye to the American case, since it is the United States that informs much of the analysis in *The Democratic State* and is the paradigmatic society for many of the theorists discussed below.

The first feature of interest is the increasingly administrative character of twentieth-century democratic government. To the liberal democratic panoply of legislature, court, and executive have been added administrative agencies that are not legislative or judicial or simply implementers of statutory law. Such agencies exercise great discretion, which is often loosely, if at all, bound by citizen preferences, statutory declaration, or judicial review (see Lowi, 1979; Stewart, 1975). Given an economy managed by such administrative officials, for example, the question naturally arises, For whom is it being administered? If those responsible for economic management have considerable discretion, it is plausible that they will use it systematically to favor business interests (i.e., those crucial to the economy's workings) over citizen opinion.

The same kind of argument can be made about the administrative apparatus of contemporary government in its guise of provider of social welfare. Social-welfare programs are designed at least partly to pacify the have-nots and are generally aimed at creating a work force that is amenable to the requirements of a property-based market system. The features of policies that have these purposes are unlikely to spring from popular preferences (Bowles and Gintis, 1976; Piven and Cloward, 1971 and 1977).

The weakening of political parties has very likely increased the discretion of public officials generally. However imperfect, parties have been a principal means of transmitting citizen opinion to political authorities and of enforcing accountability. The decline of parties opens the way for government that is dominated by policy networks, iron triangles, and coterie politics—in short, by groups of like-minded politicos who are able to keep out intruders and successfully to promote their own policy preferences (Heclo, 1978). Government begins to resemble a policy machine whose inputs and outputs are increasingly detached from broad-gauged citizen preferences. Parties provide no guarantee against the detachment of public officials from citizen opinion (and under some circumstances may increase it), but they have been important historical means by which society has attempted to control government.

The diagnosis of public authority that has been loosened from its moorings in consent and representation is further supported by our increased understanding of the significance of business concentration. The state as the handmaiden of capital is a more plausible interpretation when the process of capital accumulation is visibly organized through large-scale business corporations. It is one thing for capital accumulation to occur through the market and through financial institutions that are able to work in anonymity. But the creation of companies the size of the Fortune 500 suggests that organizations large enough to internalize at least some of the process of capital accumulation might easily decide to ask for and *get* help from government in doing so (Galbraith, 1967; Herman, 1981). A government already organized to manage the economy might indeed be receptive to corporate needs and might begin to render decisions according to whether they facilitate or retard capital accumulation. Public officials who are seen talking regularly to corporate statesmen about the health of the economy are unlikely candidates for analyses built around popular consent.

The facts of life in the contemporary international economy also reinforce state-centered formulations. Although some countries have been consistently mercantilist during the modern era, liberal societies have typically been more hesitant to deeply involve public officials in bolstering

3

the country's international trading position. This has now changed. Not the least reason is a more competitive and interdependent international economy in which industrial and commercial abilities may be spread more widely than ever before. Public officials now have substantial incentives to take a strong lead in harnessing the nation's assets. Whether such efforts are in the service of business interest or some conception of national interest (Krasner, 1978) is less important than the evidence that public officials take the lead in shaping national policy. A review of negotiations over the international monetary system suffices to show just how large state discretion looms in a matter of fundamental domestic importance. Contemporary debates over industrial policy suggest that state direction of national assets to promote international competitiveness is now a widely contemplated step.

The marked discretion of state officials, weakly bound by popular control, should not surprise us. Has not the rise of America as a world power in the atomic age prepared us to think in statist terms? How else are we to interpret the content of nuclear policy and the activities of the national-security apparatus but in state-centered terms? While there seems to be little doubt that the development of nuclear weapons and national-security agencies was a response to popular worries, policy in these areas has evolved almost entirely from the preferences of those who staff the bureaus of the executive establishment. If ever the "state" is at work, it is here. The doctrine of "national security" and the various governmental organs that elaborate it and provide the material bases in budget, weapons, and armies provide fertile ground in which state theories can flourish (Schurman, 1974; Halperin et al., 1976; Ross and Thomas, 1976).

This list of features of twentieth-century democratic politics strongly suggests that governmental activity is systematically shaped by forces beyond those generated by popular control. The discussion also indicates that governmental action does not merely reflect features of society but also actively shapes them. Government's sheer size, organizational ability, and range of activities point to this conclusion. These observations have prompted state-centered analyses of democratic politics, both of Marxist and of non-Marxist varieties.[5] These analyses have attempted to capture the active quality of government and the variety of forces that systematically shape its actions.

CLASS LACKEYS, CLASS FIDUCIARIES, AND STATE MANAGERS

In recent Marxist theories of the state, capitalism is no mere economic order but is a complex social formation that joins the economic and the

4

political. Having learnt that the connection between what capitalists may be assumed to want and what public officials actually do is often tenuous, many Marxists have discarded theories that turn on having an organized class instruct public officials and have adopted arguments about the "relative autonomy" of the state. This phrase is meant to indicate that political activity is indeed determined by the mode of production, but only "in the last instance" (Althusser and Balibar, 1970; Poulantzas, 1974).

The state, though ultimately in the service of capital, may act in ways "contrary to the short term economic interests of the dominant classes" (Poulantzas, 1974:190). Still, its very workings serve to prevent class cohesion by defining workers as individual citizens of a supposedly neutral state. The state does this juridically, since its organizing legal principles establish workers as individuals, preventing them from seeing the reality of the class struggle and their common position in the mode of production. Even as the state may accommodate some of the demands of the dominated classes, it still individualizes workers, thus preserving the capitalist mode of production which depends on (among other things) a competitive labor market (Gramsci, 1971; Poulantzas, 1974).

There are other versions of how and why the democratic state consistently acts to guarantee the interests of capital. Some theorists worry less about autonomy and take as their central proposition that the state "organizes" capitalism in ways that capitalists cannot do themselves. Class lackeys have turned into class fiduciaries. Because capitalists are competitors who operate in diverse ways, they are unlikely to be able to organize themselves into class-conscious organizations capable of articulating clear class interests. If the democratic state serves capital, these theorists argue, it must be because of features of the state itself, such as how it raises its revenues (Offe, 1974 and 1975; Block, 1977). Now this sounds very much like those who talk about the state's being determined in the last instance by the mode of production. And indeed, the difference in views is not always easy to detect. But theorists like Poulantzas seem to argue that the juridical character of the democratic state itself stems from the features of the capitalist mode of production, while those who might be labeled fiduciary theorists seem to argue that the features of the state that guarantee its fidelity to capitalism arise from the historical development of the state. In the hands of a theorist like Offe, the argument reads as if the interests of capital are what state managers say they are and that the continuation of capitalism depends on the exertions of the state. Class interests and class conflict play a decidedly secondary role in such arguments.

A number of questions remain unresolved in Marxist analyses of the democratic state. How important is the apparatus of elections and popular control in explaining the direction of state actions? Is popular control the

Stephen L. Elkin

façade behind which the real work of running capitalism gets done? If the state is relatively autonomous, how autonomous is that? Is it autonomous enough to dig the grave of capitalism (a possibility that Braybrooke rather slyly entertains in his essay below)? If the state's autonomy is considerable yet, in the end, state action is "determined" by the requirements of capital, what precisely does the determining? Is it simply that capitalists are ultimately powerful enough to give orders? Or are there reasons that public officials, without being pressured, will choose to behave in the necessary ways, as, for example, Offe sometimes implies? If the latter is the case, what are the implications for a theoretical tradition founded on the assertion that modes of production are somehow decisive in explaining the character of political life?[6]

Non-Marxists have also been impressed by the increasing pervasiveness of the state in democratic societies, but they have not started from the premise that its form and content must somehow be explained by the capitalist mode of production.[7] Nevertheless, they have been struck by the importance, for political life, of a property-based domestic and international market system and have assumed that the principal features of the political order cannot fail to be influenced by the manner in which much of collective life is organized. To suppose otherwise is to entertain an absurdity, they imply, and in this they not only have Marx as a teacher but also Aristotle and Madison (see, e.g., Lindblom, 1977; Krasner, 1978; Plattner, 1982). But the implications of having the state guarantee that much of the society's productive apparatus will be controlled by a small portion of the citizenry are not as clear-cut to these theorists as to most Marxists. This is especially true because these non-Marxists recognize that the state is also organized around institutions of popular control that its officials likewise protect. This fact seems to be just as prominent to these theorists as how the productive capacity of the society is organized. Nevertheless, these non-Marxists observe that popular control is far from perfect, allowing many crucial decisions to be made in ways that are more or less completely shielded from popular scrutiny (Lindblom, 1977; Dahl, 1977).

Out of such observations has grown up an eclectic political economy whose starting point is typically the state officials themselves or whatever institutional arrangements are labeled the state. Whether, by what, and how the state is shaped are subjects left for investigation. Beyond that it is not easy to characterize what I have already labeled an eclectic body of literature. It is, however, possible to say what theoretical imagery does *not* dominate.

In the arguments of these political economists, state officials are not driven by the claims of interest groups, by self-interest narrowly defined, or by the "electoral connection." State officials are neither agents of powerful

6

groups, businessmen dressed up as public officials, nor vote maximizers, although each of these roles of course may shape their behavior. Nor are they class lackeys or class fiduciaries. In short, state officials are thought to have *choices,* and these choices are crucial to whether the political economy flourishes, remains stable, declines, or crashes. But state officials don't operate in an empty world. The world is structured; it presents obstacles and opportunities, both of which may be promptly ignored since these structural arrangements require interpretation.

Theorists have constructed a number of positions that are consistent with this imagery. Some have argued that state officials are attempting to manage a political economy whose basic dynamic is the competing pulls of market and popular control. Their work suggests how the preferences of large numbers of citizens, given voice by the apparatus of popular control, may impede the running of a market economy. Profits and votes pull in different directions (Elkin, 1982; Lindblom, 1977; Macpherson, 1966; Wolfe, 1977).

There are Marxist versions of such arguments which are, however, distinguished either by a belief in the laws of development of the capitalist mode of production or by the view that the tensions just considered are, at bottom, *class* tensions (see, e.g., O'Connor, 1973). When such theorists speak about structural dynamics, they typically mean the motion imparted by class struggle (see, e.g., Bowles and Gintis, 1982; Przeworski and Wallerstein, 1982). By contrast, the political economists under discussion are not class theorists. For such a theorist as Lindblom, the central building blocks of societies are *control systems,* not classes. It is the competition between business and popular control that provides the central dynamic of what he terms market-oriented polyarchies.[8] These political economists also tend to doubt that there are capitalist laws of development, or they suppose that there are other operative "laws" having to do, for example, with the path of democratization in Western societies. The implication is that the tension between market and popular control is not going in any particular direction but is an essential feature of the regime, to be managed intelligently or not by public officials.

Other political-economy-minded theorists doubt whether it is accurate to speak of tensions at all or, if they exist, whether it is quite so difficult to manage them as implied (Miller, 1982; Plattner, 1982; Zuckert, 1982). After all, they argue, property rights and the rights that undergird the apparatus of popular control have long been thought to be *compatible,* because they stem from the same principles. Political leaders presumably know this, and while some of their rhetoric may suggest an awareness of tensions between big business and the people, more often they appeal to the belief that free enterprise and democracy are mutually supportive. That was the Founders' hope, these theorists argue, and most citizens believe they are the beneficiaries of the founding design. In these analyses, too, the skill of state officials in interpreting the character of the political economy is essential to explaining both how officials act and the overall direction of the political economy.

More internationalist-oriented arguments about political economy may also be found, in which state managers attempt to serve the national interest as they navigate in a complex world system. In these analyses the principal dynamic is typically the conflict between the managers who defend and advance their conception of the nation's interests and those who defend bureaucratic preserves and seek to advance domestic political goals (see, e.g., Schurman, 1974; Krasner, 1978). So far there exists no compelling synthesis that combines an analysis of the state as an actor in the world arena and interpretations of state-society relationships.

Marxist and political-economy analyses of the democratic state do merge at one specific point: an increase in the influence of the democratic state has not been accompanied by increased confidence in public authority. In Habermas's influential formulation, we are experiencing a "legitimation crisis" (1975) in which the beliefs necessary to sustain a managerial state are weakening. Perhaps perversely, the shift from market decision to public decision has been accompanied by a decline in trust in government. Here, as in other cases, political scientists who are engaged in elaborating theses on the state may only be reflecting the transitory experience of ordinary citizens. If this is the case, we can expect to find that as these citizens learn to live with the new forms of collective problem solving and as those who have lost out under the new regimen or who are philosophically ill-disposed to accept it are finally defeated, the rash of worried inquiries into the future of the democratic state may decline.

LIBERAL AND DEMOCRATIC RESPONSES

How has our political thinking responded to analyses of the democratic state? In particular, how have assertions that systemic forces shape state activity and that the state shapes society influenced thinking about the prospects for liberal societies? The question of liberal prospects, of the continuation of a society built around individual autonomy, must be counted as the central question for our political thinking, regardless of whether we wish for a new society or only for retention of what is best in the present one.

Regrettably, many political scientists seem to be unconcerned. Many who are empirically minded remain indifferent in their work to some of the central features of twentieth-century democratic politics and to efforts, like the ones just canvassed, that seek to interpret those features. It is difficult not to be contentious here, but the essential point seems to be that much of political science simply takes for granted its own foundations in a particular liberal view of the relationship between state and society. In this view, politics is implicitly understood as a deputy for society, designed to resolve conflicts among social groups which they cannot resolve for themselves. The results are acceptable, it is believed, because the deputies are instructed and their actions are reviewed. Society is viewed as directing the state, and the principal link between the two is the apparatus of popular control. Since many political scientists appear to be only dimly aware that these are their underlying presuppositions, they do not perceive the challenge inherent in state-centered analysis that is critical of such views.[9]

The difficulties of perceiving the challenge are compounded for many empirically minded political scientists because any intimation that state-centered analyses are fundamental is all too easily translated into the belief that some analysis of the power elite is being called for. And since it is widely believed that arguments such as those of C. Wright Mills cannot withstand either empirical or analytic scrutiny, the tendency to ignore state-centered analysis is strengthened.

Furthermore, many of these political scientists are reluctant to consider questions such as the prospects for liberal society because they sense that they will need either to join hands with political philosophers or to study the subject themselves. This they are reluctant to do. The celebration of the fact/value distinction, the praise of "scientific" political science, and the effort by the empirically minded to turn political philosophers into "normative" specialists (in which guise they may easily be disregarded, since no right-thinking American believes that anyone possesses a special expertise in "values")—all conspire against the acceptance of state-centered analyses.

Some students of politics have been more aware of how profound a challenge "stateness" poses to a liberal account of the workings and purposes of contemporary Western societies. One large group has responded by arguing (sometimes implicitly) that liberal theory can accommodate the challenge, because in its various forms it provides the guidance to interpret what is occurring and directions on how to respond. Three versions of this response may be discerned, each of which takes as central that a political order organized around the self-directed pursuits of individuals is still desirable and possible. These versions may be labeled: radical, expansionary, and chastened liberalism.

Radical liberals wish to go back to what they believe are the roots of liberal society. They argue that the growth of the democratic state must be

9

reversed, because it has resulted in an increase in bureaucratic discretion and in collective decision making, both of which have diminished liberty. The remedy is to restructure the society so that it will rely as little as possible on collective decision making and as much as possible on contract and private cooperative agreements. Free-market advocates (M. Friedman, 1962), libertarians (D. Friedman, 1973), contractarians of minimalist persuasion and their public choice fellow travelers (Nozick, 1974; Buchanan and Tullock, 1962), and Hayekians (Hayek, 1973)—all join in the effort to rescue liberal society from the state. Most of these theorists understand the rescue operation as securing a society of autonomously choosing individuals, a rescue operation made necessary because these (same?) individuals have (mistakenly?) constructed a quite different social order. The most thoughtful of these theorists recognize the dimensions of the reconstruction task.

Expansionary liberals come in two varieties: optimistic and temperate. The optimists are inclined to view the rise of the democratic state as an opportunity to use public authority for the creation of just the sort of rights-based society that liberalism has promised but, in their view, has not secured (see Ackerman, 1984; Dworkin, 1977; Okun, 1975; Rawls, 1971; Reich, 1964). The state, rather than being the enemy of autonomous individuals, is or can be either the creator or the guarantor of individualism. The forms of relations among citizens and between citizens and officials are now visibly a question of choice, it is argued, subject to reconstruction through law and legislation. The distinction between state and society is not to be dissolved, but the balance is to shift so that the state is the creative element that remakes society in the state's liberal image. There is little agreement about the sources of evaluative guidance for this effort at social reconstruction, if indeed there be any. What the most thoughtful theorists do agree on is that the activist democratic state may not be easy to guide in the manner that liberal theory requires.

The temperate expansionary liberals are better tutored than their brethren in the ways of power and the limits of social rationality. They still hope, however, for a state that will be capable of tempering the arbitrary exercise of private power. Here we find Lindblom (1977; with Cohen, 1979) and Dahl (1982; with Lindblom, 1953), for example, who understand the limits of bureaucratized social problem solving and the difficulties of controlling political leaders but who reason that only state authority is capable of remaking property relations and the internal life of the business corporation. These are said to place severe constraints on the day-to-day freedom and the popular control of authority that liberalism promises. The least optimistic among these theorists, which may include Lindblom himself, wonder whether state officials can in fact escape the grip of the business corporation in order to undertake the necessary reforms.

Chastened liberals worry deeply that in the end, an activist state will break down any distinction between state and society, between public and private, and will usher in the end of liberalism. A state that is capable of regulating everything will be thus tempted, they argue, and will proceed in ways that are arbitrary and produce unwarranted privilege. Chastened liberals believe that liberal theory provides the necessary diagnosis and remedy, this time in the form of constitutionalism. The positive administrative state is here to stay, they say, but it needs to be constitutionalized. The leading contemporary statement is by Lowi (1979), who is perhaps less persuaded than are other chastened liberals that state officials have great autonomy since he thinks that grants of discretionary authority are rapidly given content by interest-group preferences (cf. Lowi, 1979, with, e.g., Wilson, 1980). Constitutionalism, for Lowi, means freeing public authority from the power of interest groups and tying it to explicit statements of public objectives that are offered by the legislative process.

Other defenders of liberalism, equally drawn to constitutionalism but doubtful that state officials are as tied to interest groups as Lowi supposes, are also skeptical about the possibility of constitutionalizing administrative discretion through a strengthened legislative process (see discussion in Stewart, 1975; Wilson, 1980). Some theorists rely instead on educating administrators in a constitutional ethos and on the checks and balances of the original constitutional design (Rohr, 1983; Storing, 1980).

Yet another group of theorists have concluded that the rise of the state has rendered implausible a liberal account and justification of our present political order. The state-centered analyses surveyed so far teach, they argue, that political reconstruction of the most profound kind is called for. In the phrasing of a recent book, what is wanted is "strong democracy" based on "talk"; that is, deliberation about what is common to us as citizens (Barber, 1984). These democrats, as it is appropriate to call them, equate a state-centered politics with an undesirable bureaucratized political life dominated by expertise at the expense of the ordinary citizen's judgment.[10] Such a political life promotes passivity when active citizenship is needed. If the various shades of liberals look to Hobbes for inspiration, these "democrats" look to Rousseau, who suspected any separation between citizens and collective decision making (see Pateman, 1970; Walzer, 1976; Unger, 1983).

If liberals, even optimistic liberals, rely on the distinction between public and private as the cornerstone of the good society, democrats wish to tie politics as closely as possible to the ordinary life of the citizenry, to break down what they believe is the artificial barrier between state and society. A state-centered politics cannot provide the widespread opportunity to struggle and deliberate over the content of the common good. Such a politics asks

11

too little of its citizens, democrats say, and consequently may get too little when the collective good of the society is threatened. The more thoughtful democrats also concede that strong democracy may ask too *much* of citizens and use their participation in ways that are profoundly pernicious (Barber, 1984; Sandel, 1982).

THE ESSAYS

Much contemporary American political science, especially in its more determinedly empirical branches, has ignored the theoretical challenge posed by the increasing centrality of the state in the life of liberal democratic societies. In many professional students of politics this inattention helps to produce a bland, unexamined faith that they are studying a sound constitutional regime whose mainspring is the electoral connection. The tacit assumption is that nuclear arsenals of the present size, international monetary policy, and accelerated depreciation schedules, to mention just a few items, are consonant with the broad citizen preferences. The mainstream of late-twentieth-century American political science seems no better prepared to confront the principal political facts of the twentieth century than did its intellectual progenitor, mid-century behavioral political science. *That* political science flourished after genocide, the explosion of nuclear bombs, the rise of fascism, and the eradication of democratic regimes. Much contemporary political science appears to inhabit a mental world in which the legitimacy of liberal democracy is either not a problem at all or is thought to be one of psychology, not of something actually having gone wrong. That liberal democratic regimes are *at best* precarious achievements seems not to have sunk in.

For any single set of papers to remedy these deficiencies would be a great achievement. The authors of the papers that constitute this volume have more modest ambitions. Their work seeks to show how the rise of the democratic state calls into question at least the most facile explanations of the workings of liberal democratic politics and the least reflective justifications that have been offered in its defense. None of the papers advances specifically Marxist analyses of liberal democratic politics, although most of the authors are conversant with such work, as the papers themselves make clear. Instead, their principal intellectual ties are to the body of literature herein labeled eclectic political economy and to the variety of liberal and democratic theories that seek to interpret the rise of the democratic state. Two general questions guided the writing of the essays: What is the character of the democratic states operating in advanced capitalist economies? and, What may we hope for from the political life of such states?

The opening essay, by Roger Benjamin and Raymond Duvall, argues for having a variety of types of states operate in capitalist economies. This must be the starting point for an inquiry such as ours since, unless the character of states varies under capitalism, no inquiry into the *democratic* state can have much if any meaning. Capitalism itself would determine the essential features of the state, and claims of democratic control would be bogus or at best a distraction from the serious business of the state to maintain capitalism. Benjamin and Duvall also discuss the related theme of the autonomy of the state and consider the complexities that lie behind this concept. They then turn to the transformation of the democratic state under capitalism, emphasizing that changes in the kinds of goods that citizens wish to obtain through the market and through state provision have had a substantial impact on the character of political activity. Increasingly, they say, citizens in advanced capitalist or postindustrial societies are concerned with the "social relations of production"—that is, with quality-of-life issues, regulation of externalities, and positional goods. The politics of such a society, they imply, is likely to turn increasingly on expertise and ideology—on ideas in general—rather than on a struggle for material possessions.

David Braybrooke, whose essay comes next in the volume, builds much of his argument concerning the prospects for a significant transformation of the democratic state under capitalism around just such political changes. For Braybrooke, the state may be sufficiently autonomous to transform itself in directions that are contrary to the wishes and interests of controllers of capital. He argues that within the state apparatus there is a large array of professionals who have a strong interest in moving beyond the status quo. Their cumulative efforts, Braybrooke contends, may avoid the legitimation crisis recently described by Habermas. Habermas attributes this crisis in part to an increase in state intervention to deal with the new kinds of goods mentioned by Benjamin and Duvall. But the normative justification for such extensive involvement of the state is missing, says Habermas. Braybrooke considers how it might emerge.

Braybrooke argues, in effect, that ideology, styles of collective problem solving, the varieties of professional expertise, the apparatus of popular control, and the control of productive assets must all be analyzed in order to understand the future of the democratic state. His paper may be read as an example of how Marxist themes may be employed within a more comprehensive explanatory framework that is also sensitive to normative concerns. Without directly claiming to be so, the paper is a subtle critique of much Marxist and liberal theorizing as well as an instructive effort in combining normative and explanatory analysis.

All the essays in the volume reject the image of public officials as cyphers and of state action as serving a dominant class. But whether public officials are best understood as entrepreneurs, running something like a particularly powerful business firm selling in a political marketplace, or whether they must be understood as having more complex motives is a question on which the authors are divided. Peter H. Aranson and Peter C. Ordeshook, whose paper comes third in the volume, lean heavily on the idea of the state as being an extension of market transactions. Working from a public-choice perspective, they treat the state much like a business firm (or a set of firms) engaged in a series of transactions with citizen-consumers. Officials are assumed to be dependent enough on votes and citizens are assumed to be informed enough about how to pursue their interests so that there will be no question of state action being in the service of a single class interest. Interestingly, Aranson and Ordeshook share some of the worries of theorists on the Left that state action is, in their terms, "welfare-degrading." But their version is that the state is too attentive to *multiple* particular interest groups, which have succeeded in using public authority to supply themselves with benefits, shifting the costs to the collectivity as a whole.

The principal theme of Aranson and Ordeshook's essay is the failure of the present form of the democratic state to do an adequate job of translating broad citizen preferences into public action. As Braybrooke does, they move naturally from the explanatory to the normative, directing their analysis to how individual choice may be strengthened as the informing principle of democratic government. The very questions asked by all of these theorists are value laden; the criteria for judging the justice of the democratic state provide guidance for what is important to explain.

My essay, which comes next in the volume, also moves from explanatory matters to the justice of liberal democratic states. I argue that state officials are not closely bound by voter and group preferences, although the apparatus of popular control does matter. Neither are they in the service of a dominant class interest. My argument is consistent with Braybrooke's. The state operates in a capitalist economy, and institutions of popular control are at work; but public officials have an agenda of their own. For me, this principally means that they have their own ideas about how to generate high levels of economic performance and that they seek to deflect citizen demands that may impede their own efforts to induce growth.

My deepest concerns are normative; I ask whether liberal democratic states are nothing more than tools of domination and arenas of class struggle. I contend, instead, that they are *mixed* states and that, as such, they embody competing claims to just rule. The liberal democratic state is not derivative of economic arrangements, nor is it divorced from them. It is neither the handmaiden of capital accumulation nor an agent effectively

14

directed by popular control. Its workings are more complex, as are the grounds of its justification.

The three essays by Aranson and Ordeshook, Braybrooke, and Elkin are all liberal analyses of the workings and reform of the democratic state. In the concluding essay, Norman Furniss considers some democratic remedies and analyzes the kinds of political orders that reform of democratic states under capitalism might produce.

Furniss asks in effect, What may we hope for from democratic political life? He argues that the "regime crisis" of advanced democratic capitalist states will most likely result in either a successful defense of the welfare state or in its retrenchment. Neither result, however, is particularly appealing because the theoretical foundations and the economic basis of the welfare state are becoming increasingly shaky. Moreover, neither of course produces any serious reforms of democratic capitalism. But there *are* important reform currents at work which, Furniss argues, are intriguing in theory if far less likely to be realized than is the continuation of the welfare state. He considers two reform proposals: socialism in production and autogestionnaire democracy. The first aims to cut away at the distinction between state and market and at the present definition of property rights, which is at its core. The second looks to "civil society" as the locus for reform, as opposed to state, party, and political program. One might suppose that with autogestionnaire democracy, Western political thought has come full circle, back to Rousseauist images of state and society.

In Furniss's view, what we may hope for is more of the same, but the same is morally suspect. Whether wide-ranging reform will be possible depends in part on the development of a morally inspiring vision of a more fully democratic society. He says, however, that it will be difficult to fill the moral void created by the increasingly problematic status of democratic capitalism.

It is striking that all the authors discuss the rise of the administrative state as being a possible barrier to the achievement of justice in democratic states. The essays show a deep concern with the decline of public forums that encourage, for example, justification of any proposed distribution of benefits and burdens. Braybrooke notes that the rise of administrative discretion has its positive side, freeing professionals to develop and advocate reformist schemes. But collectively, the authors (including Braybrooke) are drawn to decentralized nonadministrative forms of social decision making. If the democratic state is to retain its legitimacy, they imply, it must develop additional institutional arrangements that will rely heavily on participation in public forums and will allow greater possibilities for individuals to define and pursue their own interests through various kinds of mutual adjustment processes.

The authors argue, then, that students of the democratic state under capitalism ought to enlarge their pantheon of seminal theorists. Adam Smith and Max Weber should be added to Marx. We need the perspectives of all three if we are to obtain a theory of the democratic state that will pay due regard to the power of administrators and to the proper direction for reform efforts, as well as to the influence of capital. And if we follow the essayists in their concerns for a just political order, the theory of the democratic state must also take its bearings from political philosophy. This last is the most important thing we learn from the essays. The very questions that we ask about the state are formed through our thinking about what is possible and just in political life. The essays demonstrate that these normatively informed questions can be pursued through a variety of theoretical frameworks, from radically individualistic and empirical to structural and speculative.

The theory of the democratic state is not, then, a Marxist preserve, although, indeed, Marxists have done much of the serious work to date. Liberals (and democrats) can and must contribute. They must because their explanatory paradigms are radically incomplete without an analysis of the state and because the sort of political order to which their political science contributes and which it sometimes celebrates is undergoing marked change. Failure to analyze the democratic state will make these political scientists irrelevant in the most important contemporary political struggles.

A theory of the democratic state is not just an exercise in explanation and demystification. That, indeed, has been the principal emphasis to date. Instead, it is a part of the effort to examine the political regimes that men are capable of, given the kinds of beings they are. Marxists who do not join their analyses of what is to a sustained discussion of what is possible and desirable will help to usher in what is reprehensible. In this they will be joined by political philosophers who are indifferent to empirical analysis and by empirically minded political scientists who are too interested in explanation to notice the fundamental reconstruction of the political life that they are trying to explain.

NOTES

1. Cf. Carl Friedrich's remark that "only in Britain, where the idea of modern constitutionalism was developed in antithesis to the 'state' concept in the course of the revolutionary struggles of the seventeenth century, did the doctrine [equating state and sovereignty] fail" (1950, p. 17).
2. See the recent overviews by Carnoy, 1984; Jessop, 1982; and Nordlinger, 1981.

3. Some terminological matters require attention. "Democratic state" should be interpreted here as meaning the state in liberal democratic societies, i.e., societies organized around popular sovereignty and a concern for individual rights. As noted, liberalism is the justifying account of how such societies work.

4. For present purposes the state can be defined as the constitutional-legal entity that sets out the authoritative policies of the society and controls the principal means of organized coercion. Benjamin and Duvall, in their essay in this volume, provide a more elaborate discussion.

5. For an overview of Marxist theories see Carnoy, 1984; and Jessop, 1982. On non-Marxist theories see Nordlinger, 1981.

6. Cf. Raymond Williams's (1977) remark that "a Marxism without some concept of determination is in effect worthless. A Marxism with many of the concepts of determination it now has is quite radically disabled" (p. 83). See also the scathing essay on Althusser by E. P. Thompson (1979).

7. Because this is a variegated collection of theorists, it is not easy to collectively characterize their work. Convenience of exposition and space both exert a homogenizing pull which the reader should guard against.

8. Contrast here Poulantzas, 1973; and Lindblom, 1977. Offe (1974 and 1975) is an ambiguous figure in this regard since class does not play the major role in his analysis, that position being reserved for the state serving capital.

9. The empirically minded have been joined by the instrumentally minded, but with a twist. Many policy scientists ignore the rise of the democratic state simply by positing its existence and trying to promote the efficient achievement of whatever policies it produces.

10. Instead of calling these theorists "democrats," it might be better to describe them as liberals who wish to democratize liberalism. This may be Barber's view, for example. But the issue of how far democratization is to go is not addressed in enough detail in the work of democrats, although Barber goes further than most.

2

The Capitalist State in Context

Roger Benjamin and Raymond Duvall

The recent resurgence of scholarly interest in the state has resulted in an active debate about the relationship between state and society.[1] The largest contribution to this debate has focused on the state in capitalist society, and much of it has been influenced in one way or another by classical Marxian concerns about the nature of the capitalist state. This has meant, by and large, that it is not the state in the abstract that is of greatest interest; rather, the *capitalist* state in *capitalist* society is the explicit concern of theorists. As a result, much of the current debate is conducted within the framework of what is referred to as "the theory of the capitalist state."[2]

One of the central questions in the current debates about the relationship between state and society concerns the autonomy of the capitalist state. Some maintain that the state is completely autonomous, an actor with its own interests, existing unto itself and for itself (Krasner, 1978). Others, following the classical Marxian perspective (perhaps Miliband, 1969) may believe that the state exists as an instrument of the dominant capitalist class, and therefore exhibits no autonomy. At least this position is typically injected into the debate, if only as a straw-man position, and it is essentially represented by the famous dictum that "the executive of the modern state is but a committee for managing the common affairs of the whole bourgeoisie" (Marx and Engels, 1972:33). Most participants in the debate, however, seem to have gravitated toward the position that the state is to be understood as being *relatively* autonomous (see, e.g., Hamilton, 1982; Evans et al., 1985). This seems to be a safe intermediate position, but its vagueness about the extent and the form of the *relative* autonomy of the

19

capitalist state permits the debate to continue uninterrupted. What it means for the capitalist state to be relatively autonomous remains controversial.

The continuation of this debate within the framework of the theory of the capitalist state is, in many respects, to be commended. Certainly, few scholarly endeavors are of greater current importance than the effort to understand the nature and the role of the state in capitalist society—its structural basis and the significance of its operational independence.

However, we believe the foundations of the debate can be improved in at least two important respects. First, there is lack of clarity and shared meaning in the use of the term "the state" among different scholars from different intellectual traditions. Put simply, the state means different things to different people. This means that a debate about the relative autonomy of the state may be (and frequently is) unfruitful because the participants may not share an understanding of what it is that is allegedly relatively autonomous. We address this issue of conceptual clarity in the next section, where we distinguish five conceptions of the state.

Second, in much of the debate, there is not enough sensitivity to the importance of context. We find this ironic, because the clear implication of setting the debate within the framework of "the theory of the capitalist state" is that context does matter. In particular, the implication is clear that capitalism somehow constitutes or defines a unique, special context for which a theory of the state will take on a different form from what it will for the state in contexts other than capitalism. It is not the theory of the state in the abstract that sets the framework for the debate about relative autonomy; rather, it is the theory of the *capitalist* state. Capitalism, as a context, must matter.

The problem, and the source of the irony, is that this implication is not pursued to its logical end. Discussion of *the* theory of *the* capitalist state suggests that capitalism constitutes a single, undifferentiated context everywhere. In our judgment, this is an inappropriate attitude, and it certainly contributes to inhibiting fruitful debate about the relative autonomy of the state to the extent that participants in the debate have fundamentally different contexts of capitalist society in mind as they address (and talk past) one another. It can and should be recognized that there are fundamentally different kinds or forms of capitalist societies in the modern world system. These different forms of capitalism define importantly different contexts for the state, so that the extent and the form of the relative autonomy of the state are likely to differ among societies.

This does not mean that we advocate an extreme relativist or historicist view in which context is all and generalization is impossible. However, we do reject as inadequate a theory that purports to be universally applicable across all contexts (see Benjamin, 1982). Fundamental differences in context are not entirely idiographic; to reject universalism, then, does not necessarily mean to accept a doctrine of complete social uniqueness. The key to this, however, rests with the word "fundamental," which we use repeatedly in this discussion as a modifier in setting our argument about resolving the tension between universalism and contextual uniqueness. If every difference in context is equally important, then one must adopt an extreme historicist position. But if some differences are fundamental, while others are merely superficial or apparent, then one can reject universalism and recognize that context matters to the validity of theory without going to the extreme of uniqueness.

For our purposes, when distinguishing different contexts of capitalism, *fundamental* differences concern the basic organizing principles—what might be called the "laws of motion" (Marx, 1967:10) or the basic dynamic and structural underpinnings—of the capitalist mode of production in different societies. Our argument is that, in the modern world system, there *are* different kinds of capitalist societies, based on fundamentally different organizing principles or "laws of motion," and that a debate in the framework of *the* theory of *the* capitalist state is disadvantaged by a failure to take account of these fundamental differences in the contexts of capitalism.[3]

Here we skirt the issue of just how many fundamentally different contexts of capitalism there are (or might be). The taxonomic exercise of identifying contexts could be quite useful. It might include such categories as primitive capitalism, competitive industrial capitalism, and late capitalism. Or it might make use of the periodization offered by Stavrianos (1981), which distinguishes mercantile (or commercial) capitalism, industrial capitalism, monopoly capitalism, and defensive monopoly capitalism. To pursue the development of an exhaustive typology, however, would lead us away from our primary objective, which is to demonstrate *how* context can be better incorporated into theoretical debates about the relative autonomy of the capitalist state. Therefore, we ignore many different kinds of capitalism and choose here to limit our attention to two ideal types (in the Weberian sense). We call those two fundamentally different forms of capitalism advanced (or "post")[4] industrial and dependent (or "peripheral") industrializing, respectively.

We develop our argument about the contextual basis of the relative autonomy of capitalist states in three stages, after we discuss, in the next section, the alternative conceptions of the state. In the second section we specify the distinguishing features of the two ideal types of contexts of advanced-industrial and dependent-industrializing capitalist societies. Then, in the third section, we employ these contextual differences to analyze the state in context, asking how it might be conceived and understood as a different creature in the advanced-industrial and dependent-industrializing capitalist contexts. Finally, in the fourth section, we offer contrasting theoretical arguments about the character, structure, and dynamics of state autonomy in the two contexts. We argue that one will draw different conclusions about the relative autonomy of the state when different conceptions of the state are used or when different capitalist contexts are referred to.

THE CONCEPT OF THE STATE

There is considerable confusion about the term "the state." It means different things to different analysts and theorists. To us this suggests a problem that must be addressed head-on before one can hope to conduct a dialogue about such theoretical issues as the relative autonomy of the state. It makes little sense to plunge into those theoretical issues unless or until there is a shared understanding of the central concept, the state. Unfortunately, little has been published to help promote conceptual clarification and shared understanding (see, however, Nettl, 1968; North, 1979). This section is an effort in that direction.

The first place to begin is to recognize that some political scientists disparage any use of the term and do not regard the state as a meaningful concept. This position seems to have two complementary sources. One is the behavioral revolution, with its aversion to abstract concepts; the other is an extreme individualistic (and reductionist), liberal philosophical perspective—namely, that the political process involving individuals and groups in interaction (often in an institutional setting) is the only appropriate unit of analysis. The effect has been that, for much of the postwar era, many liberal behavioral scholars have denied the existence of such a thing as the state, regarding it, instead, as an abstract fiction, nothing more than the reification of complex processes of interaction among individuals and groups in institutional settings (see Lowi, 1979; cf. Truman, 1951; Bentley, 1908). Fortunately, this position is no longer ascendent in political science (Evans et al., 1985), but it still must be recognized as an influential perspective that contributes to the lack of conceptual clarity about the state.

Beyond this conception that the state is not a meaningful concept, at least five different conceptions of the state are currently in circulation. The differences among the five are not small; they range from narrowly exclusive to broadly inclusive notions, and as such they imply different understandings and theories of the capitalist state. We approach them in order from most narrow to most inclusive conceptions.

1. The first and narrowest conception is of the state as a *unit of action* or as a unit of decisional authority. According to this conception, the state is

22

an actor that makes decisions and/or policy. Essentially, when one is employing this conception, the state is virtually synonymous with the government—by which is meant the collective set of personnel who occupy the positions of decisional authority in the polity, and the collective, but diverse, set of institutional agencies through which authoritative decisions and actions are taken. Whenever "the state" is used to refer to an actor—when, for example, one talks of state *policy*, or of the state *doing* something—the reference is generally implicitly to the government or some governmental agency or bureaucratic institution(s). Hence, this first, narrow conception of the state is being employed. It is the most concrete of the five conceptions of the state—an institutionally tangible "entity" that does things and has or makes policy.

This conception of the state is compatible with the extreme liberal tenets of the behavioral revolution, in treating the state as a collection of individuals and institutions that occupy role positions (those of governing authority) and that act as a group to govern. Thus, typically those in the tradition of pluralist/interest-group liberalism who write about the state at all employ this narrow conception of the state;[5] for them the state is, in effect, the government and/or governmental institutions and hence is a decisional/policy actor. But this conception is found outside of the pluralist, liberal tradition as well. Stephen Krasner's weak state–strong state dichotomy and his arguments about a "statist" perspective (1978), while they are avowedly nonindividualistic and distinct from the liberal tradition, rest on a rather narrow conception of the state as a unit of action, which has state interests and pursues state policy. Again, implicitly, this grounds the conception of the state in governmental decisions and the actions and interests of governmental agencies. Similarly, the tradition in international relations that refers to states as actors is rooted in this first conception.

In all, the conception of the state as actor has wide currency. But it is not the only conception, and indeed, as will be made clearer below, we do not believe that it is the most fruitful conception. The remaining alternatives, however, are more abstract notions—not in the sense of being more vague but, rather, in the sense of being less tangible, less concrete.

2. The first of these alternatives (our second conception) is of the state as the *organizing principles* that give "totality," or an underlying structural coherence (at an abstract level), to the myriad and diverse agencies and institutions of governance. This is the conception of the state apparatus as an organized, coherent whole—the *structure* of the state apparatus. In a sense this conception includes or subsumes the first, narrower conception, but it also goes beyond that conception. The personnel and the institutional agencies (including the public bureaucratic, administrative agencies) of government are elements of the whole, but they are not, themselves, the

23

organizing structure and hence are not the state in this second conception. Here, the state is not an actor or a mere aggregate of discrete individual and institutional actors; rather, it is the structuring principles according to which that aggregate as a whole is organized. Attention is directed to the organization and processes of governance, not to the decisions and actions of the government and/or governmental agencies per se. The state, in this second conception, does not *act* or *do;* rather, it *is* a structure.

This means that scholars who operate with this conception recognize and acknowledge the frequently incoherent, often inconsistent, and even competitive actions and policies of the separate, diverse agencies of government, while talking of a (abstractly) coherent set of structuring or organizing principles underlying them. Public bureaucracies can compete, but they stand in structured relation to one another and, together, to society. Later we say more about just what those structuring principles are. For now, it should be enough to illustrate how this conception has been employed in the scholarship of quite disparate traditions. One example is provided by the neoconservatives and liberal socialists in the U.S. (Huntington, 1975; Bell, 1975; Etzioni, 1977/78; cf. Downs, 1967) and Britain (King, 1975; Rose and Peters, 1978), who have noted the tremendous growth of the state apparatus and its increasing penetration of society. Of course, they evaluate this change very differently; but they concur on identifying a structuring principle that concerns the functional scope of and penetration of society by the administrative agencies of government across a whole range of social and economic activities (see also Skowronek, 1982; Tilly, 1975). In a similar vein, discussions of the rise and development of the welfare state (Wilensky, 1976; Flora and Heidenheimer, 1981; Hage and Hanneman, 1980; Skocpol and Ikenberry, forthcoming) or, in a different context, the bureaucratic-authoritarian state (O'Donnell, 1973; Collier, 1979) are based on a conception of the state in terms of organizing principles, not in terms of courses of action or kinds of policy. Likewise, neo-Marxists now often refer to the managers of the state apparatus as comprising a new "stratum" in social relations of production, sometimes even a new class whose size and interests set it apart from other classes (Wright, 1978; Poulantzas, 1973; O'Connor, 1973). This is clearly an attempt to identify a structural principle that provides abstract coherence to the state.

3. The third conception of the state that can be identified also revolves around structural principles, but in this case not those that underlie the organization of the agencies of government. Instead, this conception emphasizes the structural principles that define and constitute *social relations of political power and control* in society. In that sense, it is based neither upon a particular set of individuals or their actions, as is the first conception, nor upon a particular set of concrete institutions, as is the

24

second. Rather, it is based on the less tangible, the more abstract, set of social relations that constitute effective political power in society. This is essentially a class conception: in effect, *the state is the ruling class.*

Obviously, this conception generally encompasses both of the first two conceptions in that the personnel who occupy high positions of authority— the government—and the social "stratum" of the state apparatus are generally conceived as being part of the ruling class and as serving the interests of the ruling class. But this conception goes beyond those in that it includes also all elite positions of effective political power. Just what constitutes the set of such positions changes across time as the economy and polity change and become more differentiated in roles. Whereas, for example, the controllers of the mass media are not part of the state in the first two conceptions, they may have an important place in this conception. Similarly, perhaps, do labor leaders and the intelligentsia.

Although this conception is clearly associated with neo-Marxist analysts from C. W. Mills (1959) to E. O. Wright (1978; see also Therborn, 1978; Block, 1977), it should not be confused with the classical Marxist notion of the *dominant* social class (Althusser, 1970). The latter is defined in terms of social relations of *production* and exists as the class that dominates in the primary mode of production in society—for capitalist society, this is the bourgeoisie. By contrast, the state as the ruling class is a concept that is defined in terms of the occupation of positions of political power. It may, or may not, be thought to overlap substantially with the dominant class, depending on one's theoretical preconceptions. This means that one can employ the conception of the state as the ruling class (or, more generally, in terms of social relations of political power and control) without smuggling in an implication that one is really referring to the state as "the executive committee of the bourgeoisie." In sum, this is not a conception that is a theoretical short-cut toward acceptance of a crude instrumental Marxist perspective. Whether the ruling class is an instrument of the dominant class would remain a theoretical and empirical question. Instead, this is simply a more inclusive and abstract conception than the first two in saying that the state, per se, has to be understood as being more than the organized totality of the governmental apparatus. The latter is certainly a central part of the state; but also included are extragovernmental social relations of political power and control.

4. A fourth identifiable conception is even broader. It, too, is structural, but not in terms of relations between social classes. Instead, the state is conceived of as the *enduring structure of governance and rule in society;* in effect, it is the corpus of law in both the de jure and the de facto senses (see Hart, 1977). This is a conception of the state as the entire *institutional-legal order;* it is the machinery and the means by which conflict is handled, society

is ruled, and social relations are governed. This conception visualizes the state as being all of those explicit and implicit regulations—many, but not all, of which are codified in laws and administrative rulings—that govern social and economic relationships.

It may be argued that the first and second models of the state actually derive from this deeper model. It is in terms of this conception that we would place definitions of property rights as being features of the state per se (e.g., Furniss, 1978a, 1978b), and those definitions, after all, determine what property falls into the public rather than the private domain. It is from within the body of law of a society that regulatory practices do or do not emerge. For example, changes as to what appropriately falls under private and public property rights are what creates a climate for environmental protection by the governmental apparatus. Public-choice theorists in the United States have been active in working on property-rights theory (Buchanan, 1975; Aranson and Ordeshook, infra); critical theorists in Europe also are joining the debate (Braybrooke, infra). Neither school, however, explicitly recognizes the institutional-legal order as its conception of the state. About the closest that one can come to finding this conception identified explicitly is in the standard textbook literature on international relations, where the state is typically defined as a "system of political authority."[6]

5. Fifth, and broadest in scope, is the conception of *the state as being the dominant normative order* in society. This is the most comprehensive or inclusive conception because it subsumes the entire institutional-legal order and more. It is associated with the Gramscian notion of the hegemonic state (Buci-Glucksmann, 1980; Livingstone, 1976; Showstack-Sassoon, 1978) in that its focus is on the politically relevant norms and customs existing in the value system which form a "tacit" level of rule in society. The state, in this conception, is virtually synonymous with the ideational/ideological/normative bases of social order; it is, if you will, the warp and woof of societal fabric which consists of the dominant, or hegemonic, idea systems and normatively accepted practices that structure social relations. State and society become virtually indistinguishable.

The norms attached to participation and authority differ from one society to another (also over time within a society). The nature of these norms determines the individual's relationship to the group, even to the government; for example, whether one is to be subordinate or equal. From Antonio Gramsci (1971) and Jurgen Habermas (1975) we learn that language itself reinforces the society's "system of domination." This point is accurate in a Sapir-Whorfian sense. Macrosocietal institutions may be hierarchical and reinforced by the understandings attached to the concept of authority and by the language used to describe it. Such understandings may, however, evolve as norms, and values change. If this occurs, there will be pressure to change the existing system of hegemony,[7] the existing characteristics of the state as conceptualized in the second and fourth models above. In that sense, this conception underpins and structures at least those two narrower notions of the state.

Recognizing the wide disparity in conceptions of the state—from single and unitary actor to an entire dominant normative order—we must ask ourselves how to proceed. One cannot act as though the differences do not matter; indeed, the reason that the fivefold distinction between conceptions of the state is important is that one derives very different problems, arguments, and conclusions, depending on which conception one operates with. We suspect that much of the confusion surrounding debates and discussion over the state develops from authors who shift from one conception to another without explicitly realizing or noting it (see, e.g., n. 6 above). By making the fivefold distinction, one is in a better position to choose which conception of the state to examine. Our position is that the five are not equally useful conceptions.

Viewing the state as an actor is too narrow a conception in our view. In order to make the concept a meaningful and useful addition to our tools of analysis, it is better to view it in broader, more structural terms than this first conception. This is because the state as actor is virtually fully redundant with, and duplicative of, another well-established concept—namely, the government and its agencies. Here, the term "the state" is really nothing more than a "trendy," sexy label for an older bottle. Such a relabeling buys little save confusion. As a result, we believe strongly that when one employs a conception of the state as a unit of action/decision/policy, one should instead talk of the government and/or its institutional agencies. *The state is not an actor;* rather, the government and its agencies are.

Similarly, the state is not usefully conceptualized as the ruling class or as the social relations of political power and control in society (the third conception). That concept is too ambiguous: it would be a challenge, at best, to identify the ruling class precisely, and therefore, the state would necessarily remain a loose empirical notion. The state as ruling class requires substantial reconceptualization before it can be made useful. We need a structural method of determining which elites emerge and with what kind of impact on political power and control.

Finally, the fifth conception is too inclusive: virtually everything is a part of the state when it is defined as the dominant normative order. Theoretical development is artificially truncated, because the interesting

27

questions about state-society relationships are eliminated by subsuming "the state" under "society"—the two are virtually indistinguishable under this conception.

For us, then, only the second and fourth conceptions of the state are of theoretical interest and empirical utility. Each, we believe, is open to reasonably precise identification. One can "identify" the organizing principles that underlie and give coherence to the institutional aggregate of public bureaucracy and administrative apparatus; similarly, one can "observe" the established corpus of law that constitutes a legal order. In addition, each is a theoretically "unique" concept, distinguishable from other related concepts. Neither is highly redundant with other common concepts, all-encompassing in its scope of reference, or exclusive of interesting theoretical questions by definition.

Thus, in our judgment, there are two distinct but useful conceptions of the state. The first is the continually operating (i.e., administering, regulating, etc.), relatively permanent institutional aggregate of public bureaucracy and administrative apparatus *as an organized whole*. This is State 1. The second, State 2, is the more encompassing institutional-legal order, which is the enduring structure of governance and rule in society— the machinery and the means by which conflict is handled, society is ruled, and social relations are governed. We will employ both State 1 and State 2 in the analysis that follows.[8] Thus, our concern is with the relative autonomy of the structuring principles that underlie the institutional aggregate of public administrative apparatus, as well as the relative autonomy of the institutional-legal order. We shall not consider the relative autonomy of the government (as actor or decision-making unit), the ruling class generally, or the entire normative order.

As conventionally posed, the issue of the autonomy of the state concerns the degree of independence of the state from its structural basis in society. At the most general level, the question revolves around whether the state is "mere superstructural reflection" or is an "expression" of social structure. This takes more particular form in a set of questions about the relationship of the state to the dominant social class in the capitalist mode of production: To what extent is there, or is there not, an effective class basis of the state? Is the state more than a reflection of and an agency for the interests of the dominant class? Does the state, independently of dominant class interests, transform social relations and social structure? Most concretely, do some "statist" interests transcend the class basis of the state and therefore shape and direct it?

To some people, these questions may provide an intangible and, as a result, ambiguous definition of state autonomy. We recognize that we approach the issue somewhat differently from the way in which it is

28

sometimes conceived. Frequently, emphasis is placed on actions, decisions, and rules; that is, autonomy is often thought to revolve around what the state *does*. Accordingly, the guiding questions generally are: Are the state's *actions* hostile, or at least neutral, to the wants or desires of members of the dominant class? Do its decisions and rules originate from within itself rather than emerging as responses to the wishes of capitalists?

Our problem with these questions is that they are excessively focused on action, decision, wishes, and wants. As such, it is really an issue of the decisional insularity or independence of the first conception of the state discussed above. That conception we have rejected on the grounds that it is virtually redundant with the concept of the government or other particular agencies of the state. It may well be interesting to know how much decisional or action latitude the government has vis-à-vis the desires of the capitalist class. But that is not really a matter of the relative autonomy of the capitalist state per se.

Governments and bureaucracies do and will make decisions, take actions, and institute rules to which members of the capitalist class object. Does that mean, however, that the capitalist *state* is necessarily relatively autonomous? For us, the answer is clearly no. The reason is that the two conceptions of the state that we find sensible both point less to what the state *does* than to what the state *is*. In particular, the issue is the extent to which the basic *form* or character of the state—the set of organizing principles that give it coherence or "totality"—is in accord with and in the service of the objective interests of the dominant, the capitalist, class.

Posing the issue in this way presupposes that we can go beyond the decisions of governments, the actions of particular bureaucratic institutions, and the specifics of concrete legal pronouncements in order to see a "totality"—a coherent set of organizing principles—which is the state (whether as administrative apparatus or as institutional-legal order). In addition, it presupposes that we can ascertain the extent to which that set of organizing principles is in the service of—or is neutral with respect to—fundamental class interests (as distinct from conscious or expressed desires of members of a class). These may seem heroic presumptions, especially to persons who are accustomed to thinking in terms of the decisional independence of the government or other particular agencies of the state. Certainly they lead such persons to feel that the definitional questions that are posed above are rather ambiguous and fuzzy by comparison to the tendency to think about whether governmental actions and policies differ from the wishes of capitalists. But we believe that when one captures the essence of the two conceptions of the state with which we are working, questions about whether it is "a reflection of the basic interests of the dominant class" are seen not to be inherently ambiguous.

Roger Benjamin and Raymond Duvall

DIFFERENCES IN THE CONTEXTS
OF ADVANCED-INDUSTRIAL AND
DEPENDENT-INDUSTRIALIZING SOCIETIES

In this section we delineate what we regard as the relevant ways in which advanced-industrial[9] and dependent-industrializing[10] capitalist societies differ from each other, by analyzing their respective structural expressions.[11] Three dimensions of differentiation provide the basis for our analysis. They are: (1) the complexity and/or clarity of the class structure; (2) the substantive expression or manifestation of class interests; and (3) the locus of capital accumulation dynamics, the underlying processes through which spheres of production and exchange, class structure, and class interests are transformed. Together these three dimensions enable us to sketch the two ideal types of contexts in terms of social structural configurations, objective and expressed class conflicts, and transformation dynamics. We develop the sketches by considering each of the three dimensions in turn.

COMPLEXITY AND CLARITY OF SOCIAL STRUCTURE

Complexity and interdependence are two particularly important features of an advanced-industrial society. Growth in functional specificity—especially with respect to the increasingly important service sector that has seemingly endless components—produces a complex, integrated system of production and exchange. Indeed, new sectors develop as outgrowths of others. The increased complexity itself produces "crowding" effects and the need to restore order; recognition of the interdependence of seemingly disparate sectors also develops. Diversity, specialization, and sectoral integration, then, are the structural hallmarks of the spheres of production and exchange in the advanced-industrial context. It is a world in which industrial production per se is no longer dominant and in which information becomes crucial.

By contrast, the dependent-industrializing economy is structurally simple. A small number of sectors dominate the economy, and each of the dominant sectors is, relatively speaking, internally homogeneous; that is, there is, within any sector, low functional or role specificity. In addition, sectors exist in comparative isolation from one another; indeed, they develop quite independently, as frequently in response to processes elsewhere in the world system as to domestic economic processes (Duvall et al., 1981). As a result, there is extensive variation across sectors in sectoral dynamism, the extent of capital accumulation, and returns to factors of production. Sectoral imbalance, disarticulation, and intrasectoral

30

homogeneity, then, are the structural hallmarks of the economy in the dependent-industrializing context (Sylvan et al., 1983).

In a sense, complexity begets complexity, and simplicity begets simplicity. A highly variegated system of production and exchange can be expected to contain a complex class structure. Extensive role specificity and complex integration of sectors conjoin to produce a structure of subtly differentiated classes and extensive groups which are not easily classified in the conventional class categories of the capitalist mode of production.

In a word, the advanced-industrial context is marked by a highly ambiguous class structure. To be sure, there is an unambiguous labor class, a readily identifiable capitalist class, and a petit bourgeoisie, as conventionally understood. But there is much more; or at least there is considerable uncertainty about the class status of many in terms of the categories of labor, bourgeoisie, and petit bourgeoisie (Braverman, 1974; cf. Martin and Kassalow, 1980). Consider the recent debates about the so-called middle strata. What is the class status of the salaried white-collar bureaucrats, the technicians, the intelligentsia, the professionals? When such groups constitute as much of the economically active population as they do in the advanced-industrial society, no analysis of class structure can afford to ignore them. Nor is their effect unimportant in blurring class division or the pervasiveness and depth of the objective class conflict.

To what extent are the interests of the bourgeoisie, as the dominant class in the capitalist system, objectively at odds with, or objectively compatible with, the interests of these groups? An inability of scholars to provide a definitive analytical answer to that question points to a fundamental feature of the advanced-industrial capitalist context that is important for our analysis; namely, that in advanced-industrial capitalism the class basis of the state is ambiguous (both analytically and in practice) to the extent that neither class structure nor class interest is sharply defined.

By contrast, the relative simplicity of the production and exchange systems of the dependent-industrializing context is associated with a much more straightforward class structure. Classes are more clearly defined; the objective conflict in class interests is at least analytically apparent. This is not to say that ambiguity is entirely absent; there is a significant techno-bureaucratic elite in dependent-industrializing societies (Kautsky, 1972; Duvall and Freeman, 1983). But that technobureaucratic elite is not equivalent to the "middle strata" in postindustrial society, in terms either of social pervasiveness or of effect on the clarity of the class structure. Rather, in the dependent-industrializing context, conventional capitalist and precapitalist classes clearly compose most of the society. The exact composition, of course, varies from society to society; but typically, both the peasantry and labor (including literally a reserve army of unemployed)

31

are large. The conventional petit bourgeoisie is apparent, and there generally is a (small) national bourgeoisie and a landed aristocracy. Finally, and significantly, the international capitalist class is represented, although generally not through the physical presence of members of that class.

In comparison with the advanced-industrial context, then, in dependent-industrializing capitalism the class basis of the state may be relatively unambiguous (both analytically and in practice), because class structure and class interest are substantially more sharply defined.

THE EXPRESSION OF CLASS INTERESTS

Unambiguous class structure promotes a recognition of objective class interests. Complexity and ambiguity of structure make it more difficult to recognize and to express one's basic class interests. This means, *ceteris paribus*, that the behavioral manifestation or expression of interests is more likely to follow objective class bases in the dependent-industrializing context than in the advanced-industrial context. This is to say that the expressed interest of social groups is more obviously based in and revolves around social relations of production; the production and realization of physical value tend to underlie the major manifestations of competition and conflict.

In this sense, then, the dependent-industrializing context is one in which the basic processes of capital accumulation are paramount in defining what interests are pursued by groups. How production is to be organized and how the physical value that is produced is to be realized, by whom, and to what extent are the dominant questions over which interests manifestly conflict. Politics quite literally is a matter of "who gets what."

This is markedly less true in the advanced-industrial context, where objective class interests are less recognizable. There, interests grow less out of social relations of *production* than out of what might be called social relations of *consumption*. That is, the expression of group interests concerns general "quality of life" issues—how is life to be lived, with what kinds of rights, responsibilities, and privileges—much more than issues of how production is to be organized or how the physical value that is produced is to be realized. What might be called "positional goods" (Hirsch, 1976) are of equal importance to goods that one physically possesses. Furthermore, group competition and conflict revolve much more around the creation and regulation of externalities from the processes of production and consumption (Mishan, 1972). In the advanced-industrial context, manifest group interests are more concerned with the processes of consumption saturation (with respect to physical possession goods), which are often believed to be more basic than processes of capital accumulation (see Scitovsky, 1976). This is made possible because objective class interests are ambiguous and because the levels of material consumption are so high.

THE DYNAMICS OF STRUCTURAL TRANSFORMATION

There is a reciprocal relationship between the expression of interests by groups and the basic dynamics through which social structure is transformed. Structural transformation leads to the expression of different interests, and in some part, the manifest pursuit of interests by groups helps to channel the transformation of society. In this light, the varied expression of interests in the two capitalist contexts can be expected to be associated with different underlying dynamics through which those contexts are structurally transformed. And so it is.

In dependent-industrializing capitalism, the basic dynamic rests with the production and reproduction of the means of production. The conventional model of expanded reproduction is applicable here, although the sphere of reproduction goes beyond the dependent economy itself and includes the world economy. By contrast, in advanced-industrial capitalism, the locus of the transformation dynamic has shifted; it now rests increasingly with the production and reproduction of the "means of consumption."

What, then, are the implications of this basic difference in the two contexts? Since the process now revolves primarily around the means of consumption in advanced-industrial capitalism, the accumulation and expansion dynamic is substantially diminished. Slower and slower growth is, then, the expectation for advanced-industrial capitalism (see Baumol, 1967; Benjamin, 1982; cf. Olson, 1982). This expectation is countered only to the extent that a vigorous technological research-and-development (R & D) sector remains central and/or that "growth" (of income) is sustained by the repatriation of money capital from the periphery of the world system.

By contrast, in dependent-industrializing capitalism, the focus of the process of expanded reproduction on the means of production implies that the accumulation and expansion dynamic is potentially enlarged. For example, "boom growth" is at least logically compatible with the dependent-industrializing context of capitalism. The extent to which that potential is actualized in any particular dependent-industrializing society, of course, is highly dependent on the ways in which that society is and has been incorporated into the world system. One of the major distinguishing features of dependent capitalism is the strong, indeed almost entirely determining, exogeneity of the process of expanded reproduction. Both the impetus for and the constraints on that process are imposed by processes and agencies that are operating elsewhere in the international system (see Kurth, 1979; Evans, 1979). This means that the process of accumulation is a local reflection of an internationalized process (Dos Santos, 1970; Cardoso and Faletto, 1978).

33

Roger Benjamin and Raymond Duvall

A SUMMARY CONTRAST OF THE TWO CAPITALIST CONTEXTS

In table 2.1 we attempt to represent the major distinguishing features that set advanced-industrial and dependent-industrializing capitalist societies apart as two fundamentally distinct ideal types of capitalism in the contemporary world.

TABLE 2.1
FUNDAMENTAL CONTEXTUAL DIFFERENCES IN ADVANCED-INDUSTRIAL
AND DEPENDENT-INDUSTRIALIZING CAPITALIST SOCIETIES

DISTINGUISHING DIMENSION	ADVANCED-INDUSTRIAL CAPITALISM	DEPENDENT-INDUSTRIALIZING CAPITALISM
Structural complexity	Sectors of economy are interdependent and homogeneous with high differentiation functionally within sectors.	Sectors of economy are disarticulated and heterogeneous, with low differentiation functionally within sectors.
	Class structure is ambiguous; the class of many groups is uncertain.	Class structure is unambiguous; conventional capitalist and precapitalist classes are socially pervasive.
Expression of interests	Revolves around social relations of "consumption," with emphasis on "quality of life" issues more than objective class interests.	Revolves around social relations of production, with emphasis on organization of production and realization of the value of production along objective class interests.
	Rooted in process of consumption saturation.	Rooted in process of capital accumulation.
Transformation dynamic	Production and reproduction of "means of consumption."	Production and reproduction of means of production.
	Diminished potential for growth.	Significant potential for growth.
	Expansion is dependent on maintenance of centrality of R & D sector and extraction from periphery.	Expansion is dependent on the form of incorporation into the world system.

34

The table and our previous discussion indicate that advanced-industrial capitalist society is structurally complex and ambiguous; extensively populated by groups whose social class is not easily identified; marked by a relative saturation in the consumption of physical-possession goods; typified by competition and conflict among groups over "social relations of consumption" (i.e., "quality of life" issues, "positional goods," and the creation and regulation of production and consumption externalities); structurally transformed by processes of production and reproduction that revolve primarily around the "means of consumption"; and logically tending toward slower and slower growth except to the extent that technological R & D remains central and/or income can be extracted from the periphery of the world system. Dependent-industrializing capitalist society, by contrast, is structurally simple; has a sharp, unambiguous definition of class structure in which competition and conflict among groups generally follows objective class interests about the organization of production and the realization of the value produced; is structurally transformed by processes of production and reproduction of the means of production; and may or may not exhibit substantial growth.

Our task is to apply these defining statements of two distinct and ideal-type contexts of capitalism and to analyze the different nature and role of the capitalist state that exists in each of them.

THE STATE IN DIFFERENT CAPITALIST CONTEXTS

Earlier we said that analysis can and should proceed with respect to two distinct conceptions of the state. State 1 is the relatively permanent institutional aggregate of public bureaucracy and administrative apparatus as an organized, coherent totality. State 2 is the more encompassing institutional-legal order, the enduring structure of governance and rule in society. For each of these two conceptions we shall see how the state is a different kind of creature in the two contexts of advanced-industrial and dependent-industrializing capitalist societies because different structural expressions are provided by those two contexts. How is the public institutional aggregate as a coherent totality to be understood as having a basically distinct character in advanced-industrial society, in contrast to dependent-industrializing society? And how is the dependent-industrializing legal order fundamentally different from that in advanced-industrial society? Let us consider these issues, beginning with the second, broader conception of the state.

THE INSTITUTIONAL-LEGAL ORDER
IN DIFFERENT CAPITALIST CONTEXTS

There is virtually an unlimited number of ways in which one could compare and contrast states in different contexts. When one conceptualizes the state as the entire institutional-legal order, the possible points of comparison include the whole range of expressions of the law, both codified and not codified. Hence, the task of drawing out differences in the state in different contexts could quickly become a very difficult, if not an impossible, task; every legal difference could be understood, in a sense, to be a difference in the state. But theorists of the state, including ourselves, are rarely concerned with every apparent difference. Instead, we concern ouselves with the basic, or fundamental, organizing principles of the state as an institutional-legal order. This means that we must direct our attention away from particular laws and legal provisions per se and toward the more basic principles that underlie them. Those organizing principles, in effect, constitute the structure of the state.[12]

We shall argue that the structure of the state as an institutional-legal order includes at least three kinds of organizing principles. The first of those revolves around the notion and definition of *rights:* What constitutes a right? Who has rights and of what kind? Under what conditions do rights obtain? The second organizing principle for the legal order concerns the notion and definition of *private* and *public* (or social) spheres: How are public and private domains differentiated with respect to what types of activities, social relations, and possessions? What constitutes private and public "goods" and responsibilities? Third are the organizing principles addressed to the resolution or management of the tensions among conceptions of *freedom, equality, order,* and *justice:* How is each of those terms to be understood? When tensions exist among them, however they are understood, what are the rules and mechanisms through which the tension is handled? For us, then, an effort to analyze differences in the state in different contexts must include at least an examination of how legal order differs with respect to these three sets of issues as organizing principles.

The Notion of Rights. To speak of "rights" introduces a concept with a complicated past in the history of philosophy. But we believe it is important to direct attention to an indispensable theme for understanding the essential principles of an institutional-legal order; what persons can claim as *rightfully* due them is one of the foundational elements of any legal order, or State 2. We regard "rights" as being the set of legally recognized and protected privileges or immunities that are generally but informally (e.g., traditionally) agreed to be useful, just, or moral, as well as the set of legally constituted privileges or immunities that are created or established things that one may properly claim as one's due. Examples of the former might include the trinity "life, liberty, and property"; examples of the latter might include the right of various groups to vote. To examine this set of organizing principles, then, is to focus on the basic characteristics of the array of legally recognized and/or legally created just claims that are available to persons in a society.

Because of the differences in class structure and transformation dynamics in dependent-industrializing and advanced-industrial societies, what is included in rights differs substantially in the respective legal orders. In simple or most basic terms, rights in dependent-industrializing society are centered on the "life, libery, and property" trinity, with particular emphasis on the material dimensions. In the extreme, they reduce almost entirely to property rights. Accordingly, the state is primarily an embodiment and articulation of authoritative principles regarding the ownership, control, and utilization of property, including in property, of course, the means by which production is carried out in society. Typically, individuals have the right (1) to own and to dispose of property without much restriction; (2) to employ other individuals to work on the property they own; (3) to organize into new entities (companies, firms, etc.) that have the same rights as individuals; and (4) to accrue the benefits of organized ownership of property without limitation. Concomitantly, individuals who do not own effective property do not have a right to any particular "quality of life." They have only the right to attempt to accrue benefits of property ownership and the right to sell their labor to work toward that end. Often, however, they do not have the right to organize into new entities for selling their labor (such as guilds or unions) in the same way that property owners have the right to organize into companies.

We believe that this characterization represents the essence of legal orders in the dependent-industrializing societies of Latin America and East Asia. It portrays a state that is clearly rooted in and consistent with the fundamental structural features of the dependency context. It is the legal order for a society in which (1) well-defined class interests revolve almost entirely around social relations of production and (2) the basic dynamic is the process of capital accumulation through the reproduction of means of production. Property relations are the essence of society; property rights are the essence of the state.

By contrast, rights in advanced-industrial society are much more differentiated and complex. Property rights are basic in this context too; but they are significantly infringed upon by the articulation of other rights. The way in which life should be lived itself becomes, in advanced-industrial society, a matter of rights. Persons have the "right" to be free from worry about potential harm in consuming some commodity, the "right" to an adequate standard of living, the "right" to participate, and so on through myriad "quality of life" rights, including, perhaps, even such things as the "right" to breathe clean air.[13] On the one hand, this means that the state, as an institutional-legal order, is greatly expanded relative to the dependent-industrializing state; there is a fundamental difference between the contexts of rights in the scope of the state. For one thing, the conception of rights is broadened considerably by a more liberal (re)interpretation of what the trinity "life, liberty, and property" includes or implies, so that legally recognized rights are more numerous. For another, the set of legally constituted or created rights is larger.

But simple enlargement of the set of rights is not the only difference, because, on the other hand, the extension of "quality of life" rights amounts to an infringement of property rights. The right to a healthy environment, for example, has real implications for the rights of owners of the means of production to use and to dispose of their property as they see fit.[14] Thus, the state as an institutional-legal order is different in character as well as in scope from the dependent capitalist state. The difference in character clearly reflects the fundamental differences in social structures. The advanced-industrial state is rooted in a society of ambiguous class structure, in which interests revolve, in part, around "quality of life" issues, as well, of course, as around property issues.

Private and Public Realms: The Boundaries between Individual and Collective Domains. Closely related to the difference in rights in the two contexts is a different legal status for kinds of responsibilities and "goods."[15] In dependent-industrializing societies, Samuelson's distinction between public and private goods captures much of the essence of the legal order. In that order, a certain (limited) class of things is, in effect, defined as "pure" public goods (e.g., national defense, law and order, the money supply); and these become the responsibility of the government to deliver. Most everything else is implicitly treated in this institutional-legal order as a "pure" private good—that is, their production and/or consumption are of concern to those directly involved and, hence, are not legally a matter of social or public responsibility but are, rather, to be left to the private pursuit of individuals. The distinction between the domain of individual pursuits and the domain of social concern and collective responsibility is, then, pretty sharply drawn in the dependent-industrializing state.[16]

The pure public/private distinction becomes blurred and less meaningful in the advanced-industrial context. The legal system recognizes fewer seemingly private goods as being free of negative externalities. For example, whereas citizens are expected to internalize negative pollution effects from "private" factories in dependent-industrializing societies, these effects are treated as public or collective matters in advanced-industrial legal orders. Indeed, in advanced-industrial societies there is a general reluctance to acknowledge virtually any goods as being free from externalities that negatively affect the quality of life of some groups. Under these circumstances, just what constitutes the set of private goods as opposed to public goods becomes rather ambiguous, and the distinction between the domain of individual pursuits and the domain of collective concern and public responsibility becomes blurred and the object of intense political controversy. For instance, parental authority over children becomes problematic as the pursuits of parents, the pursuits of children, and collective responsibility for children's welfare collide. This blurring of the public-private dimensions of goods in the advanced-industrial context contributes to an enlarged political arena, especially a markedly greater use of litigation (a) as citizens are driven to act collectively to ward off unwanted negative externalities that they are no longer willing to internalize and (b) as the "normal" channels of political participation are unable to produce effective responses to the complex problems being raised by extensive ambiguity in the distinction between the private domain and the collective or public domain (see Benjamin, 1982). One may thus speak of the decline of government and yet the rise of politics.

To the extent that a basic feature of the state as institutional-legal order is the definition and articulation of principles regarding public versus private concerns—collective versus individual domains—the advanced-industrial state is, at base, both more pervasive socially and more ambiguous in nature than is the dependent-industrializing state. Again, we see that State 2 is clearly rooted in and compatible with the fundamental character of the social context in which it exists.

Tensions among Freedom, Equality, Order, and Justice. We are brief here, not because the tensions are easy to resolve philosophically, but because the contrast is quite stark in the handling of these tensions in the legal orders of dependent and advanced capitalist societies. The institutional-legal order that is the dependent-industrializing capitalist state resolves the tensions unambiguously in favor of economic freedom and social order; the basic principles underpinning the institutional-legal order that is the advanced-industrial capitalist state include, as well, those of social equality and distributive justice (see Flathman, 1980; Carens, 1981).

The essence of the dependent-industrializing capitalist state is to promote and protect the opportunity of property owners to accumulate wealth and to expand the stock of property that they employ to that end—in a word, to foster capitalist development. Growth, development, and accumulation are symbols that help to effect a consensus that freedom to act (by property owners) is more important than are concerns of equity which would lead to constraints on economic freedom (for property owners). But

39

entrepreneurial freedom depends on social order and stability (O'Donnell, 1973; Collier, 1979; Cardoso and Faletto, 1978; Cole and Lyman, 1971). And so State 2 also entails a fundamental commitment to social order, which is a commitment severely to curtail the freedom to act of those who would challenge or disrupt the ability of property owners to act freely with their property. The differential among groups in regard to realization of the economic and social fruits of development is taken to be the normal order of human affairs. Social inequality is a necessary and hence acceptable by-product of development; turmoil with respect to social inequality is a fully unacceptable threat to social order, to be met with the full force of the state. Hence, *the dependent-industrializing capitalist state can be thought of as repression that is committed to entrepreneurial freedom.*

In the advanced-industrial context, economic freedom and social order come under challenge when the unwillingness of subordinate citizens and groups to internalize the negative consequences on their quality of life comes to be embodied in the basic principles of the legal order. Social equality is then legally defined and accepted as a desirable and expected social condition. And mechanisms that are distributively just (in the Rawlsian sense) are pursued, even somewhat at the expense of order-preserving outcomes.[17] The result is a rather chaotic State 2, in which tensions among freedom, equality, order, and justice are not clearly resolved in any particular directions. In this respect, *the advanced-industrial capitalist state can be thought of as chaos committed to the simultaneous provision of all the (somewhat incompatible) classical liberal ideals.*

In sum, State 2 takes on a fundamentally different form in the two types of capitalist societies, with, we shall argue below, very different implications for the relative autonomy of the state (cf. Sacks, 1920). The dependent-industrializing capitalist state is a limited state in which property rights are the hallmark, private and public domains are clearly demarcated, and the commitment is to entrepreneurial freedom in a (repressive) system of social order. By contrast, the advanced-industrial capitalist state is a socially pervasive, but somewhat chaotic, state in which quality-of-life rights are extensive, the distinction between private and public is blurred and ambiguous, and the commitment to economic freedom and social order is appreciably challenged by a parallel commitment to social equality and distributive justice (cf. Rawls, 1971; Nozick, 1981).

THE ADMINISTRATIVE APPARATUS AND CONTEXTUAL DIFFERENCES

To analyze fundamental differences in State 1, we must come to grips with the basic structuring principles that give coherence—that is to say unity or "totality"—to the aggregate public bureaucracy and agencies of the government.[18] What, then, are those organizing principles which structure the administrative state? Again recognizing that we cannot offer a fully developed theory in response to this question, we believe that at least three kinds of organizing principles require consideration. One is the fundamental scope and orientation of the state: How deeply and extensively do the agencies of state pervade and intervene into society? What is the social-economic extent of the activities of state agencies? In what direction, or with what orientation, are those activities, in the aggregate, moving society.[19] A second kind of organizing principle is the social composition of the state: To what extent are the personnel of state agencies homogeneous? In what ways are they distinct from other segments of society? The third kind involves the structural constraints on the activities of state agencies: What is the relationship in practice of the administrative apparatus to the government and to the broader institutional-legal order? Together, these three sets of basic organizing principles define the nature and structure of the state. That concept, then, does not refer simply to the separate administrative agencies in the aggregate; rather, the state is the functional scope and orientation, the social composition, and the structural constraints of these administrative agencies (and other agencies of the state). Let us consider the three in turn.

The Functional Scope and Orientation of The Administrative State. In dependent-industrializing society, the range of activities of the public bureaucracy is limited. This is consistent with the limited character of the institutional-legal order. The public bureaucracy engages in the provision of the "pure" public goods mentioned above, so that machinery exists to provide security and order (this machinery is often extremely well developed and sophisticated) and to promote the conduct of economic intercourse. Beyond that, the functional scope of the dependent-industrializing state is limited, by and large, to intervention into and involvement in the sphere of production. This involvement can be quite extensive, however. It includes a whole range of activities through which state agencies (including state corporations) attempt to encourage and promote an expansion of capital accumulation in society. These activities to trigger and channel growth in the means of production include extensive financial intermediation in the form of heavy borrowing and domestic lending to provide working capital to indigenous firms; the active promotion of exports; creation of incentives for foreign investors; and a direct entrepreneurial role through the ownership and control of dynamic industrial enterprises (Duvall and Freeman, 1981; Bennett and Sharpe, 1980). This extensive involvement on the "production side" by the dependent-industrializing State 1, in conjunction with a security machinery that is frequently well developed and

41

interventionist, tends to produce a functional orientation that can be labeled "bureaucratic-authoritarian state capitalism," or what Cardoso and Faletto (1978) call "the entrepreneurial-repressive state."

By contrast, the functional scope of the advanced-industrial state appears to be virtually unlimited. State agencies are involved in the myriad regulatory activities that derive from the complex, ambiguous character of the institutional-legal order. Almost every question of who can do what, with and to whom, is officially affected by and is under the purview of some administrative agency. Thus, in contrast to the dependent-industrializing state, the functional scope of the advanced-industrial state is not limited to the provision of pure public goods and intervention on the "production side." Rather, it also includes extensive involvement on the "consumption side," through Keynesian demand-management activities (i.e., income, price, and employment policies). Indeed, the extent of this social-regulatory, "consumption side" intervention is typically so great that, by comparison, involvement on the "production side" may appear to be less extensive than it is for the dependent-industrializing capitalist state. And this "consumption side" intervention generally seems to be consistent with the most frequently offered label for the functional orientation of the advanced-industrial state, the welfare state.[20]

The State 1 whose functional realm is limited to the provision of "pure" public goods and to active intervention to promote capital accumulation through state capitalism is rooted in a society in which the fundamental dynamic is that of capital accumulation through the production and reproduction of the means of productions. The State 1 whose functional realm is virtually unlimited, entailing vast social regulatory and welfare activities, is rooted in a society in which the fundamental dynamic is that of consumption saturation through the production and reproduction of the means of consumption.

The Social Composition of the State. The personnel of the administrative state are, in a sense, similar in both contexts. They are the "modern organization men"—highly trained professional administrators and technicians. In that respect, the dependent-industrializing state looks quite like the advanced-industrial state; indeed, one of the striking features of the contemporary era is the difficulty of distinguishing the technobureaucracies of different countries. But the social role of these state personnel is quite different in the two contexts.

In advanced-industrial society, they are part (but only part) of a socially extensive "middle stratum." The professional administrators and technicians who compose the public bureaucracy are virtually indistinguishable from the professional administrators and technicians who compose the private bureaucracies of society. Indeed, there often is appreciable mobility for members of the "middle stratum," as persons move from one administrative or technical position to another in the academy, the large corporations, foundations, other organizations in the "private sector," and the public bureaucracies of the state. Like the members of the "middle stratum" in the private sector, state personnel are drawn from diverse backgrounds. Social mobility brings them from laboring-class and petit-bourgeois families; social respectability brings them from homes of the intelligentsia, and even of the bourgeoisie. In short, in advanced-industrial society, State 1, which is composed of a group that is not distinct from much of the rest of society, is in itself heterogeneous in social background (Lindblom, 1977). What shapes a cohesive bond for this group is little more than the functional requirements of the state.

In the dependent-industrializing context, the personnel of the state are not part of a socially extensive "middle stratum." Instead, they form a small, socially distinct group—in effect, a technobureaucratic *elite* (Shils, 1968; Duvall and Freeman, 1983). As a group, they are typically Western trained and oriented and, hence, are socially distant from much of the indigenous society. So, State 1 in dependent-industrializing society is composed of a group that is quite distinct from the rest of society. Its members are, through training and acculturation, relatively homogeneous; and they have as a cohesive bond, beyond the joint operation of the machinery of state and an elite status, a shared orientation to the metropolitan "center" of the world system.[21]

Constraints on the State. Functional scope, orientation, and social composition are not the only fundamental organizing principles that give the administrative state coherence and "totality." No less important are the structural relationships that the public bureaucracy has with the central locus of governmental decision making and with the broader institutional-legal order. In particular, What shapes and directs the role of the administrative state in society and economy? How does it affect the central decisional government and/or the nature of the institutional-legal order? Here, the difference between the advanced-industrial state and the dependent-industrializing state is subtle, but nevertheless important.

In advanced-industrial society, the administrative apparatus is constrained by the institutional-legal order, which permits and fosters a set of basic challenges to the operation of the administrative machinery. The public bureaucracy in all advanced-industrial societies is being challenged by a wide array of groups, under the aegis of the legal order. Some of these groups push the public bureaucracy to promote the social equality that is legitimated by the legal order; other groups challenge the bureaucracy to provide relief from negative production and/or consumption externalities;

and still others refuse to acknowledge the legitimacy of the administrative order itself.[22] In short, the law is continually being used to reshape the nature of the authority emanating from the administrative apparatus. As a result, the state as legal order constitutes a constraining, influencing context for the state as organized machinery of governance.

In turn, the organized machinery of governance, the administrative state, constrains the central decisional government. Governments come, and governments go; but the administrative state endures. And it endures as an institutionalized aggregate of regulations and procedures (gradually changing as a reflection of the broader institutional-legal order). As such, it profoundly shapes and channels the policy decisions of government. In this way, in advanced-industrial society, the most basic relationships of constraint flow from the broad institutional-legal order to the administrative apparatus, then to the decisional center of government. In this sense, the legal order, State 2, is most fundamental in advanced-industrial society.

The direction of constraining relationships is reversed for the dependent-industrializing state. Possessing a limited functional scope and consisting of an elite that is socially distant from much of society, the public bureaucracy in dependent-industrializing society is much more a creature of the government. The role of the administrative apparatus as a whole is largely determined by governmental directive. As governments come and go, so the role and nature of the state is often altered. The not uncommon shift from a populist, quasi-welfare state to bureaucratic-authoritarian state capitalism is illustrative of this point.

In turn, the public bureaucracy importantly shapes the legal order in dependent-industrializing society. The legal order of preindustrial-dependent societies (i.e., that in existence during the phase of classical dependency or pure neocolonialism) is generally not entirely congruent with the structural requisites of the accumulation and growth of capital. The property rights of entrepreneurs are not paramount; nor is the public domain sharply demarcated from the private in a legal order that typically reflects the interests and needs of the landed aristocracy and their relationship to the broader peasantry. To make the transition from classical dependency to dependent-industrializing society, this legal order, State 2, must be changed to facilitate entrepreneurial initiative and rapid accumulation. As a general rule, to the extent that the change is accomplished, it is the administrative apparatus, State 1, that initiates and directs the process. In this sense, State 1 helps to make the institutional-legal order that is the basis for capitalist development. Direction and constraint emanate from the top; State 1 is more fundamental than State 2 in the dependent-industrializing context.

In sum, the administrative state is marked by quite different characteristics in the two types of capitalist societies, with, we shall argue, different
implications for the autonomy of the state. The dependent-industrializing
capitalist state is (a) functionally limited to the provision of "pure" public
goods and to intervention on the "production side"; (b) functionally
oriented toward state capitalism and bureaucratic authoritarianism; (c)
composed of a Western-oriented technobureaucratic elite that is socially
distinct from much of indigenous society; and (d) largely the creature of the
government and the shaper of the emerging institutional-legal order. By
contrast, the advanced-industrial capitalist state is (a) very broad in
functional scope with extensive intervention on the "consumption side" in a
welfare-state orientation; (b) composed of members of a socially extensive
and heterogeneous "middle stratum" and hence socially integrated with
much of society; and (c) appreciably curtailed by the institutional-legal
order, while being an effective constraint on the government.

These differences, as well as those developed above for State 2, are
summarized in table 2.2.

CONTEXT AND THE RELATIVE AUTONOMY
OF THE CAPITALIST STATE

There are a number of implications from our argument. We shall draw
only the points that are relevant to differences in the relative autonomy of
the state in the dependent-industrializing and advanced-industrial contexts.
The major conceptual distinction to be kept in mind here concerns the
degree of autonomy of the state versus its conformity with the fundamental
structural features of the society and the economy. These two are not the
same thing. The latter is an issue of whether the state is rooted in societal
conditions, whereas the former is a matter of whether the state has a
distinct class basis. Said differently, the autonomy of the state concerns the
extent to which the state reflects and serves the basic interests of the
dominant class; the conformity of the state with society concerns the extent
to which the state reflects societal conditions generally.

We have, we trust, provided a strong enough argument to conclude
that both types of capitalist state are deeply rooted in the respective
societies of advanced-industrial and dependent-industrializing capitalism.
Each reflects the general character of the social context in which it exists,
and hence, each exhibits conformity with social conditions. This means, for
example, that in advanced-industrial society, the state/society distinction
blurs, and the state may be said virtually to merge with society (Lindblom,
1977; MacRae, 1978). It is very difficult to tell where the private domain

TABLE 2.2
FUNDAMENTAL DIFFERENCES IN ADVANCED-INDUSTRIAL AND
DEPENDENT-INDUSTRIALIZING CAPITALIST STATES

CONCEPTION OF THE STATE	DISTINGUISHING DIMENSION	ADVANCED-INDUSTRIAL STATE	DEPENDENT-INDUSTRIALIZING STATE
Institutional-legal order	Notion of rights	Property rights are infringed upon by extensive "quality of life" rights.	Property rights are paramount.
	Public and private domains	Distinction between public and private is blurred as collective externalities are widely recognized.	Public domain is limited and clearly demarcated from private domain.
	Tensions among freedom, equality, order, and justice	Commitment to economic freedom and social order is challenged by commitment to social equality and distributive justice, with resultant ambiguity.	Commitment to economic (entrepreneurial) freedom and social order is dominant.
Administrative apparatus as organized whole	Functional scope and orientation	Virtually unlimited, with extensive intervention on the "consumption side"; welfare state.	Limited to provision of "pure" public goods and intervention on "production side"; state capitalism.
	Social composition	Socially indistinct from extensive, heterogeneous "middle stratum" of private sector.	Socially distinct as technobureaucratic elite with Western orientation.
	Structural relations with government and legal order	Constrained by legal order; constrains government.	Constrained by government; constrains legal order.

46

ends and the public one begins. In a large part this is directly due to the complex, ambiguous nature of the advanced-industrial context itself, in which manifest interests revolve around ambiguous "quality of life" issues. Where, in this context, could the regulatory machinery be said to begin or end?

Similarly, the sharp demarcation of state from society in the dependent-industrializing context reflects the structural simplicity of that type of society, in which classes are readily distinguishable and class interests dominate. The emphasis on "pure" public goods (particularly social order, economic growth, and security of entrepreneurial opportunity) and the absence of recognition of collective externalities add up to a relatively limited administrative order. The simple differentiation of the class structure and the absence of society-wide complexity and interdependence allow a straightforward identification of the line between the state and society.

In short, the capitalist state conforms to and mirrors the social structure of capitalist society.

But what, if anything, does this say about the relative autonomy of the state? To deal with that question, we must consider how the major features of the state, discussed above, relate to or reflect the interests of the dominant class in society. Because we are dealing with types of capitalist society, we have implied that the capitalist mode of production is the dominant mode of production[23] and, hence, that the capitalist class is the dominant class. To what extent, then, do the basic organizing principles that underpin and provide coherence for the legal order and the administrative apparatus of dependent-industrializing and advanced-industrial societies reflect and serve the class interests of the capitalists? Conversely, to what extent do they represent and serve interests that are independent of or at odds with the interests of the capitalist class?

As we have characterized it, the institutional-legal order that is dependent-industrializing State 2 must be seen as unambiguously a representation that is in the service of the interests of the bourgeoisie. Its principal feature is to provide guarantees for the protection and utilization of the property rights of owners and controllers of the means of production. These *are* the interests of the bourgeoisie. The dependent-industrializing State 2 in the current era of capitalism, then, is the creature of (i.e., is a direct representation of the interests of) the capitalist class, which includes both the national bourgeoisie and the international capitalists.[24] It fits well the classic Marxian model of the capitalist state and is not autonomous.

However, we argued above that of the two conceptions of the state, State 1—the organizing principles of the administrative apparatus—is the more fundamental in dependent-industrializing society. The structure of the public bureaucracy contributes to the making and shaping of the legal order, while that order has only a very limited constraining role in the organization of the administrative machinery. This means that it is more important for us to direct our attention to the issue of the autonomy of State 1.[25]

To deal with that issue, we must address the interests that are served by the basic organizing principles (and operation) of the public bureaucracy as a whole. Above, we have identified three kinds of organizing principles for the administrative state. Let us consider the class interests served by each of those.

First, the social composition of the state typically creates a strong commitment to capitalist development and, hence, an affinity with the interests of the capitalist class. In part, this is due to an ideology of developmentalism and growth among the personnel of the state, which derives largely from their Western training and orientation. That ideology and orientation, in turn, dispose the state personnel to set capital accumulation among the highest objectives of the state, thereby creating something of a natural receptivity to the needs of international capital and the national bourgeoisie. The natural receptivity is heightened by the fact that the personnel of the state—the "state managers"—constitute a relatively small elite, socially distant from much of indigenous society and, as a result, generally inattentive to labor and the peasantry.

Second, the effective constraints on the administrative state emanate largely from the government, which, typically in dependent-industrializing society, is based on a supporting coalition of international capital, local capital, and the technobureaucratic elite (Evans, 1979). Such a fragile but all-important supporting coalition fosters a desire by the government to aid the capitalist class, and this is true whether the government is military or civilian, elected or not. Whatever constraints the government is able to place on the administrative state will tend to be toward that end of aiding the capitalists, in order to retain their crucial political support.

Third, the limited functional scope and bureaucratic-authoritarian state-capitalist orientation of the dependent-industrializing administrative state means that owners of the means of production are essentially unfettered in their activities. The state's intervention on the "production side" also generally does not constitute a challenge to the interests of the capitalist class per se;[26] it is typically a complement to those interests in stimulating the process of accumulation in sectors of the economy in which the private sector is unable or unwilling to perform adequately (Duvall and Freeman, 1981).

Thus, the characteristic pattern in dependent-industrializing countries is for the public bureaucracy as a whole clearly to serve the interests of the dominant capitalist class. Each of its basic organizing principles disposes it in that direction. But it should be noted that this is a disposition, a characteristic pattern, a tendency; it is not a logical necessity. Thus, the conclusion that we must reach is that State 1 in dependent-industrializing society is typically not effectively autonomous.[27]

By comparison, the organizing principles of the administrative state appear to be relatively autonomous in advanced-industrial capitalist societies. Why is this the case? While citizens may be content to absorb the marginal impacts of "pure" public goods, collective externalities signal political conflict by their very nature. The greater the level of collective "contamination" and responsibility, the greater the call for state agencies to be responsive to political demands and to regulate or to curb the unwanted negative externalities emanating from the production and consumption of so many goods. In short, the impetus for the relatively autonomous administrative state lies with the greatly increased realm of collective responsibility. Our argument about this is made in greater detail elsewhere (Benjamin, 1982), but, in sum, collective goods result from the advanced-industrial context, with its attendant complexities and interdependence. This context produces "crowding" effects that result in many more unwanted negative "spillovers." We noted earlier that citizens regard many fewer goods as being strictly private. Virtually everything is regarded as infringing on one's "quality of life" or as affecting or comprising a "positional good." As citizens demand that the state deliver more specialized goods, including regulation, the size of the administrative order grows. Growing to a point of almost unlimited social pervasiveness, composed of socially indistinct personnel, and manifesting a mixed orientation of welfare statism and state capitalism, it develops an ambiguous and quasi-independent set of interests. Under such conditions, the public bureaucracy as a whole develops independence from any single set of class interests. It is to precisely this dynamic that most of the recent literature on the relative autonomy of the capitalist state refers.

But again, as we did for dependent-industrializing State 2, we have reached first and most easily a conclusion about state autonomy for the less fundamental of the two conceptions of the state. In advanced-industrial society, it is the general institutional-legal order that is the more basic (in the sense of providing effective constraints on the administrative state) and, hence, perhaps, the more relevant for theoretical analysis.

What judgments are in order about the interests that are represented by the legal order that is the advanced-industrial state? We think the answer must be that this is not clear. We are convinced that the legal order—which has developed historically and has been partially codified over the entire period of capitalist development—is used by diverse classes to mount a challenge to many aspects of the administrative state in advanced-industrial society. Whether the basic organizing principles of that legal order may be said to represent a fundamental challenge to the basic capitalist interests in society is, however, uncertain. There are two possible positions.[28] One may argue that despite the extensive recognition of collective externalities, the emphasis on "quality of life" issues, and the endorsement of principles of social equality, the basic bourgeois-class dominance of state and society continues to be served by the legal order. The basic fabric of the legal order may promote social stability, the effective management of labor as a factor of production, and popular political legitimacy more than a real transformation of society in which the fundamental interests of the capitalist class are seriously eroded. Alternatively, one may plausibly argue that it is time to wonder whether the characteristics of the advanced-industrial legal order described here do not suggest the need to think about a postcapitalist context and a postcapitalist state. If the administrative state dominates market processes and if the legal order is being used to challenge the basic legitimacy of the administrative state, perhaps a fundamental transformation is occurring. This transformation may be sufficiently "revolutionary" that a profound alteration in the class basis of the capitalist state is being effectuated in the context of advanced industrialism. At any rate, the interests that, at base, are served by the advanced-industrial legal order are still in doubt.

Our conclusions about the relative autonomy of the state in different capitalist contexts are summarized in table 2.3.

TABLE 2.3
CONTEXT, CONCEPTION, AND AUTONOMY OF THE STATE*

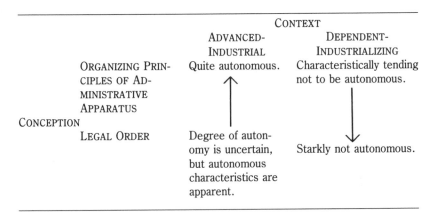

| | | CONTEXT | |
		ADVANCED-INDUSTRIAL	DEPENDENT-INDUSTRIALIZING
	ORGANIZING PRINCIPLES OF ADMINISTRATIVE APPARATUS	Quite autonomous.	Characteristically tending not to be autonomous.
CONCEPTION	LEGAL ORDER	Degree of autonomy is uncertain, but autonomous characteristics are apparent.	Starkly not autonomous.

*Arrows represent the direction of effective constraints in the relationship between the two conceptions of the state.

50

CONCLUSION

Theories of the capitalist state need to be more attentive to a number of conceptual issues. First, greater care should be given to specifying which conception of the state is being employed. Several alternative conceptions exist. Some are more useful than others, but each is apt to have different implications for the development of a theory of the state. We have tried to demonstrate these points with reference to two conceptions of the state: the public administrative machinery as a coherent totality, and the broad principles that structure the institutional-legal order.

Second, there should be greater concern than is currently expressed for the way in which social context affects the elements of a theory of the capitalist state. Implicitly, proponents of such a theory maintain that context is relevant; otherwise it would be a theory of the state rather than a theory of the capitalist state (i.e., presumably the context of capitalism per se is relevant to the nature of the state). But the implication is rarely followed sufficiently far; namely, to the explicit recognition of different contexts of capitalism. In fundamentally different types of capitalist society the nature of the state can be expected to be quite different. We have attempted to illustrate that point with reference to the contexts of advanced-industrial and dependent-industrializing capitalist societies.

Third, the conceptual distinction between the autonomy of the state and the conformity of the state with society should be kept clearly in mind. Autonomy is a more abstract notion than congruence between social structure and the nature of the state. It is generally the case that state and society conform (in the senses discussed in this chapter). But that says precious little about the autonomy—the class basis—of the state.

Pursuing these exhortations about conceptions and contexts, we have developed the argument that the relative autonomy of the state is variable and is a function of the social context in which the state exists and of the conception of the state that is employed. In particular, the state in dependent-industrializing society tends not to be autonomous, although that conclusion is clearer for the state as institutional-legal order than for the state as organized, structured, public-administrative machinery. Conversely, the state in advanced-industrial society appears clearly to be relatively autonomous, at least for the state as the organizing principles of the public bureaucracy. But for the institutional-legal order, the relative autonomy of the advanced-industrial capitalist state is ambiguous and uncertain.

This paper circulated in earlier unpublished drafts and was originally presented to the Conference Group on the Political Economy of Advanced

Industrial Societies at the annual meeting of the American Political Science Association, Washington, D.C., in August 1980. We are indebted to several colleagues for helpful comments on various of those drafts, particularly Terrence Ball, Dan Garst, Stephen Krasner, Jennifer McCoy, and Patrick McGowan. We also want gratefully to acknowledge the support of the National Science Foundation to Raymond Duvall, whose contribution to this work was funded under grant SOC7907074.

NOTES

1. The resurgence of interest in the state was indicated when the Social Science Research Council in 1983 created a continuing Committee on States and Social Structures and when the American Political Science Association in 1981 designated the state as the theme of its annual convention. It is also indicated by a marked increase in the volume of published scholarship about the state over the past decade or so. Consider, as a select few examples, Ackerman (1977), Anderson (1974), Buchanan (1975), Evans (1979), Giddens (1980), Hamilton (1982), Holloway and Picciotto (1978), Jessop (1982), Katzenstein (1977), Krasner (1978, 1984), Mandel (1975), Nordlinger (1981), Skocpol (1979), Tilly (1975), and Wright (1978).

2. Of course, not all of the literature is self-consciously a part of "the theory of the capitalist state." Some items cited in note 1 above view the relevant theoretical scope more broadly and, hence, in effect drop the confining label "capitalist" from the theoretical framework, preferring to talk instead about "the theory of the state." For reasons that will be made clear below, we believe that the presumed possibility of such a context-free theory of the state is entirely unfounded. As a result, the literature of greatest importance, in our judgment, is attentive to context, at least in limiting the scope of theory to the state in capitalist societies. But in referring to this theoretical framework in quotes, as we do in the text, we do not mean to suggest that there is a single, well-formulated, widely accepted theory of the state in capitalist society. Instead, we mean only to signal that a broad framework, not identified with any particular school of thought, has come to be accepted, if only implicitly. That this framework is broad is indicated by the explicit adoption of it and reference to the theory of the capitalist state by such diverse authors as Frankel (1982), Hamilton (1982), Jessop (1982), O'Connor (1973), Offe and Runge (1975), Poulantzas (1973, 1978), and Wolfe (1977).

3. This position is consistent with Marx's own perspective. Consider a passage from the "afterword to the Second German Edition" of *Capital,* in which Marx approvingly quotes from a published characterization of his methods by one of his critics: "But it will be said, the general laws of economic life are one and the same, no matter whether they are applied to the present or the past. This Marx directly denies. According to him, such abstract laws do not exist. On the contrary, in his opinion every historical period has laws of its own. . . . As soon as society has outlived a given period of development, and is passing over from one given stage to another, it begins to be subject also to other laws" (Marx, 1967:18). For an enlightening discussion of this issue of Marx's perspective on contextually specific laws of motion of capitalism see Farr, 1983.

4. Various terms are used in the literature to identify the different contexts to which we are referring. We do not wish to pursue the terminological debate about the best or most appropriate labels here. We do recognize, however, that labels are not simply "neutral" words; they bring with them complex connotations that include basic conceptualizations of, and even theoretical implications about, the phenomena to which reference is being made by the label: certainly the now widely used term, "postindustrial society" carries a debatable set of connotations that we would prefer to avoid in this chapter.

5. This is the literature summarized by Lowi (1979).

6. See, for example, Russett and Starr (1981:46–47), who write: "The state has no concrete existence; it is a legal abstraction. Through its government and the representatives of that government, the state undertakes legal commitments" (1981:47). More abstractly, Deutsch offers as a definition: "A *state* is an organization for the enforcement of decisions or commands, made practicable by the existing habits of compliance among the population. Such organized enforcement is an all-purpose instrument" (1978:79; emphasis in original). In these and similar definitions from texts on international relations, the state is distinguished from the government, which is the more concrete unit of decision and action through which the state (as abstract legal order) governs. Unfortunately, in spite of such formal distinctions, which are provided by standard textbook definitions, most students of international politics go on to talk about states (or nation-states) as actors. But that is inappropriate, because "systems of authority" and "legal abstractions" do not act; governments do. This represents a common, but unfortunate, conflation of the first and fourth conceptions of the state.

7. Possibly the best literature on this subject deals with the United Kingdom (Bernstein, 1974; see also Holloway and Picciotto, 1978), where, indeed, it appears that substantial disjunctures exist between the macrolevel social, economic, and political institutions, which remain hierarchical, and the microlevel context of interpersonal relationships, where equality and participation are increasingly dominant (see, e.g., Lindberg, 1975; Pateman, 1970; Braverman, 1974). Scholars who write on this topic, including those cited here, however, do not necessarily adopt the fifth conception of the state as we have characterized it. They may recognize the importance of the ideological/normative order without identifying that as the state.

8. These must be recognized to be two distinct conceptions. It would be inappropriate to suggest that the two be collapsed into a single concept of the state, as Krasner (1984) attempts to do. In his stating that we combine the two, he has misunderstood our argument.

9. In this chapter we use the term "advanced-industrial societies." As indicated above, alternative terms are frequently employed, most commonly perhaps, "postindustrial." Indeed, one of us, Roger Benjamin, has previously attempted to define the salient characteristics of postindustrialization as the point at which the service—and especially including the public—sector accounts for a greater proportion of the economy than the industrial sector. In societies such as those of Great Britain, Denmark, Sweden, and Holland, the public sector itself accounts for approximately one-half of the gross national product. For the United States, Canada, and Japan the size of the public sector is moving toward the British case (see Benjamin, 1982).

10. Dependent-industrializing societies are a subset of the broad, amorphous category of dependent countries. They have been variously labeled as the semiperiphery (in the Wallersteinian tradition of world systems), or as countries

experiencing "associated dependent development" (Cardoso, 1973); "dependent development" (Evans, 1979); or "industrialization on the periphery" (Caporaso, 1981). Essentially these labels are intended to set apart a relatively small number of countries from the bulk of peripheral or dependent societies. Whereas the latter are marked by relatively little economic growth or development and typically by the dominance in the economy of a small number of traditional export sectors, the group of "dependent-industrializing" countries often experience substantial growth, and much of that growth is based on the development of various industrial sectors. Examples of dependent-industrializing countries are Brazil, Mexico, and perhaps Argentina and Venezuela in Latin America; Taiwan, South Korea, Hong Kong, Singapore, and perhaps Malaysia in East Asia (see Duvall and Freeman, 1981, 1983).

11. This section is addressed solely to structural expressions that have a direct and important bearing on the relative autonomy of the state. It does not attempt to make a comprehensive characterization of the two contexts. Nor does it offer an analysis of the fundamental structuring principles, or "laws of motion," of advanced-industrial and dependent-industrializing capitalism. Rather, we assume that those fundamentals are different for the two contexts. Instead, we simply point to some of the important structural *expressions* of those differences. Thus, the reader should not mistake this section as our effort to describe the fundamental "laws of motion" of two kinds of capitalism. We do not offer such a description in this chapter.

12. This point seems to be worth noting. For many scholars, the concept of structure refers only to institutions or to relationships among institutions. For them, it would probably not make much sense to talk of the structure of the state when the state is conceptualized in abstract terms as the institutional-legal order. That position, it seems to us, is unfortunate. A legal system does have structure, and that structure is the set of organizing principles that, in effect, make the legal system a system rather than merely an aggregation of disparate laws. To conceive of structure only in concrete terms blinds social analysts to those abstract organizing principles which more generally constitute structure.

13. We do not mean to imply that all of these are necessarily legal rights in all advanced-industrial societies. They are simply illustrative of the ideal-type characterization of *the* advanced-industrial society. Nor would all of them fit perfectly our definition of rights. For example, the "right" to breathe clean air, per se, is not really a legally recognized or legally constituted just claim. Nevertheless in advanced-industrial societies, legal systems more and more typically include principles that essentially bestow the status of rights on such "quality of life" claims. The purpose of our illustrative list, then, is to point to the kinds of claims and privileges that come to be among the set of legal rights in advanced-industrial societies but generally not in dependent-industrializing societies.

14. Property rights do not disappear or fall by the wayside; but they can be infringed upon. Our presumption is that, because advanced-industrial is, after all, capitalist society, the infringement on property rights has real limits—in particular, the point at which the imperatives of production begin to be severely threatened or undermined.

15. Whereas rights are legally recognized or constituted just claims of immunity or privilege, goods are valued states of affairs. These are generally not *legally* recognized or constituted; rather, they are individually and/or socially defined. But the way in which the legal system handles the distinction between those goods that are matters of private concern and private pursuit, and those goods that are matters

of collective (or social, or public) concern, *is* a fundamental element of the legal order. Thus, the legal boundaries between private and public goods—or individual and collective domains—is a fundamental organizing principle of the state. These legal boundaries are not simple, explicit formulae. Instead, they are subtly implied by the corpus of laws and regulations that stipulate various issues as being of social or public concern and responsibility. By default (not by explicit demarcation), other goods are implicitly of private concern and are legally left to individual pursuit. Thus, the organizing principle in which we are interested is the number and nature of goods that are legally recognized as being matters of social concern and public responsibility.

16. It should be kept clearly in mind that we are referring here to the state as the legal order. We are not considering the broader conception of the state as a moral/normative order. If we were, our conclusions would likely be quite different. As moral/normative orders, dependent capitalist states (societies) are not typically the picture of atomized individualism that we paint here. But the legal order generally *does* recognize *few* goods as being matters of social concern and public responsibility. By legal implication, most goods remain in the domain of private individuals. The State 2 per se, then, clearly distinguishes public from private goods. In the larger moral/normative order that is society, however, many of the goods that are legally implied to be in the private domain may be regarded as matters of collective concern. They may be the responsibility of such collective institutions as the church, the community, a philanthropic organization, the extended family, or even a corporation—but not the government.

17. An important part of the Rawlsian notion of distributive justice concerns "equity of opportunity" and, concomitantly, "equality before the law" (which are distinct from what we call social equality—i.e., equality in the actual realization of social goods). Such principles of distributive justice certainly are important in advanced-industrial legal orders. But the extent to which they are permitted to undermine the commitment to principles of economic freedom and social order should not be exaggerated. Recall Anatole France's remark that "the law, in its magnificent impartiality, forbids rich men and poor men alike from begging and sleeping on park benches."

18. To repeat a point made above, it makes little sense to conceive of the state simply as the set of disparate administrative agencies, each doing its own separate thing. The state is that set of agencies as a coherent whole, or totality. Rather than being concerned with what the separate agencies do, the theorist of the state must be attentive to the organizing principles that give coherence to the disparate set. It is a matter of seeing ordering principles in apparent chaos—what the welter of bureaucratic agencies is, at base, all about.

19. To avoid possible confusion, we should note explicitly the implication of this phrase. In talking about the orientation of the state as a concept that refers to the general direction in which the myriad (and seemingly disparate) activities of the agencies of the state (public bureaucracies, etc.) are moving society, we clearly acknowledge that state agencies do move society. This does not imply, however, that the state necessarily is autonomous; that state agencies have an impact on society does not mean that, in the aggregate, they do so autonomously.

20. See Furniss and Tilton (1977). One is tempted to say that whereas dependent-industrializing society typically fosters state capitalism, advanced-industrial society generally gives rise to the welfare state. That would be misleading, however, because the advanced-industrial states, too, are heavily involved on the

"production side." Their extensive "consumption side" intervention makes their "production side" involvement appear to be less substantial than it actually is. Indeed, it may be argued that the welfare-state aspect is little more than a sophisticated form of management of labor as a factor of production (see Skocpol and Ikenberry, forthcoming). Moreover, one cannot ignore the ways in which the welfare state has recently come under severe attack by governments in several advanced-industrial countries. To what extent this phenomenon represents a fundamental change in the functional orientation of the state is still uncertain. But it seems clear that the imperatives of production and the perceived need for a stimulation of industrial expansion have bred a formidable attack on the welfare state. The industrial imperatives that underlie this attack, incidentally, constitute a major part of the reason that we are no longer comfortable with the connotations and implications of the label "postindustrial" society.

21. Members of the technobureaucratic elite from Brazil probably share more in common (in terms of interests and world view) with their counterparts in South Korea than with most of the population of Brazil. This cultural aspect of the modern world system is too often overlooked as a profoundly important part of its operation.

22. This is one of the themes of the Frankfurt school (see Habermas, 1975; Offe and Runge, 1975).

23. We presume that in most societies there are multiple modes of production in existence at the same time. That is, there exist a number (greater than one) of abstract organizing principles through which labor power is employed for productivity (i.e., modes of production). But for any society, one can identify the abstract organizing principles of the social relations of production that are the predominant, or the most characteristic, in that society.

24. It should be pointed out that we are referring to *fundamental class interests*, not to conscious interests of *individual members* of a class. Those fundamental class interests concern both the preservation of a system of relations of production (i.e., a mode of production) in which the class continues to be dominant, and the facilitation of that class's ability to achieve the maximal extraction and realization of surplus value from labor. This says nothing about conflicts of (specific, conscious) interests among segments, or factions, of the capitalist class. The national bourgeoisie may, at times, be at odds with international capitalists, and the government may be called upon to intercede in such conflicts. This does not mean that the state is or is not necessarily autonomous.

25. However, if State 2 is not autonomous and if State 2 is made and shaped by State 1, then clearly the expectation is that State 1 also is not autonomous. That is, if the structure of the public bureaucracy creates a legal order whose basic organizing principles are unambiguously in the service of the interests of the bourgeoisie, then one would expect that the basic organizing principles of that public bureaucracy would also reflect those interests.

26. Individual members and, indeed, whole fractions of the capitalist class, however, may feel quite threatened by the state's intervention on the "production side." The alliance politics of the government's supporting coalition is often affected by the perceptions of threat on the part of various factions of the capitalist class (Freeman, 1982). Nevertheless, nowhere, to our knowledge, has the state capitalism of dependent-industrializing states really threatened to displace or eliminate the capitalist class.

27. At this point it is worth reemphasizing an important conceptual distinction on which our argument rests; namely, the distinction between autonomy as a

structural concept and the divergence of policy from expressed interests as a volitional, or action, concept. The dependent-industrializing government may (and almost certainly does) make policies to which members of the capitalist class object vigorously, while the principles around which the apparatus of state is organized or structured as a totality clearly and strongly dispose the state not to be autonomous from the interests of the capitalist class.

28. It may be instructive for the reader to know that each of the two current authors is disposed to accept a different one of these two positions as being more defensible.

3

Contemporary Marxism on the Autonomy, Efficacy, and Legitimacy of the Capitalist State

David Braybrooke

Granting that the capitalist state operates with some autonomy, Marxist writers grant at least that there is some possibility of its operating to safeguard the long-run interests of capitalists against the internecine effects of their competing short-run interests. Contemporary Marxist writers agree that the capitalist state has become more active and more important. More people are involved in it, and it is involved in a greater variety of specific tasks. Has it become more autonomous? There is some confusion on this point; however, contemporary Marxist writers stress matters that come close to implying that it has; and these writers agree that it has been efficacious enough to keep capitalism going until now.

Will it be efficacious enough to keep capitalism going indefinitely? Contemporary Marxist writers are reluctant to agree that it will. They argue that, in fact, it is beset by intensifying crises about efficacy and legitimacy. Most of them incline to think that these crises cannot be resolved without transforming society radically. However, society has already been substantially transformed with the enlarged activity of the state. Given that its autonomy has enlarged, too, the question arises whether the state cannot further transform society—and itself—enough to manage the crises, even so far as bringing in a genuine form of socialism, if no managing short of this will do. This is not a question about the capacity of some machine or team, considered apart from its field of action; it is, rather, a question about what sort of field of action the state in late capitalism furnishes. What are the chances of managing the crises by continuous transformation within the normal bounds of political settlements, that is to say, without a rampage of destruction from the Left or Right?

I shall be concerned, in the discussion that follows, to explore this question as it arises in Marxist theory freely formulated in the West, in the writing chiefly of O'Connor, Mandel, Poulantzas, and Habermas. I shall, however, refer briefly to a few other writers to show how widely preoccupation with the question is shared and how much convergence there is in answers to it; and before I take up contemporary writings in detail, I shall outline the Marxist theory of the state as Marx and Engels conceived it.

THE CLASSICAL MARXIST CONCEPTION OF THE STATE

The classical conception, formulated by Marx and Engels, is more complicated, in the hands of either, than the charge that the state is merely the instrument of the ruling class. They, like Poulantzas following them, understand that the state is an arena in which several classes are represented, struggling for power (Marx, 1875; Engels, 1884; see also Poulantzas, 1978). If under capitalism it is a "committee for managing the common affairs of the whole bourgeoisie" (Marx and Engels, 1848), it is a committee that also has to take into account diverse interests, including the interests of other classes. Nor are these other classes just classes like the great landowners or the independent peasantry with which the bourgeoisie perhaps have to share dominance in the state. The dominated classes must be counted among them, too, even before they achieve formal representation in parliament.

For the state in every epoch, considered as "a material condensation" in whose name actions are taken and policies are followed,[1] is engaged in the pursuit of certain general purposes: it is said to act, and it perforce in some respects does act, on behalf of all the people who belong to it. In part, no doubt, this is so because it always suits the purposes of a ruling class to provide certain services to the classes that they rule: for example, they will protect their serfs from being killed or carried off by other oppressors. However, in part it is because the state and the purposes ascribed to it can only be understood—by the ruling class itself—as having something like full generality and, with this, some freedom to act contrary to demands by the ruling class—in other words, some autonomy. This is made plain in that pregnant medieval document Magna Carta: even laws that, in assigning different privileges, assign greater privileges to the ruling class than to other people are laws that hold for everybody. Whatever liberties they assign the less privileged classes are in principle just as much to be respected as those assigned anybody else.

This complication of inherently general purposes, of course, is much more prominent and wide-sweeping in the state of the bourgeois epoch than ever before. The bourgeoisie have proclaimed an end to privilege. The rhetoric of the state—of the political arena—in their time is the rhetoric of universal rights and justice for all. This rhetoric has not corresponded exactly to reality: the person who wrote into the Declaration of Independence the assertion that "all Men" are endowed with "unalienable Rights" to "Life, Liberty, and the Pursuit of Happiness" actually owned slaves, as did a number of other people who, with remarkably little self-questioning on this point, signed the Declaration. Nevertheless, the rhetoric of universal rights and justice for all has a force to be reckoned with. A state that uses it is subject to embarrassment from policies inconsistent with it. A state that speaks in a rhetoric of privileges for the beautiful and wellborn is not.

As I shall show, the complication of general purposes is directly reflected in Marx's and Engels's conception of the state. Nevertheless, the assertion that the state simply, steadily, and consistently serves the ruling class has some claim to being regarded as the core of their conception, especially since one may attach to that core all sorts of things that the ruling class has done, or supports having done (if they consult their interests intelligently) in the course of efforts, by themselves or by other people active in politics, to keep the system that favors them going. In the core itself, however, must be put the function of repressing any outbreaks of violence or tendencies toward such outbreaks on the part of the oppressed classes, most lately on the part of the proletariat. It is to carry out this function that an institution has arisen with troops, sheriffs, judges, and executioners at its command; and it is this function that is most continuously important to the ruling class, though that class does need, from time to time, armed protection from external enemies as well.

Yet even in carrying out this function, the state inevitably does something to serve the oppressed classes as well. It provides them, too, with some protection against violence, external or internal. It also fosters, in the sphere of comparative order that it creates, the operations of the economy, from which one may well think that the oppressed classes benefit more than they would from continual, aimless warfare. These good things flow from the protection, among other things, of private property, despite the manifold drawbacks of that institution. It is not quite clear whether Marx or Engels is ready to add to the good things the public works explicitly assigned the state by Adam Smith (roads, bridges, harbors, canals) and public services such as education (conceded by Smith as not improper; 1776). Would not doing so confuse the state—the government of men, which is going to wither away—with the administration of things, which is not? Perhaps we should understand the state as an institution centrally

61

concerned with law and order (repression) and defense that takes on to some extent the administration of things. An arena defined by certain rules and generating others expands both as regards issues to be resolved and as regards the people specially concerned with issues during various stages of policy formation. The arena will shrink on one side as the state withers away during the dictatorship of the proletariat, that is to say, during the period in which the proletariat democratically uses the inherited state apparatus for its own purposes, excluding the remnants of the bourgeoisie from political functions. It will shrink on the side where it originally was laid out, leaving only parts added later.

There is something even more important than the administration of things that is done by the state—by the bourgeois state more amply and consistently than by any previous system—and that will persist after the functions of repression and defense wither away. The state achieves at least an approximation of a genuine community embodying purposeful reason at the service of all the people who belong to it, without discrimination. As such, it invites and to some extent—to the extent of approximation— deserves the rational consent of all those people.

While discrimination, as between social classes, continues, rational consent can at best be given by some people only temporarily and with grave reservations. Certainly the proletariat can never accept as a permanent arrangement the system of exploitation tolerated—indeed fostered—in the economy by the bourgeois state on the basis of private property in the means of production. Yet even the proletariat can endorse the advance that "the democratic republic," the most fully developed form of the bourgeois state, has made over earlier forms (Engels, 1884; Marx, 1875). What the democratic republic establishes, Marx and Engels insist, is "an illusory community," "a substitute for community"; but even this is a "collective expression of individuals" (Marx and Engels, 1846). Not only in the rhetoric that it uses, but also in real effects, it goes beyond the market and civil society (society organized just so far as required to establish the market) to lay down at least some of the prerequisites of the genuine community (Marx, 1843; see also Marx and Engels, 1846).

Marx and Engels do not themselves quite get to the point of saying that to some degree, the state deliberately and systematically corrects in the public interest the bad effects of the market, which fall, of course, persistently, with most impact, upon the proletariat. However, Engels does explicitly assign to the bourgeois state the double function of, first, checking (besides possible encroachments by the workers) the aggrandizement of individual capitalists at the expense of the rest (which would often be at the expense, too, of the rest of the population; Engels, 1880) and, second, of moderating class antagonisms (Engels, 1884). In both connections, the state—those who carry the day in the arena—must affect to be acting in "the common interest" or "the public interest," and again, to some extent it must be genuinely doing so if it is to succeed. So it would be no great surprise to Marx or Engels to see the state in late capitalism doing even more than the British Parliament or Bismarck was willing to do to relieve the hardships suffered by the working class. Unemployment insurance, pensions, health services, and extensive measures of consumer protection, as well as factory legislation, thus can all be assimilated to the classical Marxist conception of the bourgeois state and its activities. On the other hand, it is not entirely easy to reconcile this conception, once these functions have been admitted, with Marx's and Engels's expectations regarding the catastrophic future of capitalism and the state.

THE CLASSICAL MARXIST PROGNOSIS · FOR THE CAREER OF THE STATE

At its simplest and most notorious, the prognosis offered by Marx and Engels envisaged the economic crises of capitalism growing worse and worse, while the proletariat—ever worse off, ever larger, ever more class-conscious—became more and more aware that it need not put up with the crises and with the system of exploitation, in crisis or out. Marx and Engels did not expect—at least they did not predict—that the system would ever, given sufficient time to get rid of gluts and depress wages, be incapable of starting up again on the economic side. It would be on the political side that the decisive breakdown would occur: the masses would not, in the end, give the capitalists and their economy any more time (Marx and Engels, 1848). The proletariat would rise in violent revolution, seize the state, and during a transitional period of class dictatorship, work through it to eliminate the distinguishing features of capitalism in favor of a system of comprehensive participant planning.

Did Marx or Engels expect that the state would be simply repressive in the face of the unrest that the crises of the economy and its discriminatory features would be arousing? Being simply repressive might well increase the chances of the simple prognosis's turning out to be true, though modern methods of repression (amplified and technologically elaborated since Marx's and Engels's time) might, skillfully used, succeed uncomfortably often. The militancy that repression might provoke could, furthermore, be anticipated and dampened by judicious measures of relief continuing provisions like those mentioned above, or by ad hoc measures. Unskillfully used, it is true, these might, through a mechanism of rising expectations, actually increase disorder. Looked at closely and skeptically, the simple prognosis

David Braybrooke

seems indeterminate on the point of truth. We know, however, what Marx would have thought of any attempt on the part of the state to forestall transformation by adopting measures of relief that substantially raised the standard of living of the proletariat. With capitalism and private property, exploitation would continue. The proletariat, however comfortable its members might be, would continue to be trapped in a system of iniquitous enslavement (Marx, 1875). It would have quite sufficient reason for intransigent opposition.

Yet Marx, with some support from Engels, also considered that advanced bourgeois societies, in which the state took the form of a "democratic republic," might be able to manage the transformation from capitalism to socialism peacefully, arriving through elections and parliamentary debate at what had to be done (Marx, 1872; Engels, 1895). (Engels seems to have considered that once arrived there, the thing would be done abruptly.) Neither Marx nor Engels had enough confidence in this possibility, or interest in it, to work it out, which is a pity, since it has implications that considerably modify both their prognosis and their conception of the state. For does not granting the possibility imply granting that at least one advanced form of the state may be capable of transforming itself, indeed of arranging for its own dissolution?

It is true that an approximation to this capacity is already implied in the dictatorship of the proletariat. There the state, under the direction of the proletariat, will set up the system of social planning and simultaneously step by step dismantle the system of repression. However, there the transformation occurs only because a united and theoretically informed proletariat imposes upon the state purposes that have not themselves been developed within the state. Self-transformation in a democratic republic would be a different matter. Here the bourgeoisie, reduced in self-confidence, perhaps, if not in relative numbers, and not organized enough or resolute enough to abandon normal peaceful politics, would accept a succession of victories in elections and in parliament by some combination of the proletariat with other dissidents; perhaps also a series of successes in economic organization: cooperative, nonprofit corporations, worker ownership, and worker control. In political discussion the bourgeoisie might even in some proportion be convinced by the arguments offered by their opponents.

For might not these arguments make abundant use of the rhetoric to which the bourgeoisie themselves have been committed? That rhetoric not only insists upon the virtues of peaceful, orderly constitutional change. It grants suffrage to all, and it insists upon universal rights and justice in terms that, in the Marxist view, cannot be made good without being made superfluous by the transformation into communism. The provisions under the democratic republic for full free debate would help make this fact (if it is

64

a fact) more and more visible and compelling. In doing so, debate, under the provisions, would make it clear that the general purposes that direct the state cannot, in their advanced forms (i.e., the forms of the bourgeois declarations, dropping all class-interested reservations), be realized except by a transformation in which the state as such will disappear (Engels, 1880; Marx and Engels, 1848). The possibility of peaceful self-transformation is the possibility that in its final form the state will be rational enough to give way to a system, yet more rational, in which its purposes are fulfilled and transcended.

What has the Marxism of our own day made of this possibility? One cannot say—one could hardly expect—that it has seized upon it with unanimous enthusiasm. Indeed, many currents of contemporary Marxism run emphatically in an opposed direction.[2] The core conception is not dead. It, with the simple prognosis, often dominates in propaganda and still supplies a standard framework of rhetorical clichés in many serious, learned, even sophisticated contributions. The survival of the bourgeois state for a hundred years after Marx's death, through two world wars and a depression deeper than anything that bourgeois apologists or Marxist revisionists like Bernstein would have thought possible, has been explained away by reference first to imperialism and second to expenditures on armaments. Is not the most commonly held Marxist view on the subject the simple thought that unless the bourgeois states were spending enormous sums on armaments, they would collapse, as was classically predicted?

This view does, of course, in effect concede that so long as the bourgeois states manage to keep up big arms budgets, they may survive without fatal amounts of social unrest. This is hardly self-transformation into a fully rational community. It is, described in disobliging terms, buying off a sufficient proportion of the masses with comforts and meantime increasing the risks of destroying the whole species. Nor is it self-transformation—in Marxist eyes—if the arms budget is set aside as a sort of unfortunate accident and the state is conceded some genuine credit for its expenditures on what O'Connor calls "social investment" (infrastructure) and "social consumption" (social insurance; O'Connor, 1973). For these things might figure among the costs of keeping going anyway.

Nevertheless, it is possible, and illuminating, to look upon the most sensitive and elaborate discussions of the state in late capitalism offered by contemporary Marxists as commentaries on the possibility of self-transformation. These discussions are for the most part, one way or another, very skeptical about the possibility. Yet some currents in contemporary Marxism, represented in these discussions, do accept—indeed explicitly accept (waiving the disobliging tone in which the acceptance may be given)—the possibility. Chief among these currents is Eurocommunism. The chief things to cite there are the official program of the Italian Communist Party and the theoretical contribution of the leader of the Spanish one.[3] Moreover, even the most skeptical currents agree with the others about the factors to be taken into account and in their general picture of the late capitalist state. Hence, in characterizing them all, it is possible to make use of the most sensitive and penetrating analysis to be found among them, that offered by Ernest Mandel (1976, 1978, 1979), though Mandel continues, somewhat inconsistently, to rely on an abrupt revolution by the proletariat and vigorously rejects the possibility of self-transformation.

MANDEL, O'CONNOR, POULANTZAS, AND HABERMAS ON THE STATE IN LATE CAPITALISM

I shall thus expound—briefly—Mandel's views as representative of contemporary Marxism; but I shall give as much attention to Habermas's, which supplement Mandel's views in part and in part conflict with them (Habermas, 1975, 1970). The conflict dialectically sharpens the issue of self-transformation. Further light on the issue can be gained by comparing Mandel's and Habermas's formulations with those of O'Connor (1973) and Poulantzas (1973, 1975, 1978).

Mandel, generalizing the classical Marxist conception, ascribes three grand functions to the state: first, repression; second, social integration—specifically the integration of the dominated class; third, establishing those general conditions of production not assured privately. As a comment on the first two functions, compatible, I think, with Mandel's view of them, one may add Poulantzas's teaching that the state is not "an instrument of force" in the hands of a dominant class (or classes) organized outside it. The dominant classes arrive within the state at whatever degree of organization they enjoy; simultaneously they settle, in struggles within the state, what scope for action the dominated classes will have and what concessions are made to their interests, concessions compatible at once with their being dominated and with their being integrated (Poulantzas, 1973, 1978).

In the course of carrying out the second function, the state, as we would expect from the classical conception, has and must have a certain amount of autonomy. Mandel is more forthright and more classical on this point than is Poulantzas. Mandel (1976) accepts it that autonomy means some freedom of action vis-à-vis the dominating class (or classes), including some freedom to act by professed public principles. Poulantzas has two views of autonomy, neither of which is explicitly aligned with the classical conception. On the one hand, he insists that what autonomy amounts to is that the several dominating classes that control "the power bloc," as well

66

as the multiple fractions into which they are divided, will each have some branch or branches of the state apparatus following policies favorable to its interests (Poulantzas, 1978). On the other hand, however inconsistent in tendency the policies of these different branches may be with each other, they may reflect an "equilibrium of force," arrived at by all contenders (including the dominated classes) within the distinctive field of action furnished by the state (Poulantzas, 1973, esp. n. 26). Autonomy so viewed would mean being just that distinctive field of action, with policy outcomes, whether in equilibrium or not, depending on the constellation of forces operating in the field.

If it is accepted, however, that the field is structured in part by professed public principles, to which the activities must give some appearance of conforming, Poulantzas's second view can be regarded as a gloss on Mandel's. When we hear of activity by the state, we are to understand activity within a distinctive field. Moreover, Poulantzas's first view is at one with Mandel's in implying that some of the policies resulting from the activity will contravene at least the short-run interests of some members of the dominating classes (Mandel, 1976; Poulantzas, 1978). Poulantzas does not say that they will be justified by an appeal to the public interest; but attempts at such justification may surely be expected. They will be made, and sometimes succeed, in justifying policies that contravene both the short-run and the long-run interests of some members of the dominating classes, though supposedly at least the long-run interests of other members will be served, along, perhaps, with the interests of people in other classes.[4]

Does autonomy cover the other possibilities of contravening the short-run interests of all the members of the dominating classes and of contravening their long-run interests? Habermas (1975) seems to allow for the former; and evidently people active in the state, consciously seeking to promote the long-run interests of the dominating classes, do sometimes find it both necessary and feasible to adopt policies contravening the short-run interests of every member. The concessions made to the welfare of the working class in "social consumption" offer manifold illustrations. Sometimes, however, the short-run interests must be supposed to be contravened inadvertently. People with the power to prevent such mishaps were not alert enough to head them off; or alert as they may be, they made mistakes about what to do. Will they not fail in the same ways to forestall some sacrifices of long-run interests, too? Indeed, these failures will often be impossible to distinguish in particular instances from the others, since the proposition that long-run interests are favored, though short-run ones are sacrificed, will in some instances not be susceptible of conclusive demonstration. Furthermore, if the diversity of the agents and the branches of politics is taken into account, as Poulantzas (1978) and others insist, so that even the dominated classes are recognized as gaining occasional advantages, one will evidently have to allow for the deliberate adoption, in some branches, of policies at odds with the long-run interests of the dominating classes. Will those classes then no longer be properly called "dominating"? But even if they and their agents are not uniformly efficient in detecting such acts of subversion, correcting them, and recouping any losses, the classes in question may still, for the time being, dominate by winning most of the time on most of the issues important to them.

Mandel (1976) writes again and again of "the growing autonomy" of the state. Certainly he holds that the state has become more active and more ambitious in carrying out its third function, of establishing the general conditions of production. It continually provides, through expenditures on armaments (and space research), on overseas aid, and on infrastructure, additional opportunities for private hands to increase their holdings of capital. It has nationalized, in one industry after another, firms that would otherwise have gone under or has supported them out of the public purse; sometimes it has nationalized whole industries (Mandel, 1976).

Some of these ventures should, no doubt, also be classified under what O'Connor (1973) calls "social expenses," since the chief immediate effect and purpose of them has been, not to increase productivity in any way, but to soften the impact of the market upon various segments of the labor force. The increasingly ambitious efforts of the state at "crisis management" call for a similar double classification. The state has thus become more active and more ambitious in carrying out its second function, social integration, too. So much is directly evident from the increase in the scope of programs to maintain, even raise, the standard of living of masses of people who would otherwise, being continually victimized by the system, be continually disaffected from it. O'Connor (1973) maintains that these are chiefly people who, as they find work, must depend for it on the competitive sector of the economy, rather than on the state sector or the monopoly sector, where the workers are much more comfortably treated to begin with. (It is consistent, of course, with there being more service to victims than previously, both that not all victims are reached and that the programs mentioned give more service to people already comfortably treated than to people more victimized.)

Does this greater activity and ambition imply more autonomy? There is a distinction to make here that Mandel does not attend to. The greater activity and ambition is common ground for all these writers. However, Poulantzas, though he insists, "The state's 'economic interventions' . . . have never been so pronounced as in the present phase, nor has the displacement of dominance in favour of the state" (1975), also declares,

"The play of its relative autonomy *vis-à-vis* the hegemonic fraction, monopoly capital, takes place within far more confined limits than was the case in the past" (1975). He offers no evidence for this assertion. Yet clearly it is possible that the state might intervene more and yet be more uncompromising in promoting the interests of the dominating classes (or of the hegemonic fraction of those classes taken together). The state might, for example, multiply subsidies to agribusinesses while it excludes farm laborers from social security; or it might subsidize firms like Chrysler only on condition that workers sacrifice wages.

Nevertheless, it is difficult to believe that the state can have become so much more active and ambitious without having become more autonomous, and become this in realizing more frequently and with, on the average, greater impact all four of the possibilities enumerated earlier of the contravening interests of the dominating classes. That is to say, the hypothesis that first suggests itself, given other components of the description offered by these writers of the increased activity and ambition of the state, is that over the whole time elapsing since Marx and Engels wrote, the state has become substantially more autonomous in all those dimensions.

It is admitted that substantial concessions have been made to the dominated classes; to keep the system going, the dominating classes have had to accept a smaller return from it than they would have got from a continuing unmodified system. Pursuing the policies that embody the concessions, is not the state in a position to bring in more easily further policies of the same sort? What would have been resisted fiercely as a radical departure a century ago will now be just one increment among others to an enormously expanded and continually growing program of state activity. It may be ampler provision for unemployment insurance; it may be increased restrictions on the power of employers to hire as they please. Whatever it is, the increment will increase the size of the program and thus make even more substantial departures feasible as increments in the future. In fact, the increments need not be favorable to the dominated class in order to put the state in a position to act with more substantial autonomy. They might, in a mixture of policies, have been more unfavorable than otherwise and still have had the effect of making an increase in "social expenses" now hardly noticeable, given the size of the program.

The hypothesis of increased autonomy (to which, in effect, I have joined a hypothesis of autonomy still increasing) needs to be tested. The best evidence of increased autonomy would be evidence of increase in autonomous activity. Without carefully designed empirical studies—of sorts conspicuously absent from Marxist writings—one cannot say how far the activity of the state has changed, compared to various points in the past, far and near. Even the extent of autonomy at any given time requires such a study. I shall try not to beg the empirical questions, but I shall argue that if autonomy is increasing, the prospects for self-transformation become more favorable. The state is not going to proceed with self-transformation in any straightforward way, however, it if proceeds at all. For though the increased activity and ambition of the state have tended to shift the issues that self-transformation involves onto the public agenda, the state cannot easily cope with them there. A second shift, in effect, displaces issues from the public agenda into the bureaucracy. This is what Mandel calls "reprivatization." Most important issues about conflicts of interest are no longer debated in the public arena, that is to say, in parliament; they are left to be settled by deals between myriad interests (predominantly, but not exclusively, capitalist interests) and various sets of bureaucrats in myriad agencies (Mandel, 1976; Poulantzas, 1978). It is, I shall argue, under "reprivatization" that autonomy will chiefly be exercised, if it is exercised to bring about self-transformation, though intermittent resort to the public agenda may also be required if self-transformation is to succeed.

Attempting to deal with the issues that self-transformation involves—attempting to deal with any of the issues in which it has become entangled—increases the already heavy burden of embarrassments that the state in late capitalism labors under. The result of its increased activity and ambition has been, Mandel claims (1976), and Habermas concurs (1975), "hypertrophy." The state has been trying to do many more things than it can do effectively. Left agrees with Right on this point, according to Buchanan (1977). It is locked into many large—indeed automatically increasing—expenditures for specific parts of its program. It is having increasing difficulty raising the money that it requires (O'Connor, 1973). It is not bringing effective means to bear upon the tasks that it has undertaken to perform. Hence it is involved in what Habermas (1974) calls a "rationality crisis."

Hypertrophy does not, however, produce the crisis all by itself. Habermas emphasizes, instead, the charge that the state has been compelled to take on new tasks inconsistent with the goals already set up for it. It cannot foster capital accumulation by large-scale interventions in the economy without, to some extent, displacing private firms and without facing the necessity of undertaking large-scale planning. It cannot carry through consistent large-scale plans without restricting private firms in their freedom to invest and in other ways. Yet the free—the anarchic—pursuit of gain by individual private firms is just what, to maintain capitalism, the state is supposed to promote (Habermas, 1975).

With the assumption of responsibilities for intervention, the basic, insuperable embarrassment of the capitalistic system comes insistently into view. The means of production call for, and to some degree get (as they must, if the system is to work at all), social planning for social purposes. Yet, with an anomaly that cannot be explained away, private appropriation of surplus value continues nevertheless (Habermas, 1975).

This embarrassment is the most important cause of the "legitimation crisis" of late capitalism, according to Habermas. Unless the state can justify both its actions and the social arrangements that it supports as serving "generalizable interests," which duly embrace and are recognized as embracing the interests of all its citizens so far as those interests can be consistently served, it will lose legitimacy (Habermas, 1975). The capitalist state cannot justify itself in this way. Formerly, it could evade the task of justification. The economy, with the theory of laissez-faire, had its own rationale, which provided a show of justification for the whole system (Habermas, 1975). Now, simultaneously with a shift of responsibilities and issues that makes evasion on that pattern impossible, the standards of justification have been raised by a general advance in discussion of such matters toward "a critical universal morality" (Habermas, 1975). This directs attention to needs that can be "communicatively shared" (Habermas, 1975:108) by agents with fully developed "communicative competence" and no defensible reason to dissemble their purposes (Habermas, 1970). Thus, the legitimation crisis is aggravated by what Habermas distinguishes as a "motivation crisis"—a crisis in social integration. Traditional norms, which dictated commitment to roles and practices in the system, have eroded in the course of the technological changes that have eliminated those roles and practices or deprived them of their traditional meaning. The norms that now apply are the newly universalistic ones (Habermas, 1975).

The embarrassment about continuing private appropriation of surplus value is not the only cause of the legitimation crisis. The rationality crisis itself has powerfully adverse effects upon legitimation. How can people regard their state as legitimate when it is manifestly incapable of doing what it undertakes to do, in part because it is trying to do too much for its organizational capacity, in part because it is trying to do inconsistent things (Habermas, 1975)? Another cause is reprivatization, which is represented in Habermas's scheme (1975) by the notion of "depoliticization" (and other notions). With reprivatization, less and less effort is made by the state to find and publicize comprehensive legitimating rationales for its policies, or even to reconcile in public arguments apparent discrepancies between the policies, taken two or three at a time. Shifted into the bureaucracy, issues may escape considerations of consistency and other general considerations that would arise about them in public forums such as parliament. Even if the diverse branches that now deal with fragments of issues are ready to offer rationales of what they do, these will often be technical and limited. They will typically take the general social arrangements of the society for granted. Moreover, they will rarely get anything like general attention by whatever public exists to follow political issues. They will be too specialized; and there will be too many of them.

Reprivatization, however, has another aspect, in which it can be regarded as mitigating the legitimation crisis. It may reduce the efforts at comprehensive justification, so that what demands do arise for justifying the basic arrangements of capitalism go, embarrassingly, unanswered. At the same time, however, it may reduce the number and intensity of demands. Since elections and parliament now make little difference to the myriad policies pursued by the ever-larger and more complex bureaucracy, people do not expect genuine efforts at comprehensive justification to be a prominent feature of electoral politics or of parliamentary debate. (The business of parliament is as fragmented as the operations of the bureaucracy.) Nor do people expect, any more than they are allowed, to make any impact on the policies pursued by the state. Formal democracy continues. From time to time, people are presented at elections with alternatives so limited that the elections amount to little more than a chance to give an empty formal assent to the system (Habermas, 1975; Poulantzas, 1978).

People turn away from political ideals (into "civil privatism") and become absorbed in their families and in their careers—"familial-vocational privatism," something that bourgeois ideology has encouraged all along (Habermas, 1975).[5] Supplied with enough material comforts, they may be content enough with this way of life in sufficient numbers to preclude any successful mass mobilization against the system. Moreover, in spite of increasing embarrassments about persistent unemployment, persistent inflation, visible confusion, and manifold inefficiency, the bureaucracy and the "monopolies" may be able to go on supplying enough material comforts to keep discontent from turning into militancy.

If Mandel is correct, the bureaucracy will do what it can to keep the system going. He does not merely, like O'Connor (1973), take every instance of trying to adjust the system so that it will work a little better as "class-conscious" in intention, evidently on the ground that while the system continues, the chief beneficiaries will be the dominating classes (O'Connor, 1973). He argues that the dominating classes can count upon the bureaucrats because the structure of the state, when the bureaucracy is so prominent, is hierarchical. The top positions in the bureaucracy go to members of the bourgeoisie; and the hierarchy selects conformists for promotion. Thus the people running the bureaucracy are more than ordinarily imbued with ideological acceptance of the state; as it stands, it is, for them, dedicated without serious qualification to serving the public interest. The main error of reformists, Mandel (1976) holds, is just their failure to understand these facts about the structure of the state and the implied commitment to keep up the present relations of production.

With these observations, Mandel completes the picture of the second shift of issues—reprivatization—as something that undoes (or forestalls) the first shift, which brought onto the public agenda issues about the fundamental arrangements of capitalism. Such issues are not going to be confronted and resolved by the public principles appropriate to the public professions and responsibilities of the state. They are not going to be dealt with that way outside the bureaucracy; they are not going to be dealt with that way inside it. The embarrassing comprehensive questions that they involve will be continually evaded in favor of fragmented policies, accompanied by fragmented rationales that take the virtues of capitalistic arrangements for granted.

Is this, however, all that is to be made of reprivatization? Discussion of the shifts—whether by Habermas or by Mandel—does not really get beyond the stage of once again formulating plausible hypotheses. Evidence is lacking for the relative magnitudes of the changes implied. Mandel does not allow sufficiently for the possibility that reprivatization opens up opportunities for more effective remedial actions than could be undertaken otherwise, under the full pressure of "formal-democratic means of legitimation" as Habermas (1975) envisages them. But if Mandel is correct about the ideological commitments and conforming behavior of the bureaucrats, he is in a position to dash cold water on any lingering hopes that Habermas might have of bringing about an advance toward the transformed society through fully general debate on the public agenda. Habermas, in holding that individual sectors of the economy have "privatized" the various parts of the bureaucracy (1975), so far agrees with Mandel's picture of reprivatization and, perhaps inadvertently, concedes the point.

Yet even if Mandel is correct, Habermas has some grounds for not conceding—for not abandoning his hopes of fully general debate. What does it mean to have the bureaucrats imbued with bourgeois ideology? Bourgeois ideology itself is responsive, as the classic Marxist conception of the state allows, to the fully generalizable interests that would be invoked in the sort of debate that Habermas imagines. Consistently with that ideology, the bureaucrats may be expected to use the sort of autonomy that they enjoy along with reprivatization, sometimes at least, to attend to interests other than those of the dominating classes. Poulantzas (1978) argues that in fact, precisely because they regard the state as charged with defending the public interest against the monopolies and other favored economic elements, some bureaucrats will quite readily take up the cause of the dominated classes, though not to the extent of encouraging them to form their own organizations outside the hierarchy.

Is even that qualification insurmountable? Habermas, on this point following Offe, disagrees with Mandel on the ideological complexion of the bureaucracy. As the state has grown in the number and intricacy of the functions that it has assumed, it has had to recruit "professionalized" additions to its civil service. These elements consist of "concrete" rather than "abstract" labor; that is to say, of people oriented to the production of use values rather than exchange values. In other words, they are people who, through their professional training, in which they are accustomed to having technology rationally used to achieve purposes defined otherwise than by profitability in the market, are bound to be impatient with the irrationality of the capitalistic system. It may be their impatience that will turn out to be decisive against tolerating the system any longer (Habermas, 1975; Offe, 1972). Autonomy with reprivatization may give them the chance to act and to seize upon the most promising means, even when these are new forms of organization outside the bureaucracy. They may be expected to be ready to defend their actions on general principles, and they may be called upon to do so in the media and in the parliament, at least on issues selected for special prominence. So, to some extent, may more conventional bureaucrats, acting though they may be on the supposition that the received institutions of the state will continue.

THE TASK OF SELF-TRANSFORMATION: ROUTE AND GOAL

The conventional bureaucrats will thus be making their contributions to keeping up public debate. The unconventional ones—the new professionals—will be resorting to public debate on occasion to justify what amounts to significant departures from the status quo. If Habermas and the other writers are correct, moreover, in their belief that departures can be more firmly justified by the standards of public debate, the unconventional ones will have the advantage in the arena. The beginnings of a map for the most favored route to the transformed society thus emerge.

Under reprivatization, on one side, bureaucrats with the new orientation will be taking initiatives in policies and organization that may culminate in transformation. For each initiative they will enlist the support of the specialized public that keeps abreast of the activity of the branch or agency in which the initiative comes forward. On the other side, organizations outside the bureaucracy will be taking initiatives, too, some of them capable of cumulation in a progressive direction. These organizations will seek the support of the branches or agencies concerned with the specialized publics in which the organizations figure. It is there, for the most part, that the "masses" will be active—in labor groups, consumer groups, peace groups, rights groups, environmental groups.

I speak of two sides in order to make sure of a balanced picture. It is not to be assumed that the new bureaucrats will be able to make cumulative initiatives stick on their own, without some form of mass support. It is not to be assumed, on the other hand, that a mass movement fragmented into specialized publics, overlapping to a degree, no doubt, but not systematically coordinated, can succeed without allies in the bureaucracy (including the courts and sometimes joining up with members of the legislature). However, to speak of two sides underrates the extent to which, under reprivatization, the activities of the branches of the bureaucracy, taken severally, are intertwined with those of the specialized publics. Overall, Poulantzas repeatedly insists that the state is best looked at, not as an apparatus, but as an arena of activity, in which the public takes part along with the official personnel of the state. Looked at closely, it is a complex of such arenas. In their multiplicity lies the autonomy of the late capitalist state.

From time to time the new bureaucrats and their allies will be called upon to justify their initiatives in public debate, and they will be well placed to do so. Sometimes, they will find themselves allied with more conventional forces inside and outside the bureaucracy. Often—very likely most of the time—a departure toward transformation may equally well be described, to the satisfaction of almost everybody, as a concession designed to maintain the system. When a departure does have to be defended as such, it will be possible to argue that it accords better than the status quo with public standards.

Many of the initiatives will not be selected for general attention in the media and in parliament. Indeed, the people taking the initiatives may be supposed to be occupied normally in putting through incremental changes too small and too various for the status quo to focus organized attention upon. Thus the pluralism and fragmentation of policy making in the capitalist state offers a substantial opportunity for self-transformation. Occasionally, however, the transforming bureaucrats may themselves wish to resort, at specially favorable junctures, to the media and to parliament, to consolidate one series or another of past gains and to establish in general legislation a more progressive climate for further departures.

I say this is the most favored route to the transformed society. I do not say it is a reliable route. If it is the most favored route, the prospects of reaching the transformed society may not be very encouraging. In fact, I do not think they are. What we are talking about is an outside chance, and it

75

may be optimistic to think it is as large as a chance of one in ten. The bias of political activity in the late capitalist state may run strongly against cumulative changes in the direction of transformation. The bias may even be increasing. Poulantzas (1978) claims that a prominent current development in the late capitalist state is "authoritarian statism," "marked by the hold of the summits of the Executive over the upper administration and by the increased political control of the former over the latter''; the executive itself has become "personalized" in one man "at the top of the Executive."

Poulantzas may have been thinking too much of France; the evidence from other capitalist countries (e.g., Canada) would be more mixed. Moreover, Poulantzas himself qualified "authoritarian statism" as a "tendency." "Underlying the process of concentration are important inner-state contradictions . . . growing contradictions." "Contradictions between monopoly and other fractions of capital, or between the power bloc and the popular masses, are expressed right at the heart of the State, in its central regions and summits. Inevitably, therefore, they traverse the focal point represented by the top man. There is not *one* president, but *several in one*" (Poulantzas, 1978). Given that the representative function of the political parties has been curtailed because the parties have been shut out of the "water-tight container" in which "the state bureaucracy has shut itself up" (Poulantzas, 1978), these are the contradictions already allowed for in the thesis of reprivatization. They do not encourage confidence in the effectiveness of the state, either as an arena in which capitalism will be maintained or as one in which it will be transformed.

The most likely prospect before the state in late capitalism may be that it will stagger on indefinitely, not changing enough to satisfy the minimum conditions for transformation into socialism or changing, so far as it does change, in an unwelcome direction. My picture of the prospects is, however, no more inconclusive than the picture offered by Habermas (1975) or O'Connor. O'Connor, who considers only the scope that conventional politicians and conventional bureaucrats have for action described as maintaining the system, holds that the state might not only survive but survive robustly if it succeeded in building up a "socio-industrial complex." There, over the heads and over the opposition of organized labor in both the state sector and the monopoly sector, it would join with the monopolies in bringing about an adequate flow of resources to workers in the competitive sector. He is inclined to think that this will not happen; but the alternative, one gathers, is not a sure prospect of transformation. It is, as probably as not, an indefinitely long process of deterioration (O'Connor, 1973).

Mandel (1979), alone among these writers, retains the classical confidence in transformation by a proletarian revolution. It is difficult, however, to see what basis he has for thinking any such thing will happen in the Western liberal democracies; and even more difficult to understand is his confidence that if it does happen, the transformation will be to his liking. Is the labor movement in Western countries going to be so much more militant and unified than it has been hitherto? Deteriorating though it will perhaps be all along, may not the system be able to temporize indefinitely with any workers' demands that threaten even remotely to turn into armed revolt? Reprivatization allows at least a good deal of scope for temporization. Would not an attempt at a revolution, even if it got under way, be the surest means of mobilizing the bourgeoisie with repressive instruments that are still essentially at their command? Mere approximation to such an attempt in Spain, Chile, and Guatemala sufficed for such mobilization.

Moreover, anything about the circumstances that improves the chances of a revolution's succeeding is likely to aggravate the reasons for apprehending that it will not bring the desired transformation. A revolution is more likely to succeed amid chaos, in which the courts and the police no longer function in a regular way. But what then is going to happen, for example, to civil liberties, which Mandel (1979), along with the other writers that I have drawn on, fervently champions, both as a feature of the transformed society and as a condition of the efforts to bring that society about (Poulantzas, 1978)? Hitherto, civil liberties have flourished only when they have had special institutional backing from the courts and parliament. Are they to be left to the discretion of popular feeling in a time of maximum popular excitement?

Mandel (1979) pictures revolution and its aftermath, the dictatorship of the proletariat, as a process during which parliament loses power while soviets—workers' councils—gain it. Poulantzas (1978), equally concerned with the preservation of representative institutions from the beginning of transformation and throughout, is more inclined to keep parliament going. But what, in a revolutionary situation, where the revolutionists' impatience with dissidents will be maximized, is going to ensure that representaive institutions, in whatever form or mix of forms they exist, will be genuinely responsive?

To succeed, the revolution may have to have monolithic organization. If so, success will be achieved only by sacrificing liberties and representation on the way, and only by committing the transformation to a form of organization entirely unsuited to bringing them back and improving on them, even as they now exist in the late capitalist state. Moreover, even if the revolution could succeed without monolithic organization, that is, in the circumstances, the sort of organization that it is likely to get.

Revolution is thus not a promising means of transformation. If we dwell upon its disadvantages, it will seem less favored than the route that I am outlining. But does not that route run, fatally, upon the other horn of an all-too-familiar dilemma? Does the route amount to anything more than Revisionism, with its fatal tendency to being coopted and assimilated by the system? I do not think it can be denied that some such dangers will be found along the route. However, they are much less considerable than the dangers to which Revisionism has time and again succumbed. The trap that Revisionism—the social democratic parties of western Europe—fell into was the trap first of seeking a majority in parliament and then of carrying on a responsible government on the basis of such a majority. To do these things, acting as a political party in a parliamentary system, the social democratic parties have had to commit themselves to compromise programs that placate widespread fears of radical change and accordingly offer to temporize indefinitely with the entrenched interests received from the past. The route that I am outlining—plural incremental departures, initiated under reprivatization by unconventional bureaucrats or by allies active in their specialized publics, with occasional resort to fully general debate—does not require any such commitment.

The initiators of these departures need not abate a jot or tittle of the overall program of transformation to which they have come to subscribe (as the result of a variety of influences—education, reading, discussion, loose connections with formal or informal organizations). They may have to accept it that their initiatives will often be undone or offset by reactionary initiatives taken elsewhere in the bureaucracy and in other specialized publics. They do not have to endorse those opposed initiatives or even desist from arguing against them and trying to get them undone in turn. When they are called upon to defend the departures that they initiate, they will do so by arguing that unless current arrangements are modified in the ways implied by these departures, the arrangements will be beset by increasing difficulties. Unless the poor are organized to help themselves, their condition and the condition of the cities will deteriorate; unless community development corporations are set up, welfare payments will continue to rise, and there will be nothing to show for them in renovated housing. In general, it will be possible to argue sincerely on these lines, even with people who will look upon the departures as concessions that will help maintain the current system. The initiators can consistently, for their part, look upon these departures as so many cumulative steps in transforming the system. The initiators are not even debarred from being frank about their views: their conventional allies may not take alarm from remarking the disagreement about the significance of the departures; they may just go on disagreeing.

Will the initiatives that fall into the progressive category cumulate if they are not coordinated by a party or organized movement, whether or not it is one that works mainly for victory at elections? I do not know; but logically, it is no more necessary for the cumulation of progressive initiatives that they be coordinated by some overall agency than that they fall into the progressive category (tending toward transformation) exclusively, and not simultaneously into the system-maintaining category. Moreover, it accords with the deterministic side of classical Marxist theory that the initiatives cumulate as responses in the superstructure to exigencies resulting from changes in the relations of production, without anyone, or any set of people, deliberately planning for cumulation. Coordination of a sort, sufficient for cumulation, might be furnished by one initiative's being conceived to exploit the opportunity—or at least the example—set by another, and by having media to publicize, among intersecting audiences in the bureaucracy and outside, such opportunities and examples.

A prima facie case can thus be made for the route via reprivatization. We cannot go further in discovering how promising the route may be, however, without knowing more about the goal to be reached. Are even the most unconventional, even the most progressive bureaucrats and their allies in specialized publics directing themselves, so far as they need to in these early stages, toward the arrangements of the transformed society? It is not enough, especially in view of the character that known postrevolutionary societies have actually assumed, to talk broadly about abundance and social planning in a classless society. It is not enough to justify expecting that the transformed society will, once installed, be more agreeable than the welfare state in late capitalism; it is not enough to tell whether social change is moving in the direction of a society about which one could confidently have such expectations. To be sure, not everything about the transformed arrangements can be specified in advance. To a very large extent, as Marx insisted, it is only reasonable, indeed necessary, to leave the institutions of the transformed society to be shaped by the perceptions and inventions of the people who are going to live in it. Their circumstances and their attitudes are going to be substantially without precedent in our un-transformed society. We need, however, to know more about the trans-formed society than Marx was willing to say to know whether it will be desirable and whether we are on the way to it.

Reflections by contemporary Marxist writers on the disillusioning features of postrevolutionary societies help on both points. Mandel (1979), Poulantzas (1978), and Carrillo (1977), for example, agree that prominent among those features, besides the suppression of civil liberties and the extinction of representative institutions, has been the rise of a monolithic bureaucracy supporting a new privileged elite. One can directly infer that among the features of the transformed society are to be civil liberties, effective provisions for representation, and some alternative to an all-powerful central bureaucracy. To these we may add that there must be some system for matching, indeed surpassing, capitalism in the production and distribution of economic benefits. It must be no worse than late capitalism in providing regular employment, interesting work, and a high standard of living for everybody. Indeed, in at least one of these categories, it must do better. Marxists have continually expected that it would do better in all.

The condition about preserving civil liberties will readily be met on the route via reprivatization. That route presupposes keeping up parliament until what effective representation it does give is given by superseding institutions (e.g., workers' councils), and it presupposes keeping up the courts at least until they have no useful functions to perform. Currently they not only serve to protect civil liberties; they are from time to time used to enlarge them and the rights against discrimination with which they intersect. Moreover, even in the best-realized of transformed societies, courts are likely to be needed indefinitely in these and other connections: justice for persons at odds with various social organizations; resolutions of private quarrels; family law; some criminal proceedings. Courts are not very soon going to lose so many functions that they cease to be robust enough and prominent enough to command respect for civil liberties.

So long as parliament is preserved, moreover, giving some effective representation, the conditions for representation will be met at least in part. Will the route be favorable for developing the alternative provisions for representation that these writers regard either as indispensable comple- ments to parliaments (Poulantzas, 1978) or as devices infinitely superior, by which parliament will be essentially supplanted (Mandel, 1979)? It is not just a question of representation. Part of the superiority of these new devices, such as workers' councils, supposedly consists in their providing for more participation, through representation and alongside it. Will the bureauc- racy—even the unconventional elements in the bureaucracy—be ready to assist such devices into being? Will the bureaucracy be willing to initiate cooperation with devices created outside—in the labor movement, in consumer groups, among environmentalists, in neighborhoods—and to persist in such cooperation?

Poulantzas (1978), as I have already noted, apprehends that the answer to both questions would be negative; organizational imperialism and self-interest would dictate otherwise. However, it is far from evident that these factors would always outweigh reforming convictions; it is not even evident that they would work out to negative answers. In Canada and the United States, the record is full of examples of organizations—ranging from neighborhood groups and the groups of welfare recipients to national farm organizations—that the bureaucracies have themselves created to mobilize, branch by branch, the specialized publics that they need. Moreover, the very notion of reprivatization implies that a host of specially mobilized publics, organized to various degrees, will be present to deal with the fragmented bureaucracy. There is, of course, ample evidence that the corresponding organizations exist in abundance and that the bureaucracy is prepared to cooperate with them (Truman, 1951). Many of them—most of them—are currently more interested, no doubt, in preserving dubious privileges accorded them under the present system than in assisting in departures toward a transformed society; but that is not by itself relevant to deciding the point about organizational imperialism and self-interest. The existence, history, and influence of such organizations demonstrate that those factors do not preclude fostering representative devices outside the bureaucracy. Among them already are organizations that call for progressive departures, and in important respects (e.g., in making alternative jobs available) these offer the same basis for cooperation with bureaucrats.

Whatever its disadvantages, a fragmented bureaucracy already offers some relief from a monolithic one. Will the progressive organizations that it fosters, among others, furnish a decentralized alternative as well as a fragmented one? The grand historical alternative to bureaucracy, fragmented or otherwise, has been, of course, the market. Marxists have only belatedly and reluctantly come to accept the market as a device to be joined with centralized planning and reduce its difficulties (Lindblom, 1977). Marxists have perhaps not even yet fully appreciated the virtues of the market as an alternative to bureaucracy. Even under capitalism, however, it implies a pluralism of power that helps to protect the liberties of small groups and individual persons. It is not just the courts and parliament that make a difference in this respect between late capitalist states and postrevolutionary societies like the Soviet Union. It is also the pluralism of employers, based on a pluralism of property holders. Exclusion from employment, even exclusion from employment suited to one's skills—as in Czechoslovakia currently—suffices for a good deal of effective repression.

The objective, then, in perfecting an alternative to a monolithic bureaucracy might be taken to be to decentralize to a pluralism of small-scale powers without giving those powers the privileges, in personal enrichment and class distinction, that are objectionable in capitalistic private property. What form might these powers take? Some of the forms have already appeared in advance of any general social transformation: consumers' cooperatives; producers' cooperatives;[6] worker-owned firms; nonprofit community-development corporations; firms (like some newspapers) that have become in effect nonprofit foundations. To these may be added multiple devices for local government—not just towns, but water districts, school districts, neighborhood school committees, communes. Some of these forms—not just the communes—may be small enough to dispense with hierarchy. With all these organizations in the picture, one can draw—

quite consistently with Marx's approval (1871), in *The Civil War in France,* of the thoroughgoing decentralization of administration envisaged by the Commune of 1871—on some suggestions brought up within the public-choice school, chiefly by Vincent Ostrom (1976), as to how all these organizations are to be related.[7]

Imagine having organizations of various sorts on the production side of the economy and other organizations of various sorts on the consumption side. Those kinds of productive organizations that were considered particularly prone to acquire undue privileges might be excluded, or admitted only under stringent precautionary regulation. Even producers' cooperatives or worker-owned firms pose dangers of monopolistic behavior (as has long been a commonplace; Bernstein, 1961 [1899]). Precautions would have to be taken against the dangers, and the precautions would be the more necessary, the larger the scale at which economies of production were maximized. Forms of provision for some needs might best be produced by single productive organizations, if they can be restrained from exploiting their monopoly positions. Whatever the size, an effective precaution might be the one lately suggested specifically for producers' cooperatives— namely, that the organization not own the capital that it uses but borrow the capital from other organizations that make a detached evaluation of its prospects (Vanek, 1977). The lending organizations, set up to act in the public interest, would have the power to check people in the borrowing organization from restricting the size of operations or making undue personal profits. As a last resort, the lending organizations would have the power to recall the investment, though if the borrowing organizations are to be independent employers, they, in their turn, will have to be protected against arbitrary recall.

In general, the efficient size of the productive organizations will vary, as, independently, will the efficient size of the organizations on the consumption side. This is so whether we take efficiency in a narrow sense, analogous to that achieved by a profitable unregulated firm in a competitive market, or in a more stringent sense, imposing the condition that all externalities be internalized. (In the first case, we would not be demanding that all the good externalities that people wish to include in the social product have been internalized and paid for by the beneficiaries or on their behalf, as social decision prescribes. An example would be lower transportation costs for everyone, once docks and tracks were built to serve a particular enterprise or industry. Nor would we be demanding that the costs minimized in achieving efficiency account for all the bad externalities—for example, congestion, or pollution—that people are ready to put up with only if costs overall are minimized. In the second case, we would be demanding both these things.)

Some of these organizations, concerned with those forms of provision for needs that come in the form of private goods, would be organizations for cooperative purchasing. One might include families (households) among them. Where larger organizations offered no advantages in purchasing that families or single persons could not match, the organizations would not, in circumstances permitting free adaptation to opportunities, appear or persist. On the production side, too, the goods in question would, in some cases, be produced by single persons and, in others, by small groups, though if the technology of modern industry is to be kept (as Marxists assume), many private goods will be produced by rather large organizations.

On the consumption side, there will also be organizations concerned with the purchase of public goods, for example, education, water-supply systems, systems of sanitation. Here the member-consumers would join not just to enjoy the economies of purchasing in bulk; besides buying together the goods in question, they would consume them together. One may imagine them choosing between productive organizations specializing in public goods and capable of supplying those goods on more or less attractive terms. In some cases, several would be contracted with to join in the production of the good in question.

Suppose the organizations are bounded both geographically and in respect to the forms of provision with which they are concerned. Each will make its own decisions but will respond to the cues given it by the decisions of other organizations; in other words, the organizations will be coordinated by something like a market process. But now, trying to imagine how the economy might be organized without a centralized bureaucracy, have we not found our way back to laissez faire and all the miseries—as well as the dubious benefits—of economic competition between organizations and between persons? Where is the planning and cooperation that Marxists had hoped for?

In part, the planning and cooperation will devolve upon organizations small enough to carry on planning for the needs of their members by the continuous direct participation that Marx treated as one of the basic remedies for alienation (Braybrooke, 1958; Thayer, 1981). Some of these organizations might be communes in which production and consumption were combined; and these communes might, as small-scale societies, come closer to realizing the hopes for the transformed society than anything else in it. In part, the planning and cooperation will be found in negotiations between organizations for the supply of goods private and public. There will be some competition on both sides, but if the organizations on the production side are not seeking ever-greater profits, but simply to break even, the competition need not be so strenuous as to distort personal relations within the producing organizations or between people on the two sides of the transactions. Indeed, the consuming organizations might normally have members who participate in the planning of the productive organizations that are dealt with; and vice versa (Thayer, 1981). On the consumption side, organizations and persons might be seeking to maximize gains, but they need not do so in rivalry with one another, and the occasions for rivalry could be diminished by assuring everyone of economic security and by approximating equality of incomes.

Security and equality are matters that will probably require some central planning—and a central authority capable of collecting taxes and regulating market processes. So will environmental matters. Exactly what tasks the central planning body should have and how it should carry them out are not subjects that can be explained in detail here. One might infer, from the apparent difficulty of carrying out the theories of central planning that have been formally outlined (Milleron, 1972), that economics may not have advanced to the point of being able to furnish such an explanation anywhere. What is crucial for present purposes is to say that the central planning body should have a relatively small role and limited powers and, even so, be as responsive as effective representation for the whole society can make it. It will have a relatively small role if it does not attempt much prescriptive planning. It may confine itself to adjusting the results of market processes, and even here rely on combinations of taxes (including social-insurance charges) and subsidies to accomplish its aims, rather than prescribe, say, safety standards and emission standards (Thurow, 1980). Presumably, the information that it needs to monitor market processes throughout the economy and make the required adjustments could be organized in large-scale computers. The computers would not themselves pose dangers of repression; they would perhaps help to minimize the corps of inspectors otherwise required.

Effective representation will demand, besides universal suffrage, some provisions for identifying, on occasion, alternative slates or representatives committed to different central-planning policies. No doubt the present political parties of the liberal democracies in late capitalism are very imperfect means of identifying such slates and of offering a choice between them. Contemporary Marxists might nevertheless give some thought about how, in the transformed society, precautions are to be taken against there being no means at all. Meanwhile, as I have already said, the continuation of parliament, with the present parties and some possibility of starting up new ones, roughly meets the requirement. Moreover, in parliament and in the parties (whether or not they are parties disciplined enough to have an identifiable programmatic commitment), there is a corps of politicians who are to some degree oriented toward making the system responsive.

How is the central planning body in the transformed society to be made responsive? If the electorate divides on issues with which the central planning body is occupied, part of the electorate is going to lose when the body goes ahead with a certain policy. The people who are thus disappointed, however, might simply swallow their disappointment and wait their turn for success on future issues. Moreover, people who lose out on one issue may, more often than not, win on others: No one may belong to a group that consistently loses, or even loses most of the time.

All of this may happen automatically, without anyone taking any special care to make it happen. In healthy political systems, however, politicians make it their business to take special care. Observing the disappointment of the people outvoted on one issue, some politicians would perhaps move for an immediate compromise, pressing the central planning body to allocate part of the resources initially committed to the winning policy to meeting some of the demands of people who supported the alternatives. If circumstances did not favor an immediate compromise, politicians, mindful of the present disappointment, would be looking for opportunities to capitalize on it in winning political support on later issues.

Of course, the process is a fallible one. Opportunities to do quite different things, serving other people, may continually seem more promising to the politicians than the project of compensating for the disappointment. In the end, nothing may come of the project. Nevertheless, the process, combined with the process of changing from one issue to another and automatically reassorting voters, may produce compensations often enough to make people outvoted on any given question reasonably content with the system in the long run and to remove any grounds for holding the system to be persistently unjust to any one group. The answer to keeping the central planning body responsive lies in making sure that it is controlled by a system of effective representation in which such a process operates.

In this regard and in regard to the other conditions to be met by the transformed society, approximations to meeting the conditions already exist in the late capitalist state; they need not be abandoned even temporarily en route to the transformation. Moreover, those approximations open up the possibility of distributing the people who are in outlook prepared to move on such a route to the transformed society, inside and outside the bureaucracy (and other parts of the state apparatus) in sufficient numbers and with sufficient power to set off on the route. Offe (1972) and Habermas (1975) suggest that such a distribution of activities may already exist. Such activities have legitimate positions in the capitalist state, and they are in positions from which greater legitimacy may be attained. It is on them that efficacious use of the autonomy of the state depends and, as well, progress toward transformation. Whether they are actually moving on the route that I have sketched and how far they can be expected to get on it, if they are, are matters on which social experiment and observation must speak, rather than a speculative survey of possibilities.

NOTES

1. Poulantzas says, "The (capitalist) State . . . is . . . the material condensation of . . . a relationship of forces among classes and class fractions" (1978:128); and though he denies that the state is a full-fledged "Subject" on the next page, he freely writes on the page previous of the state's having a role and in this role "organizing" the dominant class or classes.

2. Among these currents figure, besides the official Marxism of the Soviet Union and its satellites as set forth, for example, in the East German writings cited by Habermas, the thinking of Mandel and other Trotskyists (see Jürgen Habermas, 1973; Mandel, 1979).

3. The Italian Communist Party and its subscription to Eurocommunism are illuminatingly discussed by Paul Thomas (1979); for the views of the Spanish leader Santiago Carrillo see his book (1977).

4. The passage just cited from *Late Capitalism* perhaps covers this possibility too.

5. Habermas oddly mentions utilitarianism as a characteristic feature of "familiar-vocational privatism," ignoring its remarkabe record of public-spirited reform, in the first half of the nineteenth century especially.

6. The suitability of producers' cooperatives is somewhat problematic.

7. The public-choice school, of course, could hardly intend anything less than to supply Marxism with suggestions. However, it is not really surprising that suggestions should be found there. The public-choice school agrees with contemporary Marxism in deploring the "hypertrophy" of the state and the antilibertarian character of centralized bureaucracy. Moreover, the central, defining preoccupation of the public-choice school is what Buchanan and Tullock (1962) call "the constitutional problem"—the problem of assigning variously to the market, or to voluntary organization, or to compulsory organization (the state) the production of different goods, private and public, so that these will be forthcoming in the quantities best suited to the preferences of the people participating. So defined, the school is not committed a priori to capitalism at all, even if the market is taken to require, which it does not, private property with all the features that private property has under capitalism.

4

Public Interest, Private Interest, and the Democratic Polity

Peter H. Aranson and Peter C. Ordeshook

The outlines of a consensus[1] have emerged concerning the appropriateness of public-sector activities in representative democracies.[2] This consensus holds that most public-sector programs in these nations are inappropriate, or are carried on at an inappropriate level, or are executed in an inappropriate manner. The evidence underlying this consensus grows out of four strands of research. First, public-sector size has increased at a rate that exceeds increases in private-sector size but without an increase in public-sector productivity (Borcherding, 1977a, 1977b; Meltzer and Richard, 1978; Nutter, 1978). Both theoretical[3] and empirical[4] evidence suggest respectively that the public sector cannot be and is not as efficient as the private sector. Hence, unless there is some unexplored reason for increases in public-sector activity, as additional resources shift from the private to the public sector, a net decline in the economy's total productivity occurs, with a resulting erosion of individual welfare. Second, Western democracies have developed extensive regulations, ostensibly to improve individual welfare; but the actual statutes often embrace the least effective and least efficient means to accomplish this end (Commission on Law and the Economy, 1979; Aranson, 1979; Aranson and Ordeshook, 1981b; Noll, 1971; Breyer, 1979; Poole, 1982). In the United States the Equal Employment Opportunity Commission (EEOC; Lindsay and Shanor, 1982), the Environmental Protection Agency (EPA; Ackerman and Hassler, 1981; Aranson, 1982; Maloney and McCormick, 1982; Marcus, 1980; Margolis, 1977), the Pure Food and Drug Administration (FDA; Peltzman, 1973; Wardell and Lasagna, 1975; Weimer, 1982), the National Highway Traffic Safety Administration (NHTSA; Peltzman, 1975), the Occupational Safety and Health Administration (OSHA; Smith, 1982), and the New Deal agencies (Hawley, 1969) provide examples of this phenomenon. Third, many public-sector programs redistribute wealth from lower-income to higher-income persons (Stigler, 1970). Two well-documented examples are state-supported higher education (Hansen and Weisbrod, 1969; Hansen, 1970) and loan-guarantee programs (Hardin and Denzau, 1981; Lowi, 1979). Fourth, antitrust and antimerger statutes, rather than promoting a competitive economy, have protected inefficient firms and have further entrenched inferior management.[5]

None of these phenomena rests on a coherent normative theory of the state, although economists who are not familiar with progress in public choice often use elements of one such theory, welfare economics, to justify the adoption of these welfare-degrading programs.[6] Nor is there a constitutional theory that explains why public policy fails to be welfare regarding.[7] But because representative democracies purport to be representative, the observation that their citizens acquiesce in the ongoing degradation of their own welfare compels explanation.

This essay reviews a body of research on the general problem of the failure of representative democracy.[8] Section 2 develops some commonly invoked standards for welfare judgments about public policy and rehearses the argument that welfare-related justifications for public-sector activities are often overdrawn. Section 3 develops demand-side models of the political process in representative democracies. These models consider the political character of the undifferentiated electorate and the problem of the formation and maintenance of interest groups, with special attention to the nature of their public-policy demands. Section 4 explores the supply side of the public sector by separately considering legislatures, bureaus, and courts. Section 5 then examines alternative formulations of public-sector supply-side characteristics by reporting a general model of candidate and executive decision making based on the nature of public-sector demand. Section 6 reflects on future prospects and possible correctives for present failures and offers some commentary on the limitations inherent in any correctives.

THEORY OF THE STATE

To conclude that most public-sector programs in representative democracies are inappropriate, or are carried on at an inappropriate level, or are executed in an inappropriate manner, requires an underlying theory of the state that provides criteria of appropriateness. It would be hyperbole to claim that such a theory prevails in Western intellectual communities. Nevertheless, certain elements of welfare economics have merged to form a body of prescriptive sentences about public-sector activity (e.g., see Baumol, 1965; Buchanan, 1971; Musgrave, 1959). Indeed, some scholars in modern public finance still regard these sentences as providing the animus for actual decisions taken in the public sector,[9] although most scholars now hold that welfare theory is purely normative and cannot explain actual practice.

Here, we use welfare theory as a tool of criticism of representative democracies, not as a cynosure for public-sector decision making. Commonly accepted elements of welfare theory provide a convenient set of standards for judging the appropriateness of various public-sector activities. While these standards form an intellectual justification for the liberal democratic state, we find no reason to believe that voters and politicians actually try to follow them. Indeed, as we report here, both theory and practice argue persuasively that voters and politicians ignore them, leaving their fulfillment at best a matter of pure happenstance.

The logical structure (as distinct from the historical development) of welfare theory has two variants. The first depends on an individualistic methodology and Pareto optimality.[10] In this variant an institutional arrangement, specific statute, or regulation is welfare-preferred if at least one person is better off, and no one is worse off, under it than under some alternative institution, statute, or regulation. Using a strict Pareto criterion, one cannot balance one person's loss against another's gain, nor can one weight different persons' gains or losses differently. In this sense, the Pareto criterion is highly individualistic and neutral in deciding among the conflicting claims of various classes of persons. Therefore, socialist or other class-related bodies of prescriptions would not rest comfortably beside the Pareto criterion.[11]

A second variant of welfare theory tries to construct a social-welfare function, either by summing individual utilities or by maximizing the utility of a "representative" person. This variant loses its individualistic character and internal consistency. For as the body of knowledge beginning with Arrow (1963; see also Plott, 1976) demonstrates, the possibility of constructing an internally consistent social-welfare function that simultaneously satisfies a set of reasonable criteria is logically impossible. In place of such a function, many scholars, using a "second best" framework, have pursued wealth maximization as a standard of action.[12] But wealth maximization, like welfare maximization, remains uninteresting until conflicting claims force it to make judgments that rest on interpersonal welfare comparisons, which remain inappropriate under the first variant of welfare theory.

There is one way to incorporate the judgments made under the second variant into those made under the first. This method is especially applicable at the constitutional level of decision making. Suppose that some people are choosing a set of rules, a constitution, to govern their subsequent public-sector decisions. One proposal might be to mandate subsequent actions that maximize wealth, with or without compensation to the losers.[13] Constitution writers might well choose such an arrangement, even though any one of them might be a net loser in a particular decision rendered under it.[14] Prior unanimous consent for a constitutional order thus may signify that the regime is Pareto preferred, even though subsequent decisions made under it may be Pareto neutral, and occasionally, myopically, even Pareto inferior. When we find such an arrangement after the constitution is formed, we may regard one of its particular derivative policies as Pareto inferior, even though we would judge the entire constitutional order as Pareto preferred if we compared it, *in toto*, to some other arrangements.

Here, we use the first variant of welfare theory, but from time to time we elliptically intersperse the discussion with this constitutional hybrid, because we are concerned with outcomes that occur as a consequence of explicit constitutional arrangements and practices. If representative democracy fails, by not reaching Pareto-preferred states, then we must judge that failure either on an individualistic basis or on a wealth-maximizing criterion, with the explicit understanding that the loss of wealth, from a constitutional perspective, has unacceptably but avoidably eroded individual welfare. With these qualifications in mind, we identify somewhat arbitrarily the commonly accepted functions of the state in the view of welfare theory and describe the often-overlooked boundaries that this theory places on social choice.

WELFARE AND STATE FUNCTIONS

Welfare theory usually begins by recounting the efficiency properties of pure competitive markets. This beginning in no sense incorporates a historical or ideological supposition about the superiority of such markets as compared with other social arrangements.[15] It merely identifies an institution under which people's individual decisions maximize welfare by achieving Pareto optimality and the greatest possible total wealth, and by sending resources to their subjectively most highly valued uses.[16] The assumptions that underlie a pure competitive market include many buyers and many sellers ("many" means that no single producer or consumer alone can affect market outcomes), perfect information, zero transactions costs, an explicit (and efficient) property-rights system (e.g., effortless monitoring and enforcement of rights and contractual obligations), undifferentiated goods, long-run free (unimpaired) entry of buyers and firms, and the absence of collusion among buyers or sellers (see Henderson and Quandt, 1971, chap. 4). If, but certainly not only if, all of these conditions are met, then there are no wasted resources, all resources flow to their most highly valued uses, and wealth is maximized. The allocation of resources that exists in the presence of such a market is Pareto optimal, because there no net wealth goes unproduced, and no reallocation could occur without harming at least one person.[17]

There are two classes of departures from the pure competitive model. To the first class belong those departures that are self-correcting, because incentives exist for secondary or parallel markets or for integration or other contractual arrangements, to arise and restore efficiency. For example, in the absence of perfect information, markets, abstractly considered, may fail to maximize welfare. This absence may also signal profit opportunities from creating markets in information, however, such as occur with various brokerage and agency functions. Whether such markets can operate successfully may depend in turn on various aspects of the market for information, such as whether the information bought and sold can remain divisible (see Ackerlof, 1970; Alchian and Demsetz, 1972; Hayek, 1945; Hirshleifer, 1971; Hirshleifer and Riley, 1979; Knight, 1921; Machlup, 1962; Rothschild, 1973; Stigler, 1961). If so, then the imperfect-information departure from the conditions of the pure competitive model merely induces the development of a secondary market, requiring no further political specification of property rights nor other governmental actions.[18] Several other departures from the assumptions of a pure competitive market, most notably those involving transactions and monitoring costs, can similarly create private entrepreneurial opportunities for organizational changes that restore efficiency (Alchian and Demsetz, 1972; Coase, 1937; Klein and Leffler, 1981; Klein, Crawford, and Alchian, 1978; Rubin, 1978; Marvel, 1982).

The second class of departures from conditions of pure competition are those that further market processes cannot easily circumvent. These traditionally have been identified as instances of "market failure," because some alternative allocation of resources not theoretically achievable in the marketplace improves upon the theoretical marketplace allocation (Bator, 1968). Stated differently, voluntary action within the structure of the market relation cannot reach this theoretically identifiable allocation. Since the allocation is Pareto superior to the one that the market reaches under present governmental arrangements, some political alteration of property rights or statutory or regulatory structure may be advocated to achieve the Pareto-preferred result. That is, the presence of the alleged market failure creates a justification for the public sector to perform some new function or to alter the manner in which it performs an existing one.[19]

Public Goods. The resources bought and sold in the pure competitive market are private goods, because they share two important characteris-

91

tics. First, either law or practice or technology has created defensible property rights to them, which effectively can exclude from ownership or consumption those who have not produced or paid for them.[20] Second, in principle it is possible to create such property rights, because the goods that they circumscribe are not theoretically indivisible. A violation of either condition makes it possible that those goods to which the violation applies— public goods—will either be suboptimally produced or not produced at all (Samuelson, 1954). Classic examples of goods whose divisibility is theoretically impossible (or nearly so) include national defense and public peace, neither of which can be withheld from nonpayers. Of course, several goods (e.g., national parks) and services (e.g., education) are at least partly divisible in principle but have not been totally made so, either because property-right specifications are incomplete or because political decisions have been taken to make them free or nearly free to all users. The paradigmatic example of market failure concerns the inability to supply public goods or the suboptimal supply of such goods in pure competitive markets. The concept of a public good has become so ubiquitous and organic that it has lost much of its analytical power (e.g., see Steiner, 1974; Kahn, 1966). Here, though, we refer to a good as public only if its supply would create the particular incidence of costs and benefits that classical welfare theory would contemplate.

The public-goods problem arises in several instances that may or may not merit public-sector attention. All involve the failure to pay or contribute to the production of a jointly produced or consumed good or benefit; the relevant failure is called shirking, chiseling, or free riding, depending on the conditions under which it occurs.

Shirking arises in joint production processes, most notably those of the firm or franchise, in the presence of positive monitoring costs. For example, each worker in a complicated joint production process, in which no single worker's individual contribution is readily separable, has an incentive to shirk, thus collecting the benefits of others' efforts. The addition to the firm's net present value created by monitoring and by appropriate incentive structures (e.g., creating a market for management and control) goes in part to those monitored, to induce them not to shirk, and to monitors, who are themselves monitored by others and are ultimately disciplined by market forces (Alchian and Demsetz, 1972; Jensen and Meckling, 1976). The addition to joint product consequent to these monitoring activities is the public good.[21]

Chiseling occurs in the presence of cartels. Generally, a cartel agreement restricts output, thus raising the equilibrium price of each unit of output to the level that, by assumption, would be the profit-maximizing price if all cartel members formed a monopoly. A single cartel member chisels on the agreement by expanding output to capture the profit opportunity in the (higher) cartel price. If all cartel members chisel, then the cartel falls apart. The added profit to the cartel from successfully enforced cartelization is the public good.

Free riding occurs in several contexts. The term's traditional usage refers to those who enjoy the putatively higher wage rates and improved working conditions derived from union striking and bargaining efforts, without themselves paying union dues or the costs of striking. More recent usages expand the concept to cover failures to support traditionally nondivisible governmental services, such as national defense, public safety, conflict resolution (courts), and a host of other public-sector activities concerning which some imagination may be required to discover actual nondivisibility.

Welfare prescriptions related to the public-goods problem may reflect the context in which it arises. For example, in the case of shirking, all losses (suboptimal production levels) are internalized to the particular firm. Furthermore, external market forces discipline firms that fail to resolve these problems but reward firms that succeed. Hence, public policy should encourage or at least not hinder a firm's internal ability to monitor, sanction, and reward, and should encourage or at least not hinder the workings of external market forces that discipline or reward individual firms.

In the case of chiseling, the formation of cartel-output agreements may impose a welfare loss on those consuming the cartel's output. In keeping with welfare theory, public policy should make efforts to cartelize difficult or at least should not encourage or require cartelization in specific industries, as commonly occurs with regulation. Stated differently, some public-goods problems, such as chiseling, may be resolved to the benefit of those affected by them, but to the detriment of others. Welfare theory tries to distinguish among such opposed claimants by ascertaining under which conditions wealth—usually measured as the sum of consumers' and producers' surplus—will be maximized.

The free-rider problem associated with labor-union activity probably falls more comfortably under the heading of redistribution, which we consider momentarily. More generally, public goods, such as national defense and public peace, or potentially private goods, such as highways and school systems, which are offered free, and therefore are made nondivisible by legislative fiat, are created by the usual taxing and spending mechanisms. Public policy should distinguish the efficient level at which to produce such goods (provided that they should be produced at all), and should encourage cost-effective means of production.

Public Bads. Public bads, or external diseconomies (sometimes called externalities or external costs), are simply the reverse phenomenon of public goods. Indeed, a mere linguistic expedient makes them equivalent. For example, consider a common waterway that adjacent residents pollute at a constant rate. Their effluent reduces the waterway's suitability for other uses, such as recreation or as a source of drinking water. If a particular person unilaterally filtered and purified the water or installed purification elements on each effluent source, then the waterway's improved quality would be a public good for all adjacent residents. Their effluents into the waterway are equivalent to the production of a public bad, an external diseconomy. The failure to specify a property right in the purity of water, or the technical inability to specify such a right in the case of a common resource such as a lake, waterway, or ambient air, makes the formation of a market in suppressing the external diseconomy, or in producing the condition that occurs in its absence, difficult or impossible.

Philosophers sometimes distinguish between acts of omission and acts of commission, to point out the differences between positive and negative acts and obligations. But in the argot of public goods and bads, no such distinction occurs. A citizen who fails to produce a desirable public good or fails to contribute to its production is said to produce a public bad, and one who fails to produce a public bad, even though it would have been individually beneficial for him to produce that bad, thereby produces a public good. Thus, shirkers, chiselers, and free riders are equivalent to producers of public bads.

Property Rights. The traditional notion of property rights concerns those situations in which the common law, statute law, or administrative rule making (regulation) create legally defensible but sometimes limited rights to acquire and alienate tangible and intangible assets. The property-rights problem, however, is actually one of public goods and public bads. For example, one form of property right is the right to be compensated for the benefits that one's actions or the use of one's assets bestows on others. If an institutional arrangement could guarantee such a right, then the public-goods problem would be solved. By a similar reasoning, a property right may also contemplate the right to be compensated for the damage that others' actions impose on us, the right to avoid such damage, or the right to contract explicitly to accept it for a mutually agreeable payment. An institutional arrangement that incorporated responses to such damage, if optimally constructed, would solve the public-bads problem.

The logical equivalence of the property-rights problem and the public goods–public bads problem has not always been explicitly drawn, although it is now widely recognized. A brief example illustrates the nature of the identity but also underscores the importance of property rights as a subject matter *sui generis.* That example concerns the allocation of rights to broadcast frequencies, which vest property rights in the recipients (Coase,

1959, 1962). This practice, carried on partially today by administrative rule making through the Federal Communications Commission, is rationalized by the expectation that in the absence of legally defensible property rights, a degradation in the value of a common resource pool—the radio frequency spectrum—would result. Naturally, a variety of possible patterns of rights to spectrum use might be adopted, only a subset of which would maximize the spectrum's value (Coase, 1959; Posner, 1977).

Contemporary property-rights theory[22] now goes far beyond the traditional concerns of regulation to embrace problems such as job tenure (Alchian, 1959; de Alessi, 1974b; Martin, 1972, 1977), industrial organization and corporate governance (Alchian and Demsetz, 1972; Coase, 1937; de Alessi, 1973; Jensen and Meckling, 1976; Klein, Crawford, and Alchian, 1978; Manne, 1965; Williamson, 1964), incentives structures within bureaucracies (Ahlbrandt, 1973a; Davies, 1971; de Alessi, 1974a; Lindsay, 1976; Niskanen, 1971; Tullock, 1965), and common ownership and usufruct rights with implications for cultural and economic anthropology (Anderson and Hill, 1975; Clark, 1973; Demsetz, 1967; Gordon, 1954; Hardin, 1968; Libecap, 1978; Libecap and Johnson, 1980; Posner, 1980; Smith, 1969; Trosper, 1978; Umbeck, 1977). In each instance, a property right or economic practice emerges (or fails to emerge) to resolve a problem of external economies or diseconomies, given the prior structure of rights.

Redistribution. The goal of wealth or income redistribution as a welfare-based function of the state is the subject of serious dispute. The theoretical justification for redistribution partly follows lines identical to those that support the public production (suppression) of public goods (bads). For example, in its utilitarian aspects, redistribution is a putative source of political stability (Brennan, 1973), public peace, and insurance (Rawls, 1971). But the more traditional theoretical justification for redistribution relies on two less practical and more esoteric grounds.

First, redistribution may rest on the assumption of diminishing marginal utility for money (Blum and Kalven, 1953; Stuart, 1967). In this view, a wealthy person loses less utility than a poor person gains by the redistribution from rich to poor. Therefore, an aggregate welfare function would be maximized if everyone's wealth became equal. This justification accords with the second variant of welfare theory but not the first. Certain authors, however, have developed variations on this theme. Their implied constitution would guarantee that a collectivity's least-well-off persons would benefit from any change in public policy (Rawls, 1971) and that any welfare gains from redistribution would not be offset by the amount by which total production falls because of a loss of incentive (Thurow, 1977).

This justification for redistribution may have some positive content (Meltzer and Richard, 1981, 1983), although in its pure second variant

95

(social-welfare function) form the concept has no generally accepted scientific credentials. Nevertheless, redistribution may have some appeal in the constitutional variant of welfare theory. That is, behind a "veil of ignorance," people might unanimously agree ex ante on some kind of redistribution. Even so, this justification for redistribution is not without serious problems.

The more general argument supporting redistribution is consonant with a public-goods claim (Hochman and Rogers, 1969; von Furstenberg and Mueller, 1971). The outlines of this argument observe the existence of interdependent utility functions, those in which A's utility depends on B's consumption (or perhaps on B's utility, if it is believed to be measurable). If A's utility were solely dependent upon the amount of B's consumption accounted for by A's contribution, then no problem would emerge, because the returns to A's philanthropy would be a divisible benefit, flowing entirely to A. But if A's utility depended on B's consumption generally, including that part of B's consumption that C contributed, then a problem emerges. If C contributes to B, thus increasing B's consumption, then that increased consumption is a public good for A. In a society of such contributors, in which each gains some positive marginal utility from his own consumption, the free-rider problem is quite general, and the state might be called upon to redistribute coercively.

Monopoly. The monopoly issue today is hotly disputed as a scientific problem. The classic welfare argument concerning monopoly[23] held that by operating over the entire industry-wide demand schedule, a monopolistic firm that maximized profits would produce less output and at higher unit cost than would a competitive firm facing a horizontal demand schedule (i.e., a fixed competitive price). A deadweight loss was said to result, because the sum of consumers' and producers' surpluses would be less than would prevail in a pure competitive market.

Until recently the literature on monopoly and monopolistic practices displayed a curious intellectual asymmetry. Scholars generally set the pure competitive market up as an ideal, found small theoretical perturbations from that ideal, linked those perturbations with real-world practices, and then recommended public-sector intervention to cure the defect. The same treatment was never accorded to the pure monopoly model, however, even though it seems far more susceptible to such a treatment than does the pure competitive model. For example, a pure monopoly model contemplates substantial barriers to entry and little product substitution, although those conditions are almost never met in the real world (Baumol, 1982).

Current scholarship (see note 1 of this chapter) now makes plain that this model of monopoly is far less robust than the pure competitive model, when robustness is measured as the degree to which the assumptions of the model can be violated by the respective markets without materially changing the outcomes. Many practices once thought to be monopolistic are now deemed highly competitive, because they lower unit production costs. For example, industrial-organization scholars seldom interpret vertical integration today as a respectable subject for antitrust prosecution, because vertical integration reduces or eliminates certain costs that consumers otherwise would have to bear (Klein, Crawford, and Alchian, 1978). Similarly, practices such as base-point pricing (Haddock, 1982), once regarded as indisputable evidence of conspiracies, are now interpreted as evidence of competitive markets. Theories of predation, likewise, no longer are regarded as intellectually respectable (Elzinga, 1970; Koller, 1971; McGee, 1958), and they have joined in the academic dust heap such outdated justifications for prosecution as administered prices (Alchian, 1970; Stigler, 1962; Stigler and Kindahl, 1970, 1973) and high industry concentration (Brozen, 1970, 1971b, 1971a; Demsetz, 1973b; McGee, 1971) as per se violations of antitrust laws.

The pure monopoly model has been linked with the public-goods problem, especially concerning natural monopolies, those firms that dominate a market and enjoy globally diminishing long-run average total cost curves, such as certain public utilities (Lerner, 1964). The connection occurs because a correctly designed public policy theoretically will increase the sum of consumer and producer surplus, and therefore social welfare. The particular public-goods application to the natural monopoly problem arises because as additional people consume additional units of the good that the natural monopoly produces, the average unit cost of production declines. Hence, new consumers effectively reduce the unit cost to prior consumers. This interpretation of the monopoly problem as a public-goods problem is obviously strained and tends to empty both the concept of monopoly and that of public goods of their assertorial power (Buchanan, 1971).

The principal problem remaining with monopoly and monopolistic practices concerns whether the problems cited belong to the first class of departures from the pure competitive model, those that are self-correcting in the marketplace, or to the second class, those that are not. Contemporary scholarship increasingly assigns these problems to the first class. Of course, the manner of correction remains in dispute. For example, there is evidence that price regulation of natural monopolies has no effect (Stigler and Freidland, 1962). And a better result may derive from auctioning off monopoly rights to private producers than from regulation (Demsetz, 1968).

WELFARE BOUNDARIES ON SOCIAL CHOICE

The presence of at least one of these five problems is a necessary condition for welfare-regarding state action, but none of these five problems comprehends a sufficient condition for state action, although each is often treated as sufficient. Some of the most important recent work in public choice seeks to provide boundaries on social choice by ascertaining under what conditions each of these problems might find a welfare-regarding improvement through state action. The general lines of research identify three broad categories of boundaries. These concern the relative benefits and costs of state action, the appropriate method, and the appropriate jurisdiction.

Benefits and Costs. The absence or suboptimal supply of a potential public good does not by itself compel a public-sector solution in the form of public production or a subsidy of the production of a public good. There is an infinite variety of potential public goods or bads that clearly should not engage public-sector solutions, if only because the opportunity costs of state action exceed any possible benefits. A national program to eradicate acne is probably an example of such a public good.

The cost-benefit calculation recommending for or against state action is far more complex than simple accounting, however, and we can usefully approach the problem of computation by considering ex ante versus ex post welfare judgments. The computation problem is especially severe in the area of regulation. Congressional enactments concerning regulation have increasingly incorporated the requirements that cost-benefit analyses be performed and that only those programs whose benefits exceed their costs be adopted. One problem with such an approach concerns the inherent inability of a centralized decision mechanism, such as a regulatory commission, to calculate all of the costs and benefits, as well as all of the postregulatory reactions, that might occur because of a certain regulation. One useful way to look at this problem is to decide whether or not a particular ''market failure'' can be corrected in a secondary market or whether it is privately irreparable. If we have theoretical reasons to believe that a secondary market or subsequent producer or consumer choice will resolve the putative market failure, then we should expect the marketplace to produce the requisite solution. But suppose that it does not and that the regulatory commission calculates the benefits of its solution to exceed the costs. Such a computation does not yet justify public-sector action.

The reasons for this demurrer are complex but worth rehearsing. One of the earliest criticisms of central economic planning, and one not yet turned aside, is that decision makers out of the marketplace and in a centralized information-collection and -processing position cannot calculate relative prices and marginal rates of substitution in the manner of the decentralized marketplace. Such people do not enjoy what Hayek calls the special knowledge of the circumstances of time and place (1945), nor can they work out the individual price-quantity ratios based on the individual utilities and marginal rates of substitution of all producers and consumers in the marketplace. The market can solve this calculation problem, however, and therefore, *ceteris paribus*, the market's allocations will be superior to those made by central planners.

This result has a direct translation concerning public regulation of the marketplace to correct a public-good, or public-bad, problem. The legislature or administrative agency cannot possibly replicate each consumer's marginal rates of substitution and each producer's combinations of production costs and reaction to uncertainty. Therefore, without compelling evidence that a putative instance of market failure is not correctable in the market itself, there is no welfare justification for state action. That is, the information in the marketplace has already judged that its contemplated market-correcting action has costs that exceed the benefits. Otherwise, some producer would have undertaken it. But even if the problem is not correctable in the marketplace, there remains no sufficient condition for a public-sector response, because its costs still might exceed its benefits.

The problem of ex post versus ex ante calculation of costs and benefits still remains. That is, we must judge state actions against the constitutional conditions that made such actions possible. Stated differently, the perceived costs and benefits of various actions will change, depending on whether their calculation is made ex ante or ex post. For instance, ex ante we might judge that the aggregate costs of allowing prior restraints on freedom of the press exceed the aggregate benefits, although surely, external diseconomies flow from the exercise of that freedom. But ex post we might decide to ban pornography, or the publication of national defense secrets, or libelous utterances. Ex ante we might judge that the costs of prohibitions on religious practices exceed the benefits. But ex post we might decide to ban polygamy or liquor sales on Sunday. Such a distinction suggests that a state action taken following a prudential ex post judgment might seriously weaken a Pareto-preferred general rule adopted ex ante, which must be constantly protected for it to survive.

Finally, state action must contemplate its object with care. Certain public-goods problems should not be resolved in the public sector, because they are collective to a particular group but are not truly "public." That is, their resolution might benefit a few to the detriment of many. For instance, in the case of shirking, a clear public-goods problem, all losses are internalized to the firm experiencing problems (suboptimal monitoring levels, and therefore, effort). Furthermore, external market forces do discipline firms that fail to resolve these problems and reward firms that succeed. Hence, public policies should encourage, or at least not hinder, a firm's internal ability to monitor, sanction, and reward, and should encourage, or at least not hinder, the workings of external market forces in disciplining and rewarding individual firms. That is, agents in the public sector probably should not concern themselves with the "small" public-goods problem of private-sector shirking, which occurs in every firm. The problem has a marketplace solution, and the public sector has no way to collect the requisite information to find it.

In the case of chiseling, the formation of cartel-output agreements may impose a welfare loss on consumers of the cartel's output. In keeping with welfare theory, public policies should make efforts to cartelize difficult, or at least should not encourage or require cartelization in specific industries. Stated differently, some public-goods problems may be resolved to the benefit of those affected by them but to the detriment of others.[24] Welfare theory tries to distinguish among such opposed claimants by ascertaining under which conditions resources will be most efficiently used.

Methods of State Action. The four principal methods of state action are governance by common law, by statute, by regulation, and by public incorporation. The welfare consequences attending each of these methods differ from the others and from problem to problem, and therefore we review each method separately.

Social scientists are largely uninformed about governance by common law. Most economists and political scientists regard a market without formal statutory or regulatory-agency control as a variety of anarchy. Even the most laissez-faire economies, however, have gone far beyond anarchical structures,[25] replacing them with a system of common law, or judge-made law. The regulatory aspects of the common law are seldom appreciated. Yet, recent research indicates that common-law processes can create dynamically efficient rules of liability for governing the areas of contracts, property, and torts (Posner, 1977; Rubin, 1977; Priest, 1977; Goodman, 1978; *Journal of Legal Studies,* 1979, 1980; Calabressi, 1970). It is not clear when an economy does (or should) move from anarchic structures to a system of laws. Property-rights theory (Aranson, 1974; Demsetz, 1967; Carneiro, 1970) suggests, however, that this change might (or should) occur when a common resource is overused, provided that the cost of the legal system itself does not overcome the benefits of divisibility or liability assignment created in law.

The efficiency of the common law rests on participants' ability to bargain, to transact, and, at a reasonable cost, to monitor compliance with the terms of a contract or a legal duty. For example, a rule governing easements in property law might state the conditions under which one person has a right to use or pass over another's property without committing a trespass.[26] The efficient operation of this rule requires that the property owner, at low cost, can monitor use of the easement to see that its terms are not exceeded, can identify trespassers, and can alienate his property rights, if they are protected by a common-law rule of easements, in a bilateral negotiation with another party, which enlarges the terms of the easement. Similar conditions apply to the person owning the easement right, including his ability to alienate that right back to the property owner.[27]

A straightforward application of simple price theory to the nexus of common-law rules and property rights provides additional boundaries on social choice. For example, consider a limited externality, such as that created by a rock group that practices in a residential basement, disturbing a cellist who practices quietly in a nearby home. The common law gives to the property owner, in this case the cellist, the right to a "quiet enjoyment" of his property. So, the cellist can enforce that right against the rock group. If the rock group wants to continue to practice, it must pay the cellist not to enforce his right. If it does so, then it must place a higher value on this arrangement than the cellist places on his quiet; otherwise, not. But if the common law gives a property right to the rock group to practice at its will, then the cellist must pay for quiet, which he will do if he values it more than the group values its right to practice in the basement. With either allocation of rights, the resource—in this instance the "use" of the "ether" for a configuration of sound waves—flows to its higher-valued use. That is, with any initial allocation of rights, with alienability of those rights, and with low transactions costs, the result is efficient. This much we know from the Coase Theorem (Coase, 1960).

Two boundaries on social choice grow out of this general principle. First, neither statute law, nor regulation, nor governance by public incorporation will resolve such externalities as efficiently as will the common law. Common-law rules ordinarily will allocate the right to the party to which it would flow most of the time as a result of explicit negotiations and will allow for contracting the right away, alienating it, if the parties can mutually gain from exchange. For reasons identical to those that give decentralized markets an advantage over central planning, other forms of governance cannot achieve the common law's level of dynamic efficiency in such cases. Therefore, governance by common law enjoys a putative superiority over other forms of governance. Second, legislatures and regulatory agencies will try constantly to overturn prior contractual agreements made under common-law rules, but such attempts should be thwarted in the view of welfare theory, because, *inter alia,* they make future agreements less valuable and thus more difficult to transact.[28]

Agreements to accept an external cost eventually may be challenged in the courts, legislatures, and commissions in cases involving far subtler arrangements. For instance, a rock quarry may have operated in an uninhabited area, which is subsequently built up as a residential neighborhood. Presumably, home buyers sorted themselves out, so that those who did not value dust-free environs quite so highly bought homes in such a place for the reduced price that sellers usually could demand for their property. That is, these buyers "came to the nuisance," and courts at law at one time followed precedent by not recognizing claims that the nuisance must cease operations, [29] although that doctrine has been breached in recent years. The successful prosecution of such a suit or its legislative or regulatory equivalent would bestow a windfall gain on the home owners and a windfall loss on the quarry owners. The long-run effects of clouding or reversing the coming-to-the-nuisance doctrine would be a reduction in both quarrying and home building in such areas, a Pareto-inferior result.

But suppose that home owners eventually come to value dust-free environs and would be willing to pay the quarry owners more than the net present value of the owners' income stream, to suspend or diminish operations. The common law allows such a result, but transactions costs brought about by a free-rider problem among the (many) home owners may make its execution difficult or impossible. Common-law rulings might facilitate such transactions, but their completion often requires the formation of some kind of sovereign body. [30] That is, in such cases the assumptions underlying the efficient operation of common-law rules are materially violated.

There are other instances in which these assumptions cannot be met. For example, common-law rules might interpret air pollution as a nuisance or a trespass. But with thousands, perhaps millions, of individual pollution emitters and receptors in a relevant "market," the calculation problem and costs inherent in forming transactions and monitoring compliance are overwhelming. Thus, there may be a welfare justification for moving from a common-law regime to one of statute law. This justification assumes that the benefits that such a statute entails exceed the costs. The costs of statute-law rules, however, may exceed those of common-law rules, even when they contemplate the same outcomes. In particular, the central characteristic that separates statute law from common law (although this characteristic need not apply universally) is that under statute law, those who enjoy rights cannot alienate them. Statute law solves an externality problem by making it impossible for those protected to alienate their rights, or for those who must bear an obligation to contract out of it.

This characteristic of statute law rides roughshod over individual preferences and therefore makes it more costly to apply than common law.

But it is also the reason for its use. Its advantages grow out of the nature of the externality involved as well as the high level of transactions cost. For instance, A may sell to a factory the right to pollute the ambient air around his home and property. But it is difficult to assemble all other home owners to agree to A's transaction with the factory. The assembly problem cuts in two directions. First, if A makes such a transaction, then the factory will almost certainly pollute the ambient air of B and C, whose assembly in large numbers for purposes of bargaining and transacting is costly. But if A and B make a transaction with the factory, then C, whose consent may also be required, might hold out for the entire surplus that the contracting parties gain from the transaction.

If an exchange involving A, B, C, and the factory were desirable in the absence of transactions costs, then a statute that specified duties among all participants might avoid these two problems of transacting. The statutory result cannot replicate the participants' individual preferences as they would be worked out in a market for rights that did not have the externalities involving A's contract with the factory, C's monopoly power, or the high transactions costs of bargaining and contracting with large numbers of people. But the statute may work a rough justice among the participants. The balancing tests involved in choosing between a common-law order and a statutory regime now seem apparent, although in practice, actual calculations based on a welfare-regarding model may be quite difficult or theoretically impossible to perform in all but the most extremely simple cases.

Governance by regulation, pursuant to statutory authorization, combines elements of both common-law and statutory governance. It is like governance by statute, because most regulatory agencies function as legislative bodies. It is like governance by common law, because most regulatory agencies also perform judicial functions in their specialized areas. The welfare-related justifications for adopting governance by regulation involve those that justify governance by statute and in addition rest on the desirability of flexibility, expertise, permanence, and the perceived inability of legislatures to engage in administrative tedium. In other words, governance by regulation is justified by amplification of the legislature (Posner, 1982; Aranson, Gellhorn, and Robinson, 1982) and, some would argue, by an intellectual structure that prefers public administration over political disposition.[31] We shall find, however, that the animus of governance by regulation generates out of motives having little or no connection with improving the legislature's ability to form welfare-regarding statutes.

Within the category of governance by regulation, there are several possible modalities. The most prominent is command-and-control regulations, under which legislators or regulators set standards that private-sector producers must satisfy. For example, the Environmental Protection Agency may set maximum discharge rates for pollutants from particular factories. Under a prescriptive election model to be described in the next section, this method presumably replicates the environmental-quality preferences of the electorate's median member. An alternative procedure is the use of effluent charges, which try to "cost" environmental damage by replicating market forces and the result that would emerge from a common-law process without transactions costs. While most economists prefer effluent charges to command-and-control regulation, there is growing interest in marketable pollution rights and "offset" and "bubble" procedures. These policies combine the notion of standards and an optimum level of environmental quality with an entitlement for producers to buy and sell rights to pollute up to that level, so that for any mandated level of use of the environment as a sink, rights would flow to their most highly valued uses.

Governance by common law, statute, and regulation all involve situations in which private action remains private, but the incentives and alternatives that participants face are shaped by rules emanating from the public sector. Governance by public incorporation involves the public adoption of the private activities involved to form a public enterprise, such as the Department of Defense, the Department of Justice, or the Post Office Department.

Welfare economics provides no clear, nonideological theory concerning the choice between other forms of governance and public incorporation. Rudiments of such a theory appear from time to time in observations that the costs of regulating private action may exceed those of a simple integration of the scrutinized activity into the public sector. For example, Henry Simons believed that natural monopolies could not be successfully regulated, and so he proposed to make them collective (Simons, 1935; Stigler, 1974). Certain other activities, such as national defense and the police power, appear to require a decision-making finality that only governance by public incorporation can achieve. Other state functions, however, such as the railroads and postal and lighthouse services (Coase, 1974), probably can be supplied more efficiently in the private sector. Questions of public- versus private-sector supply form the core of many public-policy debates of both an economic and ideological nature. But as we shall see, as with decisions to regulate, the decisions eventually taken for public incorporation have very little to do with the positive economic substance of those debates, *inter alia,* because they seldom enjoy a complete accounting of benefits and costs.

These categories of methods of governance need not be exclusive. For example, public policy may leave a particular economic activity largely unregulated except for applicable common-law rules of liability. At the same time, very closely related or identical activities somehow (only) distinguished in the contemplation of law may be subject to statutory constraints, regulation, and even public incorporation. Mail and package delivery is an example. The post office delivers first-class mail, packages, bulk mail, and some express mail. Certain of these functions are carried on in regulated sectors (e.g., airline package deliveries and Federal Express) and in unregulated sectors (e.g., local courier services). Supplying public peace is similarly carried on by public incorporation (e.g., police departments), in regulated markets (e.g., licensed detectives), and in unregulated ones (e.g., unlicensed investigators and suppliers of small weapons and burglar-alarm systems). The legislature, regulatory agencies, and the courts may differ concerning the extent to which they will allow this simultaneous activity or will require that one activity preempt another.[32]

Jurisdiction. The final boundary on social choice concerns jurisdiction. While this is a more substantial decision problem in a federal state such as the United States than in a unitary state such as Great Britain, neverthe-less, to some extent, all polities decentralize both bureaucratic and legislative decision making. The problem of jurisdictions presents something of a conceptual muddle. Managerial theory has been developed that suggests the method and optimal degree of decentralization for private-sector activities (Chandler, 1962; Alchian and Demsetz, 1972; Coase, 1937; Klein, Crawford, and Alchian, 1978). Devolution may prevail both as to the extent of geographical territory covered and the degree of functional separation and independence within the firm. To some extent, such private-sector models of firm centralization and decentralization carry forward into public-sector bureaucracies, legislatures, and courts. The problems inher-ent in producing public goods and suppressing public bads, however, make it plain that the signaling capacity of price and the market for corporate control do not operate effectively in the public sector, to give decision makers appropriate incentives concerning organizational structure. Hence, those sentences that we might utter about the optimal degree of decentralization and the appropriate jurisdiction for various public-sector tasks remain largely precatory.

Abstractly considered, we might ask that the optimal jurisdiction for internalizing an externality, say, would be no larger than the area that the externality affects. For certain kinds of external economies and disecon-omies, this recommendation seems appropriate.[33] For example, if anyone, voters in Wisconsin probably should control the environmental quality of Wisconsin lakes, not voters in Maine or Tennessee. Similarly, chemical-waste dumps would seem to be an appropriate object of state and local control, not federal regulation. A limitation of state action and decision making to the smallest jurisdiction possible (the area over which the externality from a particular source is spread) makes sense, because local political mechanisms are more sensitive to citizens' preferences than are regional or national ones[34] and because the granting of rights to voters in state A to regulate some aspect of life in state B raises the possibility of very serious and untoward strategic consequences.[35]

This recommendation has qualifications, however. For example, a crackdown on burglars in Kansas City, Kansas, will increase the burglary rate in Kansas City, Missouri. And polluters who face stringent controls in one state may move to states that exercise less-pervasive environmental-quality regulations. (Indeed, a consideration of market forces would predict and approve of such a result.) Thus, one state's decision to weaken or strengthen the costs that it imposes on a particular activity may produce a public good or a public bad for some other state. While many of these interactive problems are merely transitional, we must acknowledge their nature as jurisdictional external economies and diseconomies.

The most intriguing possibility in decentralization concerns the use of state and local control as a surrogate for marketlike competition. This notion, explicated most notably by Tiebout,[36] concentrates on the problem of preference revelation in markets for public goods. Tiebout hypothesized that competition among a large number of decentralized polities (separate sovereignties) would lead to an optimal price and supply of public goods, insofar as scale economies do not constrain decentralization. This result would solve Samuelson's problem, that a unique producer of public goods could not identify an optimal price (Samuelson, 1954), as well as Olson's problem, that such a producer also could not discern a correct level of supply for such goods (Olson, 1972).

The problem of jurisdictions, like the problem of methods of governance, does not provide for exclusive categories. Various state functions may be carried on at all levels of government, with a rich menu of combinations and permutations of jurisdictional control. Furthermore, various levels of government may use different methods of governance to address the same problem. For example, the governance of banking is carried on at the federal level by public incorporation (e.g., Federal Reserve banks), by regulation (e.g., the Federal Deposit Insurance Corporation and the Federal Home Loan Bank Board), and by statute (e.g., the McFadden Act of 1927). At the same time, only one state (North Dakota) owns a bank, but most states govern banking by regulatory commission, statute, and certainly by common law (e.g., the law of contracts and frauds). Each possible combination and permutation of jurisdictional control and method of governance results in a conceptually different distribution of costs and benefits and level of productivity.

ANOMIC ELECTORATES AND ORGANIZED GROUPS

The preceding section reviews justifications for state action, methods of governance, and problems of optimal jurisdiction. We may summarize the matter thus. First, any state action must rely for a welfare-theory justification on the presence of utility interdependencies such as occur with problems with public goods and bads, property rights, monopoly, and redistribution.

Second, state action should not contemplate intervention in all cases in which one or another of these problems is present: (1) costs of state action may exceed benefits; (2) the problem may elicit the beneficial development of subsequent markets and other appropriate reactions in the private sector; (3) a problem may not be truly "public," because its public-sector solution would aid only a limited collection of persons at the expense of everyone else; and (4) the situation in which the problem exists may have been the efficient result of an explicit contract or agreement that anticipated the problem's persistence in exchange for compensation.

Third, the method of governance should correspond to the nature and extent of the specific utility interdependence. For the largest numbers of such interdependencies, involving rules governing ordinary torts, contracts, and property disputes, governance by common law would seem most appropriate, and the imposition of other forms of governance would create welfare-degrading, Pareto-inferior outcomes. Increases in transactions costs or monitoring costs would signal the possibility that a more nearly uniform approach, such as governance by statute law, may be desirable. Governance by administrative agency would seem appropriate in the presence of a potential decisional tedium. Governance by public incorporation would only occur in those instances in which the external and decision costs of *any* private action would seem intolerable.

Finally, with suitable modifications to allow for secondary external effects, the appropriate extent of jurisdiction should cover no more than the population over which the utility interdependence prevails. Of course, no matter which problem is involved or which manner of governance or jurisdiction is chosen, welfare theory would insist that only cost-effective (technologically efficient) public policies should be adopted.

THE ELECTORATE AND PUBLIC POLICY

The development of a welfare-regarding theory of public-sector action takes as its benchmark the operation of a perfectly functioning, competitive marketplace. It then identifies various classes of situations in which the allocations in the marketplace seem inferior to those allocations that theoretically might be achievable under different institutional arrangements. Were the analysis to end there, we might suppose that the public sector effortlessly, costlessly, optimally, and appropriately achieves these putatively superior allocations, and therefore the corpus of welfare theory might find application in the service of political advocacy. Plainly, however, the analysis cannot end there, because human nature and decision making remain invariant between the private and public sectors; and therefore, as the rest of this essay demonstrates, the public sector is subject to all of the "imperfections" that welfare theory finds operating in the private sector.

The possibility of public-sector failure seems magnified beyond the limits of private-sector failure, however, because of the larger numbers of connections that successfully must prevail for the public sector to act in a welfare-regarding manner. There are at least five major connections. First, there must be an undistorted link between citizens' welfare and their political preferences. Second, a similar nexus must hold between those preferences and election outcomes. Third, election outcomes must bear an appropriate relationship to legislative outcomes. Fourth, legislative outcomes correctly must direct bureaucratic outcomes in implementation. Fifth, and to close the circle, bureaucratic outcomes must not contain within them the kinds of public-policy perversities that diminish citizens' welfare.

We begin our discussion of public-sector failure by concentrating on the connection between citizens' preferences and election outcomes, assuming that all of the other connections are correctly drawn. Here, we first describe the simple underlying model that connects those preferences for the production of various levels of public goods to election outcomes. Second, we review the argument that public goods may be undersupplied in the public sector. Third, we review a parallel argument that such goods may be oversupplied. Finally, we identify sources of instability in the model, leading us to doubt the robustness of the electoral process as a method of converting citizens' preferences into the production of correct levels of public goods.

Spatial Model in Public Goods. The basic election model for the provision of public goods found its roots in a spatial location theory, developed a half-century ago (Hotelling, 1929; Smithies, 1941). Bowen (1943) first formulated the model in a political context, and Downs (1957) gave the model its fullest verbal elaboration. Subsequent developments[37] since Downs have brought the model to a high level of complexity susceptible to empirical testing (Enelow and Hinich, 1982; Aldrich and McKelvey, 1977; Rusk and Weisberg, 1972; Weisberg and Rusk, 1970; Page and Brody, 1972; Cahoon, Hinich, and Ordeshook, 1978; Hinich, 1978; Rabinowitz, 1978). Here, we consider the model in its simplest form. Suppose that there is some public good that the public sector might produce in continuously adjustable levels, from zero to a very high level beyond anyone's preference. The dimension that measures the level of production is the "space" over which citizens form preferences and candidates compete for their votes.

Figure 4.1a depicts a possible representation of a citizen's utility function (evaluation) of different production levels of this public good. In the figure, the horizontal axis measures x, the level at which the public good will be produced. The vertical axis measures B(x), the citizen's benefit from various production levels, and C(x), the citizen's cost for those production levels. Under the usual microeconomic assumptions, B(x) is marginally diminishing and C(x), marginally increasing, with x. The citizen's most preferred level of production occurs at x*, which is simultaneously the point at which the difference between costs and benefits is greatest, the slopes of the two curves, C(x) and B(x), are equal, and marginal cost equals marginal benefit. Figure 4.1b depicts another way to illustrate the same properties. Here, we define a new variable, $U(x) = B(x) - C(x)$, measured on the vertical axis, which is the citizen's utility for various levels of production of

FIGURE 4.1a

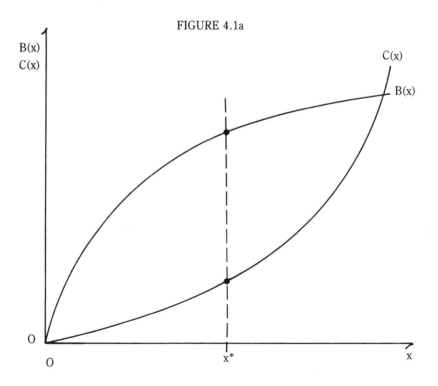

the public good. Again, x* identifies the citizen's most preferred production level for this public good.

The basic spatial model's problem is to identify the position on the dimension that a candidate will adopt as a platform (strategy) and that will subsequently win the election. To motivate the discussion, suppose that there are: (1) the citizen who most prefers x*; (2) a citizen like the one whose utility function is shown in figure 4.1b, but whose benefit and cost curves are such that he prefers a lower production level of this public good; and (3) a similar citizen who prefers a higher level than x*. If these three citizens make up the entire electorate, if all of them will vote in an election on this issue alone, and if two candidates compete by advocating various positions along this issue space, then the median citizen's most preferred position, x*, defeats all other positions. Therefore, we expect candidates to converge to this position.

Today, this model finds its principal use to describe real election processes. But the model also enjoys a normative aspect. For instance, Bowen (1943) shows that under conditions similar to those offered here,

FIGURE 4.1b

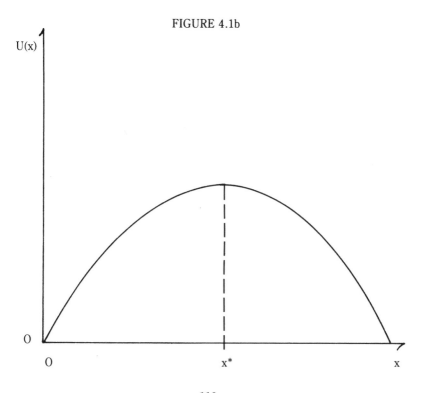

such an election would produce the public good at a level that maximized economic welfare. Similarly, Hinich and Ordeshook (1969) have used a fairly weak form of welfare comparisons, imposing symmetry, to demonstrate that this election process might also maximize social welfare.

Simple Elections and Social Imbalance. Eventually, we shall reject many aspects of this model as a description of public-policy formation. Several scholars have developed extensions and criticisms of the model, however, which accept it on its own terms but find sources of public-sector failure within its structure. The first of these criticisms, which Galbraith (1958) advanced in a different connection than the model contemplates, holds that citizens underestimate the benefits of public-sector action, leading to an underproduction of public goods. Galbraith views this under-production as a consequence of a "social imbalance." In his view, tastes for private goods, such as automobiles and sporting goods, will accurately reflect consumers' real costs and benefits. But the derived demand for parallel public goods, really quasi-public goods, such as highways and public parks, will be understated, *inter alia* because agents in the public sector lack the ability and incentive to advertise. Galbraith explains:

Advertising operates exclusively . . . on behalf of privately pro-duced goods and services. . . . Automobile demand which is expensively synthesized will inevitably have a much larger claim on income than parks or public health or even roads where no such in-fluence operates. The engines of mass communication . . . assail the . . . community on behalf of more beer but not more schools. . . .
The competition is especially unequal for new products and services. Every corner of the public psyche is canvassed by some of the nation's most talented citizens to see if the desire for some merchantable product can be cultivated. No similar process operates on behalf of the nonmerchantable services of the state. Indeed, while we take the cultivation of new private wants for granted we would be measurably shocked to see it applied to public services. The scientist or engineer or advertising man who devotes himself to developing a new carburetor, cleaner, or depilatory for which the public recognizes no need and will feel none until an advertizing campaign arouses it, is one of the valued members of our society. A politician or a public servant who dreams up a new public service is a wastrel. Few public offenses are more reprehensible. (1958:205)

Galbraith's explanation for the public-sector undersupply of public goods actually is a special case of a more general explanation, which Downs provides (1960). Downs argues that the benefits of many public goods "are remote from those who receive them, either in time, space, or comprehensibility'' (1960:551). For example, foreign aid "may prevent a hostile revolution . . . and save millions of dollars and even the lives of American troops, but because the situation is so remote, the average citizen—living in rational political ignorance—will not realize he is benefitting at all" (1960: 551). Downs believes that other governmental programs, such as water purification and various kinds of regulations, share the same problem of remoteness, and therefore they will be undersupplied. Furthermore, in Downs's view, the benefits of many governmental actions seem uncertain, because they ensure against the ravages of complex problems, which themselves might never become manifest (1960:554). While Downs acknowledges that forces such as logrolling might create a tendency for the public sector to grow too large, nevertheless he believes that, on balance, the forces that lead to a suboptimal public-sector size probably predominate.

Figure 4.2a illustrates the effect of underestimating the benefits that flow from the production of a given level of a public good. C(x) remains unchanged in figure 4.2a from that depicted in figure 4.1a. The benefit curve, B(x), shifts downward, though, to B'(x), so that at every level

FIGURE 4.2a

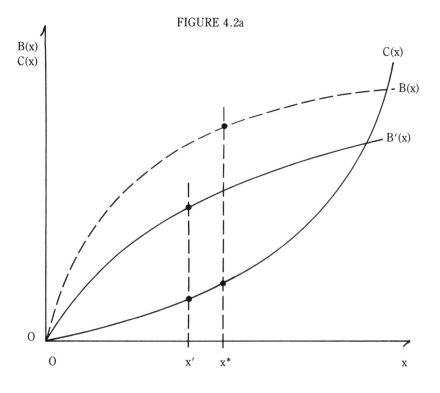

except zero, the citizen associates a lower benefit from the production of this public good. The citizen's new most preferred position under this downward revision is at x', which is to the left of and lower than x*.

Figure 4.2b shows the resulting utility function from the downward shift of the benefit curve. Notice that the *net* benefits of producing the public good are everywhere lower in figure 4.2b, compared with what they were in figure 4.1b, and the citizen's most preferred level of production, compared with that in figure 4.2a, has shifted to a lower level in figure 4.2b. If all three citizens in the hypothetical election described earlier share in this reduced perception of the benefits of this public good, so that the citizen whose utility function is depicted in figure 4.2b remains the electorate's median member, then the dominant election strategy—the equilibrium public policy that candidates will advocate—similarly shifts to a lower level of public-good production.

The social-imbalance hypothesis exhibits two fundamental weaknesses. The first is theoretical. Surely, a particular public good occasionally might get lost in the confusion of complex elections, so that citizens

FIGURE 4.2b

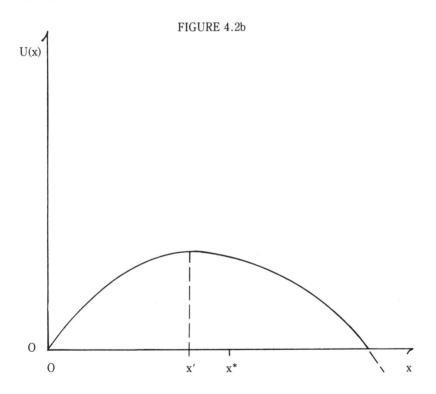

systematically underestimate its benefits. But the social-imbalance hypothesis must rest on the claim that large numbers of important public goods share in this reduced estimation of benefits. Yet, this eventuality would be such a large political imperfection that we would expect some counterforce to arise. In particular, social-imbalance theorists fail to explain why some candidate does not identify for the citizenry the full extent of its loss and thereby win the election. And as we shall see, a more general theory explains this failure; it similarly explains the nature of political advertising that now exists.

The second weakness is empirical. The public sector probably generates as much advertising as does the private sector, and perhaps more. First, political campaigning contains a large amount of advertising for particular public-sector programs (Demsetz, 1970). Candidates wish to identify themselves with their programs, and therefore campaigning and public-policy advocacy often occur simultaneously. Second, particular governmental agencies, in their lobbying activities with respect to congressional oversight, expend large amounts of money in preparing "information," which is really a public-sector form of advertising. Indeed, several executive-branch agencies have designated assistant secretaries or undersecretaries for congressional liaison who actually maintain offices on Capitol Hill. The direct "consumers" of the agencies' products are agents of the citizenry, but that observation in no way diminishes our estimates of the extent of lobbying as advertising that actually occurs. Third, most government agencies do expend large amounts on advertising in that term's more common usage (Clarkson and Tollison, 1979). The more general theoretical perspective that we shall offer will explain both the presence of high levels of public-sector advertising and the absence of advertising in favor of an enlarged production of public goods.

The Fiscal Illusion and Public-sector Size. An alternative approach to the problem of public-goods production concludes that such goods will be oversupplied because of a fiscal illusion (Goetz, 1977; Wagner, 1976). The fiscal-illusion hypothesis parallels the social-imbalance hypothesis, except that with a fiscal illusion people fail to perceive the full cost of all public programs, the real cost of particular programs, and the actual magnitude of their total tax burden.

The mechanism for inducing an illusion may take many forms. For example, many tax sources may be used, such as an income tax, a property tax, a sales tax, and an excise tax, all of which are held at fairly low levels, even though the total of taxes paid may represent a substantial proportion of a citizen's income. Alternatively, a particular tax may be collected in several small payments, as with periodic withholding of income taxes (Van Wagstaff,

114

1965) or payment of sales taxes at the time each purchase is made, again leading the citizen to underestimate his total taxes. Levies such as the corporate income tax are the most "hidden" taxes of all, because their incidences are obscure and their payers exist only "in the contemplation of law" (Aranson, 1977).

The creation of a fiscal illusion has an inherent political logic. For example, suppose that two election candidates are advocating identical public-policy programs with identical benefits. The costs of the programs may also be identical; but suppose that one candidate offers a tax plan based on a fiscal illusion to finance the program, while the other candidate does not. Presumably, the candidate who successfully induces the fiscal illusion will defeat the candidate who is more forthright about tax costs.

Figure 4.3a illustrates the nature of the fiscal illusion. In the figure the benefits from producing various levels of a public good are identical to those shown in figure 4.1a. Except at a zero level of production, however, the costs of producing various levels of the public good are everywhere lower than the associated costs in figure 4.1a. Hence, the citizen's most preferred

FIGURE 4.3a

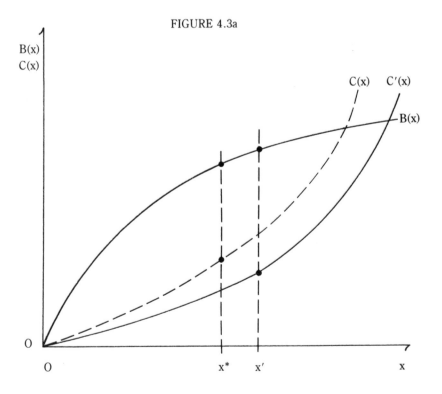

position on the issue of producing this public good is higher than it would be in figure 4.1a. Figure 4.3b shows the resulting utility function from this lowered-cost estimate. Again, the argument that prevailed in figure 4.2a concerning underproduction prevails here concerning overproduction. The citizen's utility function has shifted upward, and if the fiscal illusion similarly affects all citizens, so that the citizen whose utility function is represented in figure 4.3b remains the median voter, then the election's equilibrium strategy shifts to a higher production level.

Social-imbalance theorists rest their claims concerning public-sector spending, *inter alia*, on an argument that compares advertising in the public and private sectors. Fiscal-illusion theorists make no such comparisons, and therefore it is neither surprising nor evidently counterfactual to find that private-sector producers also try to create something like a "fiscal illusion" by such artifices as installment payments and layaway agreements. There are few external costs to the use of such artifices in the private sector, however, but the public sector encourages the production of external costs to the extent that fiscal illusions occur.

FIGURE 4.3b

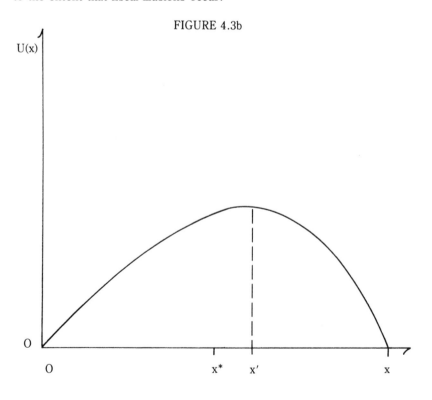

The fiscal-illusion hypothesis nevertheless shares the same theoretical weakness that afflicts the social-imbalance hypothesis. The pervasive use of fiscal illusions to generate a greater-than-optimal level of public revenues should call forth an election candidate to make the ruse plain. The failure of such a candidate to emerge requires some explanation, especially since the fiscal-illusion hypothesis enjoys more empirical validity than does the social-imbalance hypothesis. Both hypotheses point to an important governmental failure, and later we shall explain that failure more generally, as well as its particular applications to these hypotheses.

Absence of Electoral Equilibria. The final criticism of the simple model of elections with public goods as issues concerns the absence of equilibrium strategies that candidates might adopt. The absence of an electoral equilibrium is not a criticism of the model itself. It merely indicates that in certain situations the model might not predict what candidates will do, and therefore it will fail to predict the actual public policies that emerge from the electoral process. The absence of a prediction is itself a prediction, but we cannot discern the welfare consequences of an inherently unstable political mechanism, so judgments about the welfare properties of those mechanisms remain uncertain.

A simple example demonstrates the absence of an electoral equilibrium.[38] Suppose that three citizens, 1, 2, and 3, must vote on public-policy proposals x, y, and z. Citizen 1 prefers x to y and y to z; 2 prefers y to z and z to x; and 3 prefers z to x and x to y. In pairwise majority voting, x defeats y, y defeats z, and z defeats x, leading to a cyclical majority. Clearly, if either candidate in a two-candidate election chooses any particular strategy (x, or y, or z), then his opponent can always choose a strategy that will defeat him.

The theoretical absence of equilibria has generated several hypotheses concerning political responses. One hypothesis is that candidates avoid advocating specific proposals by using a strategy of ambiguity (Shepsle, 1972b, 1972a; Page, 1976; Enelow and Hinich, 1981). But knowledge about ambiguity in political platforms gains us nothing for making judgments about the welfare effects of the public sector.[39] Indeed, in itself, ambiguity represents a breakdown in the connection between citizens' preferences and candidates' election platforms.

A second alternative, but one that intervenes at the legislative stage, concerns the possibility that lawmakers use the presence of intransitivities, such as are found with cyclical majorities, to manipulate agendas to their advantage (Gibbard, 1973; Levine and Plott, 1977; McKelvey, 1976; Riker, 1980, 1958). For example, in the pairwise voting example just described, two pairwise votes are required. The motion presented for the first time in the second vote will always emerge the winner. Knowing this property of

117

intransitivities, the agenda controller can determine the election's outcome. Again, however, the presence of agenda control can tell us nothing about the welfare properties of the public policies that emerge from such processes, unless we can identify the preferences of those in control.

We have no specific response to the problem of intransitivities within the framework of this essay and its concerns.[40] Nevertheless, the general problem of disequilibria in elections and in other political processes remains troublesome for democratic theorists. We cannot comment on the virtues of that which we cannot predict, and therefore, to the extent that intransitivities or indeterminacies remain in the electoral process, to that extent social commentators at least stand mute.

PUBLIC POLICY AND POLITICAL GROUPS

The spatial theory of elections seeks to explain and predict the existence and location of equilibria in publicly supplied public goods, interpreted as election issues. Claims about the theory's empirical verisimilitude, though, must also confront the paradox: that most public-sector programs in a representative democracy are inappropriate, or are carried on at an inappropriate level, or are executed in an inappropriate manner. The problems of social imbalance and fiscal illusion merely represent two special cases of this larger paradox. Another way to state the matter is that the public sector should supply an optimal level of particular public goods in the correct jurisdiction using the proper production method. The spatial theory of elections with public goods as issues contemplates such a result, at least through the electoral process, and, by implication, through legislative, executive, bureaucratic, and judicial actions consequent to preferences revealed in elections. That such a result does not occur seems evident. That particular or generalized movements toward such a result would themselves represent the production of a public good also seems apparent. The failure to create such movements in their general or particular manifestations stands not simply as an indictment of representative democracy but also as a potential claim that this explanatory model of representative democracy, spatial-election theory, at least requires substantial modification and probably has omitted large portions of political reality that might otherwise account for the perceived inadequacies.

The Political Advantage of Organized Groups. The central inadequacy of the model and of earlier conceptions of representative democracy as cast in welfare theory is that in the model, and in earlier conceptions, political action and public policy derive exclusively from the preferences (and by implication, welfare-related concerns) of the members of an undifferentiated electorate. The omission of organized groups from this accounting of the

118

political process, and indeed a lack of appreciation of the political dominance of group members' preferences over those of the general electorate, requires correction.[41]

We begin the model's reconstruction by comparing the political efficacy of an organized group within an electorate to that of the unorganized members of the electorate in general. To cast the problem in familiar terms, consider a congressional district of about 500,000 persons, and suppose that 5,000 of them belong to an organized group. The existence of such a group connotes a superiority over the preferences of the general electorate in at least four activities.

First, the structuring of most organized groups allows for superior communications in two directions. Membership lists, mailings, and other ways of communicating with members, such as telephone pools and regular publications, enable the group's leaders to direct a remarkable amount of political and public-policy information about various officeholders and public-policy proposals to the group's members. This information often is extremely refined, addressing the particular interests of the group's members. The existence of an organized group also may enable leaders to communicate quickly and accurately to officeholders the members' preferences on a public-policy issue.

This aspect of communication deserves further elaboration. Concerning preferences on longstanding public-policy issues, an organized group's superiority over the general electorate may be somewhat diminished. On such issues candidates already may have taken positions, the citizenry's preferences already may have been revealed in elections, and some kind of public-policy equilibrium already may have been reached. There is little that is new about such issues, and organized groups may enjoy only a mild advantage over the unorganized electorate in communicating members' preferences to officeholders on such issues, and vice versa. On new and unanticipated issues, those that may never have been on the public sector's agenda, the matter is entirely different, however. At the margin of decision, group organization can make a difference concerning such issues. Group leaders do not simply summarize the members' preferences on new issues; they often "synthesize" those preferences by interpreting for members and for officeholders what impact the new issues will have on the members' welfare. Therefore, at the margins of public policy, in the creation of change, an organized group's superiority over the general electorate in communicating with officeholders and their challengers cannot be doubted. No such capacity exists for the general electorate.

An organized group's second advantage concerns public-policy transactions with officeholders. In the civics-book model, the electorate as an undifferentiated collection of persons makes a "contract" with an election

119

candidate concerning his public-policy decisions during his tenure in office. Performance under the contract is reviewed periodically, and the electorate may substitute new "suppliers" of public-sector services if superior possibilities emerge. This contract model has been subject to severe criticism concerning both its empirical reality (Ordeshook, 1970) and its desirability (Ranney, 1962; Wilson, 1925a, 1925b). But the relevant comparison is not between the ideal contract and the actual (implicit) contract that occurs, or its absence. Rather, the relevant comparison is between that actual contract and other kinds of contracts, namely those bargained out between elected officeholders, candidates, and organized groups.

The principal difference between these contracts lies in the costs of bargaining and transacting. Suppose that organized groups had no communications superiority in either direction. Even so, group leaders, as agents forming transactions, enjoy an enormous superiority over the unaggregated electorate. If an incumbent officeholder or challenger sought to bargain and make transactions with each and every member of the electorate, or even with a majority of them, the costs would be enormous, and each contract would have to be renegotiated in the light of each contract subsequently made, because positions on public goods, or external effects in general, might be involved. Assembling citizens into a group eliminates virtually all of these transactions costs and extraordinarily simplifies the officeholder's or the challenger's tasks. Therefore, at the margin the officeholder would always prefer to transact with leaders of organized groups rather than with individual citizens. The communication superiority that the organized group enjoys reinforces this advantage.

The third basis for superiority resides in the group's capacity to monitor compliance with the terms of any contract arrived at. Like communication, and indeed like transactions, monitoring goes in two directions. First, the group's leaders can monitor the actions of individual group members to see that they comply with the terms of any contract with public-sector agents. For example, group leaders might ascertain whether individual members had made campaign contributions to officeholders directly, and not to their opponents, or indirectly through the group's Political Action Committee (PAC); whether members had worked in the agent's campaign; and whether members had engaged in other supportive activities that were part of the bargain struck. In the other direction, the group enjoys an advantage in monitoring the officeholder's compliance with contract terms. Especially in labyrinthine legislative processes, it is difficult to find out whether a particular legislator acted favorably or unfavorably toward any given legislative proposal. Organized groups can develop expertise in learning about such matters, and they can monitor more easily than can an individual citizen the quality of the legislator's intercession with the bureaucracy.[42]

Finally, the organized group is superior in assuring compliance and in sanctioning noncompliance with the contract's terms. Of course, groups differ in their ability to sanction their members' noncompliance. For example, in earlier times, membership in county medical societies was required to practice medicine in certain areas and to have privileges in certain hospitals; and membership often accompanied enforced political support (Kessel, 1958). Today, medical societies have a greatly diminished capacity to ensure compliance with organizational directives. But an organized group's ability to sanction an officeholder's noncompliance with the contract's terms is clearly superior to that of unorganized citizens. Endorsements can be quickly withdrawn, and condemnations can just as quickly be applied.

The Nature of Interest-group Demands. In considering the putative political superiority of organized groups over unorganized members of the electorate, we must next inquire about the character of the public-policy demands that such groups might make. Again, the "civics book" model provides one interpretation of group action: groups form to pursue the public good. Indeed, some group political action appears superficially to correspond to this model. For example, the League of Women Voters increasingly has taken positions on large public-policy issues; the Nader groups and Common Cause similarly attack alleged inadequacies of public policy; and specialized groups, such as the Sierra Club, Friends of the Earth, and the Izaak Walton League, advocate their interpretations of what the public interest requires. Elsewhere, we discern in such groups' actions a clear diversion from welfare-maximizing policies (Aranson and Ordeshook, 1981b; see also Berry, 1977); and we discuss this diversion in the section of this essay devoted to bureaucracies. For the moment, we rely mainly on the common observation that most groups do not seem to devote their political resources to the pursuit of public goods, collectively supplied. Here, we wish to model the group decision-making process to explain this phenomenon.

We begin with a simple model of two interest groups, which between them share a positive preference for the production of a particular public good (it is public because the members of both groups would benefit from its production) but which individually prefer the collective production of different private goods. Furthermore, each group has a political budget, allowing it to lobby either for the public good or for its particular divisible, private good. Finally, assume that both the private-goods and public-goods programs are indistinguishable in the benefits that they would create as well as in their costs. Let B represent the benefit to each group of supplying

121

Peter H. Aranson and Peter C. Ordeshook

either program, and let C represent its cost. Table 4.1 shows the resulting
two-person game between the two interest groups, assuming that members
of these two groups make up the entire society (Aranson, 1981). The
table's entries assume that each group is pivotal or decisive for the program
that it seeks, so that lobbying for a program is tantamount to its public-
sector supply. If each group lobbies for the program that creates a public
good between them, then each receives a benefit, B, and the costs of this
program are shared equally, so that each pays a cost of $\frac{C}{2}$, for a net benefit
to each group of $B - \frac{C}{2}$. If each group lobbies for its respective private-
benefit program, then each receives that program and receives a benefit, B.
By virtue of such a program's supply to one group, however, the cost is
collectively imposed on both groups. The resulting net payoff for each group
is $B - (\frac{C}{2}) - (\frac{C}{2})$, or $B - C$. If one group seeks the collective supply of the
public good, while the other seeks the collective supply of its private good,
then the group that seeks the public good receives a benefit, B, but it pays a
cost of $\frac{C}{2}$ for its share of the public good and $\frac{C}{2}$ for its share of the other
group's private good, for a net payoff of $B - C$. But the other group receives
a benefit, B, from the public good that the first group pursued and an equal
benefit, B, from its own private-goods program; it pays a tax share of $\frac{C}{2}$ for
each program, yielding a total net benefit of $B + B - (\frac{C}{2}) - (\frac{C}{2})$, or $2B - C$.
   To analyze this game, consider the payoffs from group 1's perspective,
and suppose that group 2 decides to seek its private-benefit program. If so,
then group 1 receives $B - C$ no matter what it does, so that it is indifferent

TABLE 4.1
POLICY GAME BETWEEN TWO INTEREST GROUPS

GROUP 1'S STRATEGIES	GROUP 2'S STRATEGIES	
	Seek public good	Seek private good
Seek public good	$B - \frac{C}{2}, B - \frac{C}{2}$	$B - C, 2B - C$
See private good	$2B - C, B - C$	$B - C, B - C$

SOURCE: Peter H. Aranson, *American Government: Strategy and Choice* (Boston, Little,
Brown, 1982), p. 237.

122

between these two strategies. Suppose, however, that group 2 seeks the public good. Under these conditions, group 1 will receive a net payoff of $B - \frac{C}{2}$ for pursuing the public good and $2B - C$ for pursuing its private-benefit program. Hence, for group 1 to pursue its private-benefit program, $2B - C$ must exceed $B - \frac{C}{2}$, which reduces to the condition that B exceeds $\frac{C}{2}$. That is, the group's benefit from either program must exceed its tax share, one-half of the program's cost. Since the game is symmetric—both groups share the same payoff structure—this is a general condition leading to the collective supply of two private-benefit programs and the nonsupply of a public-goods program. Furthermore, notice that if B is less than $\frac{C}{2}$, then both groups will refrain from making any public-sector demands, because either program would have a negative net benefit.

This game is a prisoners' dilemma. Assuming that B exceeds $\frac{C}{2}$, each group will seek its private-benefit program; it receives $B - C$ rather than $B - \frac{C}{2}$, for a net loss in this process of $\frac{C}{2}$ for each group. If we add up the net payoffs if each group seeks a public good, as compared with the case in which each group seeks its respective private benefit, we find that the social cost of this process is C.

This simple two-person game illustrates a disturbing result, namely that the structure of payoffs to groups in a representative democracy leads each group to seek the collective supply of private benefits for itself, rather than a jointly consumed public good. Hence, if public-policy outcomes bear some relationship to the demands placed on elected officeholders, and if organized groups enjoy a political advantage over unorganized collections of citizens, then we must reject the notion that representative democracies can easily produce public goods, as a welfare-regarding model of the public sector would predict. Unless we can find some way out of this dilemma, we must conclude that these polities, in the main, produce private benefits at collective cost.[43]

The situation that table 4.1 models seems highly abstract and devoid of political or economic content, however, and a slightly more complicated model might provide further insight into the process of group-demand formation (Aranson and Ordeshook, 1978). Accordingly, suppose that each group has a political budget, exogenously determined, which it can spend to lobby for either a public-sector program that produces a public good or one that creates a private good, which only members of the group consume. But suppose that there are now n groups of equal size. Furthermore, assume that the benefits and costs of the private and public goods might be different, so that B and C represent the benefit and cost of the public good, while B' and C' represent the benefit and cost of each private good. Assume that the n groups bear equal tax shares. Finally, suppose that before any group

political action occurs, there are underlying expectations or probabilities of
P and P′ associated with the respective public-sector supply of the public-
and private-benefits programs. The decision to allocate resources in pursuit
of one program or another raises these probabilities by incremental amounts
of dP and dP′, respectively. In this n-group setting, an interest group
lobbies for the public-benefits program if,

$$dP/dP' > \frac{(B' - \frac{C'}{n})}{(B - \frac{C}{n})}.$$ (1)

To analyze inequality (1), we shall hold all other variables constant, to
trace out the effects that changes in each variable would have on the
choice between lobbying for a private-benefits program or a public-
benefits program. First, suppose that dP = dP′. That is, a change in
lobbying or other related activities produces an equal change in either P (dP)
or P′ (dP′). The left-hand side of inequality (1) now becomes 1, and
therefore a group will lobby for the publicly supplied public good if $(B - \frac{C}{n})$
exceeds $(B' - \frac{C'}{n})$.

Now if C = C′, then the relevant decision is one of comparing benefits
(B and B′) from each program (assuming that in each instance a benefit will
exceed the tax share; otherwise, no public-sector lobbying will occur). This
comparison of benefits without reference to cost is not entirely revealing,
since it raises purely empirical questions about the perceived benefits of
public-sector programs. If the social-imbalance hypothesis holds true,
however, then public-goods programs that are objectively worth as much as
private-goods programs nevertheless will not experience full valuation by
the citizenry, and therefore organized groups will lobby instead for their
private-benefit programs.

Beyond the application of the social-imbalance hypothesis, though, we
can say little. Both empirically and theoretically, public-goods programs are
inherently neither more nor less valued than are private-goods programs,
especially if programs are considered at the margin. For instance, the most
general finding concerning public-sector budgeting is that the base budget of
the previous year's allocation remains more or less untouchable, and
political action concentrates on increments to this base (Davis, Dempster,
and Wildavsky, 1966). Hence, organized groups seldom need to concern
themselves with the value to them of the entire annual allocation for a public
good such as national defense. Rather, such conflict as exists concerns
increments to the previous year's budget. And in this decision setting, a 5
or 10 percent increase in national-defense expenditures, say, may not have
an appreciably greater benefit (and probably will have a smaller benefit) than
the absolute value of a similar increase in a particular group's private benefit
(holding costs constant).

Now, suppose that $dP = dP'$, but $B = B'$. A group's decision reduces to one of comparing costs of private- and public-benefits legislation. Here we can say more empirically, although not necessarily theoretically, than we could in comparing benefits. Public-sector action commonly finds justification in the size or cost of the programs undertaken. Beyond the free-rider problem, it is often argued that if very large expenditures are involved, capital markets may not operate as efficiently as they do with smaller programs, in which an investment in one program, even by a private-sector lender, represents but a small portion of that lender's loan portfolio. Thus, because of the very large cost of public-sector programs such as highway systems, national defense, and educational plants, the central government, as a "perfect insurer" (risk-spreader), is called upon to finance the relevant program.

If real public-goods programs are exceedingly large and "lumpy," however, then that would imply that C is greater than C'. Therefore, at the margin of decision, no organized group would lobby for the more expensive public-goods program. Hence, the central economic characteristics of such programs—largeness and lumpiness—which provide a justification for their public-sector creation, simultaneously provide the conditions under which we cannot expect them to find political support among organized groups.[44]

Finally, consider the relevant increments to probability, dP and dP', and let B equal B' and C equal C'. Inequality (1) thus reduces to $dP > dP'$: a group will lobby for a public-goods program if that choice contributes more to the probability of enactment than does the alternative choice of lobbying for a private-benefits program. Except for this probability calculation, the model represented in inequality (1) is identical to the model represented in table 4.1, in the game between two organized groups. In table 4.1 the decision situation represents a game with decision making under conditions of uncertainty concerning the other player's choice. Here, the others' choices are taken as given, because the underlying probabilities represent estimates of what other groups are going to do and how the agents in the public sector will respond. That is, the decision situation that inequality (1) represents concerns decision making under conditions of risk. Differently stated, the game in table 4.1 represents a two-person free-rider problem, while the situation in inequality (1) represents an n-person free-rider problem.

While several formulations of P, dP, P', and dP' are possible, one way to look at the problem is to assume that dP and dP' are both functionally identical increments to probability whose values depend upon their underlying probabilities P and P'. The most common assumption is that there is saturation: as P, say, grows larger, dP declines as a consequence of applying equal units of political resources. Under this hypothesis, important inferences emerge. For instance, the decision makers of any particular group would usually believe that no other group would lobby for the private benefits that their group wishes to have supplied. Hence, P' equals zero. P, however, is bounded by zero but may take on a larger subjectively estimated value if a group's decision makers believe that there is any chance at all that some other group (or perhaps a median preference in the general electorate) would demand the public supply of the public good. If so, then the group in question would find P greater than P', and dP' greater than dP; and thus the group would lobby for its private-benefits legislation.

Even if P equals P', so that dP equals dP', the same result pertains. With this equality of probabilities, the situation as inequality (1) describes it is the n-person version of the prisoners' dilemma in table 4.1. Hence, given our findings in that situation, we have no reason to expect that organized groups will pursue public-benefits legislation.

The discussion thus far assumes that groups allocate their political resources to pursue either a public good or a private, divisible benefit. But groups might oppose each others' demands for private benefits, and a full accounting of interest-group decision making must expand groups' opportunity sets to include this possibility. First, if the structure of costs and payoffs associated with a particular program represents a direct transfer from one group to another, with no other groups being directly concerned, then the resulting game is zero-sum-like, and we can expect opposition from the disadvantaged group. These cases characteristically occur in certain regulatory situations in which competing producers of substitutable goods and services would alternatively be favored or disadvantaged by regulation.[45] These cases stand outside of the analytical framework constructed here, because they contain no prior assumption about cost spreading. Thus, we can say little about the welfare properties of the resulting public policies. Presumably, one group or the other might win, but we cannot be sure that a market process, whether or not devoid of imperfections, would have selected that particular winner.

Second, in the presence of cost spreading, but in the absence of a zero-sum structure, there remains the possibility that interest groups will oppose each others' demands for private benefits. Nevertheless, we might reject this possibility, because if a single group decides to mount opposition to another group's demands, then all other groups will benefit that would otherwise bear the tax share for supplying that program. That is, the supply of opposition would be tantamount to the supply of a public good for all other groups. And according to the analysis just reported, such opposition should not occur.

If a small number of groups are involved, however, then tax shares may be sufficiently large to generate opposition. We have constructed a three-person game in normal form to examine this possibility (Aranson and Ordeshook, 1978). This game, which allows no coalitions among groups, partitions the set of likely situations into two categories. First, suppose that B' exceeds C'. In this situation, all groups will pursue the public-sector supply of their private benefits. Second, if B' is less than or equal to C', then the possibility of opposition depends on the relative magnitudes of the probabilities, benefits, and costs. While no general results emerge from this inquiry, some reasonable constructions of these variables suggest that benefits need only represent some fraction of costs for opposition not to occur. In particular, if B' exceeds two-thirds of the cost of each program, then independent action in pursuit of each group's private-benefit program will occur, but not opposition.

Extending this three-person game to a more nearly general n-person form requires greater specificity about the probabilities of legislative success. Nevertheless, the results deduced reveal more about underlying political processes. For example, suppose that P_x is the probability that a group will successfully secure B' in the public sector and that x is the number of groups lobbying for their respective benefits. Let $P_x = P_{x-1} + dP_{x-1}$. The group prefers to lobby for the public-sector supply of its own private benefit rather than against the public-sector supply of all other groups' benefits if

$$P_{x-1}[B' - \frac{C'}{n}] + dP_{x-1}[B' - x\frac{C'}{n}] > 0. \tag{2}$$

Suppose that the probability that a group succeeds in securing the public-sector supply of B' equals the proportion of groups not opposing that supply. One formulation of this probability is that $P_x = \frac{x}{n}$. Inequality (2) becomes under this formulation,

$$B' > (\frac{C'}{n})\frac{(2x+1)}{(x+1)} \cong 2\frac{C'}{n},$$

for large values of x. Hence, if B' exceeds only twice the amount of each group's tax share for each program, then all groups will lobby for their respective private-benefits legislation. This is a remarkably weak condition. Each group's net payoff becomes B' − C', which by assumption may be negative.

P_x may also reflect a majority-rule variant. Suppose that n is odd and that $P_x = 0$ if x is less than a majority but equals 1 otherwise. In such a situation, the group will pursue its private-benefit legislation, and not oppose the demands of other groups, if,

$$B' > C' \frac{(n+1)}{2n} = \frac{C'}{2},$$

for large values of n.

We have also investigated a more general noncooperative n-person model, allowing for continuous adjustments in the amounts of resources allocated to support and opposition (Aranson and Ordeshook). Let P_i represent the probability that group i's private-benefit program passes; x_{ii} is the level of resources that group i allocates for this purpose; and x_{ij} are the levels of resources that it allocates to defeat group j's bill, for all j. If there is a budget constraint, if equal tax shares prevail, and if the various x_{ij}'s are arguments in a function determining P_i, then group i's payoff, V_i, becomes

$$V_i = (B'_i - \frac{C'}{n})P_i - (\frac{1}{n}) \sum_{j=1}^{n} C'_j P_j. \tag{3}$$

By placing additional restrictions on P_i, a general result emerges from equation (3). In particular, suppose that P_i is monotonically increasing and marginally diminishing in x_{ii}, strictly convex and monotonically decreasing in x_{ij}, and that benefits, costs, and budget constraints are equal for all groups. In equilibrium, the P_i's are equal, and each group's payoff becomes $P_i(B' - C')$. This result is invariant with respect to the relationships of benefits to costs and the level of resources expended in opposition. In equilibrium, except in those peculiar instances of corner solutions, P_i exceeds zero, and the public sector grows, at some net cost if C' exceeds B'.

There remains the possibility that groups will organize among themselves in a cooperative-game context to form coalitions opposed to the private-interest process. This possibility seems reasonable, because cooperative decision making is one way in which players may extricate themselves from prisoners' dilemmas. Yet, the possibility also remains that a majority of groups will form a coalition to secure their respective private-benefits legislation, to the detriment of the remaining minority.

Using a three-person cooperative game, the findings in this regard are thus. First, if one group, for whatever reason, decides to oppose the other two groups' public-sector demands, then those two groups will form a coalition in pursuit of their benefits, the only limit being that B' exceeds two-thirds of C'. Second, if one group pursues its own private benefit, then the other two groups will form an opposing coalition. Once that coalition forms, however, it is individually rational for each of its members to defect. That is, the opposing coalition is unstable, and in the end all three groups will seek their respective private benefits. Third, if a grand coalition opposed to this private-benefit process does form, then each member of the coalition will defect and pursue its own private benefits, if B' exceeds merely one-third of C'. Finally, if a group stands alone to oppose the other groups' demands, then it can do better for itself by joining the other two groups in politically pursuing its own private benefit. In sum, under very reasonable conditions, all coalitions in opposition to the private-benefit process are inherently unstable.

Efficiency and Inefficiency. The preceding discussion raises the possibility that each program's costs, although spread across all groups, will exceed its benefits, thus producing a Pareto-inferior result. Indeed, in our two-person prisoners' dilemma formulation, this inefficiency is embedded in the process, because the groups fail to pursue a jointly preferred public good, and thus produce a social cost of C. Hence, from an opportunity-cost perspective, we already know that the process is inefficient: the groups could not achieve a mutually preferred public-policy outcome.

Second, welfare theory provides no justification for these kinds of public-sector activities. That is, economists give no welfare-related credence to this variety of simple redistribution, absent an eleemosynary motive. Moreover, in the absence of specific forms of market failure, these programs would be welfare-inferior. If this were not so, then the groups presumably could purchase these programs in the private sector, where, in the absence of market failure, their production would be more efficient. Furthermore, there remains an additional cost of simple politically sanctioned transfers, which is the cost of the political action itself, a source of rents for politicians (see McCormick and Tollison, 1981; Aranson and Shepsle, 1983).

The only remaining justification for these transfers of benefits from the fisc—and ultimately, from other taxpayers, consumers, and producers—to private, divisible interest groups is that of political pluralism. For example, Dahl identifies one particular mechanism of political competition underlying this process but judges its effects as benign, and perhaps desirable (1961). In his study of New Haven politics, Dahl documents the manner in which the political parties alternated competitively in bringing one group of new immigrants after another into the political process. Presumably, each group received an identifiable benefit from this activity, and because the benefits ostensibly exceeded the costs, in Dahl's view, the resulting pluralism appeared to him to be appropriate.

The second variant of welfare theory might approve of such a result. Behind a veil of ignorance, people might choose a political order that sequentially produced programs for identifiable groups, provided that the benefits of each program exceeded the costs. Since the probability of being in such a group is very high, everyone benefits from this arrangement. Even in political theory, however, this benign judgment of pluralism has received substantial challenge, most notably from Lowi (1979).

We have sought to find general tendencies toward efficiency or inefficiency in the private demands that interest groups place on the public sector. But general sentences have been difficult to utter. Presumably, with scarce political resources the possibility of purchasing efficient (benefits in excess of costs) programs in the private sector will temper the number of such programs sought in the public sector. As an empirical matter, our inability to find patently efficient public-sector programs gives us some confidence in this conclusion. The literature suggests a fairly substantial cost differential in favor of private-sector production (Borcherding, 1981; Borcherding, Pommerehne, and Schneider, 1981), while the lure of cost spreading provides the animus for the public-sector production of inefficient programs. Furthermore, the cost of foregoing the public pursuit of public goods in all of their manifestations must represent a social cost exactly analogous to the alleged costs of market failure. That is, groups use the fisc in the manner of an overgrazed commons (Shepsle, 1983; Aranson, 1983).

Beyond these observations, we have tried to construct examples in which groups have a choice of purchasing various goods and services in the public or private sectors (Aranson and Ordeshook, 1977). The preceding discussion indicates that in the large-number case there are virtually no constraints on the relationship of benefits to costs. Explicit examples reinforce this conclusion. We can construct situations in which interest groups will pursue both inefficient and efficient programs in the public sector, but we cannot construct situations in which interest groups will purchase inefficient programs in the private sector. Therefore, at best the relationship of efficiency to interest-group public-sector activities is random. Yet, when we overlay all of the considerations just mentioned, including the findings of empirical work, we rest comfortably with the presumption that the public sector remains an explicit source of divisible benefits for identifiable groups, with corresponding programs whose costs exceed their benefits.

A final perspective on interest-group public-policy demands sets aside the costs and benefits of particular programs and looks instead to the nature of political action. This approach concentrates on expenditures for securing public policies, including money and other resources allocated to lobbying, campaigning, and more obscure payments for buying public policies. We use the term "political services" to capture all of these activities and ask what is the economic nature of these services? In particular, we wish to know if such services are normal economic goods, in the sense that expenditures on them increase proportionately with increases in wealth, or whether they are inferior goods, because expenditures on them decline proportionately with increases in wealth.

To get at this problem, we construct each group's decision structure so that it must allocate a proportion of its budget to buying goods and services in the private sector or to buying political services in the public sector. Assuming that investments in political services exhibit diminishing marginal returns, we find that political services are inferior goods (Aranson and Ordeshook, 1981a). That is, they are much like hamburgers and hot dogs, in that as people grow wealthier, they begin to substitute other foods, such as steaks and lobsters. Of course, if the interest-group public-policy demands identified here are satisfied sequentially over time, and if they reduce aggregate and individual wealth, then that datum alone will lead interest groups to purchase proportionately greater amounts of political services.[46]

THE INSTITUTIONAL MATRIX

The preceding discussion assumes implicitly that the institutions of government—legislatures, bureaus, courts, and executive administrations—are responsive to the underlying public-sector demands of interest groups for private, divisible benefits. Each model reviewed assumes that public-sector satisfaction of these demands is either a step function or a monotone increasing function of the political resources allocated to pursuing the associated programs. If we could rely on this assumption, then our analysis would draw to a close, because we can find no way to aggregate demands for public goods, including the public good of opposition to inefficient private-interest legislation. A full analysis, though, requires that we examine the institutions of government, to ascertain how they respond to demands for the collective supply of private goods. This section attends to the reactions of legislatures, bureaus, and courts. The next section closes the circle by interpreting executive-branch (presidential) and legislative decision making, using a more general election model in which candidates build platforms out of the satisfaction or denial of demands for private-benefits legislation.

LEGISLATURES

Traditional Antecedents. Before proceeding to a formal modeling of legislative decision making with regard to interest groups' private-benefit demands, we can best make sense out of, and reinforce our eventual findings about, legislative responses to such demands by rehearsing Mayhew's partition of congressional action (1974). Mayhew divides congressional activity into three categories: position taking, advertising, and credit claiming.

Position taking seems analytically equivalent to the adoption of election strategies concerning public goods. It consists of voting on roll calls and of announcing one's position on larger public-policy issues. The problems with position taking thus resemble those that candidates encounter in traditional spatial election models. First, because the voter identifies the strategy

131

chosen with the production of a particular level of a public good (unless it is the precise level that the voter most prefers), the candidate is susceptible to his opponent's opportunistic criticism and the formation of coalitions of intense minorities (see Downs, 1957; Oppenheimer, 1972). Hence, legislators try to avoid recorded roll-call votes, to bury politically damaging legislation in committees, and otherwise to utter innocuous platitudes. Second, position taking falls prey to the larger problem of absence of electoral equilibria in a legislator's district, which allows a potential opponent to defeat the incumbent legislator on any position that he might take. Accordingly, a strategy of ambiguity may prevail.

In sum, only when there is a clear majority in a legislator's district (and perhaps not even then) will the legislator take a forthright position on a legislative issue. Otherwise, position taking may turn out to be a politically destructive activity. Mayhew's discussion is revealing:

> A solid consensus in the constituency calls for ringing declarations; for years the late Senator James K. Vardaman (D., Miss.) campaigned on a proposal to repeal the Fifteenth Amendment. Division or uncertainty in the constituency call for waffling; in the late 1960s a congressman had to be a poor politician indeed not to be able to come up with an inoffensive statement on Vietnam ("'We must have peace with honor at the earliest possible moment consistent with the national interest"). On a controversial issue a Capitol Hill office normally prepares two form letters to send out to constituent letter writers—one for the pros and one (not directly contradictory) for the antis. (1974:64)

Advertising, the second form of legislative activity, merely seeks to give legislators public recognition, much as a brand name does for private-sector firms. Advertising is noncontroversial and has most of the benefits of position taking with few of its political liabilities. Advertising seems superfluous to the legislative process, however, because no necessary public-policy consequences flow from it, except that it allocates scarce resources away from the job of legislating and toward securing reelection. As a consequence, it represents a deadweight social loss, sustaining political rents for the private-interest group that we call the legislature. It would seem neither possible, nor socially desirable, nor even constitutional, though, to do away with legislative advertising.

Credit claiming is the most complex and interesting of legislative activities. The key aspect of credit claiming is credibility. Voters understand that a single member of the House is but one out of 435, and of the Senate, but one out of 100. They also understand that the president and the administrative agencies have a strong hand in public-policy decision making.

This understanding limits the extent to which individual legislators can claim credit for even small macroeconomic changes or foreign-policy successes. For instance, no single legislator could believably claim credit for reducing the rates of inflation, unemployment, or interest. Nor could any legislator credibly claim to have brought about peace in the Middle East, reduced armaments, or increased defense preparedness. Thus, while legislators may announce their support for various measures, believable credit claiming excludes entire categories of public-policy decision making: namely, the kind that ordinarily is associated with the production of nationwide public goods or the suppression of national public bads.

By the same reasoning, legislators will not claim credit for producing private benefits for those who do not affect their electoral fortunes. But they do claim credit for public policies that directly affect those who can advance their reelection or defeat. The associated programs are most closely identified with pork-barrel legislation, creating private, divisible benefits for individual legislative constituencies (Shepsle and Weingast, 1981; Weingast, Shepsle, and Johnsen, 1981). This form of legislation finds constant reference in the scholarly literature as the centerpiece of legislative activity (Ferejohn, 1974; Fiorina, 1977; Froman, 1967; Lowi, 1964; Manley, 1970; Mayhew, 1974; Plott, 1968; Schattschneider, 1935; Schwartz, 1981; Shepsle and Weingast, 1981; Stern, 1973; Stockman, 1975; Weingast, 1979; Weingast, Shepsle, and Johnsen, 1981). But the flow of political resources across state and district lines through the development of political-action committees and other artifices has also made it possible for widely dispersed but divisible interests to have an impact on public-policy decision making.

Credit claiming is hardly new, and it has long been the staple of scholarly analysis. Indeed, the language used to describe pork-barrel legislation and its close cousins is strongly reminiscent of the public goods–private goods distinction. For example, Lowi refers to ''distributive benefits,'' which seem very much like private goods (1964); Key refers to ''particularism'' and ''particularistic causes'' (1964); Mayhew speaks about ''particularized benefits'' versus ''universalistic benefits'' (1974); and Fiorina distinguishes between ''the pork barrel'' and ''case work,'' on the one hand, and ''programmatic activities,'' on the other (1977:45–46). In each of these juxtapositions, in regard to the legislator's allocation of scarce political resources, private-benefit legislation takes precedence over the development of more universalistic, public-goods legislation. Hence, the traditional and more recent literature on the Congress concludes that the legislative process responds to and encourages interest-group demands for private, divisible benefits.

Recent literature on congressional committee structure reinforces this conclusion. Committees provide a decentralized decision-making process that encourages the uncoordinated granting of benefits that the traditional literature identifies. Legislators in committees grant reciprocity to each other by not challenging other committees' jurisdictions, and they practice universalism by which most demands finding a voice in the Congress are eventually heard and satisfied by the appropriate substantive committees (Weingast, 1979; Fiorina, forthcoming; Aranson, 1981).

Formal Analysis. Formal theories of legislative decision making concerning the choice between private- and public-goods legislation and the decision to oppose or delete existing programs have been hampered by attention to the legislative technology of logrolling. Economists have evinced an interest in logrolling, because it appeared to make majority rule in legislatures more nearly marketlike, rather than simply redistributive. That is, logrolling allows for public policies to reflect the working out of differences in valuations (intensities of preferences) (Buchanan and Tullock, 1962). More recent studies argue, however, that logrolling might be a source of degradation in legislators' welfare (Riker and Brams, 1973). If we interpret legislative activity as presenting no principal-agent problems between legislators and their constituents, then the degradation of welfare consequent to logrolling paradoxically extends as well to constituents (Aranson, 1981, chap. 9). The resulting configuration of public policies with divisible, district-level incidents had been documented as early as the works of Woodrow Wilson (1956:89). It is also theoretically possible for logrolls to eliminate all private-benefits legislation (Schwartz, 1981), although a generalized analysis of pork-barrel decision making suggests that legislators will adopt logrolling technologies to produce, not deny, such programs (Weingast, Shepsle, and Johnsen, 1981).

A more general analysis, which transcends the narrow technology of logrolling, constructs a parallel between interest-group decision making, as reported in the third section of this chapter, and legislative decision making itself. Legislators clearly enjoy incentives that differ materially from those of their constituencies and of identifiable groups. Yet, it proves useful to assume initially that legislators are merely instructed delegates for those who aggregate demands in their districts, organized interest groups.

Accordingly, suppose that a constituency *is* an interest group and that legislators face decision-making problems much like those of the interest groups discussed previously. That is, to follow the structure of analysis in the third section, legislators must either support their constituents' programs or oppose all other legislators' constituents' programs in a noncooperative context. Continuing the parallel, we find that for a three-person legislature using majority rule, all bills pass if B' exceeds two-thirds of C'.

For n-person legislatures, assuming the formulation of inequality (2) concerning P_x, all bills pass if B' exceeds one-half of C', for large values of n. If coalitions are possible, and if the benefits of each program are less than two-thirds of its cost, then a grand coalition fails to enact all three proposals. But if B' exceeds two-thirds of C', then a two-person coalition will form to grant at least two of the benefits and to deny the third. Total payoffs equal $2(B' - C')$, and if C' exceeds B', then inefficiency prevails.

The possibility of legislatively deleting existing programs requires a formulation outside of the model, because it adds a time dimension to both legislators' and interest groups' decision problems. Once a program is established, it is continuously subject to legislative recision. Therefore, both interest groups and legislators must calculate the net present values of programs that in the absence of recision would run in perpetuity. It is more convenient for us to analyze this possibility under the discussion of the judiciary, so we postpone it until that time.

A Disgression on Interest Groups. Throughout the preceding discussion, while acknowledging the political superiority of interest groups over the members of an anomic electorate, we nevertheless assume, with traditional group theorists, that the costs of organizing and maintaining interest groups remain inconsequential. Interest groups in this model are taken as given (Truman, 1951). The analysis surrounding this assumption, however, plainly recognizes that free-rider problems and associated prisoners' dilemmas pervade most aspects of political life. For example, the production of public goods and the suppression of public bads is said to require governmental action precisely because of free-rider problems. And when groups lobby for the public-sector supply of inefficient private benefits, they are engaged in an n-person prisoners' dilemma. As Olson has pointed out, if members of a group share a common goal, whose accomplishment for them would be equivalent to the production of a collective good, those persons, too, experience free-rider problems (Olson, 1971). Unless we can accommodate Olson's important insight, our analysis remains incomplete.[47] We must nevertheless account for the formation of interest groups and explain certain regularities in existing legislation with regard to such groups.

To develop this explanation we divide groups into three categories. The first category contains those groups whose existence is assured by a parallel purpose. Large, dominant firms in concentrated industries are pertinent examples, as are governmental agencies and state and local governments, which act as interest groups with respect to their congressional lobbying activities. These groups already have been formed and maintained for other purposes, the returns from which are sufficient to sustain them.[48] For such groups and their leaders, the decision to pursue

135

private benefits merely concerns the relevant private costs and benefits of lobbying activities. Such organizations experience no real free-rider problems, although smaller groups may take advantage of the political penumbra that they supply if legislatures find it difficult or impossible to fashion perfectly divisible programs and benefits that exclude such smaller groups.

A second category contains groups organized pursuant to statutes or regulations. These groups form among otherwise large-number or competitive firms in the same industry or in parallel social structures. Precisely because such groups would find it difficult to form and prevail, the respective statutes are passed and regulations promulgated. Considering labor unions, this situation is explicitly recognized, as evidenced by the labor origins of the term "free-rider." It is important to understand exactly what the legislature accomplishes by governmentally enforcing membership and contribution to such groups. Certainly, such activities overcome the free-rider problem inherent in competitive markets. But legally enforced membership also makes it far simpler for the legislator to fashion a divisible benefit and to extract a rent from the group in return. Large, dominant firms in concentrated industries require no such services, and therefore they bargain with legislators in a bilateral-monopoly context. But firms or persons in competitive economic situations require the additional legislative service of group formation and maintenance through statutory enactments and regulatory ukases. Thus, legislative services hold value to participants in competitive processes beyond the value to dominant, preexisting groups.

The third category of groups encompasses those that face pervasive free-rider problems that know no clear legislative solution. These groups include the more recently developed "public interest" organizations, such as the Nader groups and various environmental lobbies. Concerning such organizations, scholars have developed a large number of ad hoc explanations for their formation. Selective incentives may encourage contributions, and tangential product lines and services supplied only to members may also be of help. Such groups are at a competitive disadvantage in creating these selective benefits, however, if a competing firm could produce them without producing the public good as well (Stigler, 1974). Even so, in recent years, legislators have found ways to funnel benefits to such groups in the form of research grants and intervener fees (Berry, 1977; Downing and Brady, 1979).

The costs of legislative action with respect to this hierarchy of groups is the opposite of the order that welfare theory would contemplate. First, there is no sense in which groups whose prior organization is assured should be the easiest to satisfy, because their demands are solely for divisible benefits, simple redistributions from the many to the few. Second, the supply of the prerequisites of organization to groups such as labor unions perforce converts them into members of the first category of groups, but they have been "captured" by their dependence on the legislature. Third, "public interest" groups are in reality demanders of supraoptimal levels of public goods, as well as private goods. To the extent that these groups form, a median preference in the electorate remains unsatisfied.

But in legislative allocations the central aspect of interest-group politics is divisibility itself. Legislators must ensure that programs are divisible among groups, because otherwise they could not secure payment for their enactments. That is why groups truly concerned with the public interest can seldom operate successfully. They cannot assemble adequate payments to legislators for their enactments. Were a legislator to create a pure public good, then, to pay him for his actions, a voter or group would be producing a public good for all other voters and groups. Legislators can create no such benefits unless somehow they develop a way to withhold payments in the form of programs to voters and groups that do not offer payment in return. That is, divisibility reasserts itself in political exchange, much as it does in private choice, to generate marketlike properties. Without such divisibility the legislative marketplace could not operate, or at least would not operate as it presently does. Yet, the external costs of this process, explicitly brought about through a cost-spreading arrangement that treats the fisc as a common resource, work a degradation of public welfare.

BUREAUCRACY

It was precisely the recognition that the political process could be subverted to the interests of discrete groups that provided the intellectual animus for the regulatory state. As early as the writings of Woodrow Wilson (1887), and later in the works of Herbert A. Simon (1947), scholars divided politics and administration, asserting that the president and the legislature, through a political process, should decide large matters of public policy but that administration should be carried out in depoliticized bureaus. The view of bureaucracy that emerged from this conception was that of a set of organizations with large powers and wide discretion, which would scientifically and nonpolitically produce the appropriate goods and services. A secondary aspect of this argument invoked the desideratum of centralization, a practice whose theoretical and empirical justifications have been seriously weakened.[49]

Regulation, one important aspect of bureau activity, is an explicit mechanism for producing private benefits at collective cost. For example, the Interstate Commerce Commission (ICC), the earliest of the federal commissions, may have been an instrument for aiding the railroads or the farmers; but in either case the public at large had little voice in the

137

commission's public policies (e.g., see Kolko, 1963, 1965; Hilton, 1966; Fiorina, 1982a; Martin, 1972). Later, the ICC would protect railroads against truckers and then switch its support to truckers, in a never-ending regulatory battle.[50] The Federal Trade Commission emerged as a protector of high-cost products against cost-cutting competition. The alphabet agencies of the New Deal era were similarly constructed (Hawley, 1966). The Securities and Exchange Commission protected underwriters of blue-chip securities against the competition of wholesale underwriters and today protects the interests of the securities bar (Manne and Solomon, 1974; Mackay and Reid, 1979). The Civil Aeronautics Board, which is not yet entirely dismembered, protected the airlines against competitive entry, in a classic regulatory pattern (Breyer and Stein, 1974; Douglas and Miller, 1974). The Federal Communications Commission resolved the dispute between the navy and commercial broadcasters, but in the process it controlled entry and competition in the interests of the networks and local ownership.

The more recent "social" regulatory agencies seem no less interested in private-interest regulation. The Environmental Protection Agency (EPA) favors some coal producers to the detriment of others and to the detriment of the public at large (Ackerman and Hassler, 1981). The EPA's regulations also protect existing industries in the Northeast against competitive entry from nascent southwestern producers (Maloney and McCormick, 1982; Pashigian, 1982). More important, the EPA administers a large pork-barrel program of grants to state and local governments for sewer construction and related projects. The Occupational Safety and Health Administration makes it extremely costly for smaller, nonunionized firms to compete with their larger, unionized counterparts. There is no discernible evidence of improved worker safety (Smith, 1982). The litany of regulation in favor of private interests seems endless, and we repeat this list merely to provide examples. Any welfare-regarding purposes or achievements that emerge from these regulatory regimes are largely epiphenomena of private-interest motivations.

Many traditional bureaucracies, such as the Department of Defense, the Department of Health and Human Services, and the Department of Agriculture, are involved less with regulation and more with the direct production of goods, services, and subsidies. These executive departments, while explicitly or arguably engaged in the production of welfare-regarding programs (such as national defense and some forms of resource redistribution), nevertheless are fecund sources of private, divisible benefits. For example, during 1983 Senate hearings on defense appropriations, Senator Donald Riegle of Michigan and Secretary of Defense Casper Weinberger had a heated exchange concerning the Reagan administration's proposed defense build-up. Riegle charged that Weinberger was an inflexible ideologue, whose proposals for increasing defense expenditures would actually diminish the amount of national defense produced. Weinberger responded to Riegle's charges by saying that Michigan voters would be interested to learn that the lower levels of defense spending that Riegle preferred would cost the Michigan economy $150 million.

Plainly, in welfare terms, such considerations are irrelevant. For example, these reduced expenditures in Michigan would also translate into diminished tax liabilities for all taxpayers and a reduced crowding out of private borrowers from credit markets, because of diminished government borrowing. Pecuniary externalities, such as Weinberger described, also should have no consequence for the optimal level and distribution of defense spending. Legislative tactics such as those that Weinberger used appear to stand at the core of expenditure decisions for the production of many public goods besides national defense. As argued earlier, the actual level of national defense produced seems to be an epiphenomenon of these pork-barrel decisions.

Bureaucracy and the Principal-agent Problem. For many researchers the central problem of bureaucratic and regulatory decision making is the divergence between the interests of the principal (the legislature) and the agent (the bureau or agency). This problem is common to many relationships, not merely those that occur in the public sector. As Jensen and Meckling observe,

> the problem of inducing an "agent" to behave as if he were maximizing the "principal's" welfare is quite general. It exists in all organizations and in all cooperative efforts—at every level of management in firms, in universities, in mutual companies, in cooperatives, in governmental authorities and bureaus, in unions, and in the relationships normally classified as agency relationships such as are common in the performing arts and the market for real estate. (1976:309)

The principal-agent problem in governmental bureaus differs substantially from its private-sector manifestations, however. In a competitive marketplace, market forces discipline the extent to which principals can allow agents' actions to diverge from those that principals intend, and they discipline agents in their divergence from principals' wishes (Alchian and Demsetz, 1972; Manne, 1965). But in the public sector, certain additional monitoring problems diminish both the principal's and agent's ability to reduce the scope of agency costs. First, to the extent that bureaus do produce public goods or suppress public bads, the usual problems of correct pricing and output apply (Samuelson, 1954; Olson, 1972). As Mises points

139

out, in the classical welfare model of the public sector, government produces (suppresses) precisely those goods (bads) that have no natural market price (1944). Accordingly, it may be impossible to identify optimum production levels and prices.

Second, because of these price and output indeterminacies, legislative principals, encouraged by bureaucratic agents, use surrogate measures of output and price, which may bear little or no relationship to measures that would adequately monitor bureau production and costs. For example, Tullock argues that State Department officials gain more from providing benefits to specific American citizens and firms than from developing a full knowledge and understanding of the particular countries in which they serve (Tullock, 1965). Military officers gain promotion by virtue of their bridge-playing abilities, social skills, and relationships with superiors, defense contractors, and congressmen, not by virtue of their ability to provide for the common defense. Lindsay argues that bureaus often supply goods and services at zero price to users, without having any clear measures of quality. Hence, because output is readily measurable, bureaus maximize it—for example, the number of patient days in Veterans Administration hospitals—rather than provide an optimum mix of quality and quantity (Lindsay, 1976). Similarly, police create speeding traps, to maximize revenues from speeding tickets, rather than allocate forces to minimize highway accidents.

All of these divergences between the principal's theoretical welfare-regarding preference and the agent's actual allocations represent not merely agency costs but also the construction of private benefits for the agency. In short, the agencies really stand as private, divisible groups, facing a perverse set of incentives and rationally producing goods and services for themselves at collective cost.

Niskanen (1971) explicitly models the principal-agent problem in the public sector as a bilateral-monopoly situation between the agency and the legislature. In his model the bureau produces twice the output of an analogous private-sector firm, with an accompanying welfare loss. Niskanen assumes that the motivation for these high production levels, which derive from the demand schedules that bureaucrats face, takes the form of private benefits, perquisites of office, and the like, for agency personnel. While Niskanen's assumption of agency budget maximizing has been subject to substantial reworking, his insights remain the benchmark for the study of bureaucracy.

Groups, Legislators, and Bureaus. Research on the divergence between legislative and bureaucratic interests and incentives serves to demythologize bureaucracies as giving undiverted attention to legislative goals and larger public purposes. But its lack of specificity about the nature of the divergence remains problematic. For example, one could argue that legislatures tend to require by statute the underproduction of public goods and the overproduction of private, divisible benefits at collective cost, but that welfare-regarding bureaus redress the balance. Of course, this conjecture contradicts a very large number of studies that conclude that many bureaus, and especially the regulatory agencies, are captives of the industries that they were intended to regulate (Bernstein, 1955).

Furthermore, recent work on the relationships among legislatures, interest groups, and bureaus comes to a different conclusion: bureaus serve as explicit agents in the production of private benefits agreed to in bargains struck between legislators and interest groups (Moran and Weingast, 1982; Weingast, 1981). In the traditional regulatory-capture literature, the agency monitors industry practices, to enforce a cartel among firms. Cartel formation and maintenance is very difficult to achieve using statutory instruments. The unit price of the good or service must be raised to the level that a monopoly would impose, but to prevent other firms from entering the market and dissipating the rents that the cartel price creates, there also must be entry control. Because demand and factor-cost characteristics facing such an industry will change over time, there must be a constant adjustment of both price and entry rules. Hence, flexible regulation is preferred to specific statutory enactments.

The traditional model of a cartel induced by regulation suggests the presence of a concentrated benefit for regulated firms at the collective cost of users. The metaphor applied to the supporting political structure is one of "iron triangles," with a congressional oversight committee, an agency, and a regulated industry at the respective vertices. Of course, while economists can sometimes think up welfare-regarding justifications for this form of regulation (e.g., see Kahn, 1966), the actual regulatory regime imposed commonly bears no relationship to a welfare-regarding model's dictates.

More recent research suggests that this single-industry-versus-dispersed-public model of regulatory origins may be misleading, because most agencies were born in conflict among contending groups (Aranson, Gellhorn, and Robinson, 1982). One model of this process argues that the legislature delegates legislative authority to the agency and thereby creates a regulatory lottery for the competing groups and firms. Because of risk-preference characteristics, these competing groups and firms prefer the lottery to the equivalent statutory certainty. After the agency has been established, it either resolves conflict in favor of one of the groups or shifts support back and forth between them. But the agency and Congress continue to exact payments for the changing cartel protection thereby established. These recent models of regulatory and bureau processes, while not settling the principal-agent problem or the congressional versus bureau-dominance debate, nevertheless establish bureaus and regulatory agencies as important contributors to the collective production of private benefits (see Posner, 1971, 1974; see also Peltzman, 1976; Aranson and Ordeshook, 1981b).

THE JUDICIARY

The judiciary ordinarily has had no place in accounts of the welfare-degrading tendencies of representative democracies. Most scholars set courts aside, believing that they are either sufficiently depoliticized or that the judiciary's concerns remain orthogonal to the principal political issues in public-policy debates. The Supreme Court is sometimes said to follow election returns; and in civil and criminal cases, lower courts, presided over by upper-middle-class or upper-class judges, are alleged to favor wealthy litigants. Whatever the merits of such claims, here we transcend them to consider other matters—namely, common-law efficiency and the interest-group basis of Supreme Court decision making.

The Efficiency of the Common Law. Earlier, we discuss governance by common law and conclude that common-law processes tend to adopt rules of liability that allocate resources to their highest-valued uses. Although the outcomes of suits at law and in equity will disadvantage particular litigants, the results are efficient in the hybrid sense of welfare theory, because behind a veil of ignorance, constitution makers would adopt such a process for large classes of disputes.

The common law's efficiency does not depend on judges' decisions, per se. Indeed, judges might even decide cases at random, with a slight bias toward not upsetting precedent, and the efficiency result would still hold. Following Rubin (1977) the demonstration of common-law efficiency proceeds thus. Suppose that the problem under study is accident liability in tort law.[51] Let A be the tortfeasor-defendant and B, the victim-plaintiff. The court must decide whether liability for an accident is to fall on A or B. If A is liable, then he will spend (for him) an optimal amount, S_A, to avoid accidents, and with this expenditure, N_A future accidents will occur. An opposite holding, placing liability on B, will result in S_B being spent on avoidance, leading to N_B future accidents. Let X equal the cost of the present accident and of each future accident that occurs, and let T_A and T_B represent, respectively, the total costs of future accident avoidance and accident costs for A and B, if each is held liable under the different rules. An efficient rule would place liability on B, say, if

$$T_B = S_B + N_B X < S_A + N_A X = T_A.$$

142

Let R be the probability that B will prevail in court if an accident occurs and litigation ensues. If precedent favors B, then R exceeds .5, but if it favors A, then R is less than .5. We now define additional variables, V_A and V_B, the expected values to the litigants of going to trial, and C, each party's litigation cost. The expected values to the litigants of going to trial are respectively:

$$V_A = R(-X) + (1-R)T_A - C,$$

and

$$V_B = R(X) + (1-R)(-T_B) - C.$$

Here, T_A and T_B represent future costs of different liability rules, the net present values of precedents that the court affirms or overturns. The litigants settle before trial if $-V_A$ exceeds V_B. But they litigate if

$$(1-R)(T_A - T_B) > 2C. \tag{4}$$

The important term in inequality (4) is the expression $(T_A - T_B)$. Suppose that the liability rule is inefficient and should hold B liable, not A. Notice that, reflecting this inefficiency, as the difference in the stream of costs, $T_A - T_B$, increases, the defendant has an increased likelihood of challenging the inefficient precedent, even though R, by assumption, is less than one-half. Once continually challenged, precedent, perhaps randomly, switches liability from A to B. *Ceteris paribus*, the parties no longer have as great an incentive to litigate and therefore to challenge the newly established efficient precedent. Similarly, notice that expression (4) is independent of the judge's particular motives.[52]

Inequality (4) shows the robustness of common-law processes in producing efficient rules of liability for certain classes of social disputes, private disagreements whose resolutions govern larger questions about social resource allocation. The inequality also demonstrates those situations in which common-law processes may be random concerning efficiency. First, with the inclusion of T_A and T_B, the inequality assumes that the litigants have a future interest in precedent. This condition may hold true for important classes of litigants. For example, insurance companies might be intensely interested in liability rules governing tort actions arising from automobile accidents. Therefore, in rear-end collisions, say, the following driver will be held liable, not the leading driver, who stopped short. Technologically, the following driver is the least-cost accident avoider, because if the leading driver must keep a constant watch in his rear-view mirror, he might have an increased chance of hitting an object in front of him.

The presence of litigants with precedential interests, such as insurance companies, will drive common-law processes to adopt efficient rules, which in turn will govern some cases involving litigants with no interest in precedent. Precedentially uninterested persons will thus receive an external benefit from the litigating activities of larger firms, which bear part of the social costs and benefits of their activities. If no such precedentially interested participants are available for particular classes of disputes, however, and absent an interest in efficiency by judges, we might be less confident that common-law processes will produce correct results. Of course, judges experienced in following arguments concerning the public-policy consequences of their decisions, as expressed in litigants' briefs and arguments, might reflect the pleadings of the cases before them and adopt efficient rules.

A second problem emerges, because of rules of judicial economy. For example, many such rules concern "standing to sue," meaning that a "party has sufficient stake in an otherwise justiciable controversy to obtain judicial resolution of that controversy" (*Black's Law Dictionary*, 1979: 1260). Rules of standing may remove some potential plaintiffs from access to the courts and their otherwise efficient rules and results. Similarly, narrow judicial construings of what constitutes a "cause of action" may produce the same effect. For example, before the 1950s, most courts held that a trespass required a physical invasion and derivatively ruled that air pollution by unseen chemicals would not constitute such an invasion. Such rulings stymied a common-law resolution of air-pollution problems. This narrow interpretation, which seemed reasonable in an earlier age, in which air pollution was less severe and the superior good of environmental quality was less highly valued at the margin, grew increasingly unreasonable in later years. Judges began to abandon the rule in the 1950s, but before the common law could work out new liability rules, federal legislation preempted common-law processes.

Finally, inequality (4) reveals the larger problem in depending upon individual litigants to drive common-law processes to efficient rules. Litigation costs might exceed the expected benefits to any particular plaintiff, but because of scale economies in litigation, all damaged persons would receive a benefit from litigation in excess of their share of the costs, were it possible to aggregate their interests. Public-goods problems thus emerge, and unless judges will accept class actions to assemble those dispersed interests, the cost of litigation, C, might undermine the robustness of the judicial process in correcting large-scale externalities. Hence, in certain situations in which welfare theory calls for governmental amelioration, the common law may find it difficult to achieve welfare-regarding results. This problem seems especially acute when disaggregated victims confront a monopolist, who internalizes the full benefits and costs of his litigation decisions.

Not surprisingly, when statute law preempts common-law rules, there is no guarantee that the result is efficient. Indeed, in many instances of conscious preemption, the result is inefficient, because of the private, divisible interests served in the legislative process. For example, in the case of industrial accidents, workers are usually the least-cost avoiders, although there are substantial grounds in the common law for holding firms liable for patently negligent conduct. Workmen's compensation statutes, though, often eliminate considerations of contributory negligence, imposing a regime of strict liability on firms. Arguably, the result is a greater number of accidents and a greater social cost (Chelius, 1977, 1976; Smith, 1982). Organized unions, having been guaranteed formation and maintenance by statute, lobbied for such a result; but individual firms, which enjoyed no practical way to assemble their interests, seemed equally disadvantaged in the legislative process. Thus, the monopoly problem just cited in common-law litigation carries forward into the legislature. And higher consumer costs are an additional result.

Supreme Court Jurisprudence. It seems more difficult to discern welfare-relevant considerations in Supreme Court decisions than in the decisions of state courts. Large classes of Supreme Court cases involve disputes in which welfare theorists must stand mute, or nearly so. For example, we can trace out the economic consequences of decisions concerning racial integration, abortion, prayer in the public schools, and pornography. But the original litigation in such cases often aligned the parties in zero-sum conflict. Many of the attendant costs and benefits seem symbolic, and therefore an analysis of such cases, using the tools of welfare theory, while they might often be instructive, might unduly size this body of law to a Procrustean bed. Such an analysis can clarify many of the issues involved. The resulting opinions and rules, however, might not be easily susceptible of interpretation using the tools that find application elsewhere in this essay.

The Supreme Court does affect the private-goods basis of legislation, though, and we can trace out the relationship between Supreme Court decision making and this character of legislation. Examining this relationship also illuminates the dynamic time dimension to private-interest legislation. The principal work is by Landes and Posner (1975), who find a connection between two characteristics of the federal government. The first is the persistence of an independent judiciary, "one that does not make decisions on the sorts of political factors (for example, the electoral strength of the people affected by the decision) that would influence and in most cases control the decision were it made by a legislative body, such as the U.S. Congress" (Landes and Posner, 1975:875). The second is an "interest-group theory" of government, such as this essay develops.

145

To explain this connection requires a recognition of the time dimension in the private-goods bargains that the legislatures generate. For instance, a particular subsidy program or entry control in a regulated industry might last for a year, ten years, or in perpetuity. *Ceteris paribus,* an interest group would prefer programs that last for longer periods than for shorter ones, and this preference holds important consequences for legislators. A congressman who expects to be in office for a limited time enjoys two important benefits from passing private-goods legislation in perpetuity. First, he need only once bear the costs of the initial legislative process. Incremental reappropriations and reauthorizations seem far simpler and less costly than initial ones, and he can immediately capitalize his share of a program's net present value, even if he only intends to remain briefly in Congress. Furthermore, this arrangement's single-payment feature circumvents his difficult contractual problem of enforcing payments in perpetuity.

Potential threats to this arrangement appear substantial. Legislators in future Congresses continuously might demand renegotiation of the original agreement and compensation for themselves. Legislative abrogation is a distinct possibility, which would reduce the net present value of the income stream to the interest group, thus simultaneously diminishing the price that the group is willing to pay to its original sponsor.

The possibility of abrogation also holds serious consequences for the abrogators, the incumbent legislators. If the members of Congress rescind agreements struck in earlier Congresses, they simultaneously reduce expectations of a long-term benefit flow among interest groups presently engaged in *de novo* bargaining with congressmen. Hence, with each abrogation of a prior agreement, an incumbent congressman reduces his expected payment from a present bargain. The entire Congress faces this problem, and it represents an institutional prisoners' dilemma for its members.

The congressional solution to this problem is institutional. Congressional procedures, such as the filibuster, bicameralism, and the capacity of committees to kill legislation, preserve the status quo by making it very difficult to terminate prior private-interest bargains. These procedures also make new legislation more costly. But Landes and Posner believe that the net benefit to the members of Congress from having status-quo-preserving procedures is greater than it would be without them.[53] Stated differently, the additional permanence of the reduced number of bills that succeed is greater than the opportunity costs of those that fail.

This assumption about the relative costs and benefits of making legislation more difficult to pass is susceptible to a different interpretation, however, one that pervades our earlier analysis of interest-group and legislative decision making in regard to a choice to pursue a private benefit or to oppose one. That analysis showed that interest groups have an incentive to seek, and congressmen have an incentive to pass, private-benefits legislation, but neither has an incentive to oppose such legislation. Landes and Posner incorporate the incentive to pass private-benefits legislation, but they worry about incentives to delete existing legislation. Yet, our earlier analysis explains that incentives to delete such legislation are equivalent to incentives to produce collective goods. We found no such incentives present. Hence, prior private-benefits legislation enjoys a presumptive permanence, even though a majority of the members of subsequent Congresses might oppose it.

The judiciary, and particularly the Supreme Court, represents a second threat to the long-run flow of private benefits from single enactments. Suppose that the judiciary were not independent, but instead were responsive to legislative changes in preferences, thus canceling certain long-term legislative contracts with interest groups. Judicial nullification may even be a preferred way for legislators to eliminate these prior bargains, because it would avoid the legislative gauntlet. Thus,

> suppose that Congress in year one "sells" the dairy industry a heavy tax on margarine, but the next year the producers of margarine offer Congress generous inducements to remove the tax. Congress is unlikely to respond to this demand by enacting repealing legislation, due to the impediments to swift legislative action. . . . But if the judges are the perfect agents of the current Congress, they will refuse to enforce the margarine tax, and the effects will be the same as legislative repeal. (Landes and Posner, 1975:879)

Hence, members of present Congresses share an incentive not merely to structure their decision-making process, to avoid legislative nullification of earlier agreements, but also to avoid compromising the independence of the judiciary.[54] To avoid conflicts with the Congress, the Court also has an incentive to affirm earlier private-interest legislation, and indeed the Supreme Court seldom overturns such legislation. Rather, the Court acquiesces in these enactments, thus reinforcing its own "independence."

The Supreme Court's activity is thus notable, not for what it does, but for what it does not do: namely, interfere with the private-interest bargains struck in the legislature. One can even sense in the Court's decisions the operation of implicit rules requiring the preservation of prior legislation. The Supreme Court goes beyond not tampering with prior enactments to finding ways to enhance their survival. For example, in statutory interpretation, the Court often examines the original congressional hearings and speeches, to discern the intent of the originating legislators. While this activity sometimes results in peculiar readings of the legislative record, nevertheless, statutory construction is a common judicial practice. Indeed, even when the Court confronts an otherwise unconstitutional statute, it usually tries to narrow the scope of the statute or otherwise interpret its terms so that it will pass constitutional muster, to preserve as much of the original bargain's intent as possible.[55]

ELECTIONS IN PRIVATE GOODS

We have come full circle from an analysis of electorates and the place of interest groups in them through the decision-making processes of the institutions of government. Our central conclusion is that most participants in the political process engage in the supply and demand of private benefits at collective cost, with scant regard for welfare-related criteria. Four tasks remain. First, we must reconcile the social-imbalance and fiscal-illusion hypotheses, which predict different public policies, with the private-goods view maintained here. Second, we must explain why the public sector does not yet account for the total gross national product. Third, we must revise our election models by departing from that of public goods as issues and moving to the notion of private goods, supplied at collective cost, as issues. Fourth, we must explain how issues cast as explicit public-goods decisions transcend that form to become decisions about private benefits, supplied at collective cost.

The accomplishment of the first of these tasks appears simple. Both the social-imbalance and fiscal-illusion hypotheses seem correct, because they do not predict mutually exclusive decisions. The social-imbalance hypothesis asserts that public goods will be underproduced. Our analysis does not predict whether such goods will be underproduced or over-produced, because the actual level of production seems epiphenomenal to the political process. For instance, we argue that the animus for national-defense production rests largely with the demands of divisible constituencies and firms, as well as with members of the military and the Department of Defense. Whether those interests coincide with the production of a proper level of national defense, or with a level of defense that is either too small or too large, we cannot say. We can merely indicate that there is too large an expenditure on private, divisible benefits, and we can identify sources of inefficiency. This means that at present expenditure levels, by making reallocations of spending, we could produce much more of the public good of national defense than we have today; or we could produce the same level of national defense at a greatly reduced cost, if we eliminated the entire private-goods nexus, and provided that there were another way to

148

assemble a demand for an optimal production of this particular public good—national defense.

The fiscal-illusion hypothesis is a close cousin to the kinds of cost spreading identified earlier. We have indicated how an effective political demand for a private, highly concentrated benefit might be formed, to the detriment of dispersed taxpayers. The inducement of a fiscal illusion merely reinforces this tendency. The social-imbalance and fiscal-illusion hypotheses thus refer to separate decision contexts. The first predicts the public-sector undersupply of public goods, and the second predicts its oversupply of private goods. Because any sensible model of electoral processes must incorporate illusions symmetrically, we construct our election model with that desideratum in mind.

Second, we must account for the public sector's failure to account for the total gross national product. To some extent an explanation for this datum rests with the simple observation that private benefits may be more easily produced collectively by having the public sector leave certain activities private. For example, regulation and the divisible benefits that flow from it could not exist without a private sector. Similarly, in many of the tax code's adumbrations, the ability to grant loopholes allows for the further production of private benefits, sometimes at the collective cost of private-sector inefficiencies pursuant to tax avoidance and the enhanced taxation of ''unprivileged'' activities. But these explanations probably remain less important than the more significant limitation, that there are macrolevel sources of inertia, preventing the public sector from growing at a faster rate than at present. Like social imbalances and fiscal illusions, the causes of this inertia should be an explicit deduction from a model of electoral processes with private benefits as issues.

An Electoral Process in Private Goods

The private-goods-election model is constructed out of assumptions concerning voters' thresholds of perception and candidates' decision procedures (Aranson and Ordeshook, 1978 and forthcoming). We assume that voters may differ systematically in their ability or willingness to perceive the net costs or benefits of alternative public policies and that candidates differ in their decision procedures between variants of global and incremental decision making. Interest groups in this model are price takers, which merely observe candidates' platforms and assess their expected welfare under each contestant's incumbency.

Voters. The discussion of the political superiority of groups over the members of an anomic electorate concentrated on the group's superior ability to monitor and enforce compliance with bargains and on its related capacity to convey political information. This process is bound to be imperfect, and therefore group members will vary in the amount of political information that they can and do absorb. The opportunity costs of collecting political information also vary systematically across the entire electorate, and these costs affect the amount of public-policy information that any particular citizen might have.[56] Here, we characterize information in each group by a distribution of thresholds of perception concerning net benefits or costs of public-policy programs. Figures 4.4a, 4.4b, and 4.4c illustrate three of the many possible general functional forms. The horizontal axis in each figure measures net benefits or costs, while the vertical axis depicts the threshold distribution's rate of change for alternative values of net benefits and costs, labeled here as X_i.

To interpret these figures, suppose that they represent the distribution of thresholds for the members of a particular group, and that an election candidate proposes a program of private benefits supplied at collective cost, which would create a net benefit or cost of X_i for each group member. The entire area under each threshold function is one. The shaded area to the left

FIGURE 4.4a

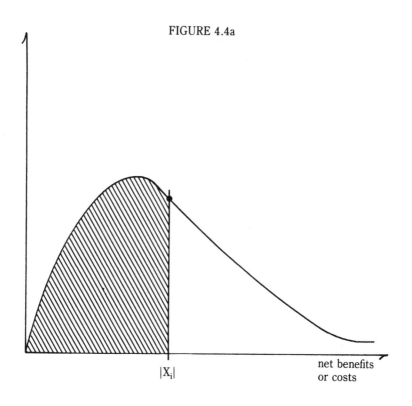

$|X_i|$

net benefits
or costs

of X_i shows the proportion of members that would perceive the net benefit or cost and act on it. Members with thresholds to the right of X_i would perceive no net change in their welfare. The distribution's skew and its general shape will affect the proportion of members that perceives a net welfare change. In figure 4.4a the members tend to be highly sensitive to small changes, while those in figure 4.4c appear largely insensitive.

It is tempting though speculative to provide interpretations of these figures. One possible interpretation is that the group whose threshold is depicted in figure 4.4a has excellent communications with its members, or that the group is small and closely knit, providing instant communications about political knowledge; by contrast, the group in figure 4.4c is only loosely constructed, with poor communications. Figure 4.4c may even represent the threshold distribution of the entire electorate.

An alternative interpretation allows for dynamic changes in thresholds as the result of changing economic and political conditions. For example, if tax shares increase rapidly because of increasing federal expenditures for various public programs, thresholds might soon pile up near zero, as citizens

FIGURE 4.4b

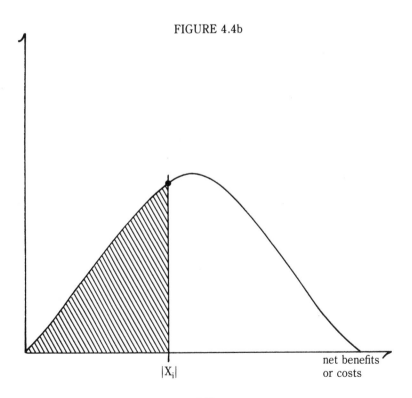

$|X_i|$ net benefits or costs

151

become highly sensitive to small changes in aggregate public-sector spending. Alternatively, during periods of economic expansion, citizens might be less aware of small changes in their tax shares and in regulatory welfare losses. While we may infer these two observations from diminishing marginal utility for wealth, they also suggest the presence of forces operating at cross-purposes. For example, if citizens become extremely sensitive to small tax-cost increases, they may also begin to demand proportionately more private, divisible benefits from the public sector, a result that the preceding analysis of political service as an inferior good would suggest. Figures 4.5a, 4.5b, and 4.5c show the respective cumulative densities of these threshold functions, $f(|X_i|)$. In these figures the vertical axis depicts the area under the threshold function, which translates into an election candidate's plurality gains or losses generated in each group from advocating a policy associated with $|X_i|$.

Candidates' Strategies. This model was originally constructed to explain the decisions of an incumbent chief executive seeking to be reelected and the decisions of his challenger. Later, though, we generalize

FIGURE 4.4c

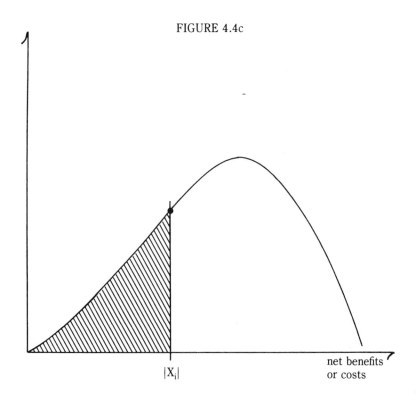

$|X_i|$ net benefits or costs

the model to include legislative decisions. The present characterization of executive decision making concerns whether such persons pass on various private-benefit programs incrementally, one at a time, or globally, all at once. The actual decision variable involved concerns the number of programs to be added, deleted, or left unchanged.

Most of the time we expect presidents and their challengers to decide incrementally, choosing to add, delete, or leave unchanged particular programs one at a time. This procedure seems attractive, first, because interest-group demands probably are pressed serially rather than all at once. Second, as noted in the discussion of the judiciary, legislators are constrained to leave most programs untouched, making changes only at the margin. Third, executives and their challengers seem physically and informationally constrained to accept what has gone before and to operate at the margin by adding or deleting programs one or a few at a time. Information costs alone preclude a "zero-base" scheme. Fourth, the strategy of ambiguity likewise restricts the number of programs on which candidates will take forthright positions.

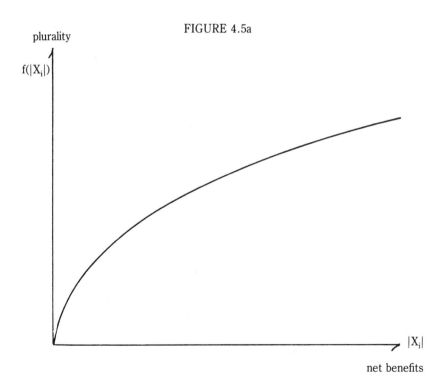

FIGURE 4.5a

plurality

$f(|X_i|)$

$|X_i|$

net benefits

Global decision making—the simultaneous considering of all present federal programs as well as those demanded or under review—may exist in an ideological space, but it is hardly realistic to believe that it prevails in day-to-day deliberations and in the private promises that candidates make to individual interest groups. Candidates who sometimes adopt global strategies or global approaches to public-policy decisions usually achieve the label of "radical." We assume that such a strategy is possible, however, if only to round out the analysis.

We also assume that each group has at most one program that can be added or deleted and that groups are of equal size. We let x equal the number of groups having programs added, and let y equal the number having programs deleted, such that x + y is less than or equal to n, the total number of groups. A candidate associates a plurality with each group, which depends on that group's net benefits or costs, X_i, and the group's distribution of thresholds. For instance, if a candidate advocates adding a benefit, B, at collective cost C for some group, if B and C are common for all of the groups' programs, and if tax shares are equal across groups, then compared

FIGURE 4.5b

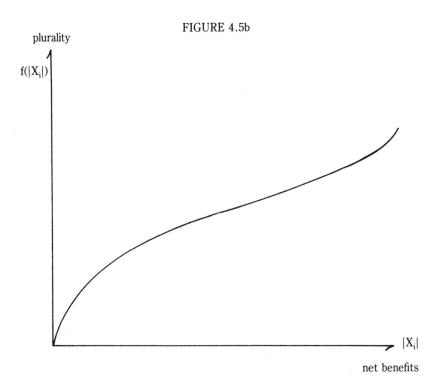

plurality

$f(|X_i|)$

$|X_i|$

net benefits

154

to the status quo of no net changes, the candidate's net plurality gain *from the benefited group* is $f(B - \frac{x-y}{n}C)$. The expression $[\frac{(x-y)}{n}]C$ represents the net addition to or subtraction from the tax or regulatory cost for each group, associated with a program addition or deletion. Since x groups have programs added, the total addition to the candidate's plurality, compared with his plurality in the status quo, is $xf(B - \frac{x-y}{n}C)$. Similarly, for the y groups whose programs are deleted, the candidate receives a plurality change (probably a loss) of $yf(-B - \frac{x-y}{n}C)$. And for the n-x-y groups whose programs or status remain unchanged, the candidate's plurality change becomes $(n-x-y)f(-\frac{x-y}{n}C)$. The candidate must choose a value of x and y to maximize his plurality, $V(x,y)$. In terms of the preceding formulations, we can state $V(x,y)$ as

$$V(x,y) = xf(B - \tfrac{x-y}{n}C) + yf(-B - \tfrac{x-y}{n}C) + (n-x-y)f(-\tfrac{x-y}{n}C). \quad (4)$$

Incremental decision making requires candidates to adjust x and y by adding or deleting programs one at a time, as an election campaign or a legislative session progresses. Global decision procedures allow x and y to

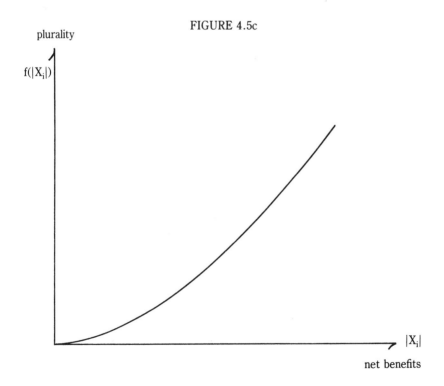

FIGURE 4.5c

plurality

$f(|X_i|)$

$|X_i|$

net benefits

155

take on any values up to an including n. An intermediate, hybrid form of global decision procedure assumes that the number of groups affected will be greater than one and less than n. That is, certain preexisting programs will not be deleted.

ELECTIONS WITH GLOBAL DECISION PROCEDURES

In earlier work, we report on the results of global candidate decision making, assuming the absence of thresholds or the presence of a uniform distribution of thresholds (1978 and forthcoming). That analysis provided few surprises, except that if the benefit of each program equals its cost in the presence of zero thresholds, then the net number of programs added or deleted may be ambiguous. The most important conclusion from examining electoral processes under these two very highly specialized assumptions is that maximum redistributive expropriations fail to occur. There is some inertia, even in these highly stylized electorates. Here, we analyze the more general cases of thresholds as depicted in figures 4.4a and 4.4c.

Sensitive Electorates. Suppose that thresholds are distributed as in figure 4.4a: citizens are sensitive to relatively small changes in their welfare. Using global decision procedures, candidates will find a strategic optimum in which each and every group's program must either be added or deleted. At an optimum strategy, however, x cannot equal y. And surprisingly, x exceeds y: more programs will be added than deleted. This last finding is independent of the relative values of benefits and costs.

Insensitive Electorates. If thresholds are distributed as in figure 4.4c, under global decision procedures, then more programs are deleted than added, provided that costs exceed benefits. If benefits exceed costs, then the actual configuration of outcomes depends on the parameters and the actual functional form of f.

ELECTIONS WITH INCREMENTAL DECISION PROCEDURES

Incrementalism seldom finds explicit definition in the literature, but our analysis requires specificity. Accordingly, we include analyses of three separate forms of incremental decision making: naïve incremental decision making and two forms of local optimization.

Naïve Incrementalism. Under naïve incremental decision making, the candidate or officeholder decides at the margin whether to add or delete some group's program. If citizens are relatively sensitive to small changes in their welfare, then the candidate adds programs one at a time only if each program's benefits exceed its costs. Otherwise, he deletes them. But if citizens are relatively insensitive, then the opposite configuration holds.

Depending on functional forms and parameters, adding programs dominates over deletion as an inverse function of the level of costs, as a direct function of the level of thresholds (insensitivity), and as a direct function of the size and support of the group that benefits.

Opportunity-cost Local Optimum. In the second incremental decision procedure, candidates serially adjust x and y to find a local optimum. For instance, suppose that a candidate's first decision is to add a program. Under an opportunity-cost local optimum, he will continue to add programs one at a time until one of two events occur. Either the marginal plurality from these additions would equal zero, or the marginal plurality from deleting a program would exceed that of adding one. When this second condition prevails, the candidate will then delete programs serially until a parallel change occurs. This decision procedure allows for recontracting of prior commitments, and it continues until the election is held or until there are no further gains as a result of additions or deletions.

Non-opportunity-cost Local Optimum. A third incremental strategy has the candidate use the same considerations as under the opportunity-cost optimum, except that he would not compare the marginal returns from additions and deletions, but would simply add programs serially until the marginal additions to plurality became zero or negative, and then he would delete programs until the same condition obtained. This procedure does not require the candidate to compare the opportunity costs of his full strategy set, and it depicts a decision maker who allows the public sector to grow until taxpayers become angry, after which he joins the tax-cutting bandwagon. Former Governor Jerry Brown of California used such a strategy in the face of Proposition 13's success in his state.

Under this decision procedure or the opportunity-cost variant, invoking the threshold distributions in either figures 4.4b or 4.4c, and allowing for recontracting of previously advocated policies, there will be a net addition of programs. That is, candidates set x greater than y.[57] Under a nonopportunity cost, local-optimum strategy, if thresholds are distributed near zero, the previously identified pattern with naïve incrementalism probably prevails, in that y exceeds x, and more programs are deleted than added. If thresholds are distributed far from zero, then under the same decision procedure, candidates add more programs than they delete.

HYBRID GLOBAL DECISION-MAKING

If candidates can operate in a greater than incremental fashion but are limited in the number of programs they can affect, then a hybrid global decision procedure prevails. For example, each of the political parties may regard a different set of programs as belonging to its traditional constituency, so that such programs cannot be deleted. If program benefits equal costs, and if thresholds are symmetrically distributed, as in figure 4.4b, then a candidate who is limited to considering only one-half of the programs under review will add more than he deletes. In a special case of figure 4.4c, using a quadratic payoff function, if a candidate adds no new programs, then he must be able to delete more than one-half of the programs under consideration, to achieve a net plurality increase. As public-sector size then grows by the accretion of more programs, the number of groups whose programs the candidate must deny, to increase his plurality, will decline. If the candidate's payoff function is concave, then these results are reversed. Accordingly, under a hybrid global decision procedure, welfare-sensitive electorates will produce a smaller public sector. The opposite result holds with thresholds distributed far from zero, the case of convex payoffs.

LEGISLATIVE DECISION MAKING

Constituency as Interest Group. To make sense out of legislative decision making by using the preceding election model in private benefits, suppose that a constituency is an interest group, so that a pure pork-barrel relationship prevails. Furthermore, suppose that separate threshold distributions describe each constituency. This formulation of the legislator's problem allows for the deletion of programs as well as their addition.

The analysis of the legislator's decision becomes more difficult than that for chief executives and their opponents, because legislative coalitions become possible. But suppose that a winning coalition has formed and that it will add or delete programs under a generalized incremental decision procedure. Because legislative coalitions may be unstable, winners and losers can change places quickly. We assume that all winning legislative coalitions will adopt identical decision rules, and that if the number of groups with programs added is less than a majority, then the coalition will delete only the programs that members of the losing coalition support. Let $P(W)$ represent the probability that a legislator belongs to a coalition of w legislators, and suppose that all coalitions are equally likely to form. Under this assumption, a legislator's expected payoff becomes,

$$V(x,y) = P(W) \left[\frac{x}{w}\right] (B - \frac{x-y}{n} C) + \frac{w-x}{w} f(-\frac{x-y}{n} C)$$

$$+ [1 - P(W)] \left[\frac{y}{n-w} f(-B - \frac{x-y}{n} C) + \frac{n-w-y}{n-w} f(-\frac{x-y}{n} C)\right]. \quad (5)$$

Because $P(W) = \frac{w}{n}$, equation (5) becomes equation (4), and the earlier findings of this election model remain invariant between executive and legislative decision making, if constituencies are equivalent to interest groups.

PUBLIC AND PRIVATE INTEREST AND POLITY

Nonconstituency Interest Groups. If constituencies are not the fundamental interest groups, but if interest groups are national, finding representation in most or all constituencies, then there is bound to be no real public-
policy conflicts among legislators. If this condition prevails, then each
legislator is equivalent to an executive or his challenger, and the results
from the election model carry over unchanged.

Heterogeneous Constituencies. Some interest groups may have members in certain constituencies but not in others. There may be neither
rhyme nor reason to the actual distribution of groups in constituencies, and
therefore there are no general findings from the election model in private
goods. If payments from interest groups to legislators are politically fungible
and transferrable across district boundaries, however, so that legislators
share in the rents from added programs or in the marginal plurality from
deleted ones, then the preceding election model again finds use.

IMPLICATIONS FROM THE MODEL

Table 4.2 summarizes certain of the findings from the election model.
While these results are overgeneralized and do not contain many of the
caveats in the original research, for purposes of speculation we discuss
them here somewhat more liberally than a closer reading might allow.

Strategic Premises. Most conjectures about this election model require
an empirical interpretation of the kinds of conditions in the electorate or in

TABLE 4.2
SUMMARY OF DECISION PROCEDURE AND THRESHOLD EFFECTS
ON PUBLIC-SECTOR GROWTH

| | THRESHOLD DISTRIBUTION | |
	Near zero	Far from zero
DECISION PROCEDURE		
Global	Net growth	Qualified net reduction
Nonopportunity cost incremental	Net reduction	Net growth

SOURCE: Adapted from Peter H. Aranson and Peter C. Ordeshook, "Alternative Theories
of the Growth of Government and Their Implications for Constitutional Tax and Spending
Limits," in *Tax and Expenditure Limitations,* ed. Helen Ladd and Nicholas Tideman
(Washington, D.C.: Urban Institute Press, 1981), p. 161.

159

political competition that would lead a given threshold condition or decision procedure to apply. For example, *ceteris paribus,* the distribution of thresholds may reflect the electorate's size. Larger electorates may be insensitive, with threshold distributions far from zero, as in figure 4.4c; smaller electorates might be sensitive, as in figure 4.4a. Using incremental decision procedures, candidates in smaller electorates would therefore create a leaner public sector, but as the electorate grows, the public sector might increase at a proportionately greater rate. Hence, those candidates or interest groups favoring (their share of) public-sector expansion should prefer centralized decision making in larger constituencies, annexations, and federalization of public-policy decision making. Devolution would be a preferred strategy for those who prefer a smaller public sector.

For those groups that find themselves in small electorates of unchanging size, but that wish to improve their chances of receiving private benefits at collective cost, an alternative strategy is to urge the agents of government to adopt global decision procedures, because this departure from incremental processes would result in a net public-sector expansion. Alternatively, if global procedures are already in place in a large electorate, such officeholders or interest groups might prefer a devolution of political authority to smaller units, because in the presence of global procedures and of citizens who are sensitive to small welfare changes that result from public-policy alterations, a net increase in public-sector size will again result.

Dynamic Aspects. Dynamic considerations invoke the possibility that thresholds and decision procedures are not merely exogenous to the political process but are also subject to manipulation. For example, as noted earlier, rapid increases in public-sector size, and the accompanying higher tax and interest rates occasioned by additional programs, might make citizens more sensitive to small changes in their welfare as their wealth declines. Alternatively, a robust economy might make citizens relatively more insensitive to public-policy-related changes in their welfare. The first possibility, of a government's growing under incrementalism in the presence of an insensitive electorate, may have characterized the development of public policies before the Reagan administration. At least in its official announcements, the Carter administration sought to use global decision procedures in the presence of an only partially sensitive electorate. As predicted, that result led to a net growth in public-sector size and, by a reasonable interpretation, the incorporation of a large number of public-spending programs into the category of "entitlements," with automatic cost-of-living adjustments, perhaps as a protective strategy, or as a legislative attempt to capitalize immediately on long-term spending programs.

The Reagan administration, faced with a greatly reduced distribution of thresholds of its own making, tried a mix of global and incremental decision procedures: global with respect to the entire body of defense programs, and incremental with regard to each reauthorization of social programs. It ended up with a net growth in public-sector size but with a concommitant shift of spending from domestic to defense categories.

One interesting aspect of the model's dynamic implications concerns the shift from cell to cell in table 4.2. We might begin with a condition of incremental decision making and an insensitive electorate, realizing net growth. As the citizenry grows poorer because of the resulting inefficiencies and higher tax costs, people will become relatively more sensitive to public-policy-related changes in their welfare. Hence, conditions will move from the right-hand to the left-hand column of table 4.2. But it remains unclear what public-policy change this shift will create, because we cannot predict the candidates' or officeholders' responses. Those who continue to decide incrementally will support a net reduction in public-sector size, but those who take a global view will advocate additions to the number of private benefits, collectively supplied. To the extent that "cost cutters" try to depart from the status quo, they will often defeat themselves by adopting global decision procedures as part of a larger public-policy attitude.

Perhaps we can best describe the experience of the United States and other representative democracies during much of the nineteenth century as a limited public sector, declining in size, in which officeholders could use global decision procedures in the presence of an electorate with thresholds distributed far from zero. That speculation gains force from the observation that in the United States and Great Britain, public-sector size relative to national product declined throughout most of the nineteenth century.

MACROECONOMIC POLICY

The preceding discussion demonstrates that under certain conditions the public sector will actually shrink. Thus, the election process itself provides a method for constraining the accretion of private-benefit programs. While this observation answers our third question about limitations to public-sector size, the conditions that prevail in most instances—incremental decision procedures with insensitive electorates—provide the theoretical assumptions necessary for net increases in public-sector size over time. Even so, we have provided an additional partial explanation of why the public sector does not yet account for the total gross national product, by beginning the theoretical construction necessary to complete the third task—namely, developing an election model in private goods. The final task is to explain how issues cast as explicit public-goods decisions transcend that form to become decisions about private benefits, supplied at collective cost.

For certain of these public-goods issues, we have already explained their transformation. Public goods—such as national defense, public peace, and environmental protection—remain at least partially public in consumption. But in their production the incidence of expenditures creates a set of private-benefit programs for individual firms and constituencies. Yet, for larger macroeconomic issues, the political engines of transformation seem less apparent. Issues such as inflation, unemployment, interest rates, and overall tax policy seem less readily susceptible to the private-benefit interpretation suggested here. Macroeconomic policies do exist, and politicians do manipulate them. The result for our analysis is thus a confrontation of two views. The first adheres to a microlevel model about the political pursuit of individual public-sector programs. The second observes the presence of macrolevel phenomena concerning these larger economic measures. Indeed, micro- and macrolevel policies may conflict, for example, because increases in private-benefit programs may occasion higher taxes and a lower gross national product.

The reconciliation of these conflicting views begins with the observation that politicians enjoy a wide variety of strategic responses to those macroeconomic outcomes that threaten or enhance the chances of election or reelection. Under a theory that we have criticized here, they may attend solely to larger macroeconomic considerations, either to gain reelection (Tufte, 1978; Nordhaus, 1975) or to develop truly welfare-regarding macroeconomic policies. But that conclusion rejects the notion that elected officeholders and challengers respond principally to organized groups, rather than to the entire anomic electorate. A closer examination of specific policies suggests that even when macroeconomic problems do occur, the demands of particular groups prevail in the fashioning of public-sector responses. Unemployment, interest rates, taxes, and deficits provide four examples (Aranson, 1983).

Unemployment. The traditional analysis of unemployment distinguishes between its cyclical and structural variants. Cyclical unemployment (and employment) occurs with the ebb and flow of the economy, as a result of changes in demand brought about by economic recession and expansion. Structural unemployment occurs as the result of a mismatch between the skills of the affected labor-market sector and the skills demanded in both the private and public sectors. The commonly suggested set of programs to reduce each form of unemployment depends upon its cause. Many economists, adopting a rational-expectations view, believe that cyclical unemployment requires no public-sector solution, because workers in cyclical industries receive a wage premium to compensate them for periods of unemployment. The high hourly wages of auto workers provide one example. Retraining programs or a negative income tax may be the most efficient solutions for structural unemployment.

Enacted solutions to unemployment problems contain few of these elements or considerations. Rather, as in other areas of political life, here, too, legislators respond to the demands of the organized, who tend to be unionized workers in cyclical industries, seeking additional public-sector support to compensate them for periods of unemployment over and above the compensation that they receive in their wage differential. For example, these groups constantly demand and sometimes receive government protection from foreign competition, even when it would be more sensible to do nothing or to relocate these workers temporarily, or even permanently, in other industries. This protection hardens investments and makes relocation more costly. Elaborate unemployment-compensation schemes, which do little for the structurally unemployed, exacerbate unemployment in cyclical industries. The hard-core and the structurally unemployed, who remain largely unorganized, only receive benefits from programs demanded by their organized sponsors—members of the welfare establishment, whose jobs are secure. These programs are not designed to reduce case loads or to allocate benefits efficiently.

Hence, the private-benefit pattern prevails in unemployment policies. The unorganized go unserved. But the organized receive divisible benefits at collective cost, with the additional problem that these benefits provide incentives for the cyclically unemployed to remain so. These programs also indirectly subsidize cyclical industries. It is estimated that the addition of these private-benefit programs to the public sector has contributed to the increase from 4 to 6 percent in long-term unemployment rates since World War II (Feldstein, 1982).

Interest Rates. Economists may disagree over policies that determine interest rates. Nevertheless, interest rates appear to generate from public policies more nearly concerned with public-goods production than is the case, say, with unemployment. Yet, even here, particular policies and general macroeconomic decisions are responsive to organized-group demands, not to the service of a larger public purpose. Specific policies include bailouts for banking institutions, construction-industry subsidies, and occasionally usury laws, which work the greatest hardship on lower-income citizens, who may not be sufficiently credit worthy to secure loans at lower, statutorily regulated rates. More commonly, the larger macroeconomic policies themselves are designed to respond to the demands of large, organized groups, such as labor unions, the construction and real-estate industries, and cyclical industries in consumer-product lines.

Peter H. Aranson and Peter C. Ordeshook

Taxes. We describe earlier the manner in which tax legislation is responsive to private-interest demands. Each new "tax reform" or "tax-reduction" bill contains a laundry list of exceptions and loopholes to benefit particular classes of firms or individual taxpayers. Sometimes, statutes are written to benefit a particular firm. The inefficiencies that tax-avoidance strategies—such as the purchase of economically unprofitable tax shelters—create, the implicit subsidies of tax loopholes and their distorting effects on the economy, as well as the high cost of tax preparation, must be counted as deadweight losses for the entire economy. Hence, these programs, too, represent private benefits supplied at collective cost.

Deficits. As a political issue, deficits during the Reagan administration attracted bipartisan appeal. Deficits are troublesome to politicians, *inter alia,* because they require debt servicing, and therefore they act as a "tax" on future public spending, thereby reducing the public sector's ability to supply future private benefits. Here again, the response to increasing deficits is consistent with the public-policy patterns described earlier. Those least well organized are affected first. For example, reductions in Social Security payments are enacted to the detriment of future recipients, not present ones. These recipients, who also bear the present burden of the program's cost, remain largely unorganized. By contrast, present recipients are organized. Similarly, student-loan programs—a benefit for a largely unorganized group of recipients—are cut from the budget, but not particularized benefits for tobacco growers, a well organized group.

In sum, concerning unemployment, interest rates, taxes, and federal deficits, public-policy decisions reflect less a coherent macroeconomic policy process, and more the demands of the organized for private-benefit legislation.

THEORY AND REFORM

Our analysis here finds grounds for rejecting the descriptive and conditionally normative conclusions of two bodies of scholarship. The first is welfare economics. Despite its theoretical elegance—asserting that the state *should* produce public goods, suppress public bads, establish property rights, control monopolies, and optimally redistribute wealth—we can find no real political or economic incentives, aside from constitutional strictures, for the actual accomplishment of these objectives. Furthermore, among economists and some political scientists, welfare theory has become something of an ideology. The discernment of a welfare-regarding task finds use in justifying governmental activity whose real motives concern the development of private, divisible programs at collective cost, which com-

monly are inefficient in their jurisdictional structures, methods of governance, allocations, and production levels. Scholars commonly brush aside the
necessary theoretical limitations of welfare-related prescriptions, with
regard to costs and benefits, jurisdictions, and methods of governance.
Therefore, in its most practical form, welfare theory has become a body of
scholarship in the service of advocating the addition of private-benefit
programs in the democratic polity.

The second body of knowledge that finds criticism here, if only
indirectly, is the Madisonian view of representative democracy, as formulated in "Federalist Paper Number 10" (1961) and in the works of more
recent pluralist scholars (Dahl, 1961). Madison acknowledges economic and
other causes of political divisions and the resulting demands for public
policies that would work a hardship on the citizenry at large. Nevertheless,
he believes that a republican form of government will oppose large interests
adverse to the electorate's welfare and will disperse smaller interests that
would unduly impose on the fisc. Our analysis suggests that when large
interests collide, one or the other may prevail, but a larger public purpose
goes unserved. More important, precisely the dispersion of smaller interests in a large republic, which Madison regarded as a solution to the private-
interest problem of "factions," is the precondition for cost spreading that
our models identify as a potent source of public-sector inappropriateness.

INSTITUTIONAL SOLUTIONS

Attempts to reform political processes in representative democracies
either seek directly to limit public-sector growth or to rearrange institutions, to affect expected costs and benefits of private-goods production.
These reforms accept motivations as they exist but try to constrain the
resulting decisions. As we shall see, motivational changes at the level of
fundamental incentives seem more nearly speculative.

Tax and Spending Limitations. The most prominent of institutional
reforms are various constitutional amendments that would require a
balanced budget and a limit to spending increases as some function of
growth in the gross national product, with the provision for an emergency
override by an extraordinary congressional majority. The several variants of
this proposal contain details susceptible of political manipulation. Under
these proposals, the political branches would find an immediate constraint
on their ability to create some private benefits at collective cost. Four
beneficial, and not necessarily contradictory, tendencies would result.

First, the private-goods nexus of legislation might continue, and
programs would be sorted out according to their political profitability, much
as they are today. At the margin, however, the addition of a new program

165

would require the elimination of an old one, and new programs would compete with each other for passage. This competition might reduce the political attractiveness of such programs. First, the eliminated program's supporters would constitute a natural opposition to favored measures, because they would bear the greatest cost. Second, the expectation that programs might run in perpetuity would be substantially reduced, because all programs would be subject to recision if politically superior substitutes emerged. Hence, interest groups would be willing to pay less to have such programs enacted. Third, because of the higher political costs associated with enacting such programs, consequent to the expected opposition, interest groups would demand a smaller number of them. In short, the tax and spending limit might work a serious mischief with the present structure of interest-group politics.

Considering the now increased costs and reduced benefits flowing from the balanced-budget spending limit, a fourth tendency might emerge, in that legislators, at the margin, might search for truly public-regarding legislation. Certainly, the private-interest basis of legislation would continue; but to the extent that it became less profitable and more costly, legislators might find real optimum arrangements of public-goods production relatively more profitable. Interest groups might then discern that legislatively created rents would be lower under budget limits, but the payoff in public welfare might be commensurately greater.

Three problems emerge from attacking the private-interest problem with balanced-budget and spending constraints. First, the provision for larger budgets consequent to votes by extraordinary congressional majorities makes it possible that such majorities will indeed emerge, perhaps increasing public-sector size and the number of groups whose demands find public satisfaction. Hence, upon the artificial creation or recognition of an "emergency," a larger coalition will form, whose members pursue yet more private programs at collective cost. The likelihood and dimensions of this possibility may be suspect, however, because in the absence of such a limit, much omnibus legislation now finds support by more than the constitutionally required supermajority. Whether such coalitions would take a different form under an amendment to balance the budget and limit revenue, we cannot say.

Second, the proposal to balance the budget and limit revenue does not directly assault the fundamental motivations underlying the private-goods problem. Instead, it merely seeks to constrain the resulting legislative outcomes. Of course, as just noted, certain changes in motivations and incentives will occur, perhaps improving the nature of legislation, and perhaps not. The approach of balancing the budget and limiting revenue, however, would deny what valid lessons might be gained from welfare

166

theory. Stated differently, under the dictates of welfare theory the public sector should embrace programs whose opportunity costs are less than the opportunity costs associated with alternative public programs and potentially foregone private-sector activities. That is, public programs should pass welfare-regarding tests of their fitness. Even under such tests, however, it is plausible that the public sector might grow larger. Yet, the macrolevel constraints of a balanced-budget approach would prevent welfare-regarding expansions and thus diminish welfare. Hence, were the president and legislators suddenly converted into sincere trustees for a larger public interest, they might find themselves constrained by an approach of balancing the budget and limiting revenue, in a manner that might deny their newly found regard for the citizenry.

The third problem may seem more technical, but it is no less acute for being so. Public-sector spending represents merely one technology for producing private goods at collective cost. Other technologies include loan guarantees, tax preferences (loopholes), and regulation. If for both legislators and their clients, direct spending suddenly should became politically more costly and less certain, then a partial shift out of direct-spending activities and into these less-hampered technologies might occur. For example, the federal government might issue a greater number of loan guarantees, reducing interest rates for the benefited classes of borrowers, while carrying the implicit subsidy off the books. Or tax-code provisions might increase in their exceptions and loopholes, to benefit particular groups, thus imposing more inefficiencies and greater tax shares on those not benefited, taxpayers at large. Or the federal government might issue a greater abundance of regulations to produce a relatively larger number of private benefits through that technology. For example, if the Social Security system found itself with mounting financial problems, the members of Congress, constrained not to increase spending, might require private employers to create highly regulated private pension funds, to siphon off part of the system's fiscal problems. Again, this activity would be carried "off the books," thus evading the constraint of balancing the budget and imposing a limit on spending. In sum, a solution by parts may turn out to be no solution at all.

Regulatory Reform. Problems of tax preferences and loan guarantees might find partial solutions in a better accounting of federal liabilities, although off-budget manipulation will remain a serious problem for any balanced-budget requirement or spending limit. The collective costs of regulation, however, remain entirely off the books, and therefore it might represent a preferred method of governance in the face of tax and spending limits. Like the public production of private benefits by spending, tax preferences, and loan guarantees, the regulatory creation of private benefits

Peter H. Aranson and Peter C. Ordeshook

finds broad and nonideological recognition as a problem of representative democracy. Solutions to this problem are varied and contradictory (Breyer, 1982; Commission on Law and the Economy, 1979; Noll, 1971; Poole, 1982).

Direct assaults on regulatory processes seem much like balanced-budget and revenue-limit constraints, because they seek to alter regulatory legislation by constraining it rather than by changing fundamental motivations. For example, in the literature and in legislative proposals, one finds recommendations for and opposition to legislative vetoes (Bruff and Gellhorn, 1977),[58] cost-benefit analyses, and sunset laws, which would automatically eliminate regulatory statutes after a fixed time period. Under a legislative-dominance view of the regulatory process (Moran and Weingast, 1982), however, a legislative veto would merely tighten the control that Congress exercises over regulatory-agency activities, without breaking the fundamental interest-group nexus of regulation. Cost-benefit studies are subject to serious manipulation and may serve merely to increase the amount of documentation required before regulations are promulgated. And sunset legislation allows Congress to renegotiate basic agreements with interest groups. This possibility may affect the interest group's expectations about future income streams from regulation. Yet, because Congress can influence the direction of regulation under present arrangements without renewing the legislation, that effect may be slight for the case of regulation (Ehrlich and Posner, 1974). More important, periodic renewal may allow Congress to perfect the production of private benefits through regulation by bringing a larger number of firms and industries under the purview of a single agency.

A proposed proximate solution to the regulatory problem is the reinvigoration of the delegation doctrine in constitutional law (Aranson, Gellhorn, and Robinson, 1982). This doctrine, an ancient rule of agency law, would constrain the further delegation of delegated powers, such as those that the electorate delegates to the members of Congress. It would require the members of Congress to pass fundamental regulatory statutes and to settle political questions rather than to delegate this task to an agency, with the vague directive to regulate "in the public interest, safety, and convenience." By requiring the explicit settlement of political questions, Congress could no longer create a regulatory lottery, as it now does by establishing regulatory regimes in the presence of conflict. The resulting specificity would encourage disadvantaged firms or industries to oppose the regulatory production of private benefits for their competitors. Were opposition absent, because regulation occurred pursuant to the traditional model of a single industry's using regulation for cartel formation, then transient regulatory agencies might result. Nevertheless, the umbrella of price and entry protection that regulation would afford to such an industry would invite competition from suppliers of substitute goods and services. In the absence of specific legislation, the delegation doctrine would forbid the extension of regulatory purview to these new competitors, and therefore the entire regulatory structure as a producer of divisible benefits at collective cost might fall of its own weight.

Decentralization. A third set of reform proposals concerns the locus of political control. As noted earlier, the production of public goods evinces problems of choosing price and output levels. Tiebout (1956) argued that radical decentralization of competing jurisdictions might create a marketlike condition in which more nearly optimal decisions might prevail. For our purposes, however, three other aspects of decentralization loom large.

First, decentralization of all governmental functions to the jurisdictions in which material effects occur would eliminate or substantially reduce the opportunity for cost spreading. That is, the costs of programs for dams, highways, schools, and other public services and regulations in state or city A would be borne in that jurisdiction, not spread to state or city B. At the margin, this reduction in cost spreading might promote an enhanced attention to the relative costs and benefits of alternative programs.[59]

Second, decentralization might create more nearly homogeneous jurisdictions, in which constituents would be more difficult to isolate as divisible recipients of goods and services. Certainly, even in small modern jurisdictions, a fairly heterogeneous electorate provides opportunities for legislating divisible programs. But at the margin, decentralization would increase homogeneity, and thus opposition might be raised to the legislative creation of private-benefit programs.

Finally, if welfare models of the political process enjoy any prescriptive robustness, then a variant of Tiebout's interpolity-competition hypothesis might prevail. That is, we might rely on the original purpose of a federalism to generate experiments in governance. Those jurisdictions that succeed in limiting governance to the production of public goods at optimal levels and prices perforce will leave their citizenry better off than those that fail in these tasks. Hence, we need not prejudge the exact form of local governance. We need merely allow jurisdictions to compete not only in the public and private goods and services that they create but also in the manner of creating them.

POLITICAL INCENTIVES AND REFORM

All of these reforms, while partially constraining underlying motivations to produce private benefits at collective cost, do little to change the incentives of politicians and their clients. Nor have we described strategies of enactment: first, because we are less than entirely sanguine about the effectiveness of any of these reforms and, second, because we are less certain about the enactment strategies that might be effective or appropriate. Surely, the underlying instability of political processes, as reflected in the absence of equilibria in electorates and legislatures, might itself aid in the adoption of one or more of these reforms in a political world in which "anything is possible."

While none of these reforms attacks the underlying motivations of political persons, they do change the rules enough to divert efforts partially away from the collective production of private benefits. Whether these changes are sufficient to create a substantial impact we cannot say. If they do succeed in suppressing the collective production of private benefits, however, then the payoff structures in legislatures and among interest groups will change. These structures probably create at least a modest self-selection among political persons, especially in light of the competitive nature of politics. Politicians also gain personal capital by practicing their skills under current incentives. But those who, under reform, no longer could succeed at the collective production of private benefits may find politics to be an unappealing vocation, in which their human capital has lost value. Those who remain or those who enter into politics to fill the vacuum may be differently motivated, producing yet further changes in the rules to accelerate the deprivatization of politics. In the absence of such a change, we cannot discern a set of reforms that would fulfill the requirement that "the citizen has a constitutional right to demand that public law be public-regarding" (Mashaw, 1981:28).

NOTES

1. For example, economists of the left, center, and right now seem to agree, to an extent that they have not before, that present antitrust policies in the United States erode economic welfare. Chicago economists long have opposed current antitrust activities. See Brozen, 1970; Demsetz, 1973a, 1973b, 1968; Posner, 1975, 1976; Stigler, 1966. More recent developments have buttressed this view. See Klein, Crawford, and Alchian, 1978. Baumol (1982), in the political center, has recently summarized the Chicago School's objections to antitrust policy, and he, too, finds that policy to be destructive of welfare. Scholars on the left, such as Thurow (1980), have also joined in condemning antitrust policy. In Thurow's view, present policies ignore competition from larger and (because of scale economies) more efficient firms in other industrial nations, which are not saddled by antitrust constraints. An attack on antitrust with regard to mergers and tender offers has also developed. See Easterbrook and Fischel, 1981; and Fischel, 1978.

2. Here, we concentrate on public policy in the United States, because we are familiar with it. But our knowledge of public policy in other democracies persuades us that the problems in those nations are not unlike those experienced in the United States. See, generally, Olson, 1982; and Benjamin, 1980. For a comparison of public-sector growth rates see Nutter, 1978.

3. For example, see Lindsay, 1976; Mises, 1944; and Niskanen, 1971. For an alternative view see Baumol, 1967.

4. Classic works include Ahlbrandt, 1973b; Davies, 1971; Lindsay, 1976; and Spann, 1977. A general survey of literature comparing the efficiency of private and public production is available in Borcherding, 1981; and Borcherding, Pommerehne, and Schneider, 1981.

5. See works cited supra in note 1; Bork, 1978; and Long, Schramm, and Tollison, 1973.

6. For example, "Governmental provision of public goods is required precisely because each individual in uncoordinated [sic] pursuit of his self-interest must act in a manner designed to frustrate the provision of these items" (Baumol, 1965:21).

7. "The Constitution presumes that private activities will be constrained only to promote public purposes. The recognition first, that there is a wide range of such purposes, and second, that democratic, collective choice may pursue any or all of them in a complex and eclectic body of regulatory statutes, in no way reduces the force of the basic principle. *The citizen has a constitutional right to demand that public law be public-regarding. Otherwise, his private harm is constitutionally inexplicable*" (Mashaw, 1981:28; emphasis added).

8. Specific works include Aranson and Ordeshook, 1981a, 1977, 1981b; and Goldin, 1975. On legislative contributions to the problem see Aranson and Ordeshook, 1978; Fiorina, 1977; Mayhew, 1974; Shepsle and Weingast, 1981; and Weingast, Shepsle, and Johnsen, 1981. On bureaucracies see Fiorina, 1977, and works cited supra in note 3. On the judiciary see Landes and Posner, 1975. On the regulatory nexus see Aranson and Ordeshook, 1981b; Jordan, 1972; Posner, 1971, 1972a, 1974; and Stigler, 1971.

9. See supra, note 6.

10. In its pure form, welfare economics contemplates as Pareto *optimal* those changes that would exhaust the possible universe of alternatives and make at least one person better off while making no one worse off. Here, we forego the intellectual conceit of Pareto optimality and instead adopt the lesser conceit of Pareto-*preferred* changes, which do not necessarily exhaust the possible universe of alternatives but are consistent with present knowledge.

11. This claim seems to be true of Marxist social and political analysis. It may not have been true of Marx's thought itself, for he noted, "What is to be avoided above all is the re-establishment of 'Society' as an abstraction *vis-a-vis* the individual" (1959:104), as quoted in Sen, 1970:1 n.1.

12. This approach is implicit in most cost-benefit analysis, which has therefore been justly criticized. See Mishan, 1971. More recently, Posner (1979) resurrects wealth maximization in law and economics. See also two symposium issues of *Hofstra Law Review:* "Efficiency as a Legal Concern," vol. 8 (Spring 1980), and "Response to the Efficiency Symposium," vol. 8 (Summer 1980). For a general theoretical discussion see Davis and Winston, 1965.

13. In welfare theory, a test for Pareto optimality under wealth maximization is the compensation principal. In general, state A is Pareto preferred to state B, first, if those who prefer a change from B to A could compensate those who lose from the

171

change, secure their consent, and still be better off in A than in B and, second, if those who lose could not compensate those who gain to get them to forego the change. See Kaldor, 1939; Hicks, 1939; and Scitovsky, 1941. Whether or not ex post compensation must be paid is strenuously debated. See Scitovsky (1941), which views the payment of compensation as a "political question," about which economists have no special expertise. The opposite view, requiring compensation, is argued in Buchanan (1959).

14. The mechanism of consent is ignorance of one's state after the constitution is enacted. The idea is first developed in Buchanan and Tullock (1962), and applied as a "veil of ignorance" in Rawls (1971). In essence, those who consent to a constitutional order under such conditions are choosing a particular lottery over alternative outcomes, whose selection the constitution will eventually govern.

15. Historical and anthropological evidence suggests that tribal, communitarian arrangements predate the kind of market contemplated in the pure competitive model and precede it in economic development. See Posner, 1980. Hayek argues that market relations developmentally have followed centralized community (collective) control. This process resembles the chronological order that Marx contemplated in historical dialectic, but whereas Marx would view the reimposition of collective control as the next step in economic development, Hayek would view it as social retrogression.

16. Returns in "payoffs" other than wealth find a place in recent work in economic theory. The more nearly inclusive term "welfare" may be substituted into this discussion, so that economic theory, as applied to the public (or private) sector refers to decision making in the presence of *any* kind of scarcity. The method is entirely general, incorporating nonmonetary concerns.

17. A large class of Pareto-optimal allocations may be produced in a pure competitive market. Once one such allocation is arrived at, however, it is Pareto optimal. A change from that allocation to another, without compensation, will harm at least one person. Hence, the primacy of the initial distribution of resources figures importantly in the final Pareto-optimal outcome chosen under the prescriptive, welfare-regarding regime described here.

18. Further political specifications of property rights to information may be appropriate, to make information private. This purpose appears to be the function of patent and copyright laws as well as of various common-law protections of trade secrets. The principal argument here is that creating more extensive property rights to information may be desirable, but regulating the primary market, because of an alleged market failure created by information inadequacies, may be undesirable.

19. The particular governmental program carrying out this function may (rarely) be strictly Pareto-preferred, based on the first variant of welfare theory. More commonly, it may require explicit ex post redistributions from a few to a few, from a few to many, from many to a few, or from many to many. If the enacted program requires redistribution, then to be Pareto-efficient, the program would have been unanimously preferred behind the veil of ignorance had it been chosen there (had the participants not known their subsequent postconstitutional and legislative roles). For example, the entire citizenry—all potential plaintiffs and defendants—might agree ex ante to an active common-law process (see Rubin, 1977). Under the actual operation of such a system, however, there will be losers who would not consent ex post to specific results.

While not objecting to the existence of winners and losers as a particular statute or regulation is worked out and applied, some scholars do object to changes in the law or the constitution that may be adopted with less than unanimous or near-unanimous consent. Therefore, they reject the second variant of welfare theory and require a strict application of unanimity standards, which themselves imply Pareto optimality. For example, Buchanan (1959) argues that the political economist's task is to formulate hypotheses about public-policy changes that would garner unanimous consent. Anything less than unanimity (applying a rule of reason to exclude madmen) would vitiate the persuasiveness of the policies adopted and introduce several other problems inherent in the political system, some of which we consider in this essay. Hence, the political economist not merely must operate on the principal vectors of public policy but also must develop compensation arrangements to secure the consent of those who otherwise might be harmed by policy changes.

20. Rarely are property rights certain. More commonly they are probabilistic and more or less complete. Only in unusual polar cases can we expect them to be entirely unassailable. This complication, while analytically interesting, is not damaging to the concept of a private good.

21. The good is "public" only for the collection of persons who own the firm, not for those outside of it. Presumably, there is a unanimous ex ante social interest in finding optimal monitoring arrangements and incentive structures within the firm, those that would equate the marginal cost of these arrangements and structures (adding monitoring costs, for example) with the marginal return (the value of the last unit of the public good added). That is, ex ante, a worker whose earnings reflect productivity, a consumer whose prices reflect the costs of production, and an owner whose returns reflect profit—all would prefer such an arrangement. To the extent that a competitive market process generates efficient levels of monitoring, say, to that extent a monitoring problem within firms belongs to the first class of departures from the pure competitive model: it is self-correcting within the structure of the market itself, and it merely requires political neutrality or common-law (contractual) enforcement.

22. Excellent reviews are available in de Alessi (1980) and Furubotn and Pejovich (1972).

23. The theory is developed in an expository but careful manner in Posner (1972b); see also Kamerschen (1976).

24. The original narrative of the prisoners' dilemma, which also models the cartel problem, was a dilemma whose *failure* of resolution at the prisoners' expense served a public purpose: the imposition of a "correct" sentence (see Luce and Raiffa, 1967).

25. The properties of an anarchy in operation may differ, depending on various conditions such as shared values, the size and population of the community, and the nature and location of scarcity (see Tullock, 1972; Buchanan, 1975; and Demsetz, 1967).

26. Easements may be created by specific contractual arrangements, by adverse use (e.g., A "openly and notoriously" passes over B's land for a given period of years), or by such common-law doctrines as "easement by necessity," which prevents the formation of "land-locked" parcels of property, those without access to a common roadway.

27. These conditions are restatements and applications to the law of easement of the famous Coase theorem (see Coase, 1960).

28. An excellent example of this phenomenon concerns the legislative disposition of "due-on-sale" clauses in home-mortgage contracts. These clauses allow mortgagees, usually banks, to require the full payment of a mortgage-loan balance at

the time that title to the mortgaged property is transferred from a seller to a buyer. In periods without interest-rate inflation, buyers usually would refinance a home at the time of purchase, rather than assume an existing mortgage, if their ability to pay the seller his full equity was limited. In times of rapid increases in home-mortgage interest rates, however, it pays the buyer to do whatever he can to assume the seller's mortgage. Under conditions of stable interest rates, the actuarial life of a mortgage was about seven years. But with an increase in the interest rates, the actuarial life grew to approximately eleven years, leaving the mortgagee with a low rate of return on its loan. When this situation grew acute during the 1970s, most banks changed their standard mortgage contracts to incorporate the due-on-sale clause in future transactions. Several state legislatures then outlawed due-on-sale clauses, but the Supreme Court has overturned such actions insofar as federally chartered banks are concerned, in *Fidelity Federal Savings & Loan Association* v. *de la Cuesta*, 102 S. Ct. 3014 (1982) (see Haddock and Hall, 1983).

At first blush it might appear that a legislative reversal of the due-on-sale clause would merely create a transfer of wealth from the mortgagee to the mortgagor. Home sellers and real-estate agents, however, also claim that maintaining the assumability of mortgages would allow them to sell homes at a lower price, thereby benefiting buyers, sellers, and real-estate agents. This proposition is dubious, because it assumes that the market is not already at equilibrium and that sellers would not beneficially absorb the full value of the reduced mortgage interest rate. Furthermore, in the wake of statutes invalidating due-on-sale clauses, banks will increase their interest rates and as well might turn to short-term mortgage instruments.

The due-on-sale clause essentially transfers the risk of unanticipated changes in the interest rate from mortgagees to mortgagors. If it were more efficient, mutually beneficial, for mortgagees to bear that risk, then that result would have occurred in the market, as it did during the period of relative price stability before the 1970s. Individual borrowers and lenders could negotiate such terms themselves, or such terms might become standard contract features.

29. *Bove* v. *Donner-Hanna Coke and Coal Co.*, 236 App. Div. 37, 258 N.Y.S. 229 (1932).

30. Such a government might redistribute wealth by majority rule from the quarry owners to the home owners, with no regard for efficiency. Thus, the danger remains that a move from common law to statutory or administrative law might find its motivation in a desire to create an inefficient result, thus increasing the value of the homeowners' assets while destroying the greater value of the quarry in operation. See supra, note 28, for a similar case.

31. "Self-government does not consist in having a hand in everything, any more than housekeeping consists merely in cooking dinner with one's own hands. The cook must be trusted with a large discretion as to the management of the fires and ovens" (Wilson, 1968:374).

32. For example, see *Brennan* v. *United States Postal Service*, 439 U.S. 1345 (1978).

33. The judicial rules of venue and standing may provide appropriate models for other public-sector decisions. The Supreme Court's decisions concerning several areas of law involving the possibility of federal preemption, however, are confused and contradictory, both between and among specific subject matters. See *Middlesex County Sewerage Authority* v. *National Sea Clammers Assoc.*, 453 U.S. 1 (1981), and

174

City of Milwaukee v. *Illinois,* 451 U.S. 304 (1981). For a discussion of decentralized environmental quality control see Aranson, 1982.

34. This is not an ideological claim for "states' rights" and "local options." Rather, it rests on the simple parallel with comparative statics in economics, that with large numbers of competing producers (here, governments) the price elasticity of demand is perfectly elastic.

35. Exactly this phenomenon of strategic use of regulation to limit productivity in competing states is documented in Ackerman and Hassler, 1981.

36. Tiebout, 1956. Several empirical studies provide conflicting evidence about the Tiebout hypothesis. See Edel and Sclar, 1974; Epple and Zelenitz, 1981; Epple, Zelenitz, and Visscher, 1978; Gramlich and Rubinfeld, 1982; Oates, 1969; and Yinger, 1982.

37. An elementary review of the model is contained in Aranson, 1981, chap. 7; a more rigorous review of developments through 1972 is available in Riker and Ordeshook, 1973, chaps. 11 and 12.

38. The discussion of instability in the text concerns a simple example of three voters and three alternatives using pairwise majority voting. The more interesting developments, however, concern the absence of equilibrium in a spatial context. The first full elaboration of this problem is in Plott, 1967. For more-recent developments see Ordeshook and Shepsle, 1982.

39. This statement may be too strong, because if the citizenry is risk-averse, then ambiguity induced by any cause will reduce welfare. This judgment afflicts elections in which there is no pure-strategy equilibrium or in which the candidates are tied in equilibrium but adopt different equilibrium strategies. For a discussion of such elections see Ordeshook, 1970.

40. The absence of an equilibrium in the legislature (or perhaps, even in the electorate) will obviously have public-policy consequences generally, and especially if agenda control is present. We would have to know who was controlling the agenda, however, what their preferences were, and other institutional rules and constraints, before we could say exactly what those public-policy consequences might be. Therefore, we might not be able to predict the legislature's public-policy decisions without first studying the institution and its rules. See Riker, 1980; see also Shepsle and Weingast, 1981b; Shepsle, 1978, 1979; and Fiorina and Shepsle, 1982.

41. Of course, group theorists such as David B. Truman and Robert A. Dahl account for public-policy outcomes largely in terms of group processes. But as we argue later, their formulation of group influence, insofar as welfare judgments are concerned, is inadequate. See Dahl, 1951.

42. For a discussion of the nature of this intercession, especially in matters of case work, see Fiorina, 1977.

43. Representative democracies obviously supply public goods. Examples include national defense, environmental quality, and public peace. To sustain the models depicted in table 4.1 and later in inequality (1), in the face of this observation, requires little imagination; for such goods are public in various aspects of their consumption but are principally private in production. For instance, national-defense production creates a multitude of pork-barrel opportunities—divisible benefits politically allocated to identifiable firms and constituencies. See Weingast, Shepsle, and Johnsen, 1981; and Shepsle and Weingast, 1981. Probably, constitutional forms sanctioning the public production of goods such as national defense provide one explanation for their production. But the explanation is largely hortatory, because games such as the one depicted in table 4.1 predict that no group will lobby for the

technologically most efficient supply of an optimal level of a public good such as national defense. But they *will* lobby for the production of particular weapons systems or base locations, say, whose principal incidents remain largely private. Thus, the animus for efficiency or optimality in the good's public aspects, considering the underlying political process, seems profoundly epiphenomenal.

44. Once again, the creation of many divisible benefits from the production, and sometimes from the consumption, of such programs, simultaneously accounts for their existence and their failure to bear a systematic relationship to efficiency criteria (see note 43 supra).

45. The theoretical genesis of regulatory agencies as legislative lotteries in such situations is developed in Fiorina, 1982; see also Aranson, Gellhorn, and Robinson, 1982. A case study of such a situation is described in Hacker, 1962.

46. There appears to be a parallel process occurring in the demand for regulation. Scholars of the regulatory process have long identified the decline of an industry with increased demands for regulatory protection (see Hillman, 1982).

47. Incomplete, but not self-contradictory. After all, the thrust of our argument is that interest groups and legislatures fail to solve their prisoners' dilemma, as evidenced by the continued production of inefficient private-benefit legislation. And the production of public goods and the suppression of public bads appear to be epiphenomenal.

48. Congressional constituencies are organized to do legislative battle in the person of their congressional representatives.

49. A review of the attack on centralization is provided in Aranson, Boyd, and Lancaster, 1983.

50. For example, see the events surrounding *American Trucking Associations, Inc.* v. *Atchison, Topeka, & Santa Fe Railway,* 387 U.S. 397 (1967), in which the Supreme Court acceded to an ICC change of heart. For years the ICC had abjured authority to require railroads to offer "piggy back" services to truckers; then the ICC asserted that it had the authority to do so.

51. Posner shows that the same framework applies equally to property and contract law (1972b).

52. Precedent is usually established or changed at the appellate level, so that jury decisions seldom figure in this analysis.

53. "Under plausible assumptions the increase in the value of legislation will exceed the increase in its cost, since a modest increase in the cost of enacting legislation could multiply manifold the length of the period in which the legislation was expected to remain in force" (Landes and Posner, 1975:879).

54. Presumably, Congress could eliminate the life tenure of judges, pack the Court, or limit its appellate jurisdiction.

55. For example, see *National Cable Television Association* v. *United States,* 415 U.S. 336 (1974), and *Kent* v. *Dulles,* 357 U.S. 116 (1958).

56. There may be several sources of imperfect information. As noted earlier, in the presence of a possible coalition of minorities or cyclical majorities, candidates might obfuscate their real public-policy intentions. Furthermore, citizens might not fully understand the manner in which proposed public-policy changes, even if adopted, would affect their welfare. See Fiorina, 1982b.

57. With the symmetric density in figure 4.4b, the results require that candidates operate only on the convex portion of the cumulative density.

58. The Supreme Court has probably eliminated legislative vetoes, in *Immigration and Naturalization Service* v. *Chadha,* 103 S. Ct. 2764 (1983).

59. There is a substantial incentive for jurisdictions to export taxes and higher costs to the extent that that is possible. Severance taxes on the mining of natural resources, taxation of foreign (i.e., out-of-state) corporations, and regulatory impositions on in-state producers of exported goods and services provide three examples of this phenomenon. Judicial nullification of these actions under the "negative commerce clause" provides only a partial and uncertain constraint on this process (see McLure, 1983). A radical decentralization of governmental functions, however, might create new possibilities for judicial review of these actions.

5

Pluralism in Its Place: State and Regime in Liberal Democracy

Stephen L. Elkin

The distinguishing feature of liberal democracies is the division of labor between market and state. Ownership of productive assets is largely placed in private hands, and major social decisions, including the pattern of work organization, industrial location, compensation for labor, and choice of industrial technology, are made through private exchange relations in which owners and managers are afforded a good deal of discretion (Lindblom, 1977, esp. pts. 3, 4, 5). Social well-being thus depends significantly on market transactions. Public officials, though they share responsibility for the level of citizen well-being with private controllers of assets, cannot command economic performance but can only induce it. The concern of public officials with the well-being of citizens stems from the organization of the state: public authority is subject to popular control, and a variety of devices—most importantly, elections—exist to foster the connections between citizen preferences and public action. In addition to elections, arrangements exist that protect citizens from arbitrary acts of officials and provide them with information sufficient to develop views about public affairs.

Once we recognize this division of labor, we commonly ask: What are the effects of this sort of property-based market system on such a state? The answer to this question in turn is typically treated as a matter of power—the respective power of business interests and other actors over public officials. Opinions are divided over whether business interests are the more powerful or whether a variety of other interests have a substantial effect on the actions of public officials (e.g., Bell, 1960; Dahl, 1961; Mills, 1956; Lowi, 1979; Domhoff, 1978; Rose, 1967). This focus on power either

179

leads to the view that popular control is insignificant, because business interests are said to dominate public action, or to an underestimation of the political importance of market exchange, private property, and business enterprise, because popular control is claimed to be sufficient to substantially constrain the serving of business interests. Both lines of argument are problematic: neither succeeds in giving sufficient weight to *both* market organization of production and distribution *and* to popular control of authority.

The relationship between market and popularly controlled state, however, is not essentially a matter of the power of actors. Much can be learned about their connection simply by considering that there *is* a division of labor: this is itself the most important thing in explaining the behavior of public officials. This division between market and popularly controlled state is the crucial characteristic of liberal democratic regimes. A regime is a complex of social practices that constitutes the way of life of the citizenry. These practices help to define the manner in which citizens are related to each other; they also imply standards of conduct that are necessary in order to keep those relations in repair. "Market" and "popular control" are designations for the two major sets of practices that constitute a liberal democratic regime. Instead of investigating then the *power* of business over state officials, the question posed here is: Given a regime that is characterized by a division of labor between market and popularly controlled state, how does this division affect the actual workings of the state?

Before considering the regime argument at length, we will examine in more detail the unpromising manner in which the relationship between market and state has most often been investigated. In particular, we will consider pluralist and elitist analyses, both of which are built around arguments concerning the power of actors. Discussion of the regime itself will then proceed in several steps.[1] First, and in particular contrast to pluralist-elitist arguments, we will establish that the division of labor between market and state means that public officials *do not need* to be *pressured* into serving business interests. Second, we will give popular control its due weight in explaining the operation of the state. The aim is to show that popular control both contributes to a concern for business performance and potentially impedes it.

Finally, we will look at the implications of the view that the liberal democratic state is shaped by both a concern for business performance and the fact of popular control. The principal implication is that the state is neither an arena nor a tool of domination. The liberal democratic state is a mixed state, and as such, not only does it mediate major interests, but it also embodies competing claims to just rule. The view of the liberal democratic state that emerges from the regime argument is: it is not

180

derivative of economic arrangements, but neither is it divorced from them. Differently stated, we understand more if we speak of "liberal democracy" rather than of "capitalism." On the one hand then, I want to resist taking a too-simple view of the importance of the market for liberal democratic politics—either by essentially ignoring it or by reducing it to the power of business actors. On the other hand, I want to resist the attractions of thinking that politics is something else, in this context—namely, a very complicated and elaborate handmaiden of capital accumulation.

It is worth emphasizing that although the argument is intended to apply to liberal democracies generally, its principal empirical frame of reference is the United States. With amendments, some of which are indicated, it can be applied to other cases.

PLURALIST AND ELITIST ARGUMENTS

Much of the American study of liberal democratic politics takes the view that politics is activity directly tied to the actions of government. The most prominent and forceful expression of this position is in pluralist theory. Lowi, for instance, characterizes the pluralist view as follows: "In the pluralist system, modern developments have brought about a discontinuity between that which is socio-economic and that which is political" (Lowi, 1979; original in italics). While there clearly are connections between politics and economics—organized business's political activities, protection of property rights, regulatory legislation, and so forth—the division of labor between market and state itself exerts no profound effects. Little or nothing about the actions of the state may be inferred or deduced from the existence of private ownership of productive assets. Empirical investigation is necessary, pluralists contend.[2] Even the observation that state authority is regularly used in liberal democracies in order to create and maintain markets does not often lead pluralists to the inference that the state is in some manner serving business interests. They often argue, instead, that while business power has been a danger to democratic control at various junctures, this danger has been contained through popular movements that succeeded in gaining hold of the levers of state authority. Rather than promoting the interests of property holders, state activity has often in fact been the principal vehicle for democratic control of business power.[3]

At the heart of this pluralist view of the relation between state and market is an understanding of politics in which the exercise of power by individuals, or by groups understood as aggregations of individuals, is central. Power itself is understood, roughly, as A getting B to do something that B otherwise would not do.[4] It is seen to be exercised in two contexts:

181

actors may contend over what is to be discussed, as well as over the action to be taken (see, e.g., Bachrach and Baratz, 1970; Cobb and Elder, 1972; Crenson, 1971). Contention may involve direct struggle, or results may be achieved at a distance, with historically given advantages playing a crucial role in both cases.

The building blocks of a pluralist conception of politics are the efforts of individuals and groups to realize their own projects.[5] These projects are said to reflect their interests, which are subjectively defined. Interests are psychological matters of desire and do not arise out of any objective features of the political-economic order.[6] Society and social structure are understood as being neutral backdrops against which these actors speak. At most they are terms used to designate the array of possible protagonists and allies; or they are summary terms for historically given advantages and disadvantages.[7] They have little or no independent explanatory status. Similarly, the state is seen as a neutral arena in which actors may settle their disputes, or as a neutral instrument that the various actors may be able to use in attempting to serve their interests. It may thus be seized for use by particular interests, or particular interests may be excluded from its use. In either case the state has no intrinsic qualities other than its inherent authority; any interest may, in principle, use it.[8]

"Actors" here can include public officials and governmental agencies. They, too, can be considered to have interests, in which service they may attempt to exert power. That they are public officials or agencies thus is incidental, an additional source of power. For these government actors, too, the state can be either arena or instrument,[9] at least if not all public officials are simultaneously driven by narrow self-interest.

In the pluralist view, then, the connection between market and state is understood primarily as a struggle among various actors, including businessmen, a variety of nonbusiness groups, and public officials. Government support of markets, the extent of government regulation, and similar matters are largely viewed as one of the products of conflict among the variety of interests. There is nothing intrinsic to the basic political and economic arrangements of the society that prevents public officials from acting against the deepest interests of businessmen. How well businessmen do in the battle over the use of state authority depends largely on how politically adept they and their adversaries are and on historically given advantages. Overall, business interests, though powerful, must compete with other groups and are not able consistently to shape state action to their purposes.

This view of politics—with individuals, their interests, and the struggles between them at the center and with the state as an arena and neutral instrument—is very much a part of liberal political theory. Of particular

182

interest in the present discussion is the adoption by pluralists of liberalism's conception of value as being a subjective interest or desire.[10] In such a subjective conception, we do not finally know what actors want unless they signify it through their behavior. Thus, when pluralists discuss power, they turn to analyses of behavior: without knowing what actors want, we can hardly talk about power. If liberalism's subjective conception of value is vulnerable, so is pluralism's understanding of power. And pluralism's analysis of the distribution of power is the foundation on which its interpretation of liberal democratic politics rests.

More important for present purposes, however, is the following peculiarity. While liberalism as a theory of politics is fundamentally concerned with property and the importance of the private realm, these have been left on the shelf in its pluralist version. The study of politics has been turned into the study of governmental process and the struggle between interests. It is therefore highly ironic that the version of liberal political theory that is embodied in pluralist thought should largely treat the political significance of business in terms of interest groups. That is its principal failure: it does not take its own liberalism seriously. Only half of society is intensively investigated, and the connection between public and private is conceived of as being little more than a question of the power of particular actors. It seems unlikely that the central fact of the division of labor between market and state can be so accommodated: market exchange, property, and business enterprise are pervasive features of liberal democracies, not merely a limited piece in an explanation of how the liberal democratic state operates.

The pluralist version of state-market relations in liberal democracy is, of course, not the only one. A common alternative is the ruling-class thesis, whose central premise is that businessmen are not just another interest, but also the most powerful one.[11] The influence that market exchange, private property, and business enterprise have on state action is construed in terms of the political power of an economic group. Proponents of the thesis, in fact, honor liberal thought with their dominating concern for the place of business, but the honor is a perverse one. They are perhaps best seen as disappointed liberals: they think in terms of actors and their power but argue that because business exerts such power, the claims of liberalism (particularly in its pluralist guise) that it enhance freedom are not met.

In its simplest form, the ruling-class thesis ties state action to market processes by positing a socioeconomic elite. This group is variously defined in terms of wealth, ownership or control of the means of production, or social status. The group is said to rule, both directly, through its members holding positions in the state, and indirectly, through agents who do its bidding or otherwise have coincident interests. Elaborate attempts may be made to show that this group or class is aware of its common interests and that it is able to communicate them to the necessary officials. The more sophisticated discussions also establish that the ruling group manages to serve its interests in the face of resistance by non-ruling-class types who have access to elections and other forms of popular control. Such arguments cite the ability of the ruling elite to eliminate resistance at its source by inducing a general outlook and a set of preferences consistent with ruling-class desires. Invoked also are more readily observable efforts to control the public agenda and to triumph in particular policy disputes. State action is in the service of class interest because there is a high-status, wealth-owning class that is powerful enough to see that it happens.

Formulated in this manner, the ruling-class thesis can clearly be seen to share major premises with pluralist theory: it sees the state as a set of levers to be grasped; major actors as interests (albeit differently defined); and the exercise of power by actors as the central political act (see Offe, 1974; also Poulantzas, 1973). In the pluralist view sketched above, these premises lead to the conclusion that no one interest dominates the state, even if some actors are more powerful than others. Proponents of the ruling-class view, of course, reach a different conclusion. The difficulty lies in sustaining it.

In the most favorable circumstances for the ruling-class thesis, class interests can be established,[12] and major opposition is silenced. If the thesis cannot be sustained under these conditions, its credibility is greatly weakened. But even then, the difficulties appear to be insuperable because an improbable degree of rationality on the part of the putative rulers is required. Rule in the ruling-class thesis depends heavily on a form of comprehensive planning that cannot be done (see, e.g., Braybrooke and Lindblom, 1970; Simon, 1976; Hayek, 1973; Banfield, 1961). The class, directly or through its agents, must be able to identify decisions that are crucial to its interests and to analyze them in sufficient detail to devise a course of action—all in a rapidly changing environment. The difficulties are patent.

The second important aspect of rule, which creates a cultural climate conducive to serving ruling-class interests, is probably less demanding of rational calculation, since it is not a matter of specific decisions but of general atmosphere. Still, a generalized investment problem presents itself to a putative ruling class if that class wishes to stay in business over time: What aspects of cultural transmission are crucial to maintaining the appropriate climate? But whether the existing cultural homogeneity can be explained by reference to so centralized a process is doubtful. Moreover, if we concede that cultural values are genuine and widespread, it is unclear in what sense the ruling class can be said to rule, at least in its own interests.

We may say, then, that if there is an aspiring ruling class, it may *try* to rule; but the complexity of social action will defeat it. This conclusion also suggests that all class arguments—including a ruling-class view—face another difficulty. In a complex, uncertain world, fundamental class interests, as such, are likely to have limited behavioral significance. The concrete interests of the actors are more likely to emerge out of social interaction than to be discovered through ratiocination. This has particular relevance for the ruling-class thesis, since interaction with public officials provides one way for the class to learn about its interests. The difficulty is that these interests will, to a large extent, be defined by public officials, who for a variety of reasons need to make sense out of what may often be inchoate demands and proposals. Agent and principal have undergone a reversal.

An additional difficulty with the ruling-class thesis is that it inevitably does not take proper account of popular control: class rule requires a clearing of the popular decks. Such a view is made suspect, however, by instances of successful popular mobilization in the face of business interests: for example, environmental and safety regulation most recently. Proponents of the ruling-class thesis might argue that some instances of rule are more important than others and that the class has the knowledge as well as the ability to act on it. Popular control is then not vitiated but is reduced to operating in areas where ruling-class interests are said not to be central. This argument requires heroic assertions about the sort of knowledge that a ruling class possesses and tends to make the argument drift into post hoc trivialities: if members of the ruling class did not fight over this matter, it is evidence that they did not need to.[13]

Arguments about social complexity and popular control need not, however, shatter the credibility of the ruling-class thesis. Proponents could attempt the difficult task of elaborating a conception of rule that would be expansive enough to accommodate various forms of indirect control without weakening assertions about class dominance. They might argue that businessmen are in a position akin to that of monopolists in the market.[14] As a group, they have substantial control over many of the resources—particularly organization, expertise, and finance—that public officials and citizens require in order to serve their own purposes. As a consequence, officials and citizens regularly turn to business organizations to accomplish public purposes, and businessmen thus find themselves in a favored position for serving their own interests. While this line of argument is promising, it finally leads to the regime argument that will be presented below. The ruling-class thesis, which turns on business power, is then transformed into a quite different argument in which public officials play the crucial role. On the other hand, if we stay within the boundaries of an argument about business power, treating monopoly as a source of power, the difficulties of accommodating the fact of popular control remain.

If the state in liberal democracies cannot be understood by examining actors and their respective power, what are the alternatives?[15] One alternative is to pursue an essentially functionalist approach, which argues, broadly, that capitalists on their own cannot carry out the necessary tasks for the continuation of a capitalist society. A variety of reasons might be suggested for this, an important one being that capitalists are, by their very nature, fragmented and competitive. They thus require the existence of an agency—the state—which must be autonomous enough to organize and assure continuity in the features that are necessary for the reproduction of the society. An obvious problem here is how to turn what is necessary in order for a result to occur into an explanation of its actual appearance, an objection that is common to functionalist arguments.[16] A more serious objection for present purposes is that all state actions, and politics more broadly, seem to become functional for capitalist reproduction.[17] This may not be inherent in the argument, but any attempt to show which actions are necessary for reproduction and then to explain why other sorts of actions arise—particularly, ones that are directed at impeding business interests—is likely to prove difficult.

It may be possible to argue that some measure of popular control is, in fact, an essential feature of the capitalist system and, thus, that when the state works to reproduce the system, it is doing more than serving the interests of capital. Unless this line of argument is developed considerably beyond its present position, however, we simply have an elaborate way of noting that in liberal democracies, popular control and the promotion of business interests can operate simultaneously.[18] We are still left with the theoretical problem of how the two are joined together in practice.[19] It is to this and related tasks that the discussion now turns.

THE REGIME ARGUMENT

We may best start by reiterating the opening remarks concerning the liberal democratic division of labor. Liberal democracy is a type of regime where the distinction between "public" and "private" is central, signifying the distinction between authority and production and how each is to be organized. When we talk about the regime, we are then referring to the basic organizing principles of the society. The state itself is the constitutional-legal entity that sets out the authoritative policies of the society and wields much of the organized means of coercion. The extent of its legitimacy may range anywhere from mere acquiescence to active support.

A state that is operating in a liberal democratic regime requires "satisfactory" economic performance from the private holders and managers of productive assets, and it needs this for at least two reasons.[20] First, most of its important officials are directly subject to popular approval through elections or indirectly through appointment by those who have been elected. Sustained poor performance, and thus low or declining levels of material well-being, will mean electoral difficulties and possibly electoral rout.[21] Even many of those whose appointments do not depend on electoral returns are also concerned about consistently poor economic performance, since it may result in an undesired rearrangement of their responsibilities.

Second, state activities require revenues, the production of which is not in the hands of state officials.[22] Economic performance to produce revenue is required for a variety of reasons, ranging from officials paying for their prerequisites to financing policies that are central to their careers and to their conception of larger national purposes. The performance of owners and managers of productive assets is of even more concern to the state to the degree that a substantial portion of national revenues originates through trading abroad. If the nation is highly integrated into the world economy, owners and managers in effect become public officials, helping to earn the nation's keep. So much is obvious. The implications are less so.

A first step towards seeing the implications is to summarize the preceding discussion as a basic premise of the liberal democratic state: officials of the state are beholden to the citizenry but cannot meet the citizens' concerns, serve their own careers, or manage the state without a satisfactory level of economic performance. Public officials cannot run the state without at least the tacit cooperation of owners and managers of productive assets. Of course, the extent of officials' concern will vary, not least because the citizens' interest in economic performance and their ability to forcefully express their views are subject to variation across space and time. Public officials *will*, however, be concerned about the level of economic performance.

None of this would be a problem if businessmen on their own would engage in the necessary activities. Economic performance would be high enough so as not to outrage citizens, and at least modest levels of state action would be possible. But whereas businessmen will clearly make some investments, take some risks, and employ some labor, even in difficult times, the great productive apparatus that is required to employ a growing population, to generate future investment capital, to provide public services, and otherwise to pay the public bill will not arise unaided. Commanding businessmen to perform will clearly not be sufficient, precisely to the degree they are guaranteed disposition over productive assets. As Lindblom puts it, owners and managers must be *induced* to perform, and public officials have long engaged in making such inducements (Lindblom, 1977, chap. 13). At the heart of the matter is likely to be the large scale of investment that is required and the high degree of uncertainty, which necessitate some fragile combination of the following: daring entrepreneurial vision—or at least ''animal spirits''—and the promise that risks can be controlled, that rewards will be high, and that compensation for failure is possible. These last three are at the center of the state's inducements to perform.[23]

Public officials therefore really have two tasks (Block, 1977). On the negative side, they must try to avoid reducing the confidence of businessmen. Low confidence means low investment. Erratic management of the currency or talk about nationalization will distress businessmen and make them less inclined to take risks. On the positive side, actual inducements must be offered. These may run from tax incentives and state provision of research money and research findings, to facilitating the granting of various permits. The latter may involve punishing rapacious officials and replacing them with those who will perform in nonarbitrary ways. Not only are the alternatives manifold; they can be organized in a variety of ways. In some liberal democratic states, everything may be accomplished centrally, while in others—the United States case being a conspicuous example—much will be done locally (see, e.g., Elkin, 1978). Thus, there are many ways to be concerned with economic performance, but once again, public officials *will* be concerned.

It is important to emphasize the differences between the view that is elaborated here and any theory built around the great power of owners and holders of productive assets. We might be tempted to conclude from the preceding discussion that the connection between market and state is much as the ruling-class thesis proposes, with perhaps a clearer understanding of just why property holders are so powerful. Public officials are more or less completely dependent on owners and managers for economic performance and thus are subject to manipulation: businessmen are powerful because they are needed, or so it would be argued. If there were no more than this to the regime argument, it would indeed be in danger of collapsing into an assertion about the power of actors. The essential feature of the liberal democratic regime, however, is not that owners and managers can exert power but is the very shape of the regime itself, particularly the division between market and popularly controlled state. Public officials do not have to be told to worry about economic performance or to facilitate it: they understand that for them to do their job as public officials, to stay in office, and to serve their ambitions, the owners and managers of productive assets must do *their* job.[24]

Differently stated, officials do negotiate with particular business interests, and power struggles may well result. But their real interest lies in the level of economic performance more generally, and that is not a matter of particular businessmen coordinating their efforts,[25] deciding to invest or not, and bargaining with or attempting to coerce government, but of large numbers of businessmen responding as individuals to market incentives.[26] Officials, then, are concerned with the workings of a social process, namely, the market. Indeed, if business-state relations consisted predominantly of officials dealing with business spokesmen who were in a position to coordinate the actions of large numbers of their fellows, power considerations would play a larger role in explaining state action. For in addition to business groups trying to extract particular concessions, other businessmen would be attempting more generally to press class interests.

There is another reason that the argument presented here is not essentially about power: the division between market and state is a two-way street. Businessmen are not unschooled in the workings of the political economy. They know that if they demand too much—and if they do it in a clumsy overweening fashion—their position may become precarious. For their part, public officials see the performance of owners and managers as a central question because the latter have a *choice*. They may, for example, consume substantial portions of their capital in ways that do little for future productivity, or they may export it. But the choice is theirs, because property rights are extensively enforced; if owners and managers do not exercise discretion, they may find that the basis for their choice has been eroded. To this we may add that the division between market and state means that those who control productive assets also require various state authorizations; this, too, is understood. To be sure, the disposition of businessmen to restrain their desires is probably less powerful than that of public officials to see that economic performance is substantial: the consequences for public officials are more proximate and tangible. But as public officials pursue their concerns about economic performance, they are likely to find businessmen exercising some restraint. In summary, it is the mix of popular control and the possibility of choice in the form of property rights that provides the underlying dynamic for business-state relations.

If the story were to end here, the relationship between public officials and controllers of assets would be close and intimate, or distant but amicable. Public officials would need only to maintain business confidence and, where appropriate, directly to facilitate performance. There would be little to prevent them from taking their cues from businessmen. Businessmen could happily be left to sort out among themselves what was necessary for their performance and to convey through various means the results of their deliberations. In some contemporary liberal democratic regimes this indeed may approximate present arrangements, and historically it may well have been true at one time of most. These cases must be explained, however, because it is not obvious why popular control of authority should only find expression in an essentially passive form—simply providing the motive for public officials' concern with economic performance—and should be confined to judging the overall results. Even if citizens agree that a substantial portion of the social product should be directed towards ensuring high levels of economic performance, the question of how much may be consumed and paid out in the form of wages and public benefits is likely to be a continuing source of dispute. And even if the mass of citizens have little sense of the connection between the present division of the social product and future performance, they will certainly have an opinion on what constitutes a fair division and how those who lose out should be treated.

This potential for conflict is built into the very arrangements of liberal democratic regimes. The very existence of public forums for consideration of the public's business invites the transformation into a public matter of what might initially be thought of as a private grievance. Furthermore, because the means of achieving satisfactory economic performance—namely, the market—will force citizens to change jobs, move, or otherwise greatly alter the basic features of their life circumstances—something that we may reasonably assume they do not wish to do—they will probably turn to the available instruments of popular control to prevent it. They will, for example, seek to constrain business choice, provide compensation to those who lose out, and resist aids to business performance that contribute to major alterations in basic features of their lives.[27] Perhaps it is the notion of a "free market" that blinds us to what is otherwise obvious. Having a choice between alternatives is freedom, the freedom of the marketplace. But the ability to keep one's life circumstances as they presently are is also freedom.[28] This the market does not offer. Citizens know this and act on the knowledge when possible.

In other words, citizens will inevitably be drawn towards employing institutions of popular control in ways that will make it more difficult for public officials and businessmen to arrive at any agreement, even a tacit one, about how economic performance is to be assured. The reasons for citizens so acting may be other than specified here; that is of no consequence. It matters only that they will inevitably be drawn to act in a fashion that will make it difficult to promote economic performance. That citizens also wish for economic growth is, of course, true. Indeed, as I have said, the concern of public officials for business performance partly rests on this wish. Popular control is, however, just that: citizen concern with the full range of public matters.

The extent to which citizens make known their views and press them with vigor will vary, but the potential is always present, requiring that measures be taken to ensure that popular control does not greatly interfere with the assessment of how to promote economic performance. Unless popular control is constrained, the liberal democratic regime will collapse or be transformed. Either private control of productive assets will be markedly reduced, or businessmen will cease to perform, or both. The means by which popular control is constrained and the degree of constraint that is achieved are the principal features that distinguish liberal democratic states from one another. A number of means are, however, common to all; they simply follow from basic features of liberal democracy and operate quite apart from conscious efforts to reduce the impact that citizens have on the relations between public officials and controllers of assets.

Consider, first, that the strength of popular control is in the electoral arena. The threat of electoral penalty strongly motivates officials; and indeed, without elections, other forms of popular control would be considerably less effective. But the potency of popular control diminishes the further we move from the electoral arena, and by the time we get to decisions made by executive agencies, it is clearly weak and indirect. Yet, the administrative arena can and does serve as a forum for negotiating at least some of businessmen's concerns and some of what they may wish for by way of inducement. Liberal democracy allows for the broad facilitation of economic performance simply because the reach of popular control is limited.

Additionally, even if the methods of maintaining business confidence and facilitating performance appear on the public agenda, owners and managers have fundamental advantages in the discussion. As is already apparent, they need not press for access to public officials; the most visible of them may even be solicited. Moreover, the very fact of owning productive assets provides controllers of these assets with the solution to a problem that other interests must struggle with and indeed may not master. Opinion without benefit of organization and other resources is weak. Business enterprises, especially larger ones, are, however, already organizations with a complement of human and financial resources that may be employed to pursue other than business ends.

Finally, it is not only public officials who realize that social well-being depends heavily on business performances; so, inevitably, do many citizens, to whom businessmen appear to be more than a sectoral interest. This, plus a natural tendency to approve of those who flourish under the existing social rules, provides a substantial reservoir of positive opinion upon which public officials and businessmen may rely.

One implication of these built-in advantages must be emphasized: they operate with a kind of historical carry-over. As a group of citizens at a given

191

moment attempt to offer an assessment of the distribution of the social product, they are, for example, attempting to do so in the context of a set of institutional arrangements. These arrangements are themselves at least partly the results of historical disputes in which the built-in advantages have operated. In short, the built-in advantages cumulate. This has the simple but profound consequence that the ordinary flow of public action works to screen out challenges. Those citizens, for example, who think that the operation of banking laws is unnecessarily weighted in favor of promoting business performance not only must object to particular actions but must also undo the institutional arrangements that created the agencies to take the actions.

Even as there are, however, certain features of liberal democratic states that work to limit the expression of popular control, citizens will still offer assessments of how to deal with the question of economic performance. Expressions of citizens' opinions are constrained, rather than squashed, not least because there will always be available some public officials who derive advantage from mobilizing citizens to challenge the present form of concern for business performance. However, there will be limits to the number of public officials so inclined and to the distance that they will be willing to travel. This is, after all, a dangerous road, since a citizenry that is in full cry may come to look askance at the present institutional arrangements that the existing, as well as the aspiring, officials wish to help manage. Additionally, even combative disaffected politicians are likely to be leery of inducing deep dismay in businessmen, since eventually these politicians either will have to operate a political economy in which businessmen are central or will have to deal with the consequences of poor performance that attend any major transformation. In their turn, however, businessmen are likely to recognize that officials must be seen to be responsive to strong expressions of citizen opinion, quite apart from any preference they have in the matter.

It will help to summarize the argument to this point. The facts of private control of productive assets and popular control of authority mean that public officials are inevitably drawn to promote economic performance. Because promoting satisfactory performance requires at least the tacit cooperation of controllers of productive assets (they will not do what is necessary on their own), their definition of what is required to gain the desired result will weigh heavily in the choices that officials make. Even though controllers of assets may not always agree among themselves or with public officials on what will serve economic performance, such agreement is not necessary for us to say that inevitably the state broadly serves business interests.

When we say then that the state promotes business interests, we are making two closely related but distinct points. First, officials are concerned about economic performance, and in their efforts to facilitate it, they attempt to see that business enterprise will flourish. Of course, particular enterprises will suffer at any given moment, but the aim is to see that in a general way, controllers of assets will reap enough rewards to induce them to continue performing at a satisfactory level. Second, in their efforts to facilitate performance, the actual definition of what is necessary is heavily shaped by what businessmen say is required. For both of these reasons, the interests of owners and controllers of assets are well served.

Public officials, however, are not unconstrained in their concern for economic performance, because citizens may and do offer their own assessments on such matters as the distribution of the social product. But basic features of regime and state operate to prevent any regular complication of the complex mutual accommodation between controllers of assets and public officials. Breaches of these limits do sometimes occur, but in no way do they alter either the disposition of public officials to facilitate economic performance or the prominent role of businessmen in defining what this requires.

The practices of public officials give actual content to the formal institutions that are crucial to operating the state. By their efforts to pay attention both to businessmen's definitions of how to promote economic performance and to assertions of popular control, public officials make possible the coexistence of contradictory claims. They in fact lead an elaborate minuet. If there are limits on popular control, but a danger that such limits may be breached, how is business performance to be maintained? If businessmen demand too much to perform, including a substantial reduction in the exercise of popular control, what will prevent a shift from citizen acquiescence to mass mobilization?

Neither overweening businessmen nor a citizenry that is in full democratic cry can be accommodated for very long in a liberal democratic state. Ambitious politicians who are bent on exciting the citizenry need to be reminded by their peers of the consequences of excessive incitement for the state as a whole: businessmen will reduce their performance. Businessmen who are attempting to have most or all of their dealings with the state handled administratively, out of citizen view, or who are resisting democratic prerogatives to control market behavior need to be reminded that failure to concede some regulation raises the possibility of even greater efforts at popular control. They also need to be reminded that national security may demand that their prerogatives be curbed. Citizens need to be reminded that even as efforts are being made to protect and promote their ability to participate in politics, so that they may be a credible deterrent to the more greedy and overbearing among owners and managers, the health of society depends on business investment.

There is no guarantee, however, that officials will prove capable of managing the state in the manner just indicated or of maintaining these practices over time. The incentives to do so—which presumably include some mix of approval of the regime's features, of the state that has been built on them, and of a desire to pursue a career within such a state—are diffuse and long-term. Short-term gains are tempting because of their promise of immediate tangible rewards. Encouraging businessmen who think they need more inducements to invest, or exciting already mobilized citizens to demand even more, is probably easier than reminding either of them about what is required to run a liberal democratic state. In any case, even if most public officials were to take the longer view, they might be incompetent or overwhelmed by the uncertainty of social affairs. Perhaps more importantly, a vital liberal democratic state rests on more than having public officials manage state institutions. At the least, the desire for popular control must be continually renewed outside of state institutions, as must the desire individually to accumulate capital, which lies at the heart of the enterprise-based market. For any or all of the above reasons, the balance between popular control and the promotion of business performance may shift enough to transform the liberal democratic state and the regime on which it rests. This line of argument will be pursued further in a later section.

Our sketch of a theory of the liberal democratic state is not yet complete.[29] The discussion has centered on the state's facilitating economic performance, and the significance of popular control has been largely interpreted in this light. Such a focus, while it is essential to any state theory, leaves too much unsaid. We cannot yet differentiate, for example, between policy making concerning tax incentives to stimulate investment and the protection of civil liberties, nor are we yet clear as to whether all state actions that might in some way facilitate economic performance are to be treated equally. Unless we can elaborate the theory further, we will inevitably be drawn into increasingly implausible assertions about the actions of public officials and the controllers of assets, since virtually all policy choices in one way or another potentially impinge on economic performance. If we mean to argue that the state inevitably facilitates economic performance, we must show that this does not mean that all aspects of public action are equally relevant to this concern. At issue is the extent to which the interests of business dominate across the spectrum of policy domains and, concomitantly, the extent to which popular control, and thus a variety of other than business concerns, shapes policy discussion (see Stone, 1980, 1981).

Given the argument outlined so far, the connection made by public officials and businessmen between economic performance and any particular policy question is a good first step towards explaining this variation across policy domains (Stone, 1980; Elkin, 1980). A well-understood connection will more readily focus the thinking and action of public officials and will make them more receptive to the approaches of business spokesmen. By the same token, owners and managers will take some trouble to indicate their preferences in the matter. Moreover, if the process of mutual accommodation between public officials and businessmen spills out into the public arena, officials are more likely to resist proposals that are offered by citizen spokesmen as they (officials) attempt to arrive at a course of action aimed at actually facilitating economic performance.

If no close connection is perceived, public officials are more likely to be guided by the variety of interest group and broader citizen concerns. But state action is still not completely free of the interests of business, as may also be inferred from the propositions already advanced. When policy choice involves complex implementation of programs and when business organizations that are capable of carrying them out are already in existence, public officials will be drawn to options that make use of such organizations. The officials' desire to be successful, whether in terms of career or larger purposes, impels them in this direction. The very fact of private ownership creates this incentive (Stone, 1980). A revealing example here is the American preference for health-insurance schemes that rely on private insurers. In addition, of course, the relevant business enterprises themselves are likely to promote private alternatives, and businessmen in general argue that economic performance is itself at stake. Still, when the connection between the policy at issue and economic performance is seen to be weak, the pulling and hauling characteristic of a developed interest-group politics is most likely to occur. It is then that business groups are one among many. The other typical form of politics under these conditions is the coziness of "iron triangles."

Perhaps the best way to see the connection between these two types of policy domains (where economic performance is and is not seen to be at issue) is to note the rapidity with which iron triangles, or vital contests between equally matched interest groups, can turn into a discussion dominated by a concern with the interests of business. On their own, businessmen probably cannot bring about such a rapid shift and, indeed, may lose out to other interests; but once public officials believe that economic performance is at stake, the transformation of one sort of policy domain into another can be quick indeed.

It is important to emphasize that the proposition "The state promotes business interests" is not first and foremost an assertion about the outcome of a series of decisions but about the disposition of public officials to facilitate economic performance and why they are likely to be guided by businessmen in this regard. Empirically, the concern for business interests is likely to dominate a wide range of outcomes, but businessmen can and do lose. It is perhaps most revealing of the nature of the argument being presented that, in comparison to pluralist or ruling-class views, it is not essentially an argument about the exercise of power. It is most assuredly an argument about advantage (but not only that, as we shall see). However, the promise of the theoretical argument is precisely that we can now see the state as being active and independent, neither neutral in its actions nor up for grabs in a scramble for power among interests. *And* we can say all of this without having to rely on implausible arguments about concentrated power and its exercise; the arguments follow from the very character of the regime. Pluralist views of liberal democratic politics go astray in that they do not take the regime seriously as it shapes the actions of the state. The ruling-class thesis goes astray in thinking that the impact of the regime can be reduced to a study of the power of a business elite; that is, in a different manner, the thesis does not take the regime seriously.

The shift away from explanations that rely on the power of actors is part of a larger and common theme in social science: the search for systemic explanations. Aside from the shortcomings already noted, the *form* of actor-power explanations is inadequate. Both pluralist and ruling-class notions are essentially simple causal explanations, dealing in efficient causes. They locate an agent or agents who are supposed, by their actions, to produce an outcome. The regime argument directs our attention to the character of the whole and says, in effect, "Don't look for particular actors and efficient causes." A state of affairs is not explained by an agent and its actions but by the set of relations in which the agent is embedded. The explanation of why the state serves business interests is not only *not* business power, *neither* is it, at bottom, the disposition of public officials. Businessmen have an attentive audience, and officials are disposed in particular ways because of the very form of the regime.[30]

IMPLICATIONS OF THE REGIME ARGUMENT

We now have sufficient understanding of the workings of the liberal democratic state, built upon a regime argument, to consider some of its implications and thus to make a preliminary assessment of its promise.

We can start by indicating how the regime argument helps us interpret the rise of the welfare state. We can now see that the welfare state is not necessarily a way station to anything else but is, in fact, simply one of the

196

historical forms that liberal democratic politics and the liberal democratic state have taken. At their center, the welfare state and the managed economy still have public officials who are concerned with promoting business performance. Also, popular control is still limited, even though citizens are perhaps better able to articulate independent conceptions of what promotes economic activity. The story of change in the twentieth century is a liberal democratic story, even as it has revealed some of the possible variations on that theme.

In the same vein, as the state has become increasingly involved in aiding and regulating business enterprise, managing the business cycle, and distributing benefits to citizens, there has been considerable discussion about the increase in the scope of government (see, e.g., Crouch, 1979; Gough, 1979; O'Connor, 1973; Weinstein, 1968). Is this increase the result of struggle by ordinary citizens or a means by which capitalists have sought to deal with their difficulties?

To use present terms, did it grow out of assertions of popular control or concern for business performance? On the basis of the preceding analysis, we can see how both have been at work and how politicians have probably played a central role in effecting the changes. Over time there have been shifts in the degree to which citizens have been organized to press their assessment of economic performance and how it might be facilitated. Politicians have been instrumental both in stimulating this organization and in using it to convince businessmen that economic performance could be enhanced by various forms of state-provided economic and social security. They have also indicated that in the absence of such concessions, citizens might offer even more troublesome assessments of economic performance and how it might be promoted. Similarly, politicians have also shaped and interpreted cues from businessmen about the kinds of public action that would induce satisfactory economic performance. Any story that interprets the rise of positive welfare-oriented states as the means by which either capitalists solved their problems or the working class dealt with theirs overlooks that it is more nearly a case of liberal democratic politicians solving *theirs*.[31]

This line of argument can be extended to clarify the status of pluralist politics, whether we mean a more or less vigorous pluralism (Wilson, 1979) or interest-group liberalism and the private appropriation of public authority (Lowi, 1979). Interest groups are revealed as being one of the forms that popular control has taken in such states. More important, we can see that the mobilization of interests in various forms, though real, cannot be the central form of political activity, as is implied by pluralist theories of politics. Citizens *do* present assessments of economic performance and of how satisfactory levels may be achieved; businessmen *do* try to protect their prerogatives and argue for a variety of inducements to perform. And indeed, a whole array of interests press their cases. But all of this takes place within the broader activity that follows from the character of the regime. Conflict between the different interests has an important place, but it is not at center stage. That is reserved for the intricate process of accommodation between businessmen, public officials, and citizens concerning the terms under which economic performance will be facilitated and business interests will be served.

In general, neither pluralism *nor* well-developed social-welfare programs are inconsistent with the state's having an inevitable concern for business interests. The welfare state leaves intact the major features of the liberal democratic state; pluralism as a form of popular control also leaves intact the concern for business interests and the limits on citizen assertiveness.

An additional advantage of the view of the state presented here is that it helps us to sort out a number of claims that have been made concerning business-state relationships in liberal democracies. First, those who argue that the state is in the service of capital—whether as an agent or in some other way that is central to the reproduction of capitalism—are likely to have difficulty with the suggestion that state action is in fact adding to present economic difficulties (Bowles and Gintis, 1980). Given recent economic performance among liberal democracies, however, it is useful to allow for the possibility that the state will be capitalism's gravedigger. The argument outlined here has the room. Within its terms we can simultaneously say that the state must be devoted to facilitating business performance, even as public officials may, in fact, get it all wrong, and as a result performance declines.

Second, we can make sense of businessmen's assertions that state action is not helping economic performance, even as we argue here that the state inevitably aims to help it. State officials are at various junctures likely to arrive at independent judgments about what is necessary for satisfactory performance and may insist for a considerable time to businessmen that businessmen are the ones who have it all wrong. As a consequence, businessmen may lose struggles over gaining new prerequisites or protecting existing ones and, believing that these prerequisites are necessary to economic performance, may conclude that public officials do not share their concern for the economy. At various times, moreover, public officials may do for businessmen what they cannot do for themselves—namely, devise a plan of action that will overcome the diversity of their interests and their short time horizons.

More generally, two common and seemingly diametrically opposed observations about the present character of business-state relations can now be reconciled. Some observers contend that the state is promoting capital, while others argue that businessmen feel constrained and overwhelmed by an expansive state. We can now say that there is some truth in both observations. The state may assert a conception of how to facilitate business performance that businessmen find disagreeable; and the state will assert and indeed attempt to act on such a conception—if that is what the workings of popular control require at the moment. Businessmen in liberal democracies are not a ruling class that dominates the state, nor are they merely a particularly powerful interest group. But then, neither is the state neutral with regard to the well-being of business. The liberal democratic state cannot be captured in any of these simplifications.

On more concrete matters, the regime argument also turns out to be helpful in explaining some of the fundamental features of making policy decisions. Even if the characterization of the state activity presented above proves to be no better at accounting for particular policy outcomes than, say, a more standard combination of bureaucratic and interest-group politics, it has some significant advantages.[32] Most important, we can account for some central aspects of the pattern of policy discussion itself. Being able to explain the subject and the form of policy discussion is at least as important as being able to explain the actual outcomes, because outcomes are often strongly influenced by the former.

The regime argument suggests, for example, that the central concern of public officials and businessmen is not that business interests dominate policy decisions but that they always be present. Public officials and businessmen may rest reasonably satisfied as long as the basic relationships that prompt and allow officials to be particularly attentive to business concerns remain intact. Less obviously, the regime argument also affords us insight into the centrality of courts and regulation in liberal democratic policy discussions.[33]

A danger in liberal democratic politics is that facilitating economic performance might be viewed as nothing more than the promotion of a particular interest. If this view becomes widely accepted, the state becomes increasingly difficult to operate. The problem recedes, however, to the degree that institutions of popular control direct public officials to engage in such activities, most obviously by passing laws to this end. We thus witness the growth of legislation that is supposed to express public sentiment about public matters but that is visibly designed to benefit the business sector. This, in turn, is justified by the assertion that the health of this sector is particularly valuable to the whole community. Nevertheless, this approach is inherently precarious, not least because others may try to press the claim that their performance is essential too. The dilemma is that institutions of popular control may soon not be perceived as such at all; and public officials

Stephen L. Elkin

who are anxious to face down overweening businessmen in the name of the larger community may discover that they are trying to do so within institutions that only respond to particular claims.

Legislation, in any case, is a cumbersome instrument if the problem is a repetitive one. Hence, a major part of the burden of reconciling a concern for business performance and popular control passes to regulatory agencies (or their equivalents) and to the courts. It now becomes clearer why in liberal democracies—especially when facilitating business performance has turned into direct promotion—regulatory agencies and the courts are central institutions. They carry out a fundamental task of the liberal democratic state and will *inevitably* be criticized. Voices will be heard, on the one hand, saying that regulatory agencies are acting as custodians of business interests and need to be strengthened as agents of popular control (Nader and Green, 1976); on the other hand, many will argue that the agencies do not promote business interests because they are either self-serving (Wilson, 1980) or have been captured by those who, in the service of some vague public interest, wish to impede business performance (Weaver, 1978). Similar criticisms are and will be made about the courts, which have the unenviable task of interpreting many of the regulations that are issued (see Elliot, 1974; Glazer, 1975; Chayes, 1976; Freedman, 1978). Over time, then, policy discussion in liberal democracies assumes a pattern, as criticisms of the means to reconcile business performance and popular control become regularized and even stylized. The means themselves eventually seem to lose their virtue. A pattern of "let's try this"—only to discover that we have tried it once before—becomes apparent.[34] The particular policy outcomes themselves are likely to be less important than the fact that the same problems keep reappearing, with the same solutions attached and with the same criticisms that the solutions are not adequate.

Two often-noted features of reform efforts in liberal democracies now also come into view. State control of business corporations has increased, and popular control has been expanded, at least with regard to particular matters. Reform, then, is clearly possible. This is consistent with what conventional views of liberal democracy teach us—namely, that through organized exertion, political and economic arrangements may be noticeably altered. Such changes, however, are not easily accommodated with a ruling-class analysis except at the cost of eviscerating the argument. Nor are the apparent limits to reform easily explained by talking about the general play of interests, and particularly about the power of organized business to resist. Once we have understood the disposition of public officials and its source in the division of labor, the obstacles in the way of substantial reform become apparent, as do the inadequacies of pluralist and ruling-class accounts of its characteristic pattern in liberal democratic states.

200

Most important of all, the regime argument makes it clear that the state is not an extension of class war by political means. The implications of this understanding reach beyond the particular point. It is in the extensions of this, normative, analysis that the real power of the regime argument becomes apparent.

We have already argued that the state is neither a neutral arena nor merely an instrument of domination by a powerful class. Might it not, however, be a battle ground for large-scale interests into whose service public officials have been recruited? The practices that we have described—broadly, of public officials promoting economic performance while at the same time responding to assertions of popular control—might lend themselves to such an interpretation. The state might be seen as an ensemble of activities embodying the struggle between those who are striving to create a new political economy and those who are working to protect the existing arrangements, of which they are the major beneficiaries—in short, a struggle between labor and capital.

This is, in fact, a tempting interpretation, precisely because the liberal democratic state does seem to have contending forces at its heart. If we were to adopt it, however, the state would become the realm of "unfreedom" (Kelly, 1979), just as much as if it were merely an instrument of domination by a powerful class. The fact that the struggle may be a relatively even one between two (or more) interests does not alter the fact that it is a struggle for domination. Nor does anything fundamentally change if we root for one side to win. The prize is still the chance to use the state to further class (or other) interests.

The problem remaining is to establish the credibility of yet another alternative: the state is neither a neutral, passive arena nor only a potential or actual instrument of domination. If we look more closely at the political practices described earlier, this alternative comes into view. Starting from the idea of a regime will help us to see that the liberal democratic state is a mixed state in the sense that it embodies at least two genuine claims to rule.

C. B. Macpherson provides a useful beginning point.[35] He characterizes the political practices that are associated with the concern for economic performance as being liberal. The central impulse of liberalism is the promotion of individual choice. A primary vehicle for the exercise of such choice, he argues, is a market system based on private property, although liberalism has also been concerned with such rights as the exercise of the franchise and of free speech. Liberal advocates have also praised ambition and the desire to accumulate wealth as being integral features of a society that rests on individual choice. Liberal political practice then, we may say, is devoted to supporting the realization of market and political choice (Sartori, 1965; Friedman, 1962). A concern for economic performance is a liberal practice, because it rests on promoting to high levels the operation of property rights and free exchange in the marketplace.[36]

Popular control, by contrast, is best understood as embodying democratic political practices. The central democratic impulse is participatory. Its emphasis is communal—collective rule by all—not individualistic; and its preeminent theorist is Rousseau, just as liberalism's is Hobbes. The democratic impulse is also egalitarian, because rule by all requires not only political equality but also economic equality sufficient not to vitiate the premise of equal participation. Its egalitarianism may also spring more directly from discussions of what constitutes a fair distribution of wealth. Clearly, the democratic impulse is a potentially far-reaching one, but for reasons that are partially enumerated or implied above, its embodiment in liberal democracies is restricted to what we have termed popular control— or democracy as method rather than substance[37]—and the extent of that has, in turn, been circumscribed.

To call the political practices that are associated with the operation of popular control "democratic" is not to deny that there has been a substantial convergence between liberalism and democracy around some of the desirable features of the state. The observation about democracy as method suggests the point. Both liberalism and democracy promote free elections, a variety of political rights, and civil liberties. But such agreement on particulars does not mean that liberals and democrats share fundamental concerns. The democratic impulse is not limited to the forms of popular control that we have described, and the potential issue of the democratic impulse, even in its limited form, is a substantial restructuring of property rights and market operations. Similarly, the distinctive claim of liberalism is that it promotes individual choice and employs state action in ways that are least damaging to that individualism, even if extensive activity by that state may be called for.

Nothing that has been said so far rules out the possibility that the liberal and democratic practices that I have described are no more than polite names to cloak efforts to dominate. We might be merely talking about the struggle between capitalists and proletarians and thus be back to a version of the idea of the state as unfreedom. The regime argument would then teach us that the state is not merely in the service of capital, but the argument could do no more.

The question at issue is how we may know that when liberal or democratic claims are made, they are not only attempts to gain advantage but are genuine assertions about how political rule should be organized. Since the question is a central one in political theory, it can hardly be settled here. But we can start by pointing to some historical evidence. Liberalism was understood—certainly by its principal early advocates—to be more than a claim that individual freedom and property holding should be advanced; it was also a claim about a freer society altogether. Similarly, the theorists of democracy clearly thought they were arguing not only for a class interest but also for a society in which men would more likely be free and would more nearly realize their potential (see Macpherson, 1966). In the contemporary world, the efforts that are made by public officials in liberal democracies to facilitate business performance are translated, in some quarters at least, into a concern for fostering ambition, individual freedom, and the accumulation of wealth—all of which are understood to be elements of the common good. Similar translations of efforts to extend popular control are also made.

There is, however, a more theoretical point to make. Politics is not a private affair, taking place in the closet. As Hanna Pitkin comments, "there is no such thing as private politics, intimate politics" (1972:204). Politics is essentially a public activity, and as such, it is an activity in which justification is essential: I am unlikely to gain any adherents if I claim that a particular mode of organizing the society advances *my* interests only. Nor can I hope to run a society only by physical force, because even armies must have adherents and because, in any case, force has limits as a durable mode of social coordination. In short, I must talk in terms of *our* interests, about why promoting virtues such as the ones that I and others possess is good for *us* as a community. There is, of course, nothing to prevent someone from proceeding in completely cynical fashion, simply casting around for a doctrine that has a large enough appeal to suit his or his group's purposes. If he continues to assert his doctrine, however, even as its popularity is lapsing, this seems more likely to stem from genuine belief in its merits than from tactical considerations directed at maintaining his following.[38]

The doctrines of liberalism and democracy, then, are not only concerned with who should rule—and thus about advantage—but about how they should do so and why. Both particular interests and public interests are being asserted. Similarly, liberal and democratic practices are more than attempts to promote particular interests; they express claims about just rule.

If we are willing to concede this, the liberal democratic state does indeed become a genuine mixed state. We may call it "democratized liberalism" (Macpherson, 1966; Sartori, 1965, chap. 15), an appellation that gives pride of place to liberalism but that clearly identifies popular control as being a vital force. This is an important conclusion, because it helps us to avoid the temptation of seeing liberal democratic politics as a morality play. Rather than a struggle between progress and reaction, or between the general interest and particular interests, or between any variation on these themes, liberal democratic politics becomes precisely that intricate minuet

Stephen L. Elkin

that I described earlier. The minuet now has an important additional feature: that of maintaining a state that embodies competing, widely shared normative claims. Liberal democratic politicians are neither mere power brokers, moving between various interests, nor spokesmen for class interests. More important, they are the central actors who are engaged in the mixing of competing and attractive claims to rule.[39] In the story of liberal democratic politics, pride of place must go, not to interests and classes, but to the institutions of the state as they are operated by public officials (cf. Huntington, 1968, chap. 1).

Understanding the liberal democratic state as a mixed state is not only valuable in itself; it also points to a weakness in current theoretical discussions of a possible legitimation crisis in market-oriented societies. Some theorists treat democratic institutions as providing an imprimatur. They are presented as a source of legitimation for what otherwise might lack it, namely, the accumulation of capital and the promotion by the state of economic performance. In this view, *liberal* political practices are the beneficiaries of legitimation, not a part of it. Legitimation is seen as a kind of function, something that the state does in order to keep itself and the larger regime intact. In particular, democratic forms, symbols, and even democratic substance are understood to be products that are produced in order to allow something else to happen.[40] To be sure, these theorists admit that governing through democratic forms is risky, because the electorate may take democracy seriously; but this chance must be taken, since liberal practices such as promoting economic performance are said to lack legitimacy.[41]

The complement to this view of democratic institutions focuses on another product as crucial for legitimation, namely, economic growth. Both views see the state as being a machine that is manufacturing a kind of political widget in the form of so many units of legitimation. But as we have said, the liberal democratic state is in fact an intricate set of practices that are both claims for advantage and claims about how the community should be ruled. The acts of legitimation, then, are the state itself in motion. Legitimation is not a *product* of the state; in a real sense, it *is* the state—at least to the degree that the practices are indeed freely expressed claims about how the community should be ruled. As Bernard Crick remarks, "the moral consensus of a free state is not something mysteriously prior to or above politics: it is the activity (the civilizing activity) of politics itself" (1964:24).[42]

With these remarks about legitimacy in mind, we can assess some current proposals on how to respond to the present decline in economic growth and productivity.[43] Some on the Left seem to talk as if their only real interest was to extend democratic practices. In the work place, for

204

example, they seem not to notice that any decline in legitimacy that follows from reduced growth can be met not only by increased democratization but also by putting greater emphasis on the heart of liberal practices, namely, individual choice. Citizens who have a sense of freedom in their daily lives— who are, in a word, involved in liberal practices (which, translated, might mean fewer regulated markets)—may be less concerned about declines in growth. Of course, many promoters of corporate well-being seem not to understand this either: liberal practices are not just instruments to promote high growth and profits; they are also forms of relation between citizens which embody a (partial) way of life. Many on the Right seem also not to recognize that citizens who are involved in democratic practices are probably more likely to accept modest levels of real income.[44]

The preceding remarks about legitimation also suggest that the decline in liberal and democratic practices is in itself a principal source of the legitimation problem. An increase in either of these practices is not easy to imagine, because the growth of large-scale public and private organizations has meant that relationships between citizens are increasingly being defined by organizational roles. The extent to which state action is tied to the requirements of bureaucratic organizations has increased markedly, and while citizens may be told and may tell each other that these are really liberal and democratic practices, the reality is otherwise. Legitimation, which arises from citizens' being related to each other in liberal and democratic ways, is thus corroded, particularly since an ethic for a bureaucratized politics seems difficult to develop (cf. Unger, 1975). The liberal democratic state is made more precarious because the growth of bureaucratic organizations makes it even more difficult for politicians to mix liberal and democratic practices.

The crisis of liberal democracy, however, cuts even deeper than the rise of administration. Once again, seeing liberal democracy as a mixed state is helpful. The state may be able to survive problems of declining productivity and capital accumulation, fiscal undernourishment (see O'Connor, 1973), overloading (see Huntington, 1968), and disaggregation (see Wilson, 1980). These all cut deep, but because they are probably imbalances within existing arrangements, profits can be raised, interest aggregation can be increased, and citizen mobilization can be reduced and a crisis thus averted. There may be "structural" reasons why necessary actions are difficult: for example, to do one thing may make other things worse. This would be serious indeed if it could be demonstrated. But potentially more serious would be a decline in the basis of liberal democratic politics itself (and in the possibility of any acceptable form of politics). Liberal democratic legitimation depends on the continuation of a public or political community that is itself increasingly precarious.

Liberal and democratic claims are addressed to a public, to the presumed beneficiaries of just rule. Liberal democracy is an unstable compound, not only because it requires assiduous efforts by politicians but also because conflict really exists between liberal and democratic claims to rule. Liberalism, as it is commonly defined, requires that coercion by all agencies—including the state—be kept to a minimum, while democratic ideas tend to promote an expansive state. The fact that these are claims about justice for the whole political order and that they are subject to compromise may soften the conflict between them but does not eliminate it. The specter of the state as unfreedom is not so easily dismissed.

To keep the compound both stable and acceptable, something else is required. Consider what happens when belief starts to disappear in the public to whom liberal and democratic claims are addressed. This may occur because widely shared belief in the possibility of having any evaluation at all disappears or because there is no longer any sense of a public or larger community to exercise that judgment. If belief in a public capable of evaluation fades, liberal democratic politics degenerates.[45] At a minimum, the effort to clothe self-interest that is induced by the knowledge that others will be asserting broadly couched claims will decline. Degeneration becomes more pronounced as politicians lose interest in maintaining the institutions that make possible the mixing of liberal and democratic claims. The politicians' exploitation of the nooks and crannies of public authority for their own advantage then really begins to flourish. At the same time, citizens increasingly come to believe that the only purpose of political institutions is to confer advantage.[46] The result? Politics increasingly degenerates into a crude pluralist or crude Marxist fantasy that sees no further than my interest and yours, my class and yours. How a liberal democratic politics can survive in such circumstances is not clear. For the truth of the matter is that it cannot. If a liberal democratic state is to survive, the political community or public must be seen as a source of evaluation. Just how this is be done is less clear.

The analysis can be extended to the regime. After all, the market itself—just as much as efforts by the state to facilitate economic performance—and the institutions of popular control themselves—just as much as the liberal and democratic practices that are the state in action—embody assertions about how the society should be justly organized. The regime is *political* just as much as the state. In either case, a picture of men who are worried only about themselves would be as much a curiosity as one in which they only worried about justice. Both state and regime join together the exercise of power and the search for common purposes. As such, they must rest on a conviction that it is possible to reason about the best ways to carry out such an endeavor.

NOTES

This paper builds on ideas that were first presented by Charles E. Lindblom (1977). Lindblom's theoretical concerns, purposes, and language are somewhat different, but it was by coming to terms with his arguments that I was able to write this essay. For an initial effort, see Elkin (1982).

In a recent paper (1980) my colleague Clarence Stone has arrived at formulations similar to some of the ones presented here. As we discussed the central ideas over several years, it is not easy to say where his ideas leave off and my own begin. Suffice it to say, the present paper could not have been written without him. Others who have contributed to the formulations here include Fred Alford, Don Babai, Diana Elkin, Ira Katznelson, Joe Oppenheimer, Ron Terchek, and Alan Wolfe.

1. The discussion here thus *starts from* the division of labor, i.e., from the regime. Aside from positing the reality of market exchange, the argument assumes the minimal operation of popular control. Officials must actually stand for office, with competition allowed. Elections must not be marred by widespread coercion and corruption, and some modest level of information about public affairs must be available. For an expanded list and general discussion see Dahl (1970). While such minimal conditions are not widespread, these are not heroic assertions about most Western societies.

It is also worth emphasizing that there are other questions to ask than the one posed here. We might, for example, inquire into whether a particular type of state is suitable to a market system based on private ownership, or we might wonder about the historical connection between popular control of authority and such market arrangements or about the origins of property-based market systems and of popular control. All are important areas of inquiry in their own right.

2. Cf. Polsby's (1980) comment on the study of community power: "The first and most basic presupposition of the pluralist approach is that nothing categorical can be assumed about power in any community."

3. Galbraith (1956) provides an exemplary rendition of this argument.

4. See Dahl's early formulation (1957) and the discussion by Lukes (1974).

5. To a greater or lesser degree these views and the ones that follow are embodied in Polsby (1980), Dahl (1961), Lowi (1979), Olson (1965), Wilson (1973), and Sayre and Kaufman (1965).

6. See Unger (1975), Lukes (1974), and Balbus (1971). That interests are subjective does not mean that no account may be given of their sources. Truman (1960), in a classic pluralist statement, seems at times to argue for an objective basis for interests; but this position, if it is held, would be inconsistent with much of the rest of the book.

7. For a fuller statement see Elkin (1979).

8. See Offe's (1974) argument on this point. Schmitt (1976), talking about English pluralists such as G. D. H. Cole, comments that the pluralist view of the state results in treating it as "nothing else than a revocable service for individuals and their free associations" (p. 45). Implicitly, many American pluralists seem to hold such a view.

9. Niskanen (1971) and Wildavsky (1979) show evidence of this view.

10. Unger (1975) argues for the connection between pluralist tenets and liberal political thought and also has a particularly sweeping and penetrating critique.

11. A contemporary and very explicit version of this view is Domhoff (1979).

12. For critical comments from very different points of view see Offe (1974) and Polsby (1980). The discussion of class interests is closely connected to the issue of "real interests" (see Balbus, 1971). Of course, not all proponents of a real-interest view hold to a ruling-class thesis. It may simply be part of an attempt to demonstrate that businessmen, or others, are exercising power when overt interaction suggests agreement (see, e.g., Crenson, 1971).

13. But see the discussion below, where a similar, if not perhaps as demanding, distinction is made between policy domains that are central to economic performance and those that are not.

14. This argument plays an essential part in Stone (1980).

15. Class theories that do not argue for a ruling class but, rather, talk about a clash between classes are typically a version of the pluralist argument, with the number of relevant interests curtailed. Aside from the criticisms I have already made, additional considerations are advanced below in connection with the state as the realm of "unfreedom."

16. Block (1977) argues that this sort of functionalist argument collapses into a ruling-class analysis because, as the argument now stands, the only guarantee that public officials serve the interests of capital (aside from some assertions about the functions of the state) is that the capitalist class can finally make it happen.

17. Cf. Lenin's (1949) remark that "the reason why the omnipotence of 'wealth' is more certain in a democratic republic is that it does not depend on . . . the poor political shell of capitalism" (p. 15).

18. For an important effort see the work of Offe. See also Habermas (1975) and O'Connor (1973). Offe and Habermas probably write out of an epistemological position that is different from the one employed here. Comparison of the merits of the various approaches would need, then, to go well beyond empirical questions. Epistemological differences frequently bedevil comparisons between Marxist and non-Marxist accounts (not to mention within each category), and in a limited space it is impossible to do more than establish a theoretical position and indicate where else the interested reader might turn for complementary formulations. For an example of the difficulties of disentangling empirical and epistemological issues see the debate between Poulantzas (1969) and Miliband (1973a and 1973b). See also Elkin (1979). In general, the epistemological issues here are not well explored in a manner that is useful to those who are trying to understand the detailed workings of actual political economies. For one effort see Wright (1979). The heart of the matter is probably the relation between parts and wholes in social phenomena. The following works are particularly revealing in this regard for the study of liberal democracy: Ollman (1977), Unger (1975), and Georgescu-Roegen (1971).

19. Another theoretical approach might loosely be called structural Marxism. The leading theorist here is Poulantzas. The complexity of the argument, the fact that he seems to have shifted ground considerably (compare *State, Power, and Socialism* to *Political Power and Social Classes*), and the fact that a number of critiques exist (Bridges, 1974; Wolfe, 1974; Laclau, 1979; Miliband, 1970, 1973a, and 1973b; Jessop, 1977; and more generally on structural approaches, Thompson, 1979 and Williams, 1977)—all indicate that there is little profit to be gained from a discussion here. Crouch ("The State, Capital, and Liberal Democracy," in *State and Economy in Contemporary Capitalism,* ed. Colin Crouch [New York: St. Martin's], 1979) suggests that the structuralist view has strong affinities with functionalist arguments. Indeed, the principal difficulty is to ascertain just what sort of argument is being made. It clearly doesn't rest on the triad of actors, interests, and power.

Because functionalist arguments also are criticized, that cannot be the basis, at least as far as Poulantzas is concerned. These don't exhaust the alternatives, to be sure, but much detective work is required.

Over and above all the reasons that I have noted for not discussing at length explicitly Marxist theory, one stands out. The real issue presented by such theories is whether they are political theories at all and whether they are in fact critiques of the possibility and desirability of politics. In Arendt's view, for example, Marx intended to bring the whole enterprise of political theory to a close (see *The Human Condition*, particularly pt. 6). Beside the consideration of this issue, other criticisms of Marxist theory are marginal. Pluralists and elitist theories are, however thin, still political theories.

20. The following recognize the importance of one or both reasons: Lindblom (1977, chap. 13), Block (1977), Offe and Runge (1975), O'Connor (1973), Bridges (1974), Bowles and Gintis (1980), Stone (1980), Crouch (1979), and Miliband (1973b, chap. 6).

21. For an early sophisticated discussion of the extent to which economic performance affects electoral fortunes see Tufte (1978). Tufte also documents how politicians, acting on the basis of that connection, attempt to manipulate economic performance for electoral advantage. A good deal of investigation will be required to estimate how poor performance must be and for how long before electoral defeat will actually loom. But even sustained mediocre performance will probably require greater efforts if politicians are reelected.

22. To the degree that citizens' concern with economic performance translates into a desire for certain kinds of publicly provided services, the two points merge.

23. See, e.g., Schumpeter's (1950) discussion of entrepreneurs and the general problem of risk and reward, and Commons (1957). For a stimulating essay see Wolin (1981).

24. Cf. Block (1977). Witness John Kennedy's statement in 1961: "This country cannot prosper unless business prospers. The country cannot meet its obligations and tax obligations and all the rest unless business is doing well. Business will not do well and we will not have full employment unless there is a chance to make a profit. So there is no long-run hostility between business and government. *There cannot be. We cannot succeed unless they succeed*" (emphasis added; quoted from Wolfe, 1981).

25. As it would be with workers. This, plus the degree of choice each has, discussed below, helps to distinguish labor from capital.

26. Block (1977) makes a parallel argument.

27. A particularly impressive current example is that workers in historically high-wage industries, such as steel or automobiles, are reluctant to give up income in order to move to other industries, particularly if that means building another union to promote and protect wage gains. They are trying and will continue to try to use state authority to prevent their having to move and to prevent reductions in wages.

28. For an exceptional essay building on the observation that the market regularly alters life circumstances see Berman (1978).

29. Nor, indeed, can a complete theory be outlined here. At a minimum, the place of the state in a changing world system must be considered. It is worth noting two obvious points of connection between the argument presented here and the workings of the world system. First, as I have already indicated, public officials, in their concern for economic performance, are likely to be more attentive to

businessmen the greater the nation's integration into the world economy. Second, while the examples below regarding variation in concern for business interests across policy areas all deal with domestic matters, the analysis may be easily extended to foreign affairs. In general, the claim on which this essay rests, however, is that it is useful to start with the domestic state and then work outward to the international system. It is not obvious how the merits of this theoretical strategy, as against starting with the international order, can be judged before theoretical work has been attempted.

30. See Thomas Kuhn's discussion of Aristotle's distinction between efficient and formal cause in "Concepts of Cause in the Development of Physics" (in Kuhn, 1977). In formal causes, Kuhn says, "Effects are deduced from a few specific innate properties of the entities with which the explanation is concerned" (p. 28).

31. See, e.g., the discussions of Roosevelt by Freidel (1973).

32. It is worth noting that we need not concede any supposed superiority in this regard to analyze built on pluralist assumptions. Past successes are not obvious, and if the distinction is refined between policy domains where economic performance is deemed to be central and where it is not, the state theory offered here may prove to be exceedingly useful in accounting for particular policy outcomes. See the discussion by Stone (1980), in the context of city politics, for how much might be understood by proceeding in the manner outlined here.

33. For a related discussion with a different emphasis see Unger (1975).

34. See the discussion of the history of economic regulation in Stewart (1975).

35. Particularly in *The Real World of Democracy;* see also Wolfe (1977).

36. Some efforts to promote economic performance can, of course, have perverse effects in this regard.

37. Compare here, Rousseau, in *The Social Contract,* to Schumpeter (1950), pt. 4. Rousseau wishes for citizens to develop a particular understanding of the connection between their own and the community's well-being, whereas Schumpeter wants a device for selecting and controlling political leaders.

38. The tactical considerations would center on maintaining a reputation for probity by not discarding doctrines of declining utility.

39. This conclusion is in the spirit of Bernard Crick's (1964) remark that "the bourgeois state, Marx said, contains 'inner contradictions' (indeed it does, that is what it is all about)."

40. O'Connor (1973), in an otherwise penetrating book, argues in this fashion.

41. Among others, see O'Connor (1973), Wolfe (1977), Offe (1974), Habermas (1975), Bowles and Gintis (1980), and Best and Connolly (1976). Not all of these theorists, however, share this functional view of legitimacy.

42. Crick (1964), p. 24. Cf. Geertz's (1980) comment on nineteenth-century Bali: "The stupendous cremations, tooth fillings, temple dedications, pilgrimages, and blood sacrifices, mobilizing hundreds and even thousands of people and great quantities of wealth, were not means to political ends: they were the ends themselves, they were what the state was for. Court ceremonialism was the driving force of court politics; and mass ritual was not a device to shore up the state, but rather the state, even in its final gasp, was a device for the enactment of mass ritual. Power served pomp, not pomp power" (p. 13). It is also worth considering the connection between this view—that is, political action as the end itself—with the argument above that theories emphasizing the power of actors (and causal theories) are flawed.

43. On the decline see Bowles and Gintis (1980), Edwards (1979), Nordhaus (1972), and Denison (1978). On the response see, e.g., the discussions cited in note 41 and *Commentary*, April 1978.

44. Cf. R. H. Tawney's comment, quoted in Michael Walzer, "Life with Father," *New York Review of Books*, 2 April 1981: "It is quite true that the bearing of risks is bracing, *if it is voluntarily undertaken*, because in that case a man balances possible gains and losses and stakes his brains and character on success. But when the majority of persons are hired servants, *they* do not decide what risks they shall bear."

45. For some suggestive arguments in this context see Joseph Cropsey (1977).

46. Consider any recent compilation of United States polling data on citizen trust in government.

6

Political Futures

Norman Furniss

I have three aims in this essay. The first is to show that advanced capitalist states are at a "historic juncture," which is characterized by a crisis or breakdown in previously stable or apparently stable international regimes. This regime crisis, when linked to domestic social and economic changes, results in a tendency toward a "new order of functioning" within and among advanced capitalist states. Second, I want to outline the implications for future political development. Unlike the "historic juncture" of the 1930s, the major impetus within advanced capitalist democracies is not toward leftist "reform" but toward retrenchment, which I will describe as a retreat from more or less comprehensive forms of the welfare state. As in the 1930s, however, there is no law that mandates that certain policy changes must take place. Britain managed to get through the 1930s without making any significant movement toward what somewhat ironically is called economic or social Keynesianism. Sweden may be able to mount a similar defense of what Timothy Tilton and I have termed the "social welfare state." My third aim is more speculative. I shall consider the arguments for radically different approaches to political and policy orientation. The need for a different approach was articulated by Sartre in his final "interview-discussion": "Either the left is going to die, in which case man dies at the same time, or new principles must be discovered for it to live by" (Sartre, 1980:399). These new principles are of two distinct types. The first focuses on the "socialism of production," which rejects the traditional distinction made in advanced capitalist states between politics and markets. The second promotes civil society *against* the state; its goal is self-management, or "autogestionnaire democracy." The first strategy is advanced most consistently in France. The second, which is not dominant anywhere, underlies the "citizens initiatives," including the "peace movement," in the Federal Republic of Germany.

Like Braybrooke in his essay, then, I intend to make a survey of possibilities. But because the four future political possibilities—retrenchment, the status quo, socialism of production, self-management—are not logically derived but empirically inferred, I must include observations and projections. Complexity, but I hope also understanding, will be increased by the need to describe distinct types of capitalist states. That there are distinct forms of capitalism is well argued in the essay by Benjamin and Duvall. I would go further and propose that within "postindustrial capitalist states" there are distinct differences that make me less sure about how far any generalizations can be supported.[1] These differences, which can be described in terms of policy patterns, certainly ought not to be associated with claims to future success. We can posit claims to inertia; we will witness the difficulties that even a Margaret Thatcher has had in altering the pattern of British policy. And we can suggest that some types of advanced capitalist states should prove more receptive to certain types of reforms. It is no coincidence, as Marxists used to say, that the "socialism of production" has been attempted in France rather than in the United States or even in Sweden.

THE NEW ORDER OF FUNCTIONING

In a major work first published in 1965, Andrew Shonfield, in *Modern Capitalism,* posed what he thought was the essential question: "What was it that converted capitalism from the cataclysmic failure which it appeared to be in the 1930s into the great engine of prosperity of the postwar Western World?" His answer was that advanced capitalist democracies in large part owed their unprecedented rates of steady economic growth and their social peace to an enlarged and facilitating public sector employing Keynesian economic management and fostering increasing private and public intellectual coherence. Shonfield saw the process as self-sustaining: "The central thesis of this book is that there is no reason to suppose that the patterns of the past, which have been ingeniously unravelled by the historians of trade cycles, will reassert themselves in the future." The reasons given were that the policy of full employment "added a new dimension to international trade" and that "the accelerated pace of technological progress . . . has made possible a high and steady increase in output per man-hour. This process will continue and may accelerate" (1965:62, 63).

Shonfield then delineated the features of this new animal, "modern capitalism." First, public authorities had a vastly greater influence on economic management. Second, this management, both public and private, developed forms of national economic planning. Third, in the private sector itself "the market has been tamed." Fourth, in the public sector, social-welfare policies had become a major preoccupation. And finally, with reference to the public at large, "it has now come to be taken for granted, both by governments and by the average person in Western capitalist countries, that each year should bring a noticeable increase in the real income per head of the population. . . . It is in fact capable of being fulfilled, at any rate for a long time to come" (Shonfield, 1965:66).

It was not Shonfield's intention to confirm the assumptions of much of the then-recent "end of ideology" literature. A major portion of his book was devoted to the political problem of how modern capitalism, operating, in his striking phrase, as a "conspiracy in the public interest," could be reconciled with notions of governance by popular consent. Moreover, one can extend Shonfield's concern to ask the more general question of whether the price of modern capitalism in terms of human autonomy or ecological balance could be too high. This concern lay behind much of the discussion surrounding the May 1968 upheavals in France and similar protests elsewhere. Modern capitalism was not attacked because it failed to deliver the goods. It was condemned because the goods were deemed tawdry and their enjoyment ultimately alienating.[2] Our purpose here is not to enter this debate and to assess, in retrospect, whether the effects of modern capitalism, on balance, were "good" or "bad." Rather, our purpose is to emphasize the stark contrast between the problems and the potentialities that were being ascribed to capitalist states during the late 1960s and the ones that were seen less than ten years later.

In broad terms the differences are clear enough. Distinguishing features are highlighted in a useful study done by the Organization for Economic Cooperation and Development (OECD), "Towards Full Employment and Price Stability" (1977). As befits an OECD report that was supervised by distinguished economists who have close ties with the government (Paul McCracken, Guido Carli, Robert Marjolin, etc.), there is much use of the optative and a tendency toward reassurance. The main argument of the report, however, emerges clearly: economic growth is desirable and possible, but only if governments recast their policies and assumptions. Governments and groups must recognize that beyond some threshold there are adverse consequences of public expenditures for economic growth and that in many countries this threshold already has been reached. All countries must "balance the books" in the medium term. Inflation is identified as being the main enemy. It has been fueled by excessive public expenditures and by groups that are seeking to maintain not merely nominal but real wages. In general, there is much concern with low profits, or, as it is usually described, a reduced "incentive to invest." Policy implications flow naturally. Market solutions are preferred. Governments need to bring home the consequences of inflationary behavior. In this connection, incomes policies are gingerly discussed. There is much more enthusiasm for a tight monetary policy. "We all agree that while there are other ways this can be done, the public announcement of targets for the rate of growth of the money supply may provide one of the best ways." And as for full employment: "We believe the route to sustained full employment lies in recognizing that governments cannot guarantee full employment regardless of developments in prices, wages, and other factors in economic life. The explanation of the paradox lies in the key role of expectations in determining economic behavior. . . . The 1974-75 recession has been a painful revelation, but it also provides a new opportunity" (OECD, 1977:193, 185).

When these recommendations are framed in terms of Shonfield's features of "modern capitalism," the contrast is pronounced. First, according to the new wisdom, public authorities should work to restore markets, not to direct them. Second, economic planning is to be replaced by monetary planning. Third, the market is too tame.[3] Fourth, the high level of public expenditures is a major concern. Finally, the public must realize that to expect regular real increases in one's standard of living is to fuel inflation and to foreclose any hopes for full employment. Together, these strictures suggest a new image of capitalism. Far from being a great engine of prosperity, capitalism is a delicate plant, capable of producing fruit in moderation, but only if given loving care. This new image of the economic system can be linked to broader changes in the nature of the state in ways, it need hardly be mentioned, that the OECD study did not project.

These changes in the nature of the state, which in sum have been described as a "new internal order" (Dommergues, 1980), can be developed along several dimensions. In most advanced capitalist democracies, the OECD policy prescriptions have been followed, producing results that Shonfield hardly would have found inspiring. For some commentators, indeed, the economic and social record of advanced capitalist states over the past few years seems at last to presage a major collapse. We must emphasize that evidence in support of this view is scanty. Economic growth continues, more or less. International trade expands, albeit more slowly. Research and development continue to be funded at high levels. The structures of the "welfare state" help to forestall physical misery, except for marginal groups. (The definition of "marginal group" varies among countries; more on this and on the welfare state below.) Average real wages in many instances have risen. On another level it is hard to affirm that advanced capitalism is beset by contradictions, if we define "contradiction" to mean a logical flaw that, over time, must destroy the structure. It is perhaps more useful to postulate that rapid change within a structure can reduce the probability of change in the structure.

I will propose that what we have described is not a collapse or the onset of a final contradiction but a regime crisis. The term itself needs elaboration. I use the world "crisis" first as presented by Paul Valéry: "A crisis is the passage from one particular mode of functioning to another" (1962:72). A major purpose of this paper is to persuade the reader that my use of "crisis" in this sense is warranted. To Valéry's definition I add the widely cited dictum by Gramsci that "the crisis consists precisely in the fact that the old is dying and the new cannot be born." This idea leaves open the future political possibilities; the emerging "mode of functioning," while it is likely to continue, need not be dominant everywhere. By "regime" I adopt the definition of a set of negotiated or mutually agreed upon rules and procedures that constrain the actions of nation states.

The regime crisis shows itself first in the decay or decline of international agreements. Nothing has replaced Bretton Woods; even partial efforts like the European Monetary System have not succeeded in bringing exchange-rate stability among the states of the European Community. The General Agreement on Tariffs and Trade (GATT) is subject to increasing constraint; it is estimated that less than a quarter of world trade is now actually "free." The international banking system similarly is in disarray. To institutional weakness is added the lessened ability of advanced capitalist states to influence other actors directly. To cite examples in the age of OPEC (Organization of Petroleum Exporting Countries) is super-fluous. The emphasis perforce has turned to indirect measures. Dirty, dangerous work is, insofar as possible, shipped out. "Less developed countries" are generally receptive. A report in the *Wall Street Journal* (17 December 1980) is instructive and worth citing at some length.

> The debate in the West over excessive regulation of factory health and safety appears a bit trivial from a Malaysian perspective. . . . Here there hasn't been any debate; cost-cutting comes first. Usually an injured or sick Malaysian worker is even barred from suing his employer for negligence. "We don't need any more litigations," says Lee Chee Wing, deputy head of the government's Social Security Organization. "We believe the employer needs a little protection." Adds a Health Ministry doctor who asks not to be identified: "The first question an investor asks is, What regulations do you have, and how well do you enforce them? If he finds these two areas are weak, he comes in."

217

Obligation for human consequences is then minimized by feigned or real ignorance. Aspirin is prescribed for lead poisoning. As for asbestos, a government study found no illness among workers. "The man who did the study says he thinks a possible explanation is the 'Asian body' is immune."

Unpleasant or polluting work that cannot be exported is subject to more subtle treatment. The most obvious method is to bring in "guest workers." An alternative is to tolerate "illegal aliens." A third option is to tolerate a "black economy." A fourth is to classify particular groups as not needing the full array of benefits or rights—such as women, teenagers. (Thus, for example, we hear in the United States the proposal that the minimum wage for teenagers be lowered. As usual, the suggestion is phrased with the best interests of the particular group in mind.) The goal throughout is to limit policy responsibility.

Pressures on individual states to conform to this pattern are also great. The sober discussion in a 1983 OECD study, "The Importance of International Economic Linkages," highlights the problem. Under the current regime, "the openness of individual OECD economics to the OECD economy as a whole . . . is such that the performance of the overall OECD economy goes far towards determining the performance of each country individually. . . . *In particular, there is a marked tendency towards international coincidence of both business cycles and policy stance.*" Moreover, this tendency would be greater if countries were to attempt individually to pursue "socialist" policies, because "pressure to respond to a change in current account position generally comes when a country moves into, or further into debt; surplus countries are often not put under equivalent pressures to adjust." Nor are the pressures entirely financial: the study reports delicately that "exchange rates are, at times, affected by incipient capital movements induced by foreign financial disturbances or political considerations" (OECD, 1983).[4] In other words, declarations that one is undertaking, to use a phrase often heard after Mitterrand's 1981 electoral victory—a "phased break with capitalism"—are likely to produce a vigorous reaction, and in France they did so.

The mode of functioning in what remains of "domestic" affairs is less novel. There appears to be a tendency (not only in the Federal Republic) to outlaw *Systemveränderer,* to make it illegal to try to change the rules of the game. Expenditures on "law and order" gain ready exemptions from budgetary restraints. Unionized workers are urged to show wage restraint and are reminded (in good OECD style) of the prospects of unemployment if wage rates go beyond what can be sustained profitably. Finally, questions are raised concerning whether past social undertakings can be maintained. Behind these questions is the assumption that the advanced capitalist state no longer can perform all of its ascribed functions. Whether due to rising expenditures or rising demands, belief that the state can construct creative new policy approaches or avoid massive policy failures has withered. Moreover, the poor economic record of the past few years is used to confirm, not the inadequacy of the OECD approach, but the necessity for greater rigor.

This position poses an immediate challenge to the viability of social democracy as a public philosophy.[5] Indeed, it is not too much of an exaggeration to suggest that social democracy was *the* public philosophy of "modern capitalism," involving, in different national contexts, the construction of a "Great Society" (Lyndon Johnson) or "das moderne Deutschland" (Willy Brandt); applying the "white heat of the technological revolution" (Harold Wilson); or "marrying one's century" (Charles de Gaulle). These visions have faded, and even in the Scandinavian bastion there are doubts (see Logue, forthcoming). Socially, there is the problem of which class is to be the beneficiary of and the support for social democracy. In a society that is predominantly urban and that is also oriented (in style, if not in numbers) around industrial occupations, social-democratic strategy is clear. In a society in which people prefer home ownership over subsidized apartment living and in which the steel industry, shipbuilding, and automobile manufacturing are declining, the foundation of social democracy is more problematic. For this type of society it is not just that manufacturing employment as a whole has declined; its internal composition is changing. In the United States, for example, from 1970 to 1977, manufacturing establishments that employed fewer than 100 workers increased their net employment by 225,000; establishments that employed from 100 to 500 workers increased theirs by 190,000; and establishments that employed more than 500 workers had a net decline in employment of 846,000. One cannot foresee that this trend will be reversed; it presages a qualitative change in the social composition of the manufacturing work force. (In some countries the change is even more striking. From 1970 to 1977, Britain lost almost 20 percent of its employment in large manufacturing establishments.)

Economically, social democracy has been linked to the assumption that capitalism is indeed a "great engine of prosperity." This assumption permits the state the luxury of being both the "ideal capitalist," of making the machine even more efficient through labor-market and other policies, and of being the "ideal social conscience," of using economic surplus for worthy ends. It also provides an effective argument against formal state ownership. To change the metaphor, why, asks one social-democratic theorist, should we disturb the capitalist "milk cow" when our goals can be achieved piecemeal without divisive confrontation (Adler-Karlsson, 1969)? When the dynamism of capitalism cannot be taken for granted, economic options are much less pleasant. On the one hand, there is less surplus to use for new projects, and funding for past commitments becomes more onerous. On the other hand, the state is urged to take various expensive measures—such as subsidies, tax cuts, and expansion of public employment—to shore up capitalism itself! The Swedish case is instructive. From 1979 to 1982 a "bourgeois" government was in power for the first time since the mid 1930s, a significant development in itself. Not surprisingly, new welfare initiatives were not launched. But at the same time, there was a large increase in the percentage of industrial production under state control and in the number of workers in what is called "sheltered employment." The reason for this anomaly is clear. In the absence of state intervention there was a risk of massive bankruptcies and of official unemployment levels that were considered to be politically unacceptable.

Perhaps the greatest challenge to social democracy, however, is to its theoretical outlook, which can be seen concretely in the issue of property rights. The "ideal" social-democratic position, as expressed by R. H. Tawney, Michael Harrington, and Gunnar Adler-Karlsson, among others, is coherent and reasonably fruitful.[6] For owners of productive property there is the effort to reinstitute the old idea of "stewardship" in property relations. Holders of productive property rights that are not fungible (who are generally capitalists) are, in Adler-Karlsson's words, to be given "a continuous set of compromises with which they will be able to agree." Over time, nonfunctional property rights are to be taken from private hands by "salami tactics" (Adler-Karlsson, 1969:65, 66). Holders of functional productive property rights are thereby put on guard: only for as long as private possession of these rights advances the public purpose are they to be spared nationalization. For individuals who do not hold productive property rights, there is an attempt to construct surrogate forms. The most significant is the idea of the property right to a job, which was elaborated at least as early as John Commons and was given forceful expression by Frank Parkin (1979a, 1979b). For Parkin, as jobs become "a form of property," class struggle is tamed. Those who are economically subordinate become politically dominant, and economic subordination loses its unacceptable face. Thus, the appeal of social democracy increased, because, for Parkin, there is no halfway house between it and the "socialism" of eastern Europe.

Leaving aside potential internal inconsistencies, we can see that the assumptions underlying the position are far from secure. "Salami tactics" are presumed to yield something of value. But when unemployment rates in most OECD countries are above 7 percent, to speak of full employment as a right is today to speak with many qualifications. More directly, if the OECD study is correct in finding that the route to sustained full employment "lies in recognizing that governments cannot guarantee full employment," then we have come across a most peculiar form of property right. The idea of a property right to a job can be advanced only when it will not be used. This is equivalent to saying that stockholders can sell shares only in a bull market. In brief, the difficulties of retaining full employment during this regime crisis indicate the extent to which major traditional tenets of social-democratic thought could rest on the viability of "modern capitalism."

We are now able to consider what political and policy possibilities exist for advanced capitalist states. In the next section we will describe the alternatives of welfare-state retrenchment and welfare-state defense. These alternatives, while they are more likely in practice, are less interesting theoretically, because they represent a response, not a solution, to the regime crisis. The possibility that this crisis could produce a "historic juncture" for reform is unfulfilled. In the final section of this paper I will present two possibilities that are intriguing in theory, albeit often less inspiring in practice.

POLITICAL FUTURES

I begin with one of the principal themes of this volume: to say that "the capitalist state" has "relative autonomy" is not to say enough. Indeed, all capitalist states are interventionist. All have modified structures of property rights, and all have intervened in various ways in the operations of the "market." This general situation does not, however, mean that all interventionist states are alike. Specifically, the major issue is not that all states have a policy of intervention but that different states have different institutional capacities and policy styles that are linked to different balances of political and social power.[7] These differences, I will propose, result in coherent policy patterns. Timothy Tilton and I have made distinctions among three kinds of public intervention in the operation of private property and unregulated markets according to the ends that advanced capitalist states pursue and the instruments that they employ. We attempt to encapsulate these types of intervention in three "models": the positive state, the social-security state, and the social-welfare state (Furniss and Tilton, 1977).

Briefly, by the term "positive state" we mean a state whose primary aim is that of protecting existing property holders from the perils of unregulated markets and redistributive demands. The "positive state" is the home of Lindblom's "privileged position of business," the dynamics of which are well developed in Stephen Elkin's essay. In the field of welfare policy (not, let us be clear, elsewhere) the positive state hesitates to do anything inconsistent with market conceptions of economic efficiency. Public programs conform, in sum, to Titmuss's "residual welfare model"

221

(1977). Within this model one can make the additional distinction between those "entitlements" that rest on the principle of social insurance, which both deflects potential redistribution to noneconomic categories and extends benefits widely, and those in which the disabled, the poor, and the "truly needy" are singled out for special treatment. The latter are particularly susceptible to cuts during times of financial stringency. Examples or approximation of the positive state have included Australia and the United States.

The "social security state" differs from the positive state on precisely this point of universality of welfare effort. Its primary aim can be described as the fulfillment of the liberal vision of equal opportunity for all through the provision of a guaranteed national minimum. No one is to be prevented from achieving his or her potential because of inadequate health care, housing, or education. Furthermore, it is recognized that the inherently nonproductive (i.e., the old, the severely disabled, and the mentally ill) have a right to state assistance. This right, however, does not extend beyond basic provision. The Beveridge Report, which provided the ideological foundation for the British welfare system after World War II, is clear on this point: "The state in organizing security should not stifle incentive, opportunity, responsibility; in establishing a national minimum it should leave room and encouragement for voluntary action by each individual to provide more for himself and his family" (Beveridge, 1942:48). The social-security state, then, has a very definite role. It is not concerned with economic organization. At the same time, however, the national minimum is to be guaranteed, not by the affected individuals or through the political process, but through the administrative procedures of the state. T. H. Marshall makes the point succinctly: The duty of what he calls the "welfare principle" is "to provide not what the majority wants but what minorities need" (1981:109, 126).

The difference between this vision and that of the "social-welfare state" is evident in the position of Ernst Wigforss, one of the leading theoreticians in the Swedish Social Democratic party. For Wigforss, the wage earner

> cannot readily agree to that view of the welfare state . . . that it should secure a minimum livelihood for all, but allow whatever goes beyond this to be won through each individual's or each group's asserting itself in an unlimited competition for standards, wealth, and power. That spirit clearly conflicts with the ideas that both the trade union movement and social democracy seek to follow in their public labors . . . that it still shall be the labor movement's ideas of equality, cooperation, and solidarity, that shall set their stamp upon society's continuing transformation. (Quoted in Furniss and Tilton, 1977:18, 19)

The achievement of this vision requires a policy mix designed to lessen the importance of market relationships in daily life—that is, to avoid economic segregation in housing and to promote the public provision of education, health care, recreation, and social activities. Concomitantly, the social-welfare state aims to redistribute resources in a more egalitarian fashion. "Solidaristic wage policy," as developed and practiced by the Swedish trade-union movement, attempts to equalize pretax incomes by capturing relatively larger wage increases for low-wage workers. Industrial democracy erodes capitalist domination within the firm. Environmental planning injects social and collective values into domains that were previously ceded to private business. These policies mandate the collaboration of producer groups (in particular, organized labor) and the state in decisions involving wages, investments, and employment. Examples include the Netherlands and Sweden.

If we look at the developments within these types of state from World War II to the first "Oil Shock," we can see broad tendencies toward consolidation and even movement toward more "developed" types of welfare states. In the United States, for example, the major expansion of AFDC (Aid for Dependent Children) and the food-stamps program pointed toward the de facto creation of a social-security state. In Britain there was a major concern about the "take-up rate"; elaborate informational programs were launched to assure that all who qualified to receive aid knew their rights. And in Sweden, proposals such as the Meidner Plan, which aimed gradually to divest capitalists of productive property rights by socializing a percentage of their profits, seemed to point beyond the social-welfare state toward some form of "socialism." These initiatives corresponded to the regime of "modern capitalism." With the current crisis the impetus has shifted from reform to retrenchment, the form of which can be understood again in terms of our three models.

In the United States the Reagan administration has attempted, with some success, to eliminate the accretion of "social-security-state" programs that were launched or given impetus in the mid 1960s. Food stamps and AFDC funds have been cut substantially. The percentage of unemployed who receive unemployment benefits is the lowest since World War II. Occupational-safety regulations are laxly enforced, union wage rates are under pressure, and so on. Some effects have been immediate. According to Census Bureau measures, the proportion of the population below the "poverty line" rose in 1981 to 14.0 percent; the percentage in 1982 again reached the level that existed before the impact of Great Society programs (*New York Times*, 27 July 1982, p. 11). Ironically, none of this has led to reduced federal deficits or even to major reductions in the overall level of spending. One reason is that the United States is a positive, not a laissez-faire, state; the line of claimants for public largesse is still large. Of particular relevance in domestic policy is the status of pensioners whose benefits have not been cut significantly and whose "poverty rate" accordingly has not risen. The results of the 1982 congressional elections further show that there are limits to making cuts in benefits. There also seems to be a consensus among Republican leadership in Congress that even the "truly needy" have sacrificed enough.

This experience had been foreshadowed in Britain, where it is fair to say that the prime minister, Mrs. Thatcher, has aimed to move away from the social-security state toward the positive state. She has had some success. Supplementary benefits for strikers' families have been cut. The earnings-related supplement on unemployment compensation has been abolished. Levels of unemployment benefits are now dropping below the levels of supplementary benefits. Capturing the essence of the changed priorities of providing social welfare is the preoccupation that fraud, not the take-up rate, is the major problem with welfare. The government, as in the United States, has set up special teams to investigate and expose fraudulent claims. Claimants now become suspects. Brian Abel-Smith concludes that "if the government continues along this road it will be the end of the post-war Butskellite consensus on the welfare state" (1980:17). At the same time, as is the case with the positive state in the United States, forces that want to retain the status quo are still strong. Within the Conservative party, even within Mrs. Thatcher's cabinet, even after her sweeping triumph in the general election, the position of what are called "the wets" has not been undermined. The British social-security state remains in reduced and meaner form.

Perhaps the most interesting example of proposed policy retrenchment however, has occurred in the Netherlands. Since World War II the Netherlands has developed a complete and structured pattern of welfare provision; only Sweden now spends more (see Furniss and Mitchell, 1984). With its "open economy" being extremely sensitive to international competition and with the departure of the Social Democratic party from the governing coalition, there has been a basic policy decision to move toward the social-security state.[8] Faced with apparently uncontrollable pressures for further public expenditures, the government presented to Parliament in June 1981 and in August 1982 two memorandums on the Reconsideration of Public Expenditures. For our purpose the significance of the memorandums is not found in the details of proposed spending cuts for public education, health, the arts, and social assistance; rather, it is found in the spirit of the memorandums. Deregulation and privatization are commended; the bureaucracy is scorned, except in its role in reducing welfare fraud. And it is made clear that the basis of security programs must be changed. In the worlds of the memorandums, the Netherlands must move *"from welfare state to guarantee state."*

To conclude this section, we should emphasize that we posit no single future for advanced capitalist states. Our concern is not with how international changes will drive states in similar directions but with how political and state structures will respond to international change. One possible response is to internalize pressures enough so as to avoid any major policy changes at all. Sweden is the current example. Unlike the rest of Scandinavia, Sweden still has a Social Democratic government in power; and unlike the Netherlands, Sweden still has structures of the social-welfare state that remain unchallenged. The price has been to set aside future welfare-state reforms. This price could be high. Previously we outlined some social and political challenges to the future viability of social democracy. Here the challenge is to the reason for the existence of social democracy. The rhetoric and declared values of the Swedish prime minister, Olof Palme, point to the nature of the problem. Palme typically speaks of himself as being "a Swedish social democrat, a European Democratic Socialist." The values of this movement derive directly from the Enlightenment. "We regard ourselves as a freedom movement. Democratic socialism is a movement for the liberation of man." The "reformist labor movement," then, is transnational (Palme, 1977). And its progress is unilinear. While one country may have progressed farther from another, all are on the same path (Brandt, Kreisky, and Palme, 1975). We need also note the stress on "reform" and on "labor." Concerning the former, Palme emphasizes that "reformism is a slow process. But it is the only way of really transforming society on the ideals of democracy" (Palme, 1980). One must also never lose sight of economic constraints (Palme, 1971), but one must never forget that the labor movement has the crucial task of extending the drive for democracy from the political so as to include the economic and social spheres. These steps the bourgeoisie, whether through cowardice or self-interest, refuses to take unaided.[9] Under the "new order of functioning," this discussion raises two fundamental questions. First, if social democracy is transnational, is its essence threatened when most parties are *retreating* down the path of social democracy or even wandering out of bounds? Can one have "social democracy in one county"? Second, even in Sweden, for how long can the reformist impetus be deferred without risking the enterprise of progressive liberation? What is the danger of having the "Swedish model" become the "Swedish aberration"?

POSSIBLE WORLDS

We have now outlined the likely futures for advanced capitalist states under current conditions of regime crisis. Most likely, retrenchment and reaction tempered by institutional and political inertia. Also possible, maintenance of the status quo. If we give equal time to less likely possibilities, it is because they pose much more exciting theoretical efforts to alter fundamentally the "political economy of the state." The first, socialism of production, proposes to eliminate the "division of labor between market and state," which is described at the microlevel in Stephen Elkin's essay and is presented at the macrolevel by Charles Lindblom in *Politics and Markets* and even more forcefully in his 1982 article "The Market as Prison." The second, autogestionnaire democracy, proposes to strengthen the authority of civil society against the state. As such, it represents an even greater challenge to traditional leftist or radical thought. It also should entail a new spirit of public discourse. I will end this essay with a few speculations about what this spirit might involve.

We begin with "socialism of production," which can be described broadly as an effort to shift the meaning of "welfare" away from consumption principles.[10] These principles we can define as state-supported action that (1) provides resources, irrespective of the market value of an individual's work, or (2) aims to transcend "the market" altogether through the provision of universal nonmonetary services. Production principles are designed to affect more the generation than the distribution of wealth. They can be defined as any state-supported action that aims to *alter* the distribution of property rights among capital, management, and labor. Any experiment in the "Socialism of Production," then, could have wide theoretical and political significance. Public officials would *no longer,* as Elkin elaborates, have to "try to avoid reducing the confidence of businessmen." Looked at another way, there might no longer be a fixation on the fiscal limits to the welfare state; and as we have seen in practice, any "fiscal crisis" tends more readily to undermine the legitimacy of social reform than of state power. Even more, it might be possible for the Left to seize the initiative in political debate. Attention might shift from how much to cut welfare spending to how to reorganize and reanimate the productive forces of society. This we will describe as the intention of the French Socialist party. Of course, the reality of the French experiment to date does not fulfill this promise. But it is, I will argue, premature to conclude that the experiment is a disaster, still less that a viable leftist political strategy based on production, rather than on consumption, is foreclosed.

The French Socialist position has been presented concisely by Maurice Duverger in a series of articles, "Three Faces of French Socialism," written for *Le Monde* in late December 1982.[11] Duverger begins by distinguishing the aims of French socialism from those of social democracy. According to Duverger, social democracy, as it is practiced in northern Europe, reflects our category of consumption principles. It is designed to redistribute incomes and to foster a feeling of security. French socialism is different. It is a "socialism of production founded on economic growth which is the only way to achieve social progress." It is based on the premise that industries that are owned or controlled by the state are the growth polls for France. For those who are interested in seeing how "socialism of production" could work, the proper model is not Scandinavia but *Japan*. Japan—like France(?)—puts production first, involves the state in basic investment decisions, and has a long-term industrial strategy. In short, both nations, in Duverger's words, have "a vision of collective interest."

This vision is not, then, a creation of French socialism; it issues from the French state. France historically has been the home of what Fred Hayward has aptly called "heroic policy-making," which is based, first, on the setting of explicit objectives for future development, together with a commitment by the government to work toward their realization; second, on the rejection of incrementalism in favor of the ordering of priorities; and third, on what one might term the guided coordination of relevant groups (Hayward and Watson, 1975). This style achieved its clearest policy expression in the French Plans of the 1950s and the early 1960s, and it formed its clearest political advocate in General de Gaulle, who saw that "as Head of State, it would be for me to [be] . . . concerned with the Plan, because it was all-embracing, because it fixed the targets, established a hierarchy of necessities and priorities, induced people in charge and even in the public consciousness a sense of what is global, ordered and sustained" (1971:134–35). The task of the Socialist government has been to reanimate this spirit and to direct endeavor toward economic growth *with* justice and solidarity.

I should note that I do not mean to imply that the French experience, with its "heroic policy making," arose from the machinations of bureaucrats or from the personal proclivities of political leaders. It issues from the nature of the French state itself, which elsewhere I have called "democratic state corporatist" (Furniss and Mitchell, 1984). The first mark of this centralized state is the form of state-group interaction. Rather than following the pattern of "liberal corporatism" as developed by Gerhard Lehmbruch, groups in the democratic corporatist state do not "penetrate" the state, nor do they bargain among themselves. Rather, bargaining takes place between the state and groups selected by the state, with decisions then being imposed on other relevant actors.[12] Second, historically, the state must have assumed primary responsibility for economic growth and, therefore, *inter alia,* for economic welfare. The final condition is that the state must be differentiated from a dominant economic class; to use an expression of some current popularity, the state must have significant "relative autonomy." On this dimension Pierre Birnbaum offers an interesting contrast between Germany and France. In Germany, "the state however developed or institutionalized nonetheless emerged as the instrument of a dominant class. Thus social domination was clearly visible through political domination. It is thus understandable that the main union was subordinate to the [social democratic] party." In France, on the other hand, "the institutionalization of the state was accompanied by marked differentiation from the dominant class. . . . Domination was thus experienced first in its political dimension" (Birnbaum, 1980:676). To summarize the argument thus far, an attempt to institute production-level policies in a democratic corporate state like France is furthered by supportive historical and institutional traditions and by a "political culture" that recognizes the legitimacy of forceful state action. The other side of the coin is the likelihood that organized working-class support, either political or industrial, will be weak. This weakness, we shall see, the French Socialist government has not overcome.

The absence of a mass base for leftist reform can be appreciated through a comparison with the Swedish case. In Sweden over 90 percent of manual workers belong to the major trade-union federation (LO), which in turn is linked closely to the Socialist Democratic party. In France, membership is much less extensive; union federations are divided on ideological lines. None of the federations are linked closely to the dominant factions of the Socialist party. Still less, in good syndicalist tradition, do union leaders want to be seen as associating too closely with the government. As Frank Wilson (1983:902) reports, the fear of being accused of collaborating with the government was as great in 1982 as it was in 1979, before the Socialist party's victory. In regard to the parties themselves, the Swedish one has a large membership, a strong-enough tradition of government to lead to "political hegemony" theses, and a full panoply of interest and research groups. The French Socialist party has a long history of divisions and a short history of political power, with many militants looking back to the events of May 1968 but drawing quite different conclusions from its failures. Membership in it, while impressive by French standards, remains relatively small. The party has approximately one member per forty voters, compared to one member per three voters in Sweden. The still-restricted social basis of party shows up well in a study of the socio-professional background of the party's 1981 parliamentary candidates. Fully 40 percent of them were teachers, another 18 percent were categorized as "cadres moyens"; 11.6 percent as "professions liberals"; and a surprisingly high 12 percent as "cadres superieurs." Workers constituted 0.7 percent of the candidates; "employes," 2.9 percent (Guédé and Rozenblum, 1981). I have not been able to find comparable data for Sweden. One study in *Dagens Nyheter* (24 December 1982) characterized 72 percent of Social Democratic parliamentarians as being "public employees"; of these, roughly half were party or trade-union functionaires.

That these employees have publicly guaranteed property rights helps to underpin the reformist nature of Swedish politics. It also helps to explain how Sweden can be said to have the highest percentage of individuals who are employed by the state of any OECD country.[13] In France, the Socialist government has been unable to substitute dialogue for command. Socialism of production does remain the goal. The nationalization program remains in place, with the public-banking sector, for example, holding 90 percent of the total deposits. The Ninth Plan accords "absolute priority" to industrial investment. And even during the current period of austerity, money for research and development continues to be increased substantially.[14] But without active participation, this type of socialism also remains, in Mark Kesselman's phrase, "socialism without the workers."[15] Proponents of "autogestionnaire democracy" would say that the absence was inevitable. They would concern themselves, not with how the state can build socialism, but with how the people can regain their freedom.

In this sense, "autogestionnaire democracy" marks a major departure from traditional leftist or radical thought. We might begin with the emphasis on civil society, as opposed to the state, and on the value of fraternity, as opposed to equality. Civil society is championed because it is the true home of the "public sphere." The importance of this "public sphere" is developed by Jean Cohen (1979:79 n.25). In reference to Habermas, he argues that his "later discursive model of truth, his reformulation of the Weberian concept of legitimazation, and his famous 'linguistic turn' clearly have their roots in the normative concept of the bourgeois public realm whose guiding principle is the attainment of a rational consensus based on the unconstrained formation of enlightened public opinion." The state constrains this formation; even more serious, it threatens to end any possibility of rational consensus by entirely absorbing civil society. This threat is developed in Habermas's concern with the "colonization of daily life" *(Lebenswelt)* through what he terms the "refeudalization of society" (see 1979).

In value orientation the focus on civil society shifts attention from "equality" to "fraternity." Equality is a state or statist ideal, and for our purposes, its problems can be discussed profitably through reference to Tawney and Marx. In his book *Equality,* Tawney rejects the charge that socialism sought to make all men the same. He rejects this goal, not because it might be impossible, an empirical matter, but because it is not morally central. His concern is not that men become the same but that they become brothers. As for Marx, it is at least possible to propose that sameness would have been dismissed as "bourgeois equality," or legislated equality. The type of equality that is worth having arises through concrete struggle, during which the involved individuals became liberated. Sartre links these two strands in his discussion with Benny Lévy. To Lévy's comment that "one must find a formulation that accepts the biological reference as an assumption but can also be expanded on a level that is no longer biological and is not mythological," Sartre replies:

> That's it. So then what is this relationship between one human being and another that will be called fraternity? It is not the relationship of equality. It is a relationship in which the motivations for an act come from the affective realm, while the action itself is in the practical domain. Which is to say the relationship between a man and his neighbor in a society in which they are brothers is, first of all, affective/practical. Originally, people shared awareness of that, you might say, but now it is a gift that has to be rediscovered. (1980:413)

What this fraternity could mean is not a mystery. In how people are conceived we emphasize the value of diversity. "It is in fact because individuals and above all groups are different in many respects that equality/ uniformity can produce only inequalities" (Rosanvallon and Vincent, 1977: 108). One must begin by acknowledging the fundamental autonomy of each individual, his right to be different. Much "socialist" argument does not start here with the consequence that what, in his Presidential Inaugural Statement, François Mitterrand was not afraid to call "the path of pluralism, in which differences come face to face with respect for others," is avoided. Much "liberal" argument ends here, thus leading, as Daniel Bell and others have perceived if not resolved, to the atomization of society and various "cultural contradictions." Autonomy, as such, is not complete. Individuals must operate in civil society. How are they to interact?

As with most political ideas, it is easier to outline what the relationships would not involve. Rejected is the reliance on state, party, and political program. "One arrives at a troubling conclusion: the historical left nourished a menacing and intolerant idea of the state. . . . We are faced with the general crisis of the historical left, la gauche étatique" (Macchiocchi, 1980:148). To condemn this *gauche étatique* is also to question the place of its traditional agent, the "class-mass" political party. In the most optimistic view, the party would have to be transformed. Jacques Julliard summarizes the position well with this advice to his French Socialist party:

Will the Socialist party . . . agree to be the Trojan horse of a civil society in full expansion, in full vitality, rather than the repository of all the old recipes and moribund doctrines? It would be wonderful—but all the same, rather surprising—if the Socialist party would substitute for the eternal cry of all victorious majorities—toutes les places et toute de suite!—the demand of *autogestionnaire democracy*—une place pour chacun! De la place pour tous! (Quoted in Berger, 1979:40)

A similar criticism can be made about party programs; by abstracting what to be real must be concrete, political programs are inherently hierarchical and elitist.

In turning from the state, party, and program as possible instruments for reform, the strategy of "autogestionnaire democracy" must look within civil society both for alternatives to the policy pattern of the new order of functioning and, ultimately, for forces that could change the nature of the state. The preliminary problem is the lack of obvious candidates. If, as Benjamin and Duvall argue in this book, we can now speak of a "postindustrial capitalist state," we can see the pertinence of the question "What is the movement that will occupy in postindustrial society the central role of the workers' movement in industrial society?" (Touraine, 1978:48). The proposition that the workers' movement may no longer be able sociologically to perform this function has, I trust, been argued sufficiently that it must be taken seriously. Even at its most effective—for example in the Swedish case discussed in the previous section—the movement is on the defensive. The "movement for the liberation of man" (in Palme's phrase) at best is stalled. Nor can we say that the French Socialist government's effort to substitute itself for the workers' movement as yet has been a success.

The alternative to the workers' movement is captured in Paul Feyerbend's slogan "Citizens' initiatives instead of philosophy!" (1980b). What we find within advanced capitalist states (proponents of autogestionnaire democracy would say within the civil societies of advanced capitalist states) is the emergence of a new type of group which is oriented around new types of political issues—such as women's rights, environmental protection, independent neighborhood democracy, and the peace movement. The groups themselves embrace what Jane Mansbridge calls "unitary democracy," which has a different approach to internal decision making. And the causes that are being advanced cut across traditional social and political patterns, thus raising the potential of political realignment. These tendencies have progressed farthest perhaps in the Federal Republic of Germany, where people have formed a plethora of *Bürger Initiativen* and where this citizens'-initiatives approach has commanded some general public support.[16] The most striking aspect of these movements, of course, is the peace movement. The peace movement consists of from two to three thousand autonomous groups that nonetheless have a marked capacity for coordination. And in contrast, for example, to the American "nuclear freeze" movement, the goal of the peace movement is linked to social transformation in ways that make the peace movement less susceptible to cooperation by the established political parties.

To be sure, nowhere are the citizens'-initiative movements dominant. Rather than discussing particular successes and failures, it seems more useful to raise a few theoretical possibilities and difficulties. We will start with epistemological orientation. To enter the world of autogestionnaire democracy is to abandon the insistence on a single truth and to embrace, instead, the analysis of a situation with its attached possibilities. The idea of possibility and its relation to necessity can be traced directly to Leibnitz: "Possibility is truth in some possible world; necessity is truth in all possible worlds." Put more formally, the distinction between necessity and possibility is that it is *necessarily true* that either "a" or "b" is correct; it is *possible* that there exists an "x," such that "a" has a relation to "x." We need not fully develop this reasoning here (Elster, 1978). It is enough to show how the perspective of "possible worlds" can lead from a commitment to a unicity of truth toward a normative position that welcomes the inevitable clashes of autogestionnaire democracy.

This perspective offers a number of advantages. First, it is actor-oriented, "intentionalist."[17] States that arise causally are excluded. Second, what is possible must be created: action can decide. Third, not all possibilities need to lead in the same direction. Fourth, on strategies, there can be no one "line." It becomes permissible to think of multiple truths and of overlapping strategies. The ideal of self-managing democracy, which celebrates uncoordinated initiatives on many fronts, is given theoretical grounding: the aim is not to create one possibility but to create possibilities from which all subsequent possibilities will lead in the desired direction. Moreover, strategies exist in time. The approach that declares that what can be done in two steps can be done in one is rejected. Finally, one is faced with the potential of inevitable failure. The set of states that come about causally in time can never be empty. A state is succeeded by another state, if only by a duplicate of itself. The set of states that is politically possible with respect to that state *can* be empty. There may be states that present the feature that purposive action is bound to fail (Elster, 1978). This I have argued, perhaps too frequently, is the situation that threatens advanced capitalist democracies. It is the reason that the addition of Gramsci's remark to our definition of regime crisis as being the transition from one form of functioning to another is not a paradox: "The crisis consists precisely in the fact that the old is dying and the new cannot be born.'' To take Gramsci's remark seriously is to enter the reasoning of possible worlds.

We are also led to consider different types of political argumentation. It is clear that the traditional political language of demands from the people (let us label them ''citizens'') and grand promises from would-be governors is inappropriate. This pattern both assumes and fosters differentiated knowledge from within civil society. This ''input-output'' exchange must be replaced by a dialogue in which the goal is action, in which the given state is seen as provisional. An idea of an alternative method of political argument can be taken from the work of Chaim Perelman. For Perelman, the aim should be to persuade, not to convice. To convince is to compel assent through a rigorous chain of argument based on formal rules of logic. To persuade is to engage in nonformal argument, to develop ''a web formed of all the arguments and all the reasons that combine to achieve the desired result'' (Perelman, 1979:18). To persuade is to lead the adherent toward action, whereas a person who is convinced could remain passive. For example, someone who is convinced of a scientific ''truth'' need not do anything different or, indeed, anything at all. This distinction, which can be traced to Aristotle's *Rhetoric* (Arnhart, 1981), also implies different sets of language structures and formal rules of logic. We are close to Habermas's idea of ''communicative ethics,'' in particular, and to ''critical theory'' in general.

Nor can the problems of ''communicative ethics'' be escaped. It is fine to say that the aim of political argument now is to break the bonds of existing expectations. It is this dynamic potentiality that motivates actors to sustain discussion; but within what institutional framework? The answer is by no means clear. As with Habermas, there is a stress on ''the need for greater participation in all areas of life where important public decisions are made; but . . . [there is] little indication as to what sorts of institutional forms are appropriate for this purpose'' (White, 1980:1015). Neither is the listing of ''procedural foundations'' an adequate substitute, for these are found to be all too congruent with the values that sustain a viable ''civil society,'' which is precisely what cannot be assumed.

Additional complexities intrude when we substitute groups for the implicit image of individual citizens as the relevant actors in deliberations. It now becomes essential that ''those who would change society should organize themselves discursively'' (White, 1981:463–64). In other words, the orientation of autogestionnaire democracy is not just preferable; it is mandatory. Similarly with political parties: a party, to refer back to the exhortation of Jacques Julliard, must be a ''Trojan horse of civil society in full expansion.'' Yet this phrase suggests an important ambiguity: How is one to organize open discussion when other (most?) major parties and groups are committed to other goals? I offer a specific example. In 1979 the French Communist Party (PCF) underwent a well-publicized conversion to "democratic self-managed socialism." As presented by Georges Marchais in his report to the Thirty-first Party Congress and confirmed a year later, this conversion was accompanied by a host of favorable references to the Soviet Union and to the socialist countries in eastern Europe. Marchais was particularly proud of their high growth rates. Meanwhile, he reaffirmed that the PCF was the repository of truth; to make the point clearer, he changed the name of the party "theory" from "Marxist-Leninism" to "scientific socialism." The problem here is not whether this conversion is sincere; the failure of the PCF to "organize itself discursively" makes its pretense illegitimate. The problem is that such a determination does not make the party go away, and it could even lessen restraints on its future behavior. What to do about those who are not thought to be likely (by whom?) to adhere to procedural rules is a pressing matter. The operation of Article 18 of the German Basic Law ("Whoever abuses freedom of expression of opinion, etc. . . . in order to combat the free democratic basic order, shall forfeit these basic rights") is not encouraging. To endow autogestionnaire democratic groups with the authority to coerce is to invest them with the mark of statehood which they need unceasingly to combat.

This reference to the coercive authority of the state brings us to our final set of difficulties. The regime crisis, which so restricts the possibility of an effective institution of the strategy of the socialism of production, impinges still more on the aims of autogestionnaire democracy. To economic constraints we can add geostrategic concerns. It is not remarkable that most Western commentary has emphasized that the Helsinki Accords helped to consolidate the Eastern Bloc. But of course the Western Alliance has been similarly affected. Talk of an end to alliances has been replaced by hopes that the existing alliances will be mutually civil. The implications for experimentation among advanced capitalist states are clear.

The French Socialist government has been able to avoid sustained pressure in part through its appeal to nationalism, in part through its control of centralizing state institutions, and in part through President Mitterrand's vocal support of the United States position on "theater nuclear weapons." A triumphant German peace movement would have none of these defenses. The Pershing II cannot suddenly be found to be a good thing to have, because the centralizing state is viewed as the enemy. And even the idea of nationalism is double-edged. When coupled with a call to end alliances, German nationalism soon inspires fears of German neutralism and, still worse, of German reunification.

In sum, theoretical difficulties and the new order of functioning present advocates of autogestionnaire democracy with immense challenges. It still must be shown that even the current modest successes are anything but defensive reactions to the dominant policy pattern of retrenchment. At the same time, we must not overlook the potential to provide "new principles for the left to live by." The orientation toward pluralism, liberating action, and decentralization can be seen as being congruent with evolving political sentiment within advanced capitalist states. There is no reason to assume that as a "possible world," autogestionnaire democracy is foreclosed. And that, for its proponents, is all that can and need be said.

NOTES

1. My ideas have been greatly influenced by the works of Pierre Birnbaum. See, e.g., Badie and Birnbaum, 1983, pts. 2 and 3.

2. In those few nations where, for various ad hoc reasons, the "automatic" prosperity of the mid 1960s seems still to apply, protests retain their "May 1968" character. A prime example is Switzerland.

3. See, e.g., the statement by Aaron Wildavsky that "of all the countries in the world today that are capitalist, none is wholly so and all are getting less so. . . . Perhaps the world gene pool of institutions would be enriched by maintaining a few examples of that vanishing breed, *corporatus Americanus*" (1978:234). Wildavsky is reviewing Lindblom's *Politics and Markets*.

4. The quotations are from pages 19 and 20; the emphasis is mine.

5. I use this term in the sense developed by Samuel H. Beer: "An outlook on public affairs which is accepted within a nation by a wide coalition and which serves to give definition and direction to government policies dealing with them" (1978:5).

6. I discuss this issue in "Property Rights and Democratic Socialism," *Political Studies* 26, no. 4 (1978).

7. Fortunately, to try to "order" these variables here would take us too far afield.

8. The remainder of this paragraph is drawn from Uriel Rosenthal, "The Welfare State: Sticks, No Carrots," a paper presented at the conference Futures of the Welfare State, Indiana University, Apr. 1983.

9. The 1981 Party Program included this typical statement: "To the Social Democratic Party, the demand for economic democracy is as self-evident as the demand for political democracy."

10. The orientation or reorientation of social democracy towards questions of production is discussed, *inter alia*, in a very useful compilation edited by Nancy Lieber, *Eurosocialism and America: Political Economy for the 1980s* (Philadelphia: Temple Univeristy Press, 1982).

11. The next three paragraphs are drawn from my paper "The French Socialist Government and Productive-Level Welfare," delivered at the conference Futures of the Welfare State, Indiana University, Apr. 1983.

12. The distinctiveness of this pattern can be seen when one compares it to the model of "Liberal Corporatism" developed by Gerhard Lehmbruch (1979) and applied to the Federal Republic of Germany.

13. See the study reported in *Die Zeit*, nos. 16–22 (Apr. 1983). Sweden was shown to have 156 state employees per 1,000 inhabitants; France, 73. The Swedish word translated above as "public employees" is *offentliganstallda*.

14. The Ninth Plan (1983–88), in according "absolute priority" to industrial investment, also foresees continued restraint on consumer and general governmental spending. Trends are summarized in the table.

FRENCH ECONOMIC PERFORMANCE

	PERCENTAGE OF INCREASE		
	1973–80	1980–83	1983–88 (Projected Ninth Plan)
Gross domestic product	2.9	1.7	2.5
Imports	6.5	5.0	6.3
Exports	6.4	3.5	7.0
Administrative budget	4.3	5.0	2.9
Household consumption	3.9	3.1	1.9
Investment	1.0	0.7	3.4
(Business investment)	1.5	1.4	5.5

Meanwhile, unemployment is expected to increase by around 600,000 individuals despite a continuing reduction in the length of the workday. Note that our concern is with the intention, not with the feasibility, of the Ninth Plan.

15. "Socialism without the Workers: The Case of France," *Kapitalistate*, nos. 10/11 (1983):11–41. Jacques Julliard calls the pattern "spectacle socialism" (Kesselman, 1983).

16. The rival would be the Netherlands, which can claim to be the spiritual home of both the peace movement and the squatters movement. The contrast with the dominant position in the French Socialist government is seen in President Mitterrand's statement of 16 November 1983 that "I am the deterrent," that the credibility of France's nuclear forces rested on his will power.

17. For an approach within the "public choice" tradition that has a number of similarities to "possible worlds" see the discussion of "artisanship" by Ostrom, 1980.

List of References Cited

Abel-Smith, Brian. 1980. "The Welfare State: Breaking the Post War Consensus." *Political Quarterly* 51 (Jan.): 17–23.

Ackerlof, George A. 1970. "The Market for 'Lemons': Qualitative Uncertainty and the Market Mechanism." *Quarterly Journal of Economics* 84 (Aug.): 488–500.

Ackerman, Bruce A. 1977. *Private Property and the Constitution.* New Haven, Conn.: Yale University Press.

———. 1984. *Reconstructing American Law.* Cambridge: Harvard University Press.

Ackerman, Bruce A., and Hassler, William T. 1981. *Clean Coal/Dirty Air.* New Haven, Conn.: Yale University Press.

Adler-Karlsson, Gunnar. 1969. *Functional Socialism.* Stockholm: Prism.

Ahlbrandt, Roger. 1973a. "Efficiency in the Provision of Fire Services." *Public Choice* 16 (Fall): 1–15.

———. 1973b. "An Empirical Analysis of Private and Public Ownership and the Supply of Municipal Fire Services." *Public Choice* 16 (Fall): 1–16.

Alchian, Armen A. 1959. "Private Property and the Relative Cost of Tenure." In *The Public Stake in Union Power,* edited by P. Bradley, pp. 330–71. Charlottesville: University of Virginia.

———. 1965. "The Basis of Some Recent Advances in the Theory of Management of the Firm." *Journal of Industrial Economics* 14 (Nov.): 30–41.

———. 1970. "Information Costs, Pricing, and Resource Unemployment." In *Microeconomic Foundations of Employment and Inflation Theory,* pp. 27–51. New York: Norton.

Alchian, Armen A., and Demsetz, Harold. 1972. "Production, Information Costs, and Economic Organization." *American Economic Review* 62 (Dec.): 777–95.

Aldrich, John H., and McKelvey, Richard D. 1977. "A Method of Scaling with Applications to the 1968 and 1972 Presidential Elections." *American Political Science Review* 71 (Mar.): 111–30.

Alt, James E. 1979. *The Politics of Economic Decline: Economic Management and Political Behavior in Britain Since 1964.* London: Cambridge University Press.

Althusser, Louis, and Balibar, Etienne. 1970. *Reading "Capital."* London: New Left Books.

American Trucking Associations, Inc. v. *Atchinson, Topeka, & Santa Fe Railway,* 387 U.S. 397. 1967 (87 S. Ct. 1608).

Anderson, Perry, 1974. *Lineages of the Absolute State.* London: New Left Books.

Anderson, Terry L., and Hill, P. J. 1975. "The Evolution of Property Rights: A Study of the American West." *Journal of Law and Economics* 18 (Apr.): 163–79.

Angelo, Richard J., and Donnelley, Lawrence P. 1975a. "Prices and Property Rights in the Fisheries." *Southern Economic Journal* 42 (Oct.): 253–62.

———. 1975b. "Property Rights and Efficiency in the Oyster Industry." *Journal of Law and Economics* 18 (Oct.): 521–34.

Aranson, Peter H. 1974. "Public Goods, Prisoners' Dilemmas, and the Theory of the State." Paper prepared for delivery at the annual meeting of the American Political Science Association, Chicago, September.

———. 1977. *The Multiple Tax on Corporate Income.* Los Angeles: International Institute for Economic Research.

———. 1979. "The Uncertain Search for Regulatory Reform." Law and Economics Center Working Paper 79-3.

———. 1981. *American Government: Strategy and Choice.* Boston: Little, Brown.

———. 1982. "Pollution Control: The Case for Competition." In *Instead of Regulation: Alternatives to Federal Regulatory Agencies,* edited by Robert W. Poole, Jr., pp. 339–93. Lexington, Mass.: D. C. Heath.

———. 1983. "Public Deficits in Normative Economics and Positive Political Theory." In *The Economic Consequences of Public Deficits,* edited by Lawrence Mayer, pp. 157–82. Boston: Martinus Nijhoff.

Aranson, Peter H.; Boyd, William A.; and Lancaster, Thomas D. 1983. "Political Science and Public Choice: A Quarter Century Retrospective." Atlanta, Ga.: Emory University Law and Economics Center Working Paper no. 83-1.

Aranson, Peter H.; Gellhorn, Ernest; and Robinson, Glen O. 1982. "A Theory of Legislative Delegation." *Cornell Law Review* 68 (Nov.): 1–67.

———. Forthcoming. "The Legislative Creation of Legislators: Public Choice Perspectives on the Delegation of Legislative Power." In *Constitutional Limits to the Delegation of Regulatory Authority Principal Paper by Aranson, Gellhorn, and Robinson,* edited by Ellen Jordon.

Aranson, Peter H., and Ordeshook, Peter C. 1977. "A Prolegomenon to a Theory of the Failure of Representative Democracy." In *American Re-evolution: Papers and Proceedings,* edited by Richard D. Auster and Barbara Sears, pp. 23–46. Tucson: Department of Economics, University of Arizona.

———. 1978. "The Political Bases of Public Sector Growth in a Representative Democracy." Paper prepared for delivery at the annual meeting of the American Political Science Association. New York City, September.

———. 1981a. "Alternative Theories of the Growth of Government and Their Implications for Constitutional Tax and Spending Limits." In *Tax and Expenditure Limitations,* edited by Helen F. Ladd and T. Nicholas Tideman, pp. 143–76. Washington, D.C.: Urban Institute Press.

———. 1981b. "Regulation, Redistribution, and Public Choice." *Public Choice* 37 (1): 69–100.

————. Forthcoming. "Incrementalism, the Fiscal Illusion, and the Growth of Government in Representative Democracies." In *The Growth of Government*, edited by William Meckling. Boston: Martinus Nijhoff.

Aranson, Peter H., and Shepsle, Kenneth A. 1983. "The Compensation of Public Officials as a Campaign Issue: An Economic Analysis of Brown v. Hartlage." *Supreme Court Economic Review* 2:213–76.

Arendt, Hannah. 1958. *The Human Condition*. Chicago: University of Chicago Press.

Arnhart, Larry. 1981. *Aristotle on Political Reasoning: A Commentary on the Rhetoric*. Dekalb: Northern Illinois University Press.

Arrow, Kenneth J. 1963. *Social Choice and Individual Values*. 2d ed. New York: Wiley.

Bachrach, Peter, and Baratz, Morton. 1970. *Power and Poverty*. New York: Oxford University Press.

Badie, Bertrand, and Birnbaum, Pierre. 1983. *The Sociology of the State*. Chicago: University of Chicago Press.

Bahro, Rudolf. 1978. *The Alternative in Eastern Europe*. London: New Left Books.

Balbus, Isaac. 1971. "The Concept of Interest in Pluralist and Marxian Analysis." *Politics and Society* 7 (Feb.): 151–77.

Banfield, Edward. 1961. *Political Influence*. Glencoe, Ill.: Free Press.

————. n.d. " 'Economic' Analysis of 'Political' Phenomena: A Political Scientist's Critique." University of Pennsylvania.

Barber, Benjamin. 1984. *Strong Democracy*. Berkeley: University of California Press.

Bator, Francis M. 1968. "The Anatomy of Market Failure." *Quarterly Journal of Economics* 72 (Aug.): 351–79.

Baumol, William J. 1965. *Welfare Economics and the Theory of the State*. 2d ed., rev. Cambridge: Harvard University Press.

————. 1967. "Macroeconomics of Unbalanced Growth: The Anatomy of the Urban Crisis." *American Economic Review* 57 (June): 415–26.

————. 1982. "Contestable Markets: An Uprising in the Theory of Industrial Structure." *American Economic Review* 72 (Mar.): 1–15.

Beer, Samuel H. 1978. "In Search of a New Public Philosophy." In *The New American Political System*, edited by Anthony King, pp. 5–44. Washington, D.C.: American Enterprise Institute for Public Policy Research.

Bell, Daniel. 1960. "Is There a Ruling Class in America?" In *End of Ideology*, edited by Daniel Bell, pp. 47–74. Glencoe, Ill.: Free Press.

————. 1975. "The Revolution of Rising Entitlements." *Fortune*, April, p. 9.

Benjamin, Roger. 1980. *The Limits of Politics: Collective Goods and Political Change in Postindustrial Societies*. Chicago: University of Chicago Press.

————. 1982. "The Historical Nature of Social-Scientific Knowledge: The Case of Comparative Political Inquiry." In *Strategies of Political Inquiry*, edited by Elinor Ostrom, pp. 69–98. Beverly Hills, Calif.: Sage Publications, Inc.

Bennett, Douglas, and Sharpe, Kenneth. 1980. "The State as Banker and Entrepreneur." *Comparative Politics* 12 (2; Jan.): 165–89.

Bentley, Arthur F. 1908. *The Process of Government*. Chicago: University of Chicago Press.

Berger, Suzanne. 1979. "Politics and Antipolitics in Western Europe in the Seventies." *Daedalus*, Winter, p. 40.

LIST OF REFERENCES CITED

Berman, Marshall. 1978. "All That Is Solid Melts into Air." *Dissent* 25 (1; Winter): 54–73.

Bernstein, Basil B. 1974. *Class, Codes, and Control.* 2d rev. ed. London: Routledge & Kegan Paul.

Bernstein, Edward. (1899) 1961. *Evolutionary Socialism.* New York: Schocken.

Bernstein, Marver H. 1955. *Regulating Business by Independent Commission.* Princeton, N.J.: Princeton University Press.

Berry, Jeffrey M. 1977. *Lobbying for the People: The Political Behavior of Public Interest Groups.* Princeton, N.J.: Princeton University Press.

Best, Michael, and Connolly, William. 1976. *The Politicized Economy.* Lexington, Mass.: Heath.

Beveridge, William. 1942. *Social Insurance and Allied Services.* New York: Macmillan.

Birnbaum, Pierre. 1980. "States, Ideologies, and Collective Action in Western Europe." *International Social Science Journal* 33 (4): 671–86.

Black's Law Dictionary. 5th ed. 1979. St. Paul, Minn.: West.

Block, Fred. 1977. "The Ruling Class Does Not Rule." *Socialist Review* 7 (May): 6–28.

Blum, Walter J., and Kalven, Harry, Jr. 1953. *The Uneasy Case for Progressive Taxation.* Chicago: University of Chicago Press.

Bodin, Jean. 1962. *The Six Bookes of Commonweale,* edited by J. P. Mayer. Cambridge: Harvard University Press.

Bogosian, Theodore. 1975. *Automobile Emission Control: The Sulfate Problem.* Cambridge: Harvard University, Kennedy School of Government.

Borcherding, Thomas E. 1977a. "One Hundred Years of Public Spending, 1870–1970." In *Budgets and Bureaucrats: The Sources of Government Growth,* edited by Thomas E. Borcherding, pp. 19–44. Durham, N.C.: Duke University Press.

———. 1977b. "The Sources of Public Expenditures in the United States." In *Budgets and Bureaucrats: The Sources of Government Growth,* edited by Thomas E. Borcherding, pp. 46–70. Durham, N.C.: Duke University Press.

———. 1981. "Comparing the Efficiency of Private and Public Production: A Survey of the U.S. Evidence." Paper prepared for delivery at the International Seminar on Public Economics/Conference on Public Production, Bonn, West Germany, August.

Borcherding, Thomas E.; Pommerehne, Werner E.; and Schneider, Friedrich. 1981. "Comparing the Efficiency of Private and Public Production: The Evidence from Five Countries." Paper prepared for delivery at the International Seminar on Public Economics, Bonn, West Germany, August.

Bork, Robert H. 1978. *The Antitrust Paradox: A Policy at War with Itself.* New York: Basic Books.

Bottomly, Anthony. 1963. "The Effects of Common Ownership of Land upon Resource Allocation in Tripolitania." *Land Economics* 39 (Feb.): 91–95.

Bove v. *Donner-Hanna Coke and Coal Co.,* 258 N.Y.S. 229. 1932 (236 App. Div. 37).

Bowen, Howard R. 1943. "The Interpretation of Voting in the Allocation of Economic Resources." *Quarterly Journal of Economics* 58 (Nov.): 27–48.

Bowles, Samuel, and Gintis, Herbert. 1976. *Schooling in Capitalist America.* New York: Basic Books.

———. 1980. "The Crisis of Liberal Democratic Capitalism: The Case of the United States. *Politics and Society* 11 (1): 51-93.

LIST OF REFERENCES CITED

Brandt, Willy; Kreisky, Bruno; and Palme, Olof. 1975. *Briefe und Gespräche.*
Frankfurt am Main: Europäische Verlagsanstalt.
Braverman, Harry. 1974. *Labor and Monopoly Capital: The Degradation of Work in the Twentieth Century.* New York: Monthly Review Press.
Braybrooke, David. 1958. "Diagnosis and Remedy in Marx's Doctrine of Alienation." *Social Research* 25 (Autumn): 325–45.
Braybrooke, David, and Lindblom, Charles. 1970. *A Strategy of Decision.* New York: Free Press.
Brennan, Geoffrey. 1973. "Pareto Desirable Redistribution: The Non-altruistic Dimension." *Public Choice* 14 (Spring): 43–67.
Brennan v. United States Postal Service, 439 U.S. 1345. 1978 (99 S. Ct. 22).
Breyer, Stephen. 1979. "Analyzing Regulatory Failure: Mismatches, Less Restrictive Alternatives, and Reform." *Harvard Law Review* 92 (Jan.): 549–609.
———. 1982. *Regulation and Its Reform.* Cambridge: Harvard University Press.
Breyer, Stephen G., and Stein, Leonard R. 1982. "Airline Deregulation: The Anatomy of Reform." In *Instead of Regulation: Alternatives to Federal Regulatory Agencies,* edited by Robert W. Poole, Jr., pp. 1–41. Lexington, Mass.: D. C. Heath.
Bridges, Amy. 1974. "Poulantzas and the Marxist Theory of the State." *Politics and Society* 4 (2; Winter): 161–90.
Brozen, Yale, 1970. "The Antitrust Task Force Deconcentration Recommendation." *Journal of Law and Economics* 13 (Oct.): 279–92.
———. 1971a. "The Persistence of 'High Rates of Return' in High-Stable Concentration Industries." *Journal of Law and Economics* 14 (Oct.): 501–12.
———. 1971b. "Bain's Concentration and Rates of Return Revisited." *Journal of Law and Economics* 14 (Oct.): 351–69.
———. 1974. "Concentration and Profits: Does Concentration Matter?" *Antitrust Bulletin* 19 (Summer): 381–99.
Bruff, Harold H., and Gellhorn, Ernest. 1977. "Congressional Control of Administrative Regulation: A Study of Legislative Vetoes." *Harvard Law Review* 90 (May): 1369–1440.
Buchanan, James M. 1959. "Positive Economics, Welfare Economics, and Political Economy." *Journal of Law and Economics* 2 (Oct.): 124–38.
———. 1971. *The Bases of Collective Action.* New York: General Learning Press.
———. 1975. *The Limits of Liberty: Between Anarchy and Leviathan.* Chicago: University of Chicago Press.
———. 1977. "Why Does Government Grow." In *Budgets and Bureaucrats: The Sources of Government Growth,* edited by Thomas E. Borcherding. Durham, N.C.: Duke University Press.
Buchanan, James M., and Tullock, Gordon. 1962. *The Calculus of Consent: Logical Foundations of Constitutional Democracy.* Ann Arbor: University of Michigan Press.
Buci-Glucksmann, Christine. 1980. *Gramsci and the State.* London: Lawrence & Wishart.
Cahoon, Larry S.; Hinich, Melvin J.; and Ordeshook, Peter C. 1978. "A Statistical Multidimensional Scaling Method Based on the Spacial Theory of Voting." In *Graphical Representation of Multivariate Data,* edited by P. C. Wang, pp. 243–78. New York: Academic Press.
Calabressi, Guido. 1970. *The Costs of Accidents: Legal and Economic Analysis.* New Haven, Conn.: Yale University Press.

241

Caporaso, James A. 1981. "Industrialization in the Periphery: The Evolving Global Division of Labor." *International Studies Quarterly* 25 (3; Sept.): 347–84.

Cardoso, Fernando Henrique. 1973. "Associated-dependent Development: Theoretical and Practical Implications." In *Authoritarian Brazil: Origins, Politics, and Future,* edited by Alfred Stepan, pp. 142–79. New Haven, Conn.: Yale University Press.

Cardoso, Fernando Henrique, and Faletto, Enzo. 1978. *Dependency and Development in Latin America.* Berkeley: University of California Press.

Carens, Joseph H. 1981. *Equality, Moral Incentives, and the Market.* Chicago: University of Chicago Press.

Carneiro, Robert L. 1970. "A Theory of the Origin of the State." *Science* 169 (Aug.): 733–38.

Carnoy, Martin. 1984. *The State and Political Theory.* Princeton, N.J.: Princeton University Press.

Carrillo, Santiago. 1977. *Eurocommunism and the State.* Translated by N. Green and A. M. Elliott. London: Lawrence & Wishart.

Chandler, Alfred D., Jr. 1962. *Strategy and Structure: Chapters in the History of Industrial Enterprise.* Cambridge, Mass.: MIT Press.

Chatelain, Jacky. 1979. "Une Nouvelle Economies, une nouvelle philosophie." *Temps modernes* 399 (Oct.): 638–75.

Chayes, Abram. 1976. "The Role of the Judge in Public Law Litigation." *Harvard Law Review* 89 (7; May): 1281–1316.

Chelius, James R. 1976. "Liability for Accidents: A Comparison of Negligence and Strict Liability Systems." *Journal of Legal Studies* 5 (June): 293–309.

————. 1977. *Workplace Safety and Health: The Role of Workers' Compensation.* Washington, D.C.: American Enterprise Institute.

City of Milwaukee v. *Illinois,* 451 U.S. 304. 1981 (101 S. Ct. 1784).

Clark, Colin. 1973. "Profit Maximization and the Extinction of Animal Species." *Journal of Political Economy* 81 (July/Aug.): 950–61.

Clarkson, Kenneth W., and Tollison, Robert. "Toward a Theory of Government Advertising." In *Research in Law and Economics: A Research Annual,* edited by Richard O. Zerbe, Jr., vol. 1, pp. 131–43. Greenwich, Conn.: JAI Press.

Coase, Ronald H. 1937. "The Nature of the Firm." *Economica* 4 (Nov.): 386–405.

————. 1959. "The Federal Communications Commission." *Journal of Law and Economics* 2 (Oct.): 1–40.

————. 1960. "The Problem of Social Cost." *Journal of Law and Economics* 3 (Oct.): 1–44.

————. 1962. "The Interdepartment Radio Advisory Committee." *Journal of Law and Economics* 5 (Oct.): 17–47.

————. 1974. "The Lighthouse in Economics." *Journal of Law and Economics* 17 (Oct.): 357–76.

Cobb, Roger, and Elder, Charles. 1972. *Participation in American Politics: The Dynamics of Agenda Building.* Boston: Allyn & Bacon.

Cohen, Jean, 1979. "Why More Political Theory?" *Telos* 40 (Summer): 70–94.

Cole, David C., and Lyman, Princeton N. 1971. *Korean Development: The Interplay of Politics and Economics.* Cambridge: Harvard University Press.

Collier, David, ed. 1979. *The New Authoritarianism in Latin America.* Princeton, N.J.: Princeton University Press.

Commentary. 1978. Symposium: "Capitalism, Socialism and Democracy" 65 (4; Apr.): 29–71.

LIST OF REFERENCES CITED

Commission on Law and the Economy. 1979. *Federal Regulation: Roads to Reform.* Washington, D.C.: American Bar Association.

Commons, John R. 1957. *The Legal Foundations of Capitalism.* Madison: University of Wisconsin Press.

Crenson, Matthew. 1971. *The Un-Politics of Air Pollution.* Baltimore, Md.: Johns Hopkins Press.

Crick, Bernard. 1964. *In Defense of Politics,* Middlesex, Eng.: Penguin.

Cropsey, Joseph. 1977a. "On the Relation of Political Science and Economics." In *Political Philosophy and the Issues of Politics,* edited by Joseph Cropsey, pp. 32–43. Chicago: University of Chicago Press.

————. 1977b. "The United States as Regime and the Sources of the American Way of Life." In *The Moral Foundations of the American Republic,* edited by Robert H. Horowitz, pp. 86–101. Charlottesville: University Press of Virginia.

Crouch, Colin, ed. 1979. *State and Economy in Contemporary Capitalism.* New York: St. Martin's.

Dahl, Robert A. 1957. "The Concept of Power." *Behavioral Science* 2:201–5.

————. 1961. *Who Governs? Democracy and Power in an American City.* New Haven, Conn.: Yale University Press.

————. 1970. *After the Revolution: Authority in a Good Society.* New Haven, Conn.: Yale University Press.

————. 1971. *Polyarchy.* New Haven, Conn.: Yale University Press.

————. 1977. "On Removing Certain Impediments to Democracy in the United States." *Political Science Quarterly* 92 (1; Sept.): 1–20.

————. 1982. *Dilemmas of Pluralist Democracy.* New Haven, Conn.: Yale University Press.

Dahl, Robert, and Lindblom, Charles E. 1953. *Politics, Economics and Welfare.* New York: Harper & Bros.

Davies, David A. 1971. "The Efficiency of Public versus Private Firms: The Case of Australia's Two Airlines." *Journal of Law and Economics* 14 (Apr.): 149–65.

Davis, Otto A.; Dempster, M. A. H.; and Wildavsky, Aaron. 1966. "A Theory of the Budgetary Process." *American Political Science Review* 60 (Sept.): 529–47.

Davis, Otto A., and Winston, Andrew B. 1965. "Welfare Economics and the Theory of Second Best." *Review of Economic Studies* 32 (Jan.): 1–14.

de Alessi, Louis. 1973. "Private Property and the Dispersion of Ownership in Large Corporations." *Journal of Finance* 28 (Sept.): 839–51.

————. 1974a. "An Economic Analysis of Government Ownership and Regulation: Theory and Evidence from the Electric Power Industry." *Public Choice* 19 (Fall): 1–42.

————. 1974b. "Managerial Tenure under Private and Government Ownership in the Electric Power Industry." *Journal of Political Economy* 82 (May/June): 645–53.

————. 1980. "The Economics of Property Rights: A Review of the Evidence." In *Research in Law and Economics: A Research Annual,* edited by Richard O. Zerbe, Jr., vol. 2, pp. 1–47. Greenwich, Conn.: JAI Press.

————. 1982. "On the Nature and Consequences of Private and Public Enterprises." (March) Xerox.

de Gaulle, Charles. 1971. *Memoirs of Hope: Renewal and Endeavor.* New York: Simon & Schuster.

243

Demkovich, Linda E. 1978. "From Public Interest Advocates to Administration Defenders." *National Journal* 10 (Nov. 25): 1892–98.

Demsetz, Harold. 1967. "Toward a Theory of Property Rights." *American Economic Review* 57 (May): 347–59.

———. 1968. "Why Regulate Utilities?" *Journal of Law and Economics* 11 (Apr.): 55–65.

———. 1970. "Discussion." *American Economic Review* 60 (May): 481–84.

———. 1973a. "Industry Structure, Market Rivalry, and Public Policy." *Journal of Law and Economics* 16 (Apr.): 1–9.

———. 1973b. *The Market Concentration Doctrine*. Washington, D.C.: American Enterprise Institute for Public Policy Research.

Denison, Edward. 1978. "The Puzzling Drop in Productivity." *Brookings Bulletin* 15 (2; Fall): 10–12.

Descartes, René. 1977. *Regles utiles et claires pour la direction de l'esprit en la recherche de la verité*. The Hague: Martinus Nijhoff.

Deutsch, Karl W. 1978. *The Analysis of International Relations*. 2d ed. Englewood Cliffs, N.J.: Prentice-Hall.

De Vany, Arthur, and Sanchez, Nicolas. 1969. "Land Tenure Structures and Fertility in Mexico." *Review of Economics and Statistics* 61 (Feb.): 67–72.

Domhoff, William G. 1978. *The Powers That Be*. New York: Random House.

Dommergues, Pierre, ed. 1980. *Le Nouvelle Ordre intérieur*. Paris: Alain Moreau.

Dos Santos, Theotonio. 1970. "The Structure of Dependence." *American Economic Review* 60 (2; May): 231–36.

Douglas, George W., and Miller, James C., III. 1974. *Economic Regulation of Domestic Air Transport: Theory and Policy*. Washington, D.C.: Brookings Institution.

Downing, Paul B., and Brady, Gordon L. 1979. "Constrained Self Interest and the Formation of Public Policy." *Public Choice* 34 (1): 15–28.

Downs, Anthony. 1957. *An Economic Theory of Democracy*. New York: Harper & Row.

———. 1960. "Why the Government Budget Is Too Small in a Democracy." *World Politics* (July): 541–63.

———. 1967. *Inside Bureaucracy*. Boston: Little, Brown & Co.

Duvall, Raymond D., and Freeman, John R. 1981. "The State and Dependent Capitalism." *International Studies Quarterly* 25 (1; Mar.): 99–118.

———. 1983. "The Technocratic Elite and the Entrepreneurial State in Dependent Industrialization." *American Political Science Review* 77:569–87.

Duvall, R.; Jackson, S.; Russett, B.; Snidal, D.; and Sylvan, D. 1981. "A Formal Model of Dependencia Theory." In *From National Development to Global Community: Essays in Honor of Karl W. Deutsch*, edited by R. L. Merritt and B. M. Russett. London: George Allen & Unwin.

Dworkin, Ronald. 1977. *Taking Rights Seriously*. Cambridge: Harvard University Press.

Easterbrook, Frank, and Fischel, Daniel. 1981. "The Proper Role of a Target's Management in Responding to a Tender Offer." *Harvard Law Review* 94 (Apr.): 1161–1203.

Edel, Matthew, and Sclar, Eliot. 1974. "Taxes, Spending and Property Values: Supply Adjustment in a Tiebout-Gates Model." *Journal of Political Economy* 82 (Sept./Oct.): 941–54.

Edwards, Richard. 1979. *Contested Terrain*. New York: Basic Books.

Ehrlich, Isaac, and Posner, Richard A. 1974. "An Economic Analysis of Legal Rulemaking." *Journal of Legal Studies*. 3 (Jan.): 257–86.

Elkin, Stephen L. 1978. "Twentieth Century Urban Regimes." Paper delivered to American Political Science Association, New York.

———. 1979. "Castells, Marxism and the New Urban Politics." *Comparative Urban Research* 7 (2): 22–33.

———. 1980. "Cities without Power." In *National Resources and Urban Policy*, edited by Douglas Ashford, pp. 265–93. New York: Methuen.

———. 1982. "Market and Politics in Liberal Democracy." *Ethics* 92 (4): 720–32.

Elliott, Ward. 1974. *The Rise of Guardian Democracy*. Cambridge: Harvard University Press.

Elster, Jon. 1978. *Logic and Society*. New York: Wiley.

Elzinga, Kenneth. 1970. "Predatory Pricing: The Case of the Gunpowder Trust." *Journal of Law and Economics* 13 (Apr.): 223–40.

Enelow, James M., and Hinich, Melvin J. 1981. "A New Approach to Voter Uncertainty and the Downsian Spatial Model." *American Journal of Political Science* 25 (Aug.): 483–93.

———. 1982. "Ideology, Issues, and the Spatial Theory of Elections." *American Political Science Quarterly* 76 (Sept.): 493–501.

Engels, Friedrich. (1880) 1918. *Socialism: Utopian and Scientific*. Translated by Edward Aveling. London: G. Allen & Unwin.

———. (1884) 1972. *The Origin of the Family, Private Property and the State*. New York: Pathfinder Press.

———. (1895) 1935. "Introduction to Marx's The Class Struggle in France." In *The Class Struggle in France*, pp. 9–30. New York: International Publishers.

Epple, Dennis, and Zelenitz, Allan. 1981. "The Implications of Competition among Jurisdictions: Does Tiebout Need Politics?" *Journal of Political Economy* 89 (Dec.): 1197–1217.

Epple, Dennis; Zelenitz, Allan; and Visscher, Michael. 1978. "A Search for Testable Implications of the Tiebout Hypothesis." *Journal of Political Economy* 86 (June): 405–26.

Etzioni, Amitai. 1977/78. "Societal Overload." *Political Science Quarterly* 92 (Winter): 607–33.

Evans, Peter. 1979. *Dependent Development*. Princeton, N.J.: Princeton University Press.

Evans, Peter; Rueschemeyer, Dietrich; and Skocpol, Theda, eds. 1985. *Bringing the State Back In*. Cambridge: Cambridge University Press.

Farr, James. 1983. "Marx No Empiricist." *Philosophy of the Social Sciences* 13 (Dec.): 465–72.

Feldstein, Martin. 1982. "Inflation and the American Economy." *Public Interest* 67 (Spring): 63–76.

Ferejohn, John A. 1974. *Pork Barrel Politics*. Stanford, Calif.: Stanford University Press.

Feyerabend, Paul. 1980a. "Democracy, Elitism, and the Scientific Method." *Inquiry* 23 (Mar.): 3–18.

———. 1980b. *Erkenntis fur freie Menschen*. Frankfurt: Suhrkamp.

———. 1980c. "Zaharon Mach, Einstein and Modern Science." *British Journal of the Philosophy of Science* 31 (Sept.): 273–82.

Fiorina, Morris P. 1977. *Congress: Keystone of the Washington Establishment*. New Haven, Conn.: Yale University Press.

———. 1982a. "Legislative Choice of Regulatory Forms: Legal Process or Administrative Process?" *Public Choice* 39 (1): 33–66.

———. 1982b. *Retrospective Voting in American National Elections.* New Haven, Conn.: Yale University Press.

———. Forthcoming. "Legislative Facilitation of Government Growth: Universalism and Reciprocity Practices in Majority Rule Institutions." *Research in Public Policy Analysis and Management.*

Fiorina, Morris P., and Shepsle, Kenneth A. 1982. "Equilibrium, Disequilibrium, and the General Possibility of a Science of Politics." In *Political Equilibrium,* edited by Kenneth A. Shepsle and Peter C. Ordeshook, pp. 49–64. Boston: Kluwer-Nijhoff.

Fischel, Daniel. 1978. "Efficient Capital Market Theory, the Market for Corporate Control, and the Regulation of Cash Tender Offers." *Texas Law Review* 57 (Dec.): 1–46.

Flathman, Richard E. 1980. *The Practice of Political Authority: Authority and the Authoritative.* Chicago: University of Chicago Press.

Flora, Peter, and Heidenheimer, Arnold. 1981. *The Development of Welfare States in Europe and America.* New Brunswick, N.J.: Transaction Books.

Frankel, Boris. 1982. "On the State of the State: Marxist Theories of the State since Lenin." In *Classes, Power, and Conflict,* edited by Anthony Giddens and David Held, pp. 257–73. Berkeley: University of California Press.

Freedman, James. 1978. *Crisis and Legitimacy.* New York: Cambridge University Press.

Freeman, John R. 1982. "State Enterpreneurship and Dependent Development." *American Journal of Political Science* 26:90–112.

Freeman, John, and Duvall, Raymond. 1983. "The Technobureaucratic State and the Entrepreneurial State in Dependent Industrialization." *American Political Science Review* 77: 569–87.

Freidel, Frank. 1973. *Franklin D. Roosevelt: Launching the New Deal.* Boston: Little, Brown.

Friedman, David. 1973. *The Machinery of Freedom.* New York: Harper & Row.

Friedman, Milton. 1962. *Capitalism and Freedom.* Chicago: University of Chicago Press.

Friedrich, Carl J. 1950. *Constitutional Government and Democracy.* Boston: Ginn & Co.

Froman, Lewis A., Jr. 1967. *The Congressional Process: Strategies, Rules, and Procedures.* Boston: Little, Brown.

Furniss, Norman. 1978a. "The Political Implications of the Public Choice—Property Rights School." *American Political Science Review* 72 (June): 399–410.

———. 1978b. "Property Rights and Democratic Socialism." *Political Studies* 26 (Dec.): 450–61.

———. 1983. "The French Socialist Government and Productive-Level Welfare." Paper presented at a conference on Futures of the Welfare State, Indiana University, April.

Furniss, Norman, and Mitchell, Neil. Forthcoming. "Social Welfare Provisions in Western Europe: Current Status and Future Possibilities." In *Public Policy and Social Institutions,* edited by Harrell Rodgers. Greenwich, Conn.: JAI Press.

Furniss, Norman, and Tilton, Timothy. 1977. *The Case for the Welfare State.* Bloomington: Indiana University Press.

Furubotn, Eirik, and Pejovich, Svetozar. 1972. "Property Rights and Economic Theory: A Survey of Recent Literature." *Journal of Economic Literature* 10 (Dec.): 1137–62.

Galbraith, John Kenneth. 1956. *American Capitalism*. Boston: Houghton Mifflin.

————. 1958. *The Affluent Society*. New York: Mentor.

————. 1967. *The New Industrial State*. Boston: Houghton Mifflin Co.

Geertz, Clifford. 1980. *Negara: The Theatre State in Nineteenth Century Bali*. Princeton, N.J.: Princeton University Press.

Gensemer, Bruce L.; Lean, Jane A.; Neenan, William B. 1965. "Awareness of Marginal Income Tax Rates among High-Income Taxpayers." *National Tax Journal* 19 (Sept.): 268–76.

Georgescu-Roegen, Nicholas. 1971. *The Entropy Law and the Economic Press*. Cambridge: Harvard University Press.

Gibbard, Allan. 1973. "Manipulation of Voting Schemes: A General Result." *Econometrica* 41 (July): 587–601.

Giddens, Anthony. 1980. *The Class Structure of the Advanced Societies*. 2d ed. London: Hutchinson.

Glazer, Nathan. 1975. "Towards an Imperial Judiciary." *Public Interest* 41 (Fall): 104–23.

Goetz, Charles J. 1977. "Fiscal Illusion in State-Local Finance." In *Budgets and Bureaucrats: The Sources of Government Growth*, edited by Thomas E. Borcherding, pp. 176–87. Durham, N.C.: Duke University Press.

Goldin, Kenneth D. 1975. "Price Externalities Influence Public Policy." *Public Choice* 23 (Fall): 1–10.

Goodman, John C. 1978. "An Economic Theory of the Evolution of the Common Law." *Journal of Legal Studies* 7 (June): 393–406.

Gordon, Scott H. 1954. "The Economic Theory of a Common Property Resource: The Fishery." *Journal of Political Economy* 62 (Apr.): 124–42.

Gough, Ian. 1979. *The Political Economy of the Welfare State*. Atlantic Highlands, N.J.: Humanities Press.

Gramlich, Edward M., and Rubinfeld, Daniel L. 1982. "Micro Estimates of Public Spending Demand Functions and Tests of the Tiebout and Median-Voter Hypotheses." *Journal of Political Economy* 90 (June): 436–60.

Gramsci, Antonio. 1971. *Selections from Prison Notebooks*. New York: International Publishers.

Guede, Alain, and Rozenblum, Serge-Allain. 1981. "Les Candidates aux elections legislatives de 1978 et 1981." *Revue française de science politique* 31 (Oct.–Dec.): 982–98.

Habermas, Jürgen. 1970. "Toward a Theory of Communicative Competence." In *Recent Sociology*, no. 2, edited by Hans Peter Dreitzel, pp. 114–18. New York: Macmillan.

————. (1973) 1975. *The Legitimation Crisis*. Translated by Thomas McCarthy. Boston: Beacon Press.

————. 1978. *L'Espace public*. Paris: Payot.

————. 1979. *Communication and the Evolution of Society*. Boston: Beacon Press.

Hacker, Andrew. 1962. "Pressure Politics in Pennsylvania: The Truckers vs. the Railroads." In *The Uses of Power: 7 Cases in American Politics*, edited by Allan F. Westin, pp. 323–76. New York: Harcourt, Brace & World.

Haddock, David D. 1982. "Base-Point Pricing: Competitive vs. Collusive Theories." *American Economic Review* 72 (June): 289–306.

LIST OF REFERENCES CITED

Haddock, David D., and Hall, Thomas D. 1983. "The Impact of Making Rights Inalienable: *Merrion v. Jicarilla Apache Tribe, Texaco, Inc. v. Short, Fidelity Federal Savings & Loan Ass'n v. de al Cuesta,* and *Ridgway v. Ridgway."* *Supreme Court Economic Review* 2:1–41.

Hage, Jerald, and Hanneman, Robert A. 1980. "The Growth of the Welfare State in Britain, France, Germany, and Italy: A Comparison of Three Paradigms." *Comparative Social Research,* vol. 3. Greenwich, Conn.: JAI Press.

Hallagan, William. 1977. "Share Contracting for California Gold." *Explorations in Economic History* 15 (Apr.): 196–210.

Halperin, Morton, et al. 1976. *The Lawless State.* New York: Penguin Books.

Hamilton, Bruce W.; Mills, Edwin S.; and Puryear, David. 1975. "The Tiebout Hypothesis and Residential Income Segregation." In *Fiscal Zoning and Land Use Controls: The Economic Issues,* edited by Edwin S. Mills and Wallace Oates, pp. 101–18. Lexington, Mass.: Heath.

Hamilton, Nora. 1982. *The Limits of State Autonomy.* Princeton, N.J.: Princeton University Press.

Hansen, W. Lee. 1970. "Income Distribution Effects of Higher Education." *American Economic Review* 60 (May): 335–40.

Hansen, W. Lee, and Weisbrod, Burton A. 1969. *Benefits, Costs, and Finance of Public Higher Education.* Chicago: Markham.

Hardin, Clifford M., and Denzau, Arthur T. 1981. *The Unrestrained Growth of Federal Credit Programs.* St. Louis, Mo.: Washington University Center for the Study of American Business.

Hardin, Garrett. 1968. "The Tragedy of the Commons." *Science* 162 (Dec.): 1243–48.

Hart, H. L. A. 1983. *Essays for Jurisprudence and Philosophy.* Oxford: Oxford University Press.

Hawley, Ellis W. 1966. *The New Deal and the Problem of Monopoly.* Princeton, N.J.: Princeton University Press.

Hayek, Friedrich A. 1945. "The Use of Knowledge in Society." *American Economic Review* 35 (Sept.): 519–30.

———. 1973. *Law, Legislation and Liberty,* Chicago: University of Chicago Press.

Hayward, Fred, and Watson, John, eds. 1975. *Planning, Politics and Public Policy.* Cambridge: Cambridge University Press.

Heclo, Hugh. 1978. "Issue Networks and the Executive Establishment." In *The New American Political System,* edited by Anthony King. Washington, D.C.: American Enterprise Institute.

Henderson, James M., and Quandt, Richard E. 1971. *Microeconomic Theory: A Mathematical Approach.* New York: McGraw-Hill.

Herman, Edward. 1981. *Corporate Control, Corporate Power.* Cambridge: Cambridge University Press.

Hicks, J. R. 1939. "Foundations of Welfare Economics." *Economic Journal* 49 (Dec.): 696–712.

Hillman, Arye L. 1982. "Declining Industries and Political-Support Protectionist Motives." *American Economic Review* 72 (Dec.): 1180–87.

Hilton, George W. 1966. "The Consistency of the Interstate Commerce Act." *Journal of Law and Economics* 9 (Oct.): 87–113.

Hinich, Melvin J. 1978. "Some Evidence on Non-voting Models in the Spatial Theory of Electoral Competition." *Public Choice* 33 (2): 83–102.

Hinich, Melvin J., and Ordeshook, Peter C. 1969. "Abstention and Equilibrium in the Electoral Process." *Public Choice* 7 (Fall): 81–106.

Hirsch, Fred. 1976. *Social Limits to Growth.* Cambridge: Harvard University Press.

Hirshleifer, Jack. 1971. "The Private and Social Value of Information and the Reward to Inventive Activity." *American Economic Review* 61 (Sept.): 561–74.

Hirshleifer, Jack, and Riley, John G. 1979. "The Analytics of Uncertainty and Information: An Expository Survey." *Journal of Economic Literature* 17 (Dec.): 1375–1421.

Hochman, Harold D., and Rogers, James D. 1969. "Pareto Optimal Redistribution." *American Economic Review* 59 (Sept.): 542–57.

———. 1971. "Is Efficiency a Criterion for Judging Redistribution?" *Public Finance* 26 (2): 348–60.

Hofstra Law Review. 1980a. Symposium issue: "Efficiency as a Legal Concern" 8 (Spring): 484–770.

———. 1980b. Symposium issue: "Response to the Efficiency Symposium" 8 (Summer): 811–972.

Holloway, John, and Picciotto, Sol, eds. 1978. *State and Capital: A Marxist Debate.* Austin: University of Texas Press.

Horwitz, Morton J. 1978. *The Transformation of American Law, 1780–1860.* Cambridge: Harvard University Press.

Hotelling, Harold. 1929. "Stability in Competition." *Economic Journal* 39 (Mar.): 41–57.

Huntington, Samuel P. 1968. *Political Order in Changing Societies.* New Haven, Conn.: Yale University Press.

———. 1974. "Postindustrial Politics: How Benign Will It Be?" *Comparative Politics* 6 (Jan.): 163–92.

———. 1975. "The Democratic Distemper." *Public Interest* 14 (Fall): 9–38.

Ikenberry, John. 1983. "International Change, State Structure and Policy Responses." Paper prepared for delivery at the annual meeting of the American Political Science Association, Chicago, September.

Inman, Robert P. 1978. "Testing Political Economy's 'As If' Proposition: Is the Median Income Voter Really Decisive?" *Public Choice* 33: 45–65.

Ireland, Thomas R. 1969. "The Calculus of Philanthropy." *Public Choice* 7 (Fall): 23–32.

Jacobs, Jane. 1961. *The Death and Life of Great American Cities.* New York: Random House.

Jensen, Michael C., and Meckling, William H. 1976. "Theory of the Firm: Management Behavior, Agency Costs, and Ownership Structure." *Journal of Financial Economics* 3 (Oct.): 305–60.

Jessop, Bob. 1977. "Recent Theories of the Capitalist State." *Cambridge Journal of Economics* 1 (4; Dec.): 353–73.

———. 1982. *The Capitalist State.* New York: New York University Press.

Jordan, William A. 1972. "Producer Protection, Prior Market Structure, and the Effects of Government Regulation." *Journal of Law and Economics* 15 (Apr.): 151–76.

Journal of Legal Studies. 1979. Symposium Issue: "Private Alternatives to the Judicial Process" 7 (Mar.): 231–417.

———. 1980. Symposium Issue: "Change in the Common Law: Legal and Economic Perspectives" 9 (Mar.): 189–429.

Kahn, Alfred E. 1966. "The Tyranny of Small Decisions: Market Failures, Imperfections, and the Limits of Economics." *Kyklos* 19 (1): 23–47.

Kaldor, Nicholas. 1939. "Welfare Propositions in Economics and Interpersonal Comparisons of Utility." *Economic Journal* 49 (Sept.): 549–52.

Kamerschen, David R. 1976. "The Economic Effects of Monopoly: A Lawyer's Guide to Antitrust Enforcement." *Mercer Law Review* 27:1061–1109.

Kateb, George. 1979. "The Moral Distinctiveness of Representative Democracy." Paper delivered to the American Political Science Association, Washington, D.C.

Katzenstein, Peter, ed. 1977. *Between Power and Plenty*. Madison: University of Wisconsin Press.

———. 1980. "Capitalism in One Country? Switzerland in the International Economy." *International Organization* 34 (Autumn): 507–40.

Kautsky, John H. 1972. *The Political Consequences of Modernization*. New York: Wiley.

Kelly, George Armstrong. 1979. "Who Needs a Theory of Citizenship?" *Daedalus* 108 (4; Fall): 21–36.

Kent v. Dulles, 357 U.S. 116. 1958 (78 S. Ct. 1113).

Kessel, Reuben A. 1958. "Price Discrimination in Medicine." *Journal of Law and Economics* 1 (Oct.): 20–53.

Kesselman, Mark. 1983. "Socialism without the Workers." *Kapitalistate*, nos. 10/11: 11–41.

Key, V. O., Jr. 1964. *Politics, Parties, and Pressure Groups*. 5th ed. New York: Crowell.

King, Anthony. 1975. "Overload: Problems of Governing in the 1970's." *Political Studies* 23 (June–Sept.): 162–74.

Klein, Benjamin; Crawford, Robert G.; and Alchian, Armen A. 1978. "Vertical Integration, Appropriable Rents, and the Competitive Contracting Process." *Journal of Law and Economics* 21 (Oct.): 297–326.

Klein, Benjamin, and Leffler, Keith B. 1981. "The Role of Market Forces in Assuring Contractual Performance." *Journal of Political Economy* 89 (Aug.): 615–41.

Knight, Frank H. 1921. *Risk, Uncertainty, and Profit*. New York: Houghton Mifflin.

Koford, Kenneth. 1982. "An Optimistic View of the Possibility of Rational Legislative Decision Making." *Public Choice* 38 (1): 3–19.

Kolko, Gabriel. 1963. *The Triumph of Conservatism*. Chicago: Quadrangle.

———. 1965. *Railroads and Regulation*. New York: Norton.

Koller, Ronald H. 1971. "The Myth of Predatory Pricing: An Empirical Study." *Antitrust Law and Economics Review* 4 (Summer): 105–23.

Kramer, Jane. 1980. "Zurich." *New Yorker*, Dec. 15, pp. 118–20.

Krasner, Stephen D. 1978. *Defending the National Interest*. Princeton, N.J.: Princeton University Press.

———. 1984. "Approaches to the State: Alternative Conceptions and Historical Dynamics." *Comparative Politics* (Jan.): 223–46.

Kuhn, Thomas. 1977. *The Essential Tension*. Chicago: University of Chicago Press.

Kurth, James R. 1979. "The Political Consequences of the Product Cycle: Industrial History and Political Outcomes." *International Organization* 33 (1; Winter): 1–34.

Laclau, Ernesto. 1979. *Politics and Ideology in Marxist Theory*. London: Verso.

Landes, William M., and Posner, Richard A. 1975. "The Independent Judiciary in an Interest-group Perspective." *Journal of Law and Economics* 18 (Dec.): 875-901.

Lang, Nicholas. 1975. "The Dialectics of Decentralization: Economic Reform and Regional Inequality in Yugoslavia." *World Politics* 27 (Apr.): 309-35.

Lehmbruch, Gerhard. 1979. "Liberal Corporatism and Party Government." In *Trends toward Corporatist Intermediation*, edited by Philippe Schmitter and Gerhard Lehmbruch, pp. 40-76. Beverly Hills, Calif.: Sage.

Lenin, Vladimir I. 1949. *The State and Revolution*. Moscow: Progress Publishers.

Lerner, Abba P. 1964. "Conflicting Principles of Public Utility Regulation." *Journal of Law and Economics* 7 (Oct.): 61-70.

Levin, Harvey J. 1962. "Federal Control of Entry in the Broadcast Industry." *Journal of Law and Economics* 5 (Oct.): 49-67.

————. 1968. "The Radio Spectrum Resource." *Journal of Law and Economics* 11 (Oct.): 433-501.

Levine, Michael, and Plott, Charles R. 1977. "Agenda Influence and Its Implications." *Virginia Law Review* 63 (May): 561-604.

Libecap, Gary. 1978. "Economic Variables and the Development of Law: The Case of Western Mineral Rights." *Journal of Economic History* 38 (June): 338-62.

Libecap, Gary D., and Johnson, Ronald N. 1980. "Legislating Commons: The Navajo Tribal Council and the Navajo Range." *Economic Inquiry* 18 (Jan.): 69-86.

Lieber, Nancy, ed. 1982. *Eurosocialism and America: Political Economy for the 1980s*. Philadelphia: Temple University Press.

Lindberg, Leon N., ed. 1975. *Stress and Contradiction in Modern Capitalism*. Lexington, Mass.: Lexington Books.

Lindblom, Charles E. 1977. *Politics and Markets*. New York: Basic Books.

————. 1982. "The Market as Prison." *Journal of Politics* 44 (May): 324-36.

Lindblom, Charles E., and Cohen, David K. 1979. *Useable Knowledge*. New Haven, Conn.: Yale University Press.

Lindsay, Cottom M. 1976. "A Theory of Government Enterprise." *Journal of Political Economy* 84 (Oct.): 1061-77.

————. 1980. "Equal Pay for Comparable Work: An Economic Analysis of a New Antidiscrimination Doctrine." Law and Economics Center Occasional Paper.

Lindsay, Cottom M., and Shanor, Charles A. 1982. "*County of Washington v. Gunther:* Legal and Economic Considerations for Resolving Sex-Based Wage Discrimination Cases." *Supreme Court Economic Review* 1:185-233.

Lively, Jack. 1978. "Pluralism and Consensus." In *Democracy, Consensus and Social Contract*, edited by Pierre Birnbaum et al., pp. 185-202. Beverly Hills, Calif.: Sage.

Livingstone, David W. 1976. "On Hegemony in Corporate Capitalist States: Material Structures, Ideological Forms, Class Consciousness and Hegemonic Arts. *Sociological Inquiry* 46 (3/4): 235-50.

Logue, John. Forthcoming. "Has Success Spoiled the Welfare State? Solidarity and Egotism in Social Democratic Scandinavia." *Dissent*.

Long, William; Schramm, Richard; and Tollison, Robert. 1973. "The Economic Determinants of Antitrust Activity." *Journal of Law and Economics* 16 (Oct.): 351-64.

Lowi, Theodore J. 1964. "American Business, Public Policy, Case Studies, and Political Theory." *World Politics* 16 (July): 677-715.

————. 1979. *The End of Liberalism: The Second Republic of the United States.* 2d ed. New York: W. W. Norton & Co.

Luce, R. Duncan, and Raiffa, Howard. 1967. *Games and Decisions: Introduction and Critical Survey.* New York: Wiley.

Lukes, Steves. (1959) 1970. "Economic and Philosophic Manuscript of 1844." In *Collective Choice and Social Welfare.* San Francisco: Holden Day.

————. 1974. *Power: A Radical View.* London: Macmillan.

————. 1977. *Essays in Social Theory.* London: Macmillan.

Macchiocchi, Maria-Antonietta. 1980. "La Restructuration idéologique." In *Le Nouvelle Ordre intérieur,* edited by Pierre Dommergues, pp. 123-52. Paris: Alain Moreau.

McCormick, Robert E., and Tollison, Robert D. 1981. *Politicians, Legislation, and the Economy: An Inquiry into the Interest-group Theory of Government.* Boston: Martinus Nijhoff.

McCracken, Paul, et al. 1977. *Toward Full Employment and Price Stability.* OBECD Publications Center.

McGee, John S. 1958. "Predatory Price Cutting: The Standard Oil (N.J.) Case." *Journal of Law and Economics* 7 (Oct.): 137-69.

————. 1971. *The Defense of Industrial Concentration.* New York: Praeger.

Machlup, Fritz. 1962. *The Production and Distribution of Knowledge in the United States.* Princeton, N.J.: Princeton University Press.

Mackay, Robert J., and Reid, J. D., Jr. 1979. "On Understanding the Birth and Evolution of the Securities and Exchange Commission: Where Are We in the Theory of Regulation." In *Regulatory Change in an Atmosphere of Crisis: Current Implications of the Roosevelt Years,* edited by Gary M. Walton, pp. 101-21. New York: Academic Press.

McKelvey, Richard D. 1976. "Intransitivities in Multidimensional Voting Models and Some Implications for Agenda Control." *Journal of Economic Theory* 12 (June): 472-82.

McLure, Charles E., Jr. 1983. "Incidence Analysis and the Supreme Court: An Examination of Four Cases from the 1980 Term." *Supreme Court Economic Review* 1:69-112.

Macpherson, C. B. 1966. *The Real World of Democracy.* Oxford: Clarendon Press.

MacRae, Duncan, Jr. 1976. *The Social Function of Science.* New Haven, Conn.: Yale University Press.

Madison, James. 1961. "Federalist Paper #10." In *The Federalist Papers,* pp. 77-84. New York: Mentor.

Maloney, Michael T., and McCormick, Robert E. 1982. "A Positive Theory of Environmental Quality Regulation." *Journal of Law and Economics* 25 (Apr.): 99-123.

Maloney, Michael T., and Yandle, Bruce. 1980. "Rent Seeking and the Evolution of Property Rights in Air Quality." Clemson University Department of Economics Working Paper.

Mandel, Ernest. 1975. *Late Capitalism.* Translated from the German by Joris DeBres. London: Verso.

————. 1978. *From Stalinism to Eurocommunism.* London: New Left Books.

————. 1979. *Revolutionary Marxism Today.* London: New Left Books.

Manley, John F. 1970. *The Politics of Finance.* Boston: Little, Brown.

Manne, Henry G. 1965. "Mergers and the Market for Corporate Control." *Journal of Political Economy* 72 (Apr.): 110-20.

Manne, Henry G., and Solomon, Ezra. 1974. *Wall Street in Transition: The Emerging System and Its Impact on the Economy.* New York: New York University Press.

Mannheim, Karl. 1953. *Ideology and Utopia.* New York: Harcourt, Brace & World.

Marchais, Georges. 1979. "Pour une avancee démocratique." *Cahiers du communisme,* June, pp. 14–80.

Marcus, Alfred. 1980. "The Environmental Protection Agency." In *The Politics of Regulation,* edited by James Q. Wilson, pp. 267–303. New York: Basic Books.

Marcuse, Herbert. 1979. "Protosocialisme et capitalisme avance." *Les Temps modernes* 394 (May): 1705–30.

Margolis, Howard. 1977. "The Politics of Auto Emissions." *Public Interest* 49 (Fall): 3–21.

Marshall, T. H. 1981. *The Right to Welfare and Other Essays.* New York: Free Press.

Martin, Albro. 1972. *Enterprise Denied: The Origins of the Decline of American Railroads, 1897–1917.* New York: Columbia University Press.

Martin, Benjamin, and Kassalow, Everett M., eds. 1980. *Labor Relations in Advanced Industrial Societies: Issues and Problems.* Washington, D.C.: Carnegie Endowment for International Peace.

Martin, Donald L. 1972. "Job Rights and Job Defections." *Journal of Law and Economics* 15 (Oct.): 385–410.

———. 1973. "Same Economics of Job Rights in the Longshore Industry." *Journal of Economics and Business* 25 (Winter): 93–100.

———. 1977. "The Economics of Employment Termination Rights." *Journal of Law and Economics* 20 (Apr.): 187–204.

Marvel, Howard P. 1982. "Exclusive Dealing." *Journal of Law and Economics* 25 (Apr.): 1–25.

Marx, Karl. (1843) 1972. "On the Jewish Question." In *The Marx-Engels Reader,* edited by Robert C. Tucker, pp. 26–52. 2d ed. New York: W. W. Norton & Co.

———. (1852) 1935. *The Eighteenth Brumaire of Louis Bonaparte.* New York: International Publishers.

———. (1871) 1940. *The Civil War in France.* New York: International Publishers.

———. (1872) 1972. Speech in Amsterdam, 8 September. In *The Marx-Engels Reader,* edited by Robert C. Tucker. 2d ed. New York: W. W. Norton & Co.

———. (1875) 1938. *Critique of the Gotha Program.* Revised translation. New York: International Publishers.

———. 1967. *Capital.* Vol. 1: *The Process of Capitalist Production.* Translated by Samuel Moore and Edward Aveling and edited by Frederick Engels. New York: International Publishers.

Marx, Karl, and Engels, Frederick. (1846) 1947. *The German Ideology.* Edited, with an Introduction by R. Pascal. New York: International Publishers.

———. (1848) 1955. *The Communist Manifesto.* Edited by Samuel H. Beer. Crofts Classics Edition. Arlington Heights, Ill.: AHM Publishing Corp.

———. 1972. *Manifesto of the Communist Party.* Peking: Foreign Language Press.

Mashaw, Jerry L. 1981. "Constitutional Deregulation: Notes toward a Public-Public Law." *Tulane Law Review* 31:28.

Mayhew, David R. 1974. *Congress: The Electoral Connection* New Haven: Conn.: Yale University Press.

Meltzer, Allan H., and Richard, Scott F. 1978. "Why Government Grows (and Grows) in a Democracy." *Public Interest* 52 (Summer): 111–18.

————. 1981. "A Rational Theory of the Size of Government." *Journal of Political Economy* 89 (Oct.): 914–27.

————. 1983. "Tests of a Rational Theory of the Size of Government." *Public Choice* 41:403–18.

Middlesex County Sewerage Authority v. National Sea Clammers Association. 1981 (101 S. Ct. 2615).

Miliband, Ralph. 1969. *The State in Capitalist Society.* London: Weidenfeld & Nicolson.

————. 1970. "The Capitalist State: Reply to Nicos Poulantzas." *New Left Review* 59 (Jan./Feb.): 53–60.

————. 1973a. "Poulantzas and the Capitalist State." *New Left Review* 82 (Nov./Dec.): 83–92.

————. 1973b. *The State in Capitalist Society.* London: Quartet Books.

————. 1977. *Marxism and Politics.* Oxford, Eng.: Oxford University Press.

Miller, Stephen. 1982. "The Constitution and the Spirit of Commerce." In *How Capitalistic Is the Constitution?* edited by Robert A. Goldwin and William A. Schambra, pp. 148–69. Washington, D.C.: American Enterprise Institute for Public Policy Research.

Milleron, J. C. 1972. "Theory of the Value with Public Goods: A Survey Article." *Journal of Economic Theory* 5 (3): 419–77.

Mills, C. Wright. 1959. *The Power Elite.* New York: Oxford University Press.

Minasian, Jora R. 1964. "Television Pricing and the Theory of Public Goods." *Journal of Law and Economics* 7 (Oct.): 71–80.

————. 1975. "Property Rights in Radiation: An Alternative Approach to Radio Frequency Allocation." *Journal of Law and Economics* 18 (Apr.): 221–72.

Mises, Ludwig von. 1944. *Bureaucracy.* New Haven, Conn.: Yale University Press.

Mishan, Ezra J. 1971. "Evaluation of Life and Limb: A Theoretical Approach." *Journal of Political Economy* 79 (July/Aug.): 687–705.

————. 1972. *Elements of Cost-Benefit Analysis.* London: George Allen & Unwin.

Moran, Mark J., and Weingast, Barry R. 1982. "Congress as the Source of Regulatory Decisions: The Case of the Federal Trade Commission." *American Economic Review: Papers and Proceedings* 72 (May): 109–13.

Munley, Vincent G. 1982. "An Alternate Test of the Tiebout Hypothesis." *Public Choice* 38:211–17.

Musgrave, Richard A. 1959. *The Theory of Public Finance.* New York: McGraw-Hill.

Nader, Ralph; Green, Mark; and Seligman, Joel. 1976. *Taming the Giant Corporation.* New York: Norton.

National Cable Television Association v. United States, 415 U.S. 366. 1974 (94 S. Ct. 1146).

Nettl, J. P. 1968. "The State as a Conceptual Variable." *World Politics* 29 (July): 559–92.

Niemi, Richard G., and Weisberg, Herbert F., eds. 1972. *Probability Models of Collective Decision Making.* Columbus, Ohio: Charles E. Merrill Publishing Co.

Niskanen, William A., Jr. 1971. *Bureaucracy and Representative Government.* Chicago: Aldine Atherton.

Noll, Roger G. 1971. *Reforming Regulation: An Evaluation of the Ash Council Proposals.* Washington, D.C.: Brookings Institution.

Nordhaus, William. 1972. "The Recent Productivity Slowdown." *Brookings Papers on Economic Activity* 3:493–536. Washington, D.C.: Brookings Institution.

LIST OF REFERENCES CITED

————. 1975. "The Political Business Cycle." *Review of Economic Studies* 42 (Apr.): 169-90.

Nordlinger, Eric. 1981. *On the Autonomy of the Democratic State.* Cambridge: Harvard University Press.

North, Douglass C. 1979. "A Framework for Analyzing the State in Economic History." *Explorations in Economic History* 16:249-59.

Nozick, Robert. 1974. *Anarchy, State, and Utopia.* New York: Basic Books.

————. 1981. *Anarchy, State and Utopia.* Totowa, N.J.: Rowman & Littlefield.

Nutter, G. Warren. 1978. *Growth of Government in the West.* Washington, D.C.: American Enterprise Institute for Public Policy Research.

Oates, Wallace E. 1969. "The Effects of Property Taxes and Local Public Spending on Property Values: An Empirical Study of Tax Capitalization and the Tiebout Hypothesis." *Journal of Political Economy* 77 (Nov./Dec.): 957-71.

O'Connor, James. 1973. *The Fiscal Crisis of the State.* New York: St. Martin's Press.

O'Donnell, Guillermo. 1973. *Modernization and Bureaucratic Authoritarianism.* Berkeley: Institute of International Studies, University of California.

Offe, Claus. 1972. "Tauschverhaltnis und politische Steuerung." In *Strukturprobleme des kapitalistischen Staates,* edited by Jürgen Habermas. Frankfurt am Main: Suhrkamp.

————. 1974. "Structural Problems of the Capitalist State: Class Rule and the Political System: On the Selectiveness of Political Institutions." In *German Political Studies,* edited by Klaus von Beyme, vol. 1, pp. 31-57. Beverly Hills, Calif.: Sage Publications.

Offe, Claus, and Runge, Volker. 1975. "Theses on the Theory of the State." *New German Critique* 6 (Fall): 137-47.

Okun, Arthur M. 1975. *Equality and Efficiency: The Big Tradeoff.* Washington, D.C.: Brookings Institution.

Ollman, Bertell, 1977. *Alienation.* 2d ed. London: Cambridge University Press.

Olson, Mancur. 1965. *The Logic of Collective Action.* Cambridge: Harvard University Press.

————. 1971. *The Logic of Collective Action: Public Goods and the Theory of Groups.* Rev. ed. New York: Schocken.

————. 1972. "Evaluating Performance in the Public Sector." Paper prepared for delivery at the annual meeting of the Public Choice Society, Pittsburgh.

————. 1982. *The Rise and Decline of Nations: Economic Growth, Stagflation, and Social Rigidities.* New Haven, Conn.: Yale University Press.

Oppenheimer, Joe A. 1972. "Relating Coalitions of Minorities to the Voter's Paradox or Putting the Fly in the Democratic Pie." Paper prepared for the annual meeting of the Southwest Political Science Association in San Antonio, Texas.

Ordeshook, Peter C. 1970. "Extensions to a Model of the Electoral Process and Implications for the Theory of Responsible Parties." *Midwest Journal of Political Science* 14 (Feb.): 43-70.

Ordeshook, Peter C., and Shepsle, Kenneth A., eds. 1982. *Political Equilibrium: A Delicate Balance: Essays in Honor of William H. Riker.* Boston: Kluwer-Nijhoff.

Organization for Economic Cooperation and Development. 1977. "Toward Full Employment and Price Stability." Paris.

————. 1983. *Economic Outlook.* Paris.

255

Ostrom, Vincent. 1974. *The Intellectual Crisis in American Public Administration*. University: University of Alabama Press.

———. 1980. "Artisanship and Artifact." Paper prepared for delivery at the annual meeting of the American Political Science Association in New York, September.

Page, Benjamin I. 1976. "The Theory of Political Ambiguity." *American Political Science Review* 70 (Sept.): 742-52.

Page, Benjamin I., and Brady, Richard A. 1972. "Policy Voting and the Electoral Process: The Vietnam War-Issue." *American Political Science Review* 66 (Sept.): 979-95.

Palme, Olof. 1972. *Socialisme à la Scandinave*. Paris: Plon. Published in Sweden as *Politik Ar Att Vilja*.

———. 1977. "Social Justice and International Law." Jackson H. Ralston Lecture. Stanford, Calif.: Stanford University.

———. 1980. "Democratizing the Economy." Address given in Washington, D.C., on Dec. 6.

Parkin, Frank. 1979a. *Marxism and Class-Theory: A Bourgeois Critique*. New York: Columbia University Press.

———. 1979b. "Socialism, Equality and Liberty." In *The Future of Socialism?* edited by André Liebich. Montreal: Interuniversity Center for European Studies.

Pashigian, B. Peter. 1982. *The Political Economy of the Clean Air Act: Regional Self-interest in Environmental Legislation*. St. Louis, Mo.: Washington University Center for the Study of American Business.

Pateman, Carole. 1970. *Participation and Democratic Theory*. London: Cambridge University Press.

Peltzman, Sam. 1973. "An Evaluation of Consumer Protection Legislation: The 1962 Drug Amendments." *Journal of Political Economy* 81 (Sept./Oct.): 1049-91.

———. 1975. "The Effects of Automobile Safety Regulation." *Journal of Political Economy* 83 (Aug.): 667-725.

———. 1976. "Toward a More General Theory of Regulation." *Journal of Law and Economics* 19 (Aug.): 211-40.

Perelman, Chaim. 1979. *The New Rhetoric and the Humanities*. Dordrecht: D. Reidel.

Perelman, Chaim, and Olbrechts-Tyteca, L. 1969. *The New Rhetoric*. Notre Dame, Ind.: University of Notre Dame Press.

Pitkin, Hanna. 1972. *Wittgenstein and Justice*. Berkeley: University of California Press.

Piven, Frances Fox, and Cloward, Richard A. 1971. *Regulating the Poor*. New York: Pantheon.

———. 1977. *Poor People's Movements*. New York: Pantheon.

Plattner, Marc F. 1982. "American Democracy and the Acquisitive Spirit." In *How Capitalistic Is the Constitution?* edited by Robert A. Goldwin and William A. Schambra. Washington, D.C.: American Enterprise Institute.

Plott, Charles R. 1967. "A Notion of Equilibrium and Its Possibility under Majority Rule." *American Economic Review* 57 (Sept.): 787-806.

———. 1968. "Some Organizational Influences on Urban Renewal Decisions." *American Economic Review* 58 (May): 306-11.

———. 1976. "Axiomatic Social Choice Theory: An Interpretation and Overview." *American Journal of Political Science* 20 (Aug.): 511-96.

LIST OF REFERENCES CITED

Polsby, Nelson. 1980. *Community Power and Political Theory.* New Haven, Conn.: Yale University Press.

Poole, Robert W., Jr., ed. 1982. *Instead of Regulation: Alternatives to Federal Regulatory Agencies.* Lexington, Mass.: D. C. Heath.

Posner, Richard A. 1971. "Taxation by Regulation." *Bell Journal of Economics and Management Science* 2 (Spring): 22–50.

———. 1972a. "The Behavior of Administrative Agencies." *Journal of Legal Studies* (June): 305–47.

———. 1972b. *Economic Analysis of Law.* 1st ed. Boston: Little, Brown.

———. 1974. "Theories of Economic Regulation." *Bell Journal of Economics and Management Science* 5 (Autumn): 335–58.

———. 1975. "The Social Costs of Monopoloy and Regulation." *Journal of Political Economy* 83 (Aug.): 807–27.

———. 1976. *Antitrust Law: An Economic Perspective.* Chicago: University of Chicago Press.

———. 1977. *Economic Analysis of Law.* 2d ed. Boston: Little, Brown.

———. 1979. "Utilitarianism, Economics and Legal Theory." *Journal of Legal Studies* 8 (Jan.): 103–40.

———. 1980. "A Theory of Primitive Society with Special Reference to Primitive Law." *Journal of Law and Economics* 23 (Apr.): 1–53.

———. 1982. "Economics, Politics, and the Reading of Statutes and the Constitution." *University of Chicago Law Review* 49 (Spring): 288–90.

Poulantzas, Nicos. (1968) 1973. *Political Power and Social Classes.* Translated by T. O'Hagen. London: New Left Books.

———. 1969. "The Problem of the Capitalist State." *New Left Review* 58 (Nov./Dec.): 67–78.

———. (1974) 1975. *Classes in Contemporary Capitalism.* Translated by D. Fernback. London: New Left Books.

———. 1978. *State, Power, Socialism.* Translated by P. Camiller. London: New Left Books.

Priest, George L. 1977. "The Common Law Process and the Selection of Efficient Rules." *Journal of Legal Studies* 6 (Jan.): 65–82.

Przeworski, Adam, and Wallerstein, Michael. 1982. "The Structure of Class Conflict in Democratic Capitalist Societies." *American Political Science Review* 76 (2): 215–38.

Puviani, Amileare. 1903. *Teoria della illusione finanziaria.* Palermo: Sandron.

Quirk, James, and Saposnik, Rubin. 1968. *Introduction to General Equilibrium Theory and Welfare Economics.* New York: McGraw-Hill.

Rabinowitz, George. 1978. "On the Nature of Political Issues: Insights from a Spatial Analysis." *American Journal of Political Science* 22 (Nov.): 793–817.

Rae, Douglas. 1979. "The Egalitarian State." *Daedalus* 108 (Fall): 37–54.

Ranney, Austin. 1962. *The Doctrine of Responsible Party Government.* Urbana: University of Illinois Press.

Rawls, John. 1971. *A Theory of Justice.* Cambridge: Belknap Press of Harvard University Press.

Reich, Charles. 1964. "The New Property." *Yale Law Journal* 73 (5): 733–87.

Reschovsky, Andrew. 1979. "Residential Choice and the Local Public Sector: An Alternative Test of the Tiebout Hypothesis." *Journal of Urban Economics* 6 (Oct.): 501–20.

Riker, William H. 1958. "The Paradox of Voting and Congressional Rules for Voting on Amendments." *American Political Science Review* 52 (June): 349–66.
————. 1980. "Implications from the Disequilibrium of Majority Rule for the Study of Institutions." *American Political Science Review* 74 (June): 349–66.
Riker, William H., and Brams, Steven J. 1973. "The Paradox of Vote Trading." *American Political Science Review* 67 (Dec.): 1235–47.
Riker, William H., and Ordeshook, Peter C. 1973. *An Introduction to Positive Political Theory.* Englewood Cliffs, N.J.: Prentice-Hall.
Rochatyn, Felix. 1981. "The Older America: Can It Survive?" *New York Review of Books,* Jan. 22, pp. 13–14.
Rohr, John. 1983. "The Administrative State and the Constitution." Paper delivered to the American Political Science Association in Chicago, Ill.
Rosanvallon, Pierre, and Vincent, Patrick. 1977. *Pour une nouvelle culture politique.* Paris: Seuil.
Rose, Arnold. 1967. *The Power Structure.* New York: Oxford University Press.
Rose, Richard, and Guy, Peter B. 1978. "The Growth of Government and Political Bankruptcy: The Political Consequences of Economic Overload." Paper presented at the Midwest Political Science Meetings in Chicago, April.
Rosenthal, Uriel. 1983. "The Welfare State: Sticks, No Carrots." Paper presented at the conference Futures of the Welfare State, at Indiana University, April.
Ross, Thomas B., and Wise, David. 1974. *The Invisible Government.* New York: Vintage Books.
Rothschild, Michael. 1973. "Models of Market Organization with Imperfect Information." *Journal of Political Economy* 81 (Nov./Dec.): 1283–1308.
Rousseau, Jean Jacques. 1968. *The Social Contract.* Translated by Maurice Cranston. Baltimore, Md.: Penguin Books.
Rubin, Paul H. 1977. "Why Is the Common Law Efficient?" *Journal of Legal Studies* 6 (Jan.): 51–63.
————. 1978. "The Theory of the Firm and the Structure of the Franchise Contract." *Journal of Law and Economics* 21 (Apr.): 223–33.
Rusk, Jerold G., and Weisberg, Herbert F. 1972. "Perceptions of Presidential Candidates: Implications for Electoral Change." *Midwest Journal of Political Science* 16 (Aug.): 338–410.
Russett, Bruce M., and Starr, Harvey. 1981. *World Politics: The Menu for Choice.* San Francisco: W. H. Freeman.
Samuelson, Paul A. 1954. "The Pure Theory of Public Expenditure." *Review of Economics and Statistics* 36 (Nov.): 387–90.
————. 1964. "Public Goods and Subscription TV: Correction of the Record." *Journal of Law and Economics* 7 (Oct.): 81–83.
Sandel, Michael. 1982. *Liberalism and the Limits of Justice.* New York: Cambridge University Press.
Sartori, Giovanni. 1965. *Democratic Theory.* New York: Praeger.
Sartre, Jean-Paul. 1980. Interview-Discussion with Benny Levy. *Dissent* 27 (Fall): 397–442.
Sayre, Wallace, and Kaufman, Herbert. 1965. *Governing New York City.* New York: Russell Sage Foundation.
Schattschneider, E. E. 1935. *Politics, Pressures, and the Tariff.* Englewood Cliffs, N.J.: Prentice-Hall.
Schmitt, Carl. 1976. *The Concept of the Political.* New Brunswick, N.J.: Rutgers University Press.

Schoyer, Trent. 1975. "The Re-politicization of the Relations of Production: An Interpretation of Juergen Habermas' Analytic Theory of Late Capitalist Development." *New German Critique* (Spring): 107–28.

Schumpeter, Joseph. 1950. *Capitalism, Socialism, and Democracy.* New York: Harper & Row.

Schurman, Franz. 1974. *The Logic of World Power.* New York: Pantheon.

Schwartz, Thomas. 1981. "The Pork-Barrel Paradox." Paper prepared for the annual meeting of the Public Choice Society.

Scitovsky, Tibor, 1941. "A Note on Welfare Propositions in Economics." *Review of Economic Studies* 9 (Nov.): 77–88.

———. 1942. "A Reconsideration of the Theory of Tariffs." *Review of Economic Studies* 9 (2): 89–110.

———. 1976. *The Joyless Economy.* New York: Oxford University Press.

Scott, Anthony. 1955. "The Fishery: The Objectives of Sole Ownership." *Journal of Political Economy* 63 (Apr.): 116–24.

———. 1980. *Writing by Candlelight.* London: Merlin Press.

Sen, Amartya K. 1970. *Collective Choice and Social Welfare.* San Francisco: Holden Day.

Shepsle, Kenneth A. 1972a. "Parties, Voters, and the Risk Environment: A Mathematical Treatment of Electoral Competition under Uncertainty." In *Probability Models of Collective Decision Making,* edited by Richard G. Niemi and Herbert F. Weisberg, pp. 273–97. Columbus, Ohio: Merrill.

———. 1972b. "The Strategy of Ambiguity: Uncertainty and Electoral Competition." *American Political Science Review* 66 (June): 555–68.

———. 1978. "The Role of Institutional Structures in the Creation of Policy Equilibrium. In *Sage Yearbook in Politics and Public Policy,* edited by Douglas W. Rae and Theodore J. Eismeier, pp. 249–83. Beverly Hills, Calif.: Sage.

———. 1979. "Institutional Arrangements and Equilibrium in Multidimensional Voting Models." *American Journal of Political Science* 23 (Feb.): 27–59.

———. 1983. "Overgrazing the Budgetary Commons: Incentive-Compatible Solutions to the Problem of Deficits." In *The Economic Consequences of Public Deficits,* edited by Lawrence Mayer, pp. 211–19. Boston: Martinus Nijhoff.

Shepsle, Kenneth A., and Weingast, Barry R. 1981a. "Political Preferences for the Pork Barrel: A Generalization." *American Journal of Political Science* 25 (Feb.): 96–111.

———. 1981b. "Structure and Strategy: The Two Faces of Agenda Power." Paper prepared for delivery at the annual meeting of the American Political Science Association in New York City, September.

———. 1981c. "Structure-induced Equilibrium and Legislative Choice." *Public Choice* 37 (3): 503–19.

Shils, Edward A., ed. 1968. *Criteria for Scientific Development: Public Policy and National Goals.* Cambridge, Mass.: MIT Press.

Shonfield, Andrew. 1965. *Modern Capitalism.* London: Oxford University Press.

Showstack-Sassoon, Anne F. 1978. "Hegemony and Political Intervention." In *Politics, Ideology, and the State.* London: Lawrence & Wishart.

Simon, Herbert A. 1947. *Administrative Behavior: A Study of Decision Making.* New York: Free Press.

———. 1976. *Administrative Behavior.* 3d ed. New York: Free Press.

Simons, Henry C. 1935. *Positive Program for Laissez-Faire.* 2d ed. Chicago: University of Chicago Press.

LIST OF REFERENCES CITED

Skinner, Quentin. 1981. "The World as Stage." *New York Review of Books*, Apr. 16, pp. 35–37.

Skocpol, Theda. 1979. *States and Social Revolutions: Comparative Analysis of France, Russia, and China.* Cambridge: Cambridge University Press.

Skocpol, Theda, and Ikenberry, John. Forthcoming. "The Political Formation of the American Welfare State in Historical and Comparative Perspective." *Comparative Social Research.* Vol. 6. Greenwich, Conn.: JAI Press.

Skowronek, Stephen. 1982. *Building a New American State: The Expansion of National Administrative Capacities, 1877–1920.* London: Cambridge University Press.

Smith, Adam. (1776) 1976. *An Inquiry into the Nature and Causes of the Wealth of Nations.* Edited by George J. Stigler. Chicago: University of Chicago Press.

Smith, Robert S. 1982. "Protecting Workers' Health and Safety." In *Instead of Regulation: Alternatives to Federal Regulatory Agencies*, edited by Robert W. Poole, Jr., pp. 311–38. Lexington, Mass.: D. C. Heath.

Smith, Vernon L. 1969. "On Models of Commercial Fishing." *Journal of Political Economy* 77 (Mar./Apr.): 181–98.

Smithies, Arthur. 1941. "Optimal Location in Spatial Competition." *Journal of Political Economy* 49 (June): 423–39.

Spann, Robert M. 1977. "Public versus Private Provision of Governmental Services." In *Budgets and Bureaucrats: The Source of Government Growth*, edited by Thomas E. Borcherding, pp. 71–89. Durham, N.C.: Duke University Press.

Stavrianos, L. S. 1981. *Global Rift: The Third World Comes of Age.* New York: William Morrow & Co.

Steiner, Peter O. 1974. "Public Expenditure Budgeting." In *The Economics of Public Finance*, edited by Alan S. Blinder et al., pp. 241–97. Washington, D.C.: Brookings Institution.

Stern, Phillip M. 1973. *The Rape of the Taxpayer.* New York: Random House.

Stewart, Richard. 1975. "The Reformation of American Administrative Law." *Harvard Law Review* 88 (8; June): 1667–1813.

Stigler, George J. 1961. "The Economics of Information." *Journal of Political Economy* 69 (June): 213–23.

———. 1962. "Administered Prices and Oligopolistic Inflation." *Journal of Business* 35 (Jan.): 1–13.

———. 1966. "The Economic Effects of the Antitrust Laws." *Journal of Law and Economics* 9 (Oct.): 225–58.

———. 1970. "Director's Law of Public Income Redistribution." *Journal of Law and Economics* 13 (Apr.): 1–10.

———. 1971. "The Theory of Economic Regulation." *Bell Journal of Economics and Management Science* 2 (Spring): 3–21.

———. 1974a. "Free-riders and Collective Action: An Appendix to Theories of Economic Regulation." *Bell Journal of Economics and Management Science* 5 (Autumn): 360.

———. 1974b. "Henry Calvert Simons." *Journal of Law and Economics* 17 (Apr.): 1–5.

Stigler, George J., and Freidland, Claire. 1962. "What Can Regulators Regulate? The Case of Electricity." *Journal of Law and Economics* 5 (Oct.): 1–16.

Stigler, George J., and Kindahl, James K. 1970. *The Behavior of Industrial Prices.* New York: National Bureau of Economic Research.

————. 1973. "Industrial Prices as Administered by Dr. Means." *American Economic Review* 63 (Sept.): 717-21.

Stockman, David. 1975. "The Social Pork Barrel." *Public Interest* 39 (Spring): 3-30.

Stone, Clarence. 1980. "Systematic Power in Community Decision Making: A Restatement of Stratification Theory." *American Political Science Review* 74 (4; Dec.): 987-90.

————. 1981. "Community Power Structure: A Further Look." *Urban Affairs Quarterly* 16 (4; June): 505-15.

Storing, Herbert J. 1980. "American Statesmanship: Old and New." In *Bureaucrats, Policy Analysts, Statesmen: Who Leads?* edited by Robert A. Goldwin, pp. 88-113. Washington, D.C.: American Enterprise Institute for Public Policy Research.

Strasser, Johano. 1979. *Grenzen des Sozialstaats?* Frankfurt am Main: Europäische Verlagsanstalt.

Stuart, Arnold J. C. "On Progressive Taxation." In *Classics in the Theory of Public Finance*, edited by Richard A. Musgrave and Alan T. Peacock, pp. 48-71. New York: Macmillan.

Sylvan, David; Snidal, Duncan; Russett, Bruce M.; Jackson, Steven; and Duvall, Raymond. 1983. "The Peripheral Economies: Penetration and Economic Distortion, 1970-1975." In *Contending Approaches to World System Analysis*, edited by William R. Thompson, pp. 79-111. Beverly Hills, Calif.: Sage Publications.

Tawney, R. H. 1931. *Equality*. New York: Harcourt, Brace.

————. 1964. *The Radical Tradition*. London: Allen & Unwin.

Thayer, Frederick C. 1981. *An End to Hierarchy and Competition*. New York: Franklin Watts.

Therborn, Göran. 1978. *What Does the Ruling Class Do When It Rules? State Apparatuses and State Power under Feudalism, Capitalism and Socialism*. London: New Left Books.

Thomas, P. 1979. "Marxism and Compromise: A Speculation." In *Compromise in Ethics, Law, and Politics*, vol. 22, edited by J. R. Pennock and J. W. Chapman. New York: New York University Press.

Thompson, E. P. 1979. *The Poverty of Theory and Other Essays*. New York: Monthly Review Press.

————. 1980. *Writing by Candlelight*. London: Merlin Press.

Thurow, Lester C. 1977. "Equity: The Implicit Agenda." In *American Reevolution: Papers and Proceedings*, edited by Richard Auster and Barbara Sears, pp. 133-41. Tucson: Department of Economics, University of Arizona.

————. 1980. *The Zero Sum Society*. New York: Basic Books.

Tiebout, Charles M. 1956. "A Pure Theory of Local Expenditures." *Journal of Political Economy* 64 (Oct.): 416-24.

Tilly, Charles, ed. 1975. *The Formation of National States in Western Europe*. Studies in Political Development, no. 8. Princeton, N.J.: Princeton University Press.

Titmuss, Richard. 1977. *Social Policy*. London: George Allen & Unwin.

Touraine, Alain. 1978. *La Voix et le regard*. Paris: Seuil.

————. 1979. "Political Ecology: A Land to Live Differently—Now." *New Society* 50 (Nov.): 307-9.

Trosper, Ronald L. 1978. "American Indian Relative Ranching Efficiency." *American Economic Review* 68 (Sept.): 503-16.

Truman, David. 1951. *The Governmental Process: Political Interests and Public Opinion.* New York; Knopf.

Tufte, Edward. 1978. *Political Control of the Economy.* Princeton, N.J.: Princeton University Press.

Tullock, Gordon. 1965. *The Politics of Bureaucracy.* Washington, D.C.: Public Affairs Press.

———, ed. 1972. *Explorations in the Theory of Anarchy.* Blacksburg, Va.: Center for the Study of Public Choice.

Umbeck, John. 1977. "A Theory of Contract Choice and the California Gold Rush." *Journal of Law and Economics* 20 (Oct.): 421-37.

Unger, Roberto M. 1975. *Knowledge and Politics.* New York: Free Press.

———. 1983. "The Critical Legal Studies Movement." *Harvard Law Review* 96 (3): 561-675.

Valery, Paul. 1962. *The Outlook for Intelligence.* New York: Harper.

Vanek, Jaroslav. 1977. *The Labor-Managed Economy.* Ithaca, N.Y.: Cornell University Press.

van Wagstaff, Joseph. 1965. "Income Tax Consciousness under Withholding." *Southern Economic Journal* 32 (July): 73-80.

von Furstenberg, G. M., and Mueller, Dennis C. 1971. "The Pareto Optimal Approach to Redistribution: A Fiscal Application." *American Economic Review* 61 (Sept.): 628-37.

Wagner, Richard E. 1976. "Revenue Structure, Fiscal Illusion, and Budgetary Choice." *Public Choice* 25 (Spring): 45-61.

Walzer, Michael. 1976. "Politics in the Welfare State." In *Essential Works of Socialism,* edited by Irving Howe, pp. 00. New Haven, Conn.: Yale University Press.

———. 1981. "Life with Father." *New York Review of Books,* Apr. 2, pp. 3-4.

Wardell, William M., and Lasagna, Louis. 1975. *Regulation and Drug Development.* Washington, D.C.: American Enterprise Institute for Public Policy Research.

Weaver, Paul. 1978. "Regulation, Social Policy and Class Conflict." *Public Interest* 50 (Winter): 45-63.

Weimer, David Leo. 1982. "Safe—and Available—Drugs." In *Instead of Regulation: Alternatives to Federal Regulatory Agencies,* edited by Robert W. Poole, Jr., pp. 239-83. Lexington, Mass.: D. C. Heath.

Weingast, Barry R. 1979. "A Rational Choice Perspective on Congressional Norms." *American Journal of Political Science* 23 (May): 245-62.

———. 1981. "Regulation, Reregulation and Deregulation: The Political Foundations of Agency Clientele Relations." *Law and Contemporary Problems* 44 (Winter): 147-77.

Weingast, Barry R.; Shepsle, Kenneth A.; and Johnsen, Christopher. 1981. "The Political Economy of Benefits and Costs: A Neoclassical Approach to Distributive Politics." *Journal of Political Economy* 89 (Aug.): 642-64.

Weinstein, James. 1968. *The Corporate Ideal in the Liberal State, 1900-1918.* Boston: Beacon Press.

Weisberg, Herbert F., and Rusk, Jerold G. 1970. "Dimensions of Candidate Evaluation." *American Political Science Review* 64 (Dec.): 1167-85.

White, Stephen. 1980. "Reason and Authority in Habermas: A Critique of the Critics." *American Political Science Review* 74 (Dec.): 1007-17.

————. 1981. Discussion on "Reason and Authority in Habermas: A Critique of the Critics." *American Political Science Review* 75 (June): 463–65.

Wildavsky, Aaron. 1978. "Changing forward versus Changing Back." *Yale Law Journal* 88 (Nov.): 217–34.

————. 1979. *The Politics of the Budgetary Process.* Boston: Little, Brown.

Wilensky, Harold. 1976. *The 'New Corporatism,' Centralization, and the Welfare State.* Sage Professional Papers, 06-020. Beverly Hills, Calif.: Sage Publications.

Williams, Raymond. 1977. *Marxism and Literature.* Oxford, Eng.: Oxford University Press.

Williamson, Oliver E. 1964. *The Economics of Discretionary Behavior: Managerial Objectives in a Theory of the Firm.* Englewood Cliffs, N.J.: Prentice-Hall.

Wilson, Frank. 1983. "French Interest Group Politics: Pluralist or Neocorporatist?" *American Political Science Review* 77 (Dec.): 67bn.40.

Wilson, James Q. 1973. *Political Organizations.* New York: Basic Books.

————. 1979. *American Government: Institutions and Policies.* Lexington, Mass.: Heath.

————, ed. 1980. *The Politics of Regulation.* New York: Basic Books.

Wilson, Woodrow. 1887. "The Study of Administration." *Political Science Quarterly* 2 (June): 197–220. Reprinted in *The Papers of Woodrow Wilson,* vol. 5. Edited by Arthur S. Link, pp. 357–80. Princeton, N.J.: Princeton University Press.

————. 1925a. "Committee or Cabinet Government?" In *The Public Papers of Woodrow Wilson: College and State,* vol. 1. Edited by Ray S. Baker and William E. Dodd, pp. 95–129. New York: Harper & Brothers.

————. 1925b. "Leaderless Government." In *The Public Papers of Woodrow Wilson: College and State,* vol. 1. Edited by Ray S. Baker and William E. Dodd, pp. 336–59. New York: Harper & Brothers.

————. 1956. *Congressional Government: A Study in American Politics.* New York: Meridian.

Wolfe, Alan. 1974. "New Directions in the Marxist Theory of Politics." *Politics and Society* 4 (2; Winter): 131–59.

————. 1977. *The Limits of Legitimacy.* New York: Free Press.

————. 1981. "Presidential Power and the Crisis of Modernization." *Democracy* 1 (2; Apr.): 9–24.

Wolin, Sheldon. 1981. "The People's Two Bodies." *Democracy* 1 (1; Jan.): 9–24.

Wright, Erik Olin. 1978. *Class, Crisis and State.* London: New Left Books.

————. 1979. *Class Structure and Income Determination.* New York: Academic Press.

Yinger, John. 1982. "Capitalization and the Theory of Public Finance." *Journal of Political Economy* 90 (Oct.): 917–43.

Zuckert, Catherine H. 1982. "The Political Theory of the Market." Paper delivered to the American Political Science Association in Washington, D.C.

Contributors

PETER H. ARANSON (Ph.D., University of Rochester), Department of Economics, and Law and Economics Center, Emory University. Author of many articles, including "A Theory of Legislative Delegation" (with E. Gelhorn and G. O. Robinson), *Cornell University Law Review*, November 1982; editor of *Supreme Court Economic Review;* coeditor of *Public Choice.*

ROGER BENJAMIN (Ph.D., Washington University), Department of Political Science, University of Minnesota; Senior Vice-Chancellor for Academic Affairs and Provost, University of Pittsburgh. Author of *The Limits of Politics* (University of Chicago); coauthor of *Community Development and Rational Choice;* coeditor of *The Changing Industry of the Pacific Basin* (with Robert Kuderle); and numerous articles in comparative politics and public policy.

DAVID BRAYBROOKE (Ph.D., Cornell University), Professor of Philosophy and Politics, Dalhousie University. Author of articles on Marx's doctrine, the dialectic of history, ethics, decision making, and the philosophy of science; a Fellow of the Royal Society of Canada; a former president of the Canadian Philosophical Association; in 1983/84, vice-president of the American Political Science Association.

RAYMOND DUVALL (Ph.D., Northwestern University), Associate Professor of Political Science, University of Minnesota. In several articles, his research has focused on the state in dependent societies. Two recent articles are "The Technobureaucratic Elite and the Entrepreneurial State in Dependent Industrialization," *American Political Science Review*, September 1983, and "International Economic Relations and the Entrepreneurial State," *Economic Development and Cultural Change*, January 1984.

CONTRIBUTORS

STEPHEN ELKIN (Ph.D., Harvard University), Department of Government and Politics, University of Maryland. Author of *Politics and Land Use Planning* (Cambridge University Press) and of numerous articles on political economy, policy analysis, and urban affairs; founder (with Martin Shefter and John Mollenkoff) of the Conference Group on Political Economy.

NORMAN FURNISS (Ph.D., Harvard University), Department of Political Science and West European Studies, Indiana University. Author (with T. Tilton) of *The Case for the Welfare State* (Indiana University) and numerous articles on political philosophy and international and comparative politics.

PETER ORDESHOOK (Ph.D., University of Rochester), University of Texas at Austin. Author (with William Riker) of the classic *An Introduction to Positive Political Theory* (Prentice-Hall, 1973).

Index

action. *See* state action

administrative state. *See* state—the administrative state

agencies, administrative, 2; as providers of social welfare, 3

anarchy, 173 n.25; and laissez-faire economies, 100

authoritarianism, bureaucratic, 45

authoritarian statism, 76

authority, public. *See* public authority

bads, public, explained, 93–94

bourgeoisie, the, 25, 31, 32, 43, 56 n.25, 60, 62; petit, 31, 32; interests of, in dependent-industrializing society, 47; and rhetoric of rights, 61

bourgeois state. *See* state—the bourgeois state

bureaucracy, 78, 83, 121; and state-centered politics, 11; and the dominant class, 48–49; and the bourgeoisie, 72; and bourgeois ideology, 73; and reprivatization, 75, 80–81; and political parties, 76; organizational imperialism, self-interest, and, 80–81; markets as alternatives to, 81; and the principal-agent problem, 139–40

bureaucratic authoritarianism, 45

business interests: as favored over citizens' interests, 3; assisted by government, 3; and public authority, 3, 180; and public officials, 3, 179, 180, 188, 189; and power, 181; in liberal theory, 183; and ruling-class thesis, 183–86; and economic performance, 187, 195; and popular control, 193; the state as promoter of, 193, 209–10 n.29; in the liberal democratic state, 193; and policy domains, 194; and program implementation, 195; and iron triangles, 195; as promoted by legislation, 199–200; courts as promoters of, 200; regulatory agencies as promoters of, 200; privileged position of, 221

capitalism, 79, 80; and public authority, 3; and control of the state, 3; as assisted by government, 3; definition of, 4–5; and public officials, 5; and class cohesion, 5; and liberal democracy, 5, 181; the state in service of, 5; and democratic control, 13; and forms of society, 20, and theory of the state, 20; differing contexts of, 21; in bureaucratic-authoritarian state, 42, 44, 48; autonomy of, 45; laws of motion of, 52 n.3, 54 n.11; governmental intervention in, 62, 68–69, 70; transformation

INDEX

from, to socialism, 64; the state in late, 66–74, 76; political parties in late, 84; and school of public choice, 86 n.7; conversion of, from failure, 214; modern, 215; features of modern, 216; and social democracy, 219

capitalist state. *See* state—the capitalist state

central planning. *See* planning, central

choice. *See* public-choice theory, school of; social choice

citizen-initiative movements, 232

citizen preferences, and the constitutional regime, 12

civil liberties, 79; and revolution, 77; preserving, and reprivatization, 80

classes: interests of dominant, 5, 67, 68, 69; tensions among, 7; in advanced-industrial society, 31; in dependent-industrializing capitalism, 31–32; and organizing principles of administrative state, 40–45, 48; in Marxist concept of the state, 60

class interests, 56 n.24; and capitalism, 5, 32

collective decision making, 11

common good, and state-centered politics, 11

common law: as method for state action, 100–102, 107; and property rights, 100–101; and allocation of right, 101; and free-rider problem, 102; efficiency of, 143–45. *See also* law; statutory law

communicative ethics, 233

consent: control systems vs. classes and, 7; and veil of ignorance, 172 n.14; unanimous, 172–73 n.19

consumption: social relations of, 32, 34, 35; means of, 33–35; and growth, 33

corporatism, liberal, 227, 235 n.12

cost-benefit analysis, 171 n.12; as boundary on social choice, 98–100

decision making, collective, 11

decision making, global: defined, 154; in elections, 156; hybrid, 157–58

decision making, incremental: in elections, 156; and naïve incrementalism, 156–57;

and opportunity-cost local optimum, 157; and non-opportunity-cost local optimum, 157; and large vs. small electorates, 160; and insensitive electorates, 161

decision making, legislative: constituency as interest group in, 158; and nonconstituency interest group, 159; and heterogeneous constituencies, 159

democracy: vs. liberalism, 11; public-sector programs in representative, 87; failure of representative, 88; representative, and welfare theory, 118, 165; convergence between liberalism and, 202–3

—advanced capitalist: and welfare state, 213–16; and economic growth, 214; and inflation, 215; and OECD policy, 216; and tight monetary policy, 216; and full employment, 216; and recession, 216; and regime crisis, 232

—autogestionnaire, 15, 213–14, 230–35; and civil society, 226, 231; as departure from radical thought, 229; equality in, 229; and unitary democracy, 231; and regime crisis, 234; and pluralism, 235

—liberal: and liberal theory, 1; as a state, 1; administrative agencies in, 2; features of, 2–4, 179; social-welfare programs in, 3; market system in, 3; Marxist analysis of, 12, 19ff.; revolution in, 76–77; as mixed state, 180; authority in, 181; and capitalism, 181; pluralist theory of, 181–83; and public/private distinction, 186; business-state relationships in, 198–99; and promotion of special interests, 199; central role of institutions in, 204; decline of public faith in, 206

—social, 227; as a public philosophy, 219; and modern capitalism, 219; economic assumption of, 219; and property rights, 220; reorientation of, 235 n.10

—strong, 11, 12

—unitary, 231

democratized liberalism, 203

distributive justice, 39, 40, 55 n.17

economy, the international: and public officials, 3–4; state-centered analysis of, 3; and domestic politics, 8

268

INDEX

equality: in institutional-legal order, 36; in advanced-industrial capitalism, 40; as statist ideal, 229; bourgeois, 230
equal opportunity, in the social-security state, 222
externalities, 82; regulation of, and group competition, 32; explained, 93–94. See also bads, public

familial-vocational privatism: defined, 72; utilitarianism as feature of, 86 n.5
fascism, 1
fiscal-illusion hypothesis, 149; and public-sector size, 114–18
freedom: in institutional-legal order, 36; economic, 39, 40; entrepreneurial, 40; in advanced-industrial capitalism, 40

global decision making. See decision making, global
goods. See positional goods; private goods; private-goods-election model; private/public goods; public goods
group interests: in advanced-industrial and dependent-industrializing capitalism, 32; and quality-of-life issues, 32; and transformation of society, 33
growth: in advanced-industrial capitalism, 33; in dependent-industrializing capitalism, 33, 53–54 n.10; in advanced capitalist democracy, 214; economic, and governmental policy, 215

hegemonic state, the, 26
heroic policy making. See policy making, heroic

imbalance. See social-imbalance hypothesis
incremental decision making. See decision making, incremental
institutional-legal order, the, 54 n.12; the state as, 25–26; in different capitalist contexts, 36–40; and rights, 37–38; pri-

vate/public distinction and, 38–39; and dependent-industrializing capitalist state, 40; and advanced-industrial capitalist state, 40
institutional reform: tax and spending limitations as, 165–67; regulatory reform as, 167–69; decentralization as, 169; political incentives for, 169–70
intelligentsia, 25, 31, 43
interest groups, 6, 14; and state officials, 11; political advantages of, 118–21; nature of demands by, 121–28; policy game between two, 122; and prisoners' dilemma, 123, 126, 135; and decision making, 126; and pluralism, 129; and free-rider problem, 135–36; and regulation, 137–39; as constituency, 158; non-constituency, 159; and public-sector expansion, 160; and popular control, 197
international economy. See economy, the international
iron triangles, 3; and business interests, 195

justice: in institutional-legal order, 36; distributive, 39, 40, 55 n.17; in advanced-industrial capitalism, 40

labor, division of, between market and state, 179–80, 207 n.1, 226
law: in institutional-legal order, 36; and administrative state, 44. See also common law; statutory law
legislative decision making. See decision making, legislative
legislative process, the: and interest groups, 131ff.; position taking in, 131–32; advertising in, 132; credit claiming in, 132–33; committees in, 134; formal theories of, 134–35; costs of, 146; and business performance, 200
legitimation: and liberal political practices, 204; as the state itself, 204; and decline in economic growth, 204–5; and decline in liberal and democratic practices, 205
legitimation crisis, 8, 13, 72; and reprivatization, 71

269

INDEX

and business interests, 198; connection between liberalism and, 207 n.10
pluralist theory: of liberal democracy, 181–83; and power, 181–82, 183; concept of politics in, 182; and concept of interests, 182; and the state, 182; and connection between market and state, 182; and ruling-class thesis, 184; and regime argument, 196
policy. *See* public policy
policy making, heroic: tenets of, 227; origins of, 227–28; and democratic corporate state, 227–28
policy networks, 3
political parties: decline of, 3; and public officials, 3; and state bureaucracy, 76; in late capitalism, 84
polyarchies, 7
popular control, 190; and governmental activity, 4; and state-centered analysis of the democratic state, 4; institutions of, 6; and markets, 7, 180; as linking state and society, 9; of authority, 179; and ruling-class thesis, 185–86; as constrained in liberal democratic regime, 191, 192; and business interests, 193; and interest groups, 197–98; regulatory agencies, 200; as democratic political practice, 202
positional goods, 32, 35, 49
positive state. *See* state—the positive state
postindustrial society, 21, 53 n.4, 231; and advanced-industrialized society, 53 n.9
postrevolutionary society: features of, 79–80; and representative institutions, 79
power: and popular control, 179–80; of business actors, 179–80; community, 207 n.2
prisoners' dilemma, 123, 126, 135, 173 n.24; and Congress, 146
private goods, 83; characteristics of, 91–92
private-goods-election model, the, 148–69; and interest groups, 149; voters in, 149–52; and opportunity cost of information gathering, 150; and candidates' strategies, 152–56; incremental decision making in, 153, 155–56; global decision making in, 154–55; implications from, 159–61. *See also* decision making, global; decision making, incremental
private property, 61, 62; public intervention in, 221. *See also* property rights

private/public distinction, in advanced-industrial society, 38
private/public goods, 55 n.16; and the legal order, 38; distinction between, 38; boundaries between, 38; and planning, 83
production, mode of, 6, 7, 21, 25, 28, 31, 56 n.23; and political activity, 5; social relations of, 13 (defined), 32, 56 n.23. *See also* socialism of production
proletariat, the, 61; dictatorship of, 62; revolt of, 63, 66; the state under, 64
property law: and common law, 100–101; easements in, 101. *See also* property rights
property rights, 15, 173 n.20, 229; and popular control, 7; in dependent-industrializing society, 37, 39, 40; in advanced-industrial society, 37, 54 n.14; and Pareto-preferred results, 91; discussed, 94–95; as problem of public goods and bads, 94; and common law, 100–101; and information, 172 n.18; and social democracy, 220; productive, 220; nonfunctional, 220; to a job, 220; as guaranteed in Swedish politics, 229
public authority: and business interests, 3; crisis of, 8; and interest groups, 11; and popular control, 179
public bads, explained, 93–94. *See also* externalities
public-choice theory, school of: and the state, 14; and property-rights theory, 26; and Marxism, 86 n.7; and use of welfare economics, 88; theory of the state in, 88–106; and the spatial model in public goods, 108–11; public-sector and welfare-regarding acts in, 108; and social-imbalance hypothesis, 111, 113, 114–17, 118; fiscal illusion in, 114–18; interest-group conflict as prisoners' dilemma in, 123, 126, 135; private-goods-election model, 148–56; and possible worlds, 236 n.17
—and elections: with global-decision procedures, 156; sensitive electorates, 156; insensitive electorates, 156; with incremental decision procedures, 156; naïve incrementalism, 156; opportunity-cost local optimum, 157; non-opportunity-cost local optimum, 157; hybrid global decision making in, 157

INDEX

strong democracy, 11, 12
Supreme Court. *See* United States, Supreme Court

unitary democracy, 231
United States, Supreme Court: and interest-group basis of decision making, 142–48; and rules of judicial economy, 144; and litigation costs, 144; jurisprudence, 145–58; and private-goods basis of legislation, 145–48; as threat to private benefits, 147; and private-interest bargains in legislature, 147; decisions and federal preemption, 174–75 n.33
utilitarianism, as a feature of familial-vocational privatism, 86 n.5

wealth maximization, in law and economics, 171 n.12
welfare economics: in public-choice theory, 88; in public-sector activity, 88–89; and self-correcting markets, 91; and market failure, 91; and public incorporation, 104; Pareto optimality, Pareto-preferred changes and, 171 n.10
welfare theory, 129; logical structure of, 89; Pareto optimality as variant of, 89; social-welfare function as variant of, 89; and Pareto-preferred states, 90; and state functions, 90–97; in service of private-benefit programs, 165; Pareto optimality and wealth maximization in, 171 n.13